Television's Guardians

James L. Baughman

Television's Guardians

*The FCC
and the Politics
of Programming
1958-1967*

The University of Tennessee Press, Knoxville

The paper in this book meets the guidelines for permanence
and durability of the Committee on Production Guidelines
for Book Longevity of the Council on Library Resources.
Binding materials have been chosen for durability.

Library of Congress Cataloging in Publication Data

Baughman, James L., 1952-
    Television's guardians.

    Bibliography: p.
    Includes index.
    1. Television broadcasting policy—Untied States.
2. Television—Law and legislation—United States.
3. United States. Federal Communications Commission.
I. Title.
HE8700.8.B38   1985   384.55'4   84-13178
ISBN 0-87049-448-1

Acknowledgments:
The author gratefully acknowledges permission to quote from
Newton N. Minow, *Equal Time: The Private Broadcaster and the Public Interest.*
Copyright© 1964 by Newton N. Minow.
Reprinted with the permission of Atheneum publishers.

For my parents

Contents

List of Tables

There will be a temptation, I realize, to treat the uproar of the autumn as one of those things which pass and are forgotten. This country cannot afford to do that. For television, which is the most powerful medium of mass communications, is of enormous importance in the life of a nation. To forget it because it is not in the headlines would be frivolous, and indeed a sign of a serious national weakness.

Walter Lippmann,
"The Administration and TV,"
New York *Herald Tribune*, 5 January 1960

Acknowledgments

Many people helped me in the preparation of this work without necessarily being responsible for its failings. Stuart Bruchey, Albro Martin, Philip Ranlet, John M. Cooper, Jr., and Eleanora Schoenebaum read and offered criticisms of the entire work, while my good friends Donald Ritchie, Bonnie J. Brownlee, Clark Judge, and Karen Blair suffered through one or more chapters. I am especially grateful to Richard M. Fried and David L. Schuyler for improving a revised draft.

Co-workers at the School of Journalism and Mass Communication, University of Wisconsin, Madison, displayed constant support during the latter stages of this work's writing and revision. Jean Rockwell and Virginia Trapino very ably retyped many, many pages without being driven to violent behavior. William B. Blankenburg strove valiantly and perhaps unavailingly to rescue me from mental and stylistic lapses.

Many archivists aided me. I am particularly grateful to Janice O'Connell of the State Historical Society of Wisconsin, Lane Moore of the National Archives and Elizabeth Mason of the Oral History Collection of Columbia University. The late Sally Fly Connell allowed me to review the papers of her father and the oral history project at Columbia that she compiled in her father's name. To be thanked, too, are Holly Cowan Shulman and Marian Seldes for permission to review their fathers' papers, then in their possession.

I wish to express my appreciation to the many individuals connected with broadcasting and its regulation who submitted to interviews. These include Kenneth A. Cox, E. William Henry, John W. Bricker, Bernard Schwartz, Arthur M. Schlesinger, Jr., Eric F. Goldman, Fred Friendly, Frederick W. Ford, Nicholas Johnson, Michael Dann, Frank Shakespeare, Tedson J. Meyers, Henry Geller, Joel Rosenbloom, Ramsey Clark, and Frank Stanton. I am especially grateful to Newton Minow, who spent many hours reviewing his career with me and allowed me to review his large and helpful manuscript collection. Most of the interviews were taped and have been deposited with the Oral History Collection of Columbia University.

Others aiding me and to be thanked include Steve Allen, Kent Anderson, Erik Barnouw, the Angelo Coclanis family, Mary Ann Coffman, David Culbert, W. Phillips Davidson, Herbert Gans, Oren Harris, Phil Holen, Roman Hruska, Kenneth Jackson, Paul Murphy, George Nash, Michael Shain, and Charles Teague.

Part of the cost of the research and writing of this work was met by grants from the Lyndon B. Johnson Foundation, the Lincoln Educational Foundation, and the Graduate Faculty of the University of Wisconsin, Madison. I am grateful to all three groups.

Finally, I wish to thank William E. Leuchtenburg. Whatever is to be admired in this book can most often be attributed to his guidance. Inadequacies are my burden.

Friends and family are, of course, to be thanked most of all. They put up with me and this enterprise for much too long.

James L. Baughman
December 1983

Introduction

In the 1960s, many liberals discovered that the federal government could be a clumsy and ineffective means of social and cultural change. Strategists for the Democratic party had been convinced in the 1950s that the problems of American society could be overcome by avoiding the inertia of leadership epitomized by Dwight Eisenhower and using governmental institutions in bold fashion. Active and purposeful presidents, department secretaries, and independent agency chairmen could move a nation. But while many of the New Frontier and Great Society programs achieved substantial gains in the areas of civil rights and consumer protection, others only proved that more care or planning had to be instituted to bring about substantial alterations in the social well-being of poor Americans. In some instances, the marketplace—in the form of the tremendous economic expansion of 1963-68—did more for Americans than any well-intended social scheme.[1]

One such episode of liberal institutional frustration involved the Federal Communications Commission (FCC) led by Newton N. Minow. He and others perhaps rather innocently hoped to change the programming of American's commercial television networks and stations. They and their agency met with little success.[2] Congress eventually had to create the Public Broadcasting System (PBS) to provide more diverse forms of programming.

Minow and others had fought for the "public interest" in broadcasting. The phrase, as applied to government regulation generally, was already under attack in the 1960s as beyond definition or otherwise nebulous.[3] Yet communications commissioners had in some ways less difficulty with the expression than did their fellow regulators. With the radio spectrum finite, the government allotted portions of the wave band only to those parties willing to serve all Americans. That meant that the preferences of minorities as well as majorities were to be heeded by the licensed parties.

What Americans tended to get, however, was "majority television." The overwhelming amount of the schedule—especially during those hours when most Americans used their TV sets—went to mass amusement, underwritten by advertisers and profiting network and production company executives and shareholders. Although most viewers rarely complained about that arrangement, rarely were they given a choice, and the dissatisfied were left without much use for their TV receivers. Seemingly nothing Minow and others did could change that circumstance.

I have assumed here that the industry—grouped as an entity—weighed decisions in essentially entrepreneurial ways; only a third force, in this instance, the FCC could alter that approach to scheduling decisions. Thus, I will not analyze the broadcasters' treatment of air time at great length, or even indict them. In explaining the origins of the Second World War and the role of those who had tried to placate the Germans, A.J.P. Taylor remarked in 1963, "I have little interest in denouncing the appeasers. I am more interested in finding out why we, the opponents of appeasement, failed."[4]

Most previous studies of the independent commissions have similarly recounted their lack of success. Emphasizing earlier periods in modern American history, too many scholars have sought to confirm a commonplace theory that each commission came to be "captured" by the industries it had been initially intended to police. Those dealing with the agencies in the post-1945 decades have been content to dismiss them with the cliches of a consumer organization publicist or hard-pressed journalist. The commissions have been regarded as corrupt, ineffective bodies dominated by nonentities sensitive only to industry opinion. If the institutions did not work according to a regulatory ideal, fault had to lie with those in the agency who lacked the proper mission for regulation.

The "captive" thesis amounted to a commonsense correlation. The losers in most of the regulatory battles involving broadcasting in the 1950s and 1960s were those few consumers who cared about the "balance" of the broadcast schedule. The industry, while frequently worried about the FCC, won most of the major skirmishes. Angry consumer advocates therefore implied that broadcasters had "captured" the agency.[5]

Although the captive thesis has been taken up by many historians of regulation,[6] it is not especially informative or inspiring. Indeed, the very simplicity of the formula probably has inhibited research into a vital component of the modern American state. The failure of regulation seemed so obvious that little or no scholarly work has been done by historians on the regulatory agency after the New Deal.[7]

In other ways, the captive thesis has had a deadening effect on the study of the administrative process. Dismissing agencies as the prisoners of "business interests" is akin to other currently tempting historical explanations, such as accounting for the inadequacies of Reconstruction with obvious and presentist references to white racism. But, as one recent scholar of postbellum America observed, however widespread, racial intolerance does not fully explain precisely *why* and *how* the Republicans' Reconstruction policies failed.[8]

After a historical review of the FCC, this book focuses on two crises, one regulatory, the other cultural, that came in the late 1950s. House hearings conducted in 1958 and 1960 found the FCC ineffective and two commissioners guilty of intimate ties to parties subject to commission proceedings. At the same time, a small but powerful group of opinion leaders began to decry the programming of network television. The networks, these observers complained, had cancelled virtually all of the programming identified with the "golden age" of television and replaced it with more action Western and detective series that left these critics deeply dissatisfied. Television had seemingly become too commercial a venture, too independent of regulatory pressures that might have prevented such an abrogation of its responsibility to all audiences.

The commission struggled unavailingly throughout the next decade to restrain television from its commercial instincts. Many of the FCC's solutions were structural, technical to the point of being tedious to the lay observer. Relying on a relatively unused portion of the broadcast spectrum, the commission hoped to encourage the founding of more stations, which would compete against established outlets by offering more diverse programming. Other responses constituted direct challenges to individual stations to increase their program balance.

Neither of these approaches—the structural nor the direct—proved efficacious. The commission itself was too weak, and Congress and the president could take exception to the mildest efforts to police television licensees. In effect, broadcast regulation could not be made to work.

With the ineffectiveness of the FCC evident to all but the most stubborn consumer groups, an increasing number turned to solutions that effectively acknowledged the agency's failure. By the late 1960s, many of the same people who had once hoped the FCC might save the medium were calling for the creation of a public, noncommercial network. In the late 1970s and early 1980s, many more placed their faith not in regulation or even public television but in new technologies. Various transmission systems, most of them ignored or thwarted by the commission earlier, promised far greater choice in programs for consumers.

The abandonment of the FCC as an instrument of better television left commercial broadcasters largely free to pursue their own ends. Given the potential for regulatory abuse, notably in the Nixon years, champions of the Fifth Estate's freedom could be grateful for a weak FCC. On the other hand, given the performance of network television since the mid-1960s, it is by no means clear that the champions of the golden age and the liberals on the FCC—television's guardians— were wrong to seek something more from the nation's most popular cultural institution.

Television's Guardians

Chapter One

"From Crisis to Crisis":
The Folklore of Broadcast
Regulation, 1912-1958

In the late 1950s, a folklore of regulation developed in American political theory. In the first six decades of the twentieth century, American reformers periodically convinced themselves that independent commissions could regulate American businesses. When this "fourth branch" of government failed to serve a "public interest" in regulation, the heirs to the liberal tradition assumed that the commissions had become captives of American business.

Broadcast regulation between 1912 and 1958 typified this argument over ineffective trusteeship. Only for a brief period, 1941-46, did the Federal Communications Commission take its tasks seriously. By the late 1950s, a function basic to the agency—the assignment of television frequencies—tempted individual commissioners into compromising what scant integrity they seemed to possess. Indeed, the FCC by the late fifties had so besmirched itself with conflict-of-interest improprieties that its initials came to stand for "From Crisis to Crisis." A woman told her very young daughter that her father, an attorney with the commission, worked as a gangster. Learning of this, the incredulous father asked his wife about her motive; she replied, "You surely don't want me to tell my friends that you work for the FCC, do you?"[1]

The Federal Communications Commission had been part of a great innovation in American government. Legislation creating the Interstate Commerce Commission (ICC) in 1887 marked the beginning of the independent commission system. Such agencies were ostensibly "independent" of the executive, legislative, and judicial divisions.[2] More commissions were formed on the state and national level during the first fifteen "progressive" years of the twentieth century.

The rise of the American administrative branch followed the emergence of complex and large-scale economic organizations. With the advent of national markets, many companies merged into giant organizations capable of manipulating traditional buyer-seller relationships and of extending their operations further by mastering new technologies, about which a senator or judge might know little. The independent agencies, however, offered an alternative to regulating from the bench or Capitol Hill. A regulatory body could concentrate wholly on the day-to-day workings of particular industries and be staffed with experts familiar with the economics of these businesses.[3]

The new agencies were to be infused with the "public interest," that is, decisions were to be made with a maximum regard for both the general welfare and popular opinion. The very power of an agency to expose industrial malfeasance would serve to check abuses, since many progressives, notably those identified with Robert M. La Follette, assumed that Americans would engage themselves in the work of the independent commissions. "We can only do what you tell us you want done,"a Federal Radio Commission (FRC) commissioner said in his agency's first year.[4]

The leaders of industry often helped to promote federal regulation. Some major business executives agreed to the premise of national regulation in the hope of influencing the drafting of the particular law establishing a commission. These managers preferred dealing with one national agency rather than many state authorities, which might prove to be more hostile to their interests—or less subject to their lobbying skills. In other instances, larger companies expected commissions to protect them—by setting rates or proper production procedures—from the excesses of competition from smaller rivals who might otherwise undermine their market dominance.[5]

The evolution of radio regulation well illustrates the admixture of the interests of entrepreneurs, product users, and the public. The immediate "problem" necessitating the regulation of broadcasting involved the technical aspects of radio: certain stations and individual operators hampered reception of radio programming. By the early and middle 1920s, a clamor for governmental intervention in radio transmission extended to the millions purchasing radio set receivers, congressmen who received letters complaining of interference, radio set manufacturers, and the more scrupulous stations.

Revisions of existing radio law had to be made. In 1912, Congress empowered the Commerce Department to assign radio spectrum frequencies,[6] but within fifteen years, the situation bordered on chaos. Demand for the limited radio air space placed enormous burdens on Secretary of Commerce Herbert Hoover. Some stations ignored restrictions that Hoover placed on their allotment of air time or frequency spacing. Aimee Semple McPherson, the popular evangelist, operated a Los Angeles station on whichever airwave her engineers and the Lord felt obliged to utilize.[7] Concomitantly, two court decisions and an opinion of the attorney general undermined Hoover's authority.[8]

The infant radio industry formed a coalition for quick relief through a revision of federal law. Radio station managers, forming the National Association of Broadcasters (NAB) in 1922, called for an expanded governmental role. Hoover himself recalled that "radio men were eager for regulation to prevent interference with one another's wave lengths," and he considered the emerging enthusiasm for additional federal authority to be "one of the few instances that I know of when the whole industry and country is earnestly praying for more regulation."[9]

Yet listeners also insisted on governmental succor. Although histories of radio regulation usually cite Hoover's recognition of industry demands for regulation, their use of his "one of the few instances" remark rarely stresses Hoover's coupling of "industry and country."[10] The country, in this case, consumers, were hardly silent about the crisis of reception. "Something," a Floridian contended in February 1925, must "be done to straighten out this uncalled for confusion on the air. All is lost, including honor." A Maryland man had bought a $750 set in late 1926 and complained of its uselessness due to station interference. Others objected to the programming of the new medium. A North Dakotan expressed horror in December 1926 at "very undesirable music," notably jazz, and pleaded for government assistance.[11]

With constituent fury impossible to contain indefinitely, Congress enacted a new radio law in 1927.[12] Hoover and the NAB had wanted the government's radio regulatory role expanded but kept within the Commerce Department.[13] Indeed, his congressional ally, Congressman Wallace White of Maine, had first proposed such a revision in 1922. The Senate, though, had looked on the White bill with disfavor. Some, judging radio to be a medium of enormous power, suspected Hoover's motives. He or an unscrupulous successor might use radio as an instrument of propaganda. Grimly, Hoover agreed to a Senate bill, offered by Senator Clarence Dill of Washington, that created a Federal Radio Commission of five members. The inquiry into the Teapot Dome scandals, disgracing two of Harding's cabinet officers for their handling of government oil leases, had convinced Dill and others of the wisdom of having public resources placed out of the control of officials of the executive branch. The Dill version became law in February 1927.[14]

The Radio Act of 1927 left much unresolved. Hoover, Dill, and others defined the airwaves as a limited, national resource, akin to public land. The FRC would determine which parties would have access to it for three-year periods. The FRC was to allocate frequencies according to the "public interest, convenience, or necessity," a phrase that originated with an amendment to the Interstate Commerce Act. Yet a radio station was not to be viewed as a common carrier. Radio programming was not to be likened to the services of a railroad or telephone company; the FRC could not censor individual programs.[15] Nor could the commission set the rates charged for air time.[16] If anything, the FRC was cast as a policeman at an intersection of the Lincoln Highway ensnarled by automobiles. He could direct but not design the vehicles.[17]

The FRC's limited programming authority resulted at least in part from the prospect of a federal radio "censor." Both Hoover and Congressman White sympathized with those who disapproved of the number of jazz concerts over the air. But White's colleagues had been wary of the government as interceder. The very creation of an "independent" radio commission, rather than an augmented authority within the Commerce Department, had been tied to this concern with governmental interference in expression. White in that spirit refrained from including the right to engage in evaluation of programming. In March 1926, the Maine Republican had written to a listener:

> Government crop reports, weather forecasts, discussions of
> public and other matters which will readily occur to you
> were more important than a jazz concert. I felt that at
> some time, some authority would have to determine
> whether on Sunday, sermons and sacred music should or
> should not have a right-of-way over the reports of a ball

game. . . . I soon found, however, that a fear existed that
such a power might amount to censorship.[18]

Strenuously avoiding the censorship feared by White's colleagues,
the FRC regarded programming cautiously. The new agency emphasized such technical matters as the absence of static, and a potential operator's scheduling intentions were not given much consideration. If anything, the commission favored those who defined the public
interest as private gain. In assigning some five hundred radio frequencies in its first year, the FRC overwhelmingly preferred commercial
over noncommercial (educational or religious) groups.[19] Finally, the
commission pursued the ICC's "case-by-case" philosophy of regulation. Tending to review each license application on its individual
merits, the FRC did not adhere to a well defined standard of the public
interest in programming. As a result, radio stations enjoyed enormous
flexibility in what they presented the American listener.[20]

Yet the Radio Commission did not obscure the public interest in
broadcasting altogether. In 1929, the FRC presented criteria for sta
tions to observe in fulfilling their obligations as users. All licensees
were to air such "public service" programming as news, weather, and
religious broadcasts and offer other types of local productions as well.
That mandate— mirroring Congressman White's concern—was upheld
by the courts as no infringement on the First Amendment.[21] Moreover, those few stations operating well outside decorum did suffer
the worst of all possible fates. By 1933, the FRC had revoked the
licenses of a Kansas quack, a Louisiana crank, and a Los Angeles anti-
Semite, all using their access to the airwaves to spread their
philosophy of ill reason.[22]

The commission's broad standards and license revocations had the
effect of negative law: that is, FRC rulings tended to prevent station
managers from committing gross abuses. Radio operators felt obligated
to air *some* news and weather reports daily and religious programs
on Sundays. But for most stations, such events constituted a very
small percentage of total programming, well below, for example, the
25 percent that some congressmen in the early 1930s thought stations should apportion to such fare.[23]

Radio in the thirties had not fulfilled the "possibility for service,
for news, for entertainment, for education and for vital commercial
purposes" envisioned by Hoover in his 1922 radio conference talk.
Instead, the successful stations aired mainly mass entertainment,

more of the jazz and other music that so discomforted Congressman White; they profited by selling time for the "advertising chatter" that Hoover, for one, had bemoaned.[24]

By the early thirties, too, network or "chain broadcasting" had come to dominate much of programming. The FRC ostensibly favored local production over network fare. Yet the commission also shared some of Hoover's earlier excitement over the cultural and educational possibilities of national transmission. The agency did little but acknowledge the steady evolution of the two great national "hook-up" systems: the National Broadcasting Company (NBC), a subsidiary of the Radio Corporation of America (RCA), and the Columbia Broadcasting System (CBS). For a variety of reasons, station executives coveted network affiliations. A New Orleans station manager contended in mid-1932 that affiliation with a network "meant a quick road to better programs, a better class of business and large financial returns."[25]

Congress failed to confront either the changes in, or performance of, radio when reconsidering radio regulation in 1934. In an apparent wish to consolidate communication regulatory bodies, President Roosevelt recommended that Congress combine the government's overseeing of telephone and telegraph, heretofore the charge of the ICC, as well as of radio, into a seven-member commission to be called the Federal Communications Commission.[26] But except for a clause regarding powers over the height of radio towers, the new commission essentially assumed the FRC's limited prerogatives. Not surprisingly, the communication industries offered no opposition to the cosmetic conglomeration. Both houses passed the measure in 1934 by voice vote after limited debate.[27]

Between 1934 and 1939, the FCC operated without much more purpose than had the FRC and hardly shared in the limelight that shone during the New Deal on such other independent agencies as the Securities and Exchange Commission (SEC). If the New Deal, as many scholars maintain, reaffirmed the older faith in the regulatory commission, that religiosity was initially absent at the FCC's offices. The new agency continued the FRC's fairly exclusive "technical" standard: awarding and renewing licenses largely on the basis of engineering criteria. To proponents of an expansive administrative state, the FCC appeared ill-led and badly managed. An aide to Roosevelt remarked in July 1937, "Quite confidentially, this commission is one of the sore spots."[28] Uneasy that the president intended to name him FCC chairman, SEC chairman William O. Douglas visited the White House in March 1939. To Douglas's great relief, Roosevelt asked him to serve on the Supreme Court.[29]

Roosevelt did reverse the FCC's course by designating James Lawrence Fly as its chairman in July 1939. An attorney for the Tennessee Valley Authority, Fly identified with the antitrust inclination of such fellow New Dealers of the late 1930s as Thurman Arnold of the Justice Department. Possessed of an unusually acerbic personality, Fly offended the most powerful individuals and groups in broadcasting. The chairman brusquely handled relations with David Sarnoff, president of RCA, and, paraphrasing John Randolph, compared the NAB to a mackerel, "in the night, it shines and it stinks."[30]

Fly's public quarreling somewhat cloaked the more substantial element to his chairmanship. Fly believed that the FCC could and should concern itself with far more than technical criteria. By increasing competition, mainly at the two major networks' expense, the FCC could augment listeners' choices. To Fly, greater selection—and not the technical quality of the broadcast—defined the "public interest" in broadcast regulation.[31]

In May 1941, the FCC issued the *Report on Chain Broadcasting*, which included regulations outlawing or modifying a wide range of network-station relationships. These guidelines were to be enforced through the commission's authority to revoke the license; the chains each held a limited number of licenses and could therefore be made subject to the agency. Designed to limit the capacity of the networks to dictate arrangements to potential affiliates, the rules made switching affiliation to third or fourth networks easier for stations. That freedom, the FCC anticipated, would both encourage new networks to present alternative forms of programming and permit licensees to pay closer heed to their communities' needs. The resulting local and national competition would be consistent with an older tenet of liberal ideology, that many voices were preferable to a few, that oligopoly in communications was dangerous to a democracy. "Competition, given a fair test," the commission contended, "will best protect the public interest. That is the American system."[32]

Most significantly, the commission's regulations caused a partial dissolution of NBC, the nation's largest radio network. The 1941 rules forbade any network to affiliate with more than one station in a community. The National Broadcasting Company had operated two systems, the "Red" and "Blue" networks, each with a separate array of affiliates ostensibly competing against each other in a given listening area. Because of the new rules, NBC would have to part with one of its chains; it elected to relinquish its Blue system, the less profitable operation. Sold in October 1943 after NBC lost its court challenge of the rules, the Blue network became the American Broadcasting Company (ABC), and a new national network, the artificial organism of the FCC, had been born.[33]

In what constituted the most important single ruling in broadcast law, the Supreme Court by a 5-to-2 majority in May 1943 upheld not only the chain regulations but the commission's right to set overall program objectives. In *NBC v. U.S.*, Justice Frankfurter, a strong proponent of the administrative state, argued that because of the limits of the spectrum, a licensee's rights could not be defended absolutely under the free speech clause of the First Amendment. Under the "public interest" criterion, Frankfurter reasoned, the commission must not confine itself to technical considerations. The 1934 act "does not restrict the Commission merely to the supervision of traffic," Frankfurter stated. "It puts on the Commission the burden of determining the composition of that traffic."[34]

Frankfurter's broad interpretation notwithstanding, the FCC remained unwilling to involve itself more directly in programming until after Fly's resignation in November 1944. Fly had expected competition to better the medium, but there were few signs that it had done so. The new chairman, Paul A. Porter, tried to move the FCC in another direction. An ardent New Dealer, Porter had labored in the Agriculture Department in the 1930s and briefly worked as an attorney for CBS. Despite that corporate affiliation, Porter held views distinct from both Fly and his former employer concerning programming. Porter contended that the FCC had every right to police programming more vigorously, and Frankfurter's NBC ruling appeared to reinforce such a belief.[35]

On the initiative of Commissioner Clifford J. Durr, another ex-TVA attorney, the commission commenced an elaborate examination of radio programming. The FCC studied the programming of six stations, comparing their schedules with what they had announced to the commission prior to their licenses' renewal. Not surprisingly, the survey uncovered gross discrepancies between programming promised and aired.[36]

In March 1946, the commission issued a report, *Public Service*

Responsibilities of Broadcast Licensees (dubbed the "Blue Book" because of its powder blue cover), which noted the infractions and stipulated new and more definite program standards. No single program received criticism. Rather, the commission called on stations to submit annual statements with a sample week's programming and to provide certain general types of noncommercial fare.[37]

With the issuance of the Blue Book, there loomed the prospect that the commission would actively regulate programming in ways never before attempted. Specifically, the agency indicated that license holders wishing to retain their franchises had to present additional local (rather than so much network) programming. News and other public affairs series should be aired without regard to their popularity. Americans stood at the threshold of what one FCC assistant termed "radio's second chance."[38]

The commission, however, never applied the Blue Book to its license renewal procedures, and the violations it had uncovered continued unabated. In releasing the new station regulations, "the FCC created controversy in the industry and in the press," one scholar of the agency wrote, "but little else."[39] The commission "won the battle," observed the first Hoover Commission, referring to the *NBC* case, "but lost the war."[40]

What had happened? The very pace of the expansive, postwar economy undermined regulation: most commissions did not grow in size and budget at the same level as the industries being regulated. Between 1946 and 1952, the FCC's appropriation, limited by President Truman, ranged between $5.5 million (1946) to $6.7 million (1949), falling thereafter. In contrast, the total revenues of the five national networks alone—not counting local stations, telephone companies, and Western Union—continually rose, from $86.5 million in 1946 to $276 million in 1952.[41]

Then, too, the independent agencies lost the glamour of the New Deal years, when, so the legend went, the bright young attorneys and academicians rushed to Washington to supervise the American economy. The new prosperity after the war caused many talented liberals to soften their views toward policing private enterprise; good times made the overseeing of business appear less urgent. The clever and the inspired stopped coming to Washington in the same numbers.

Indeed, many of those already in the capital and responsible for the FCC's new and vigorous approach to regulation quit the agency. Porter left in early 1946 to work in the Truman administration. His successor, Charles R. Denny, Jr., served until 1947, when he resigned to become an NBC vice president. The president's loyalty program encouraged Durr, one of Roosevelt's abler, liberal nominees, to leave in protest.[42]

All told, the quality of the commissioners declined in the years immediately following the release of the Blue Book. Truman did name some able individuals, notably Frieda Hennock and Wayne Coy, figures who freely challenged industry opinion and fought for educational broadcasting. But often, a former SEC chairman complained, "appointments too frequently sprung from fairly petty political considerations."[43] Truman had failed in 1946 to renominate Norman Case, who had served on the commission with some distinction and wished reappointment. Again, in 1947, Truman refrained from renaming an able Republican commissioner and, instead, designated an obscure and dimly qualified Ohio Republican as a sop to that state's Old Guard. Following that appointment, a concerned trade publisher implored an aide to the president, "*Please* keep the FCC from becoming mere political football."[44]

Postwar presidential appointments to the FCC had the effect of undermining the agency. It did not, after all, take very much political deadwood—only four party hacks—to create a commission majority consisting of less than highly competent and dedicated experts infused with the public interest. By 1957, a prominent critic of the mass media described the FCC as "a stuffy, bureaucratic body not particularly concerned with high principles and laggard in enforcement of those it announces."[45]

Eisenhower's presidency further downgraded the independent commission. The first Republican administration in twenty years regarded the commissions as foreign bodies infested with New Deal emigres, "prejudice[d] against the capitalist system," one aide wrote.[46] Eisenhower rarely met with commission chairmen; a communications law attorney recalled in January 1961 that "Larry Fly, Paul Porter or Wayne Coy saw the President every so often," but Eisenhower "was too busy or there was Sherman Adams [the president's chief of staff] to bar them."[47] Eisenhower's appointments, most drawn from the ranks of state utility boards, lent nothing to the commission's plummeting prestige.[48] Eisenhower so disliked patronage matters that he effectively left the filling of many agency vacancies to the Republican National Committee, which, in turn, recommended for appointment to the FCC some of the administration's more partisan and least honorable commissioners.[49]

In the 1950s, the commission entered what one former chairman dubbed "the whorehouse era." Another commissioner, borrowing on the same metaphor, described it as the time "when the Commission lost its virginity, and liked it so much it turned pro."[50] Studies by political scientists published in 1952 and 1955 supplied ample proof of agency bias in favor of the industries policed.[51] James Landis, a great champion of administrative government in the 1930s, found practicing before the FCC of the 1950s a deeply frustrating experience.[52] He among others of the late New Deal, observed one scholar of the independent agency, "Shouted 'Housanna' in 1938 and saw the promised land. Now it is the time of the abominations. The agencies have betrayed reform and abandoned decency."[53]

Nothing more exasperated the independent agency's critics in the postwar decade than the FCC's awarding of the new and limited number of television licenses. Soon after the beginning of regular telecasts in 1948, the value of a TV station in a major market jumped. Despite high start-up costs incurred from new equipment and programming, TV stations commanded increasingly impressive revenues from the sale of time to advertisers.[54] And the commissioners found themselves overwhelmed with applications for more television channels. But despite the rush for stations, the FCC failed to abide by a consistent procedure in new license cases, even after promulgating one in 1952. Instead, applicants competed against one another by stressing various strengths, any one of which might be the basis for a grant. In one instance, the placement of the men's room entered deliberations.[55]

If an independent agency ever needed the disinterested "experts" with whom progressives earlier had anticipated populating the commissions, it was the FCC in the 1950s. And yet the temptations surrounding the awarding of TV franchises proved too great for the statehouse types Eisenhower had named to the commission. By the late fifties, the FCC was a regulatory rat's nest, waiting to be exposed. The possibilities of improprieties became public in 1957 when two magazine stories asserted that the commission had granted licenses in Boston, Miami, and St. Louis for political reasons.[56] The charge of political influence, that the FCC's four-to-three Republican majority favored Republican applicants, could never be proved. A pattern did emerge, however, of *ex parte* contacts: commissioners fraternizing with and accepting gifts and loans from license applicants and their lobbyists. These reports wounded the FCC's already marginal reputation for judicious behavior.[57]

The most damning news arrived in early 1958. The House Commerce Committee's Legislative Oversight Committee had begun an investigation in 1957 of the FCC and six other independent commissions.[58] To committee counsel Bernard Schwartz, the FCC and Commissioner Richard A. Mack afforded an irresistible opportunity. Mack, a Democrat, had been named by Eisenhower to the FCC in 1955. Having earned an undistinguished record as a public utilities regulator in Florida, Mack had appeared to be malleable to Chairman George McConnaughey. Mack did McConnaughey's bidding, but he also found himself incapable of handling the commission workload. He began to drink heavily.[59] His most serious weakness, however, was not liquor but ties to an old friend from college. Thurman Whiteside, a Miami influence peddler, had been secretly giving money to Mack to help him meet personal expenses. In 1956 and 1957, Whiteside asked Mack to return many favors by voting for an applicant for Miami's channel 10, a party from whom Whiteside received remuneration for contacting Mack. House counsel Schwartz uncovered the scheme after checking Mack's office records and then wiretapping an interview with him during which the commissioner confessed to voting at Whiteside's strong urging. Facing impeachment, Mack resigned. One Democratic colleague termed the channel 10 disclosures "morally equal to those of Teapot Dome."[60]

At the time of the Mack inquiry, Schwartz established that Chairman John C. Doerfer, McConnaughey's successor, had arranged to have certain travel costs in 1954 and 1955 paid for by private broadcast interests. These items included hotel and golfing expenses, charges made by his wife during shopping trips, and his use of a plane owned by Storer Broadcasting. On one occasion, the FCC chairman had the government pay him for items already covered by Storer and the NAB.

Schwartz came close to forcing Doerfer's ouster, and all commissioners suffered from Schwartz's detailed listing of their free lunches, Christmas turkeys, and free color television sets (then precious commodities) "loaned" to each commissioner by the Radio Corporation of America. Justifications for the complimentary TV sets that followed would have sounded better on "The Luci-Desi Comedy Hour." The RCA set was "no luxury," Doerfer said. "It's part of our job to see how it works. We look to TV shows not for fun, but to learn what's going on."[61]

The commission emerged from the Legislative Oversight Committee hearings of 1958 with a thoroughly tainted record. One commissioner, having resigned in disgrace, faced prosecution. The FCC chairman had been publicly reprimanded by House members for his *ex parte* social contacts, and nearly all commissioners had been embarrassed by the disclosures of gifts and free meals. Only the committee's pursuance of the Bernard Goldfine affair, implicating Sherman Adams for interfering with the work of the other regulatory agencies, saved the FCC from even more unsettling exposes.[62]

The regulatory ideal at the FCC had been abandoned for some free turkeys and color television sets. When in 1887 Grover Cleveland named his first ICC commissioner, he selected Thomas M. Cooley, a widely respected jurist, whom many considered well suited for the Supreme Court. With the House investigation of the commissioners, Schwartz said in March 1958, "you couldn't get a man of that stature to touch a job on one of these agencies with a twenty-foot pole."[63]

Eisenhower's poor appointments only partly explain the extraordinary deterioration of the administrative ideal at the FCC. Eisenhower's critics regarded the FCC's many failings as the fault of those the president had designated to be commissioners. Yet this conclusion tended to ignore structural changes within the regulatory process, alterations which would have frustrated any number of philosopher kings allied to the New Deal's model of "active" regulation and serving on the FCC in the fifties. Between 1946 and 1958, certain groups methodically worked to restrict the administrative agency as an effective instrument of government. This anti-independent commission coalition succeeded in imposing on the FCC and other agencies procedures that, while guaranteeing the rights of parties affected by regulation, much restricted the regulator's capacity to formulate and act on policies consistently.

In the 1940s, the American Bar Association, foes of the New Deal, and political scientists had joined in a fight to confine the powers of all the commissions. Members of this informal alliance mistrusted the agencies for their exercise of both rule-making (policy) and adjudicative (license issuance) functions, that is, acting as both lawmaker and judge. Old Guard Republicans disliked bureaucratic expansiveness in any form. So, too, did many students of government viewing the fourth branch (the one not cited in *L'esprit des Lois*) with unusual hostility "The Independent Commission," one law professor noted in

1956, "has been the bete noire of political scientists for many years"[64]

Decisions of the federal judiciary added to the ranks of the agencies' adversaries. By the time of the *NBC* case in 1943, the courts had begun to give the commissions greater discretion in setting regulations and punishing those who disobeyed them. What emerged, most often in the opinions of Justice Frankfurter, was a doctrine of "administrative finality," in which the high court refrained from challenging most of the decisions of the independent commissions. The Roosevelt appointees in particular, observed one scholar, "stressed the limitations of the judge, who is expert only in matters of law. The fact-finding of administrative agencies has come to be accepted as final except under extraordinary circumstances."[65]

With the courts seemingly unwilling to check the agencies, Congress in 1946 passed the Administrative Procedure Act (APA). To encourage justices to challenge the rulings of the fourth branch, the law widened the scope of judicial review of administrative decisions. In addition the APA provided for procedures within the commissions themselves by creating a special class of hearing examiners responsible only to the Civil Service Commission to oversee contested cases. In effect, hearing examiners could not consult with individual commissioners except to present their final decision.[66]

The APA helped to shatter the harmony and purposefulness of the FCC. Commissioners wishing to make policy from individual cases could not inform examiners of the broader policy considerations. In effect, the Administrative Procedure Act made agency operations more time-consuming, less flexible, and less likely to be aimed toward broad, general purposes.[67] Two critics of the 1946 statute declared that it "proposes to place all administrative activity in a judicialized straightjacket. . . . [APA] seeks to substitute therefore a system not based on constitutional, legal, economic, or administrative reality, but upon the desire of lawyers to have the maximum opportunity to participate in the process of administration, to lock administrative action, and to subject the administration process to judicial methods and judicial controls at every turn."[68]

Even before the ill effects of the Administrative Procedure Act could be fully appreciated, Congress singled out the FCC for additional procedural impediments. Ostensibly to guarantee fair treatment, Senator Ernest W. McFarland of Arizona offered a series of amendments to the 1934 Communications Act. The "McFarland amendments," enacted in 1952, created still another bureaucratic layer immune from

Commission control—the review staff, set up to prosecute the cases before the hearing examiners. The 1952 amendments also sharply limited involvement of such "interested" third parties as consumer groups in favor of corporate ones. At the same time, the commission was now required to conduct hearings upon the insistence of any party actually seeking a license. In addition, the full commission and not a single commissioner would have to meet to handle a petitioned hearing. Finally, the amendments restricted the FCC's power in reviewing the transfer or sale of a license. Commissioner Robert T. Bartley remarked in March 1958, "A fellow being denied an application before the FCC gets more due process than a murderer."[69]

Chairman Doerfer, among others, found the Balkanization of his personnel chart a constant frustration. Accustomed in Wisconsin to arbitrating disputes in utilities regulation personally and quickly, Doerfer thought the commission unduly slow in resolving much of anything. "The Administrative Procedure Act, all these separations of functions," a colleague recalled, "really just were an aggravation and frustration to him."[70]

With thick lines separating the commission bureaucracy from the commissioners themselves, decisions made in the 1950s were often uninformed by the agency's own staff when compared with the representations of private interests. The commissioners frequently overruled the formal, written opinions of FCC examiners and the review staff: it legally was easier to confer with an applicant than an FCC underling.[71] In the Miami and Boston dockets, both marred by scandal, a commission majority disregarded the detailed findings of the hearing examiner, evidencing not just the commissioners' whimsy but the legally prescribed distance between them and their bureaucracy. "Insulating the Commissioners from the staff," one scholar found, "further increases the Commission's dependence upon partisan, self-serving evidence and testimony."[72]

Because the full commission had to meet whenever an unsuccessful petitioner insisted on reconsideration of an order, Doerfer calculated in June 1956 that about 30 percent of his and the staff's time involved protests alone. The "protest" provisions of the McFarland amendment, one legal scholar determined, "have placed the Commission in an administrative straitjacket. The public's interest in receiving greater service has been sacrificed, through loss of discretion, to the purely private interest of competitors seeking delay and obstruction. The attempt to legislate 'fairness' has only led to a greater 'unfairness' with the public the principal loser."[73]

Not only had national legislators determined to handcuff the FCC with procedural regulations, but by regarding these bodies as "arms of Congress," congressmen freely issued opinions to individual commissioners on cases involving constituents. In 1953, Senator Joseph R. McCarthy of Wisconsin attempted to set commission policy regarding the number and use of TV channels allocated for Milwaukee; he wished to change one channel reserved for educational use and deny another to a political adversary, the *Milwaukee Journal*.[74] During the Miami proceedings, six senators wrote on behalf of an applicant. For many legislators, such participation came naturally. When Senator John Carroll of Colorado sought in July 1959 to limit congressional intercession in commission proceedings, Senator Everett M. Dirksen successfully frustrated the effort. Aligning himself with Dirksen, Senator Mike Mansfield, the Senate Democratic whip, said, "I feel no compunction at all about calling agencies." A TV trade journal observed that "backdoor approaches to agencies may be improper when made by non-politicians, but members of Congress are politicians elected by constituents whose interests (including TV channels) must be served."[75]

Congress further disrupted the regulatory process through its power of the purse. As early as 1927, with the establishment of the Federal Radio Commission, Congress had put off funding the new agency. Secretary of Commerce Hoover ended up providing office space and salary money for the agency he had not sought in the first place.[76] The first Hoover Commission noted in 1949 how Congress used appropriations to convey its displeasure with agency policies. Indeed, in given years, legislators did reduce appropriations below FCC and Budget Bureau requests. A commission too "independent" of Congress risked more cutbacks. Between 1949 and 1955, the FCC awaited congressional support for funding a special study of the networks to replace the 1941 *Report on Chain Broadcasting*.[77]

The House and Senate Commerce committees that oversaw FCC activities frequently engaged themselves in the technical questions that the commission had been established to answer. In the late 1940s and early 1950s, Senator Edwin C. Johnson of Colorado, chairman of the Senate Commerce Committee incessantly lectured the commission about detailed matters regarding television about which even the FCC's beleaguered engineering staff knew far more.[78]

Finally, the state of public opinion helped to shape the FCC's fate.

A basic consideration of those first favoring the independent commission had been that the public would, in organized or spontaneous fashion, involve itself in the workings of the fourth branch. Yet the decade after the Second World War saw little activity by consumer and other public interest groups in general, and virtually none among broadcast service users.[79] Americans, in general like many liberals, apparently had lost much of their antagonism toward large-scale capital.[80] As a result, observed Bernard Schwartz, for the commissioners, "The public tends ever increasingly to become identified with the interest of the dominant groups in the regulated industry."[81]

The press, which might have informed Americans of the commission's activities, gave the FCC scant coverage. In April 1952, when the commission issued a master plan for the allocation of TV channels throughout the nation, such major newspapers as the *New Orleans Times-Picayune*, the *Washington Post*, and the *Baltimore Sun*, failed to mention the decision.[82] The public thus often lacked basic information on the agency. Just under 60 percent of those people surveyed in February 1959 could not identify the initials FCC; many more could not state the commission's functions.[83]

Between 1946 and 1958 it would have been astonishing for the FCC to have taken seriously the regulatory ardor of the Fly and Porter years. Certain presidential appointments, especially under Eisenhower, proved disastrous. Some who did serve with merit did not secure reappointment. Congress imposed rigid procedural formulas on the FCC, all the while insisting that the commission work more speedily. Powerful congressional leaders hampered FCC operations by interjecting their views in quasi-judicial proceedings. Finally, the general public mood favored free enterprise over regulation. All told, if one were concerned about the programming over American television in the late 1950s, about the last place to expect initiatives would have been at the Federal Communications Commission.

Chapter Two

"The TV Problem":
1958-1960

Scandals at the FCC coincided with growing criticism of the agency's chief ward, television. By the late 1950s, as the public learned of various improprieties at the commission, a small but influential body of writers argued that the "quality" of TV programming had begun to decline. Indeed, after a decade of experimentation and promise, some of these critics argued that TV had become a national problem. The most popular mass medium in America was dominated by three national corporations, and the FCC, unable even to allocate individual station licenses, was being asked to do something about network programming.

Early in 1958, as the House Commerce Committee conducted its inquiry into the FCC, just over four out of every five American homes had a television set. Television had entered the living room with a speed and completeness that exceeded that of any other household technological innovation, including the telephone or radio. Between 1948 and 1958, the number of homes with TV receivers rose from 172,000 to 42 million. It became difficult to travel anywhere in America and not find rooftops decorated with TV antennas and the evening organized around the television schedule.[1]

National chains—the American Broadcasting Company, The Columbia Broadcasting System, and The National Broadcasting Company—established what the tens of millions of Americans watched.[2] Almost from the beginning, the networks provided

individual stations with the greater part of their schedule. The proportion of network programs a station carried ranged from 51.6 percent in June 1953 to 57.5 percent in June 1958, and in the evenings,
network fare made up for 95 percent of a station's schedule.[3] In
November 1955 a telecaster in Iowa complained that "entirely too
many station operators want only to be network relay stations."[4]

Between 1958 and 1960, network television came under increasingly bitter attack. By the end of this period, newspaper and magazine
critics had been joined by intellectual and political leaders regretting
certain changes in the networks' programming practices, or
associating the medium with some of the worst, ongoing tendencies
in American society. Indeed, the breadth of these attacks upon television left many TV industry leaders feeling victimized. One major
advertising agency president complained in November 1960, "Television is inevitably made the whipping boy for fatness, indolence and
even the shoddy morality of which I'm afraid much of this country
is guilty today."[5]

Certain censures of television had been expressed throughout the
first decade of network telecasts. Many intellectuals condemned the
very emergence of commercial television as part of a larger and
negative formulation against modern mass culture.[6] Similarly, some
parent groups and psychologists continually protested the violence
portrayed on TV.[7]

Some critics, however, complained about television only at the end
of the decade. They did so less out of an enthusiasm for the programming of television's early years than out of disgust for what had replaced it. Put differently, television to them changed dramatically between the early and late 1950s. And these alterations did not suit the
tastes of the medium's regular and new critics.

Three groups formed this contingent of unhappy watchers. First
were the televison reviewers and feature writers for major and influential magazines and newspapers, mainly on the East Coast. Such
analysts as Gilbert Seldes of *The Saturday Review*, Marya Mannes
of the *Reporter*, and Jack Gould of the *New York Times*, in turn, persuaded their readers, only occasionally interested in the medium, that
something was amiss.[8] Finally, certain artists joined in. They were
the "creative talent" tied to the older television—writers, directors,
and actors—whose programs were cancelled as the medium shifted
to different formats.

Much evidence contradicts the first principle of these critics—that

TV programming changed in substantial ways by the late 1950s. Available data, based on typologies of programs, do not suggest that television programming underwent a shift during the decade. If anything, studies of the three networks' schedules tend to underscore either the constancy with which certain program forms (like situation comedies) appeared on the schedule or the cyclical popularity of other genres. These surveys, in sum, seem to belie the possibility of a distinct, golden age of early television.[9]

Early television, however, did differ in many ways from that which came over the air in the late 1950s. Programs in the mediums's first decade, for example, were far more likely to be presented live rather than on film. Far more originated in New York than Los Angeles; networks even telecast some series from Chicago in the early 1950s.

Another attribute of the golden age was the weekly "dramatic anthology." Mainly broadcast over NBC and CBS, the anthologies were ordinarily sixty minutes long and were staged live from New York from an original script. Such programs as "Studio One" (CBS, 1948-57), "Producers' Showcase" (NBC, 1947-58), and "Robert Montgomery Presents" (NBC, 1950-57) usually had only one sponsor, which, along with the network, granted producers a remarkable freedom. One producer, Fred Coe, established his own company of writers and performers and supervised from 375 to 400 individual productions. In May 1953, Coe's "Philco Playhouse" presented *Marty*, the story of a Bronx butcher, written by Paddy Chayefsky. Starring Rod Steiger, *Marty* proved to be perhaps the most memorable effort of the anthology form.[10]

In retrospect, the high point of the golden age may have been the live "spectacular," a special program usually running from 90 to 120 minutes, which Columbia and NBC ran from 1953 through 1957. Sylvester L. Weaver, Jr., program chief at NBC, was the first to commit himself to the concept. When NBC presented such "spectaculars" as *Peter Pan* with Mary Martin as Sir James Barrie's flying waif, CBS soon followed with special productions of Noel Coward's *Blithe Spirit*, a musical *Cinderella*, and *High Tor*.[11]

Although the quality of television news, in contrast, generally lagged badly behind the original entertainment produced by the networks, there were exceptions. Weaver developed "The Today Show," beginning in January 1952, a morning two-hour news and informational program.[12] Less original in conception than "Today" was "See It Now" (CBS, 1951-58), narrated and coproduced by the medium's Pericles,

Edward R. Murrow. The critical success of "See It Now" owed much to Murrow's reputation in radio, while the program's organization originally resembled that of *The March of Time* newsreel.[13]

Murrow commanded a small but powerful following of TV critics and fellow journalists. "See It Now" often covered controversial topics, notably on March 9, 1954, when Murrow narrated a highly critical report on Senator McCarthy. That segment received extravagant praise, to the envy of NBC news and managerial personnel; David Sarnoff publicly complimented Murrow for his telecast. A writer for *Variety* exclaimed that the McCarthy program "was worth a dozen variety shows and maybe a couple of hundred conventional drama segments."[14]

The golden age of television tended, then, to include much that satisfied many critics while raising the expectations of others. There were early and at times savage criticisms of young TV.[15] But few reviewers had the perspicacity to anticipate a deterioration of television programming. Robert Saudek, producer of "Omnibus," denied ever believing in a golden age but did remember expecting television to improve from the rough beginnings.[16] Spectaculars often enormously pleased critics, with any number of them defending CBS and NBC—and their power over programming—because of these special entertainments[17] They also led some to assume that there would always be a measure of "balance" between commercial fare for the masses and programming aimed at somewhat higher tastes. In May 1955, Jack Gould of the *New York Times* argued that television had to be regarded as a "medium of compromise. It's the nature of the beast. It must appeal to the biggest audience it can get. This may put good minority programs on at bad hours. But the overall effect of television on the country has been beneficial."[18]

Many of the features of Gould's "medium of compromise" vanished within a very short period. Between 1956 and 1958, most anthologies, live productions, and Murrow's "See It Now" left the air. Hollywood displaced Broadway as the center of program production. And among some, a sense of yearning for those lost elements of the medium emerged to inspire new or more urgent criticisms.

Such displeasure was partly explained by the programs that were made for the "new" television of the late 1950s. Those who mourned the passing of the golden age often had highly selective memories. They tended to forget the awkward and simply embarrassing programming of the era. Live drama could be pretentious and fraught with technical mistakes. Dreary situation comedies and talent-free musical hours often filled a network's evening schedule. "Nothing is more responsible for the good old days," Franklin P. Adams once observed, "than a bad memory." Yet feelings of nostalgia, a romantic longing for a recent or distant era, sociologist Fred Davis notes, normally arise not from a specific sense of the past. Rather they flow from a dissatisfaction with the present.[19] The types of programs that came to supplant those of the golden age—not necessarily the programs of that earlier epoch—caused a critical anguish. Thus, for example, those bemoaning the passing of "The Voice of Firestone," a musical program, would have been far less likely to vent their frustrations had the networks substituted equally satisfying programs for such series.

Instead, the three national chains replaced certain series or anthologies first with quiz programs, then with Westerns and detective dramas, few of which appealed as much to the elites as the earlier fare had. Columbia excised Murrow's "See It Now" to make room for "Do You Trust Your Wife?" a quiz program hosted by Edgar Bergen, who appeared with his wooden assistants Charlie McCarthy and Mortimer Snerd.[20] And, ABC cancelled "The Voice of Firestone" for the 1959-60 season, replacing it with "Bourbon Street Beat," a filmed series about New Orleans private investigators.[21]

The prime-time quiz program posed the first threat to the old order. With the success of CBS's "The $64,000 Question," which began June 1, 1955, the number of evening prime-time quiz programs rose sharply. Created by Louis Cowan, "Question" differed from earlier programs in the amounts of cash prizes and melodramas. Such gimmicks helped the show to draw huge audiences and induced much imitation. In early 1957, Charles Van Doren, an instructor of English at Columbia University and scion of a prominent family of writers, captured the hearts of millions with his boyish good looks and modest manner on "Twenty-One."[22] By December 1957, quiz programs accounted for thirty-seven hours of the networks' weekly schedule. "For a while," one congressman complained, "every time we turned the dial we had a quiz we could look at."[23] The quiz shows' arrival all but doomed the relatively less popular anthologies and news programs. "When 'The $64,000 Question' was born," recalled one TV anthology writer, "commercial television was never the same again."[24]

The quiz-show boom cloaked still another, even more lasting

development: the advent of the filmed action-adventure series, the Western. Cowboys had always been on TV, but in December 1954 and January 1955, episodes of ABC's "Disneyland" based on the life of Davy Crockett drew remarkable ratings—while fueling a coonskin cap craze among children—that deeply impressed advertisers. That fall, ABC scheduled three new Westerns, "Wyatt Earp," "Cheyenne," and "Broken Arrow."[25] (Such horse operas became known as "adult" Westerns to distinguish them from old Hollywood serials shown on TV earlier and because of their explicit treatment of violence, and relatively complex portrayal of human motives.[26]) By the end of 1957, the TV Western had begun to displace the quiz show as the most popular programming in evening prime time. "All Hollywood is divided into two groups," wrote Terrence O'Flaherty, critic for the *San Francisco Chronicle*: "those who are acting in Westerns and those who are writing satellite jokes."[27] Charles Van Doren may have earned $129,000 on "Twenty-One" in 1956-57, but Hugh O'Brien, who played Wyatt Earp, made just over $500,000 in 1958.[28]

Westerns had become both popular and commonplace by the end of 1959. In early 1959, eight of the ten top programs, according to the A. C. Nielsen rankings, were Westerns; *Time* magazine, in typical fashion, did a cover story replete with a value-laden quote by a Hollywood script writer: "Why do so many people spend so much time staring at the wrong end of a horse?"[29] So many Westerns appeared in evening prime time that Groucho Marx complained in February to a friend, "The air is now completely filled with cowboys, fertilizer and inanity."[30] That fall, however, more horse operas followed; 28 of the 125 network series were Westerns. O'Flaherty wrote in October 1959 of "watching westerns so much lately I'm able to recognize not only the actors but the horses."[31]

The new horse operas, like the quiz programs, carried their price. In February 1957, NBC cancelled "Robert Montgomery Presents," even though the series had a sponsor for the 1957-58 season. Lever Brothers dropped the one hour, "Lux Video Theatre" for a half-hour series, and NBC abandoned other anthologies for "The Californians" (September 1957), "Bat Masterson" (October 1957), "Jefferson Drum" (April 1958), "Buck Skin" (July 1958), and "Cimarron City" (September 1958).[32] As listed in table 1, of twenty-five anthology series broadcast in the 1950s, twenty-one, or 84 percent, left the air by 1958. In the fall 1959 season, the president of the CBS Television Division

Table 1. Selected Drama Anthology Programs, 1948-1958

1.	Actor's Studio	ABC	1948-49
		CBS	1949-50
2.	Alcoa Theatre	NBC	1955-60
3.	Armstrong Circle Theater	NBC	1953-57
		CBS	1957-63
4.	Cameo Theatre	NBC	1950-55
5.	Campbell Soup Soundstage	NBC	1952-54
6.	Cavalcade of America	NBC	1952-53
		ABC	1953-57
7.	Chevrolet Tele-Theatre	NBC	1948-50
8.	Climax	CBS	1954-58
9.	Danger	CBS	1950-55
10.	Fireside Theatre	NBC	1949-58
11.	General Electric Theatre	CBS	1953-62
12.	Goodyear TV Playhouse	NBC	1951-60
13.	Kraft Television Theatre	NBC	1947-58
14.	Lux Video Theatre	NBC	1949-58
15.	Pepsi Cola Playhouse	ABC	1953-55
16.	Philco TV Playhouse	NBC	1948-55
17.	Playhouse 90	CBS	1957-61
18.	Producers' Showcase	NBC	1954-57
19.	Pulitzer Prize Playhouse	ABC	1950-52
20.	Robert Montgomery Presents	NBC	1950-57
21.	Schlitz Playhouse of Stars	CBS	1951-55
22.	Studio One	CBS	1948-58
23.	Twentieth Century Fox Hour	CBS	1955-57
24.	U. S. Steel Hour	CBS	1953-63
25.	The Web	CBS	1950-54

Note: Anthologies included in the table ran two years or more. Certain programs such as "Ford Theatre" (1949-57) were not listed because they often featured musical-variety or documentary material. Others were not included because they were aired on an irregular basis. Finally, certain programs listed in some compilations as "dramatic anthologies" I have considered regular series. Each episode of "The Millionaire" involved a specific circumstance and not an original one. Similarly, I did not count programs such as "The Loretta Young Show" which regularly starred an individual actor; they were largely vehicles for the billed player.

Source: Tim Brooks and Earle Marsh, *The Complete Directory to Prime Time Network TV Shows* (New York, 1979); Vincent Terrace, *The Complete Encyclopedia of Television Programs*, 2 vols. (South Brunswick, N. J., 1976).

discovered to his horror that 35 percent of CBS's nighttime schedule was taken up by one of three forms: Westerns, mystery-detective series, and adventure programs. He was satisfied only when he realized that NBC and ABC offered even less diversity.[33]

Ever greater numbers of television shows came out of the "can." The few anthologies such as "Playhouse 90" and "The Goodyear TV Playhouse" that remained were no longer aired live. The June 1953 rate of live programming stood at 81.5 percent; five years later it had slipped to 69.7 percent and slowly ebbed to below 50 percent by the decade's end (see table 2). The *New York Times* noted in July 1957 that TV "for better or worse clearly seems to be moving to a philosophy of film."[34]

Critics uniformly mourned the passing of video's equivalent of the theater. Terrence O'Flaherty termed the passing of the last "Kraft Television Theatre" drama in September 1958 "the saddest news of all."[35] Writing in February 1959, John Crosby observed a "Playhouse 90" rehearsal in New York that evoked a "forlorn" quality, "forlorn because every time I see a live dramatic production anymore I think this may be the last one."[36]

To the critics' alarm, Hollywood surpassed Broadway as the supplier of programs. Originally, many motion picture companies had boycotted the new medium as a threat to theatrical films.[37] The networks had turned to New York theatrical talent for some programs. By the mid-fifties, however, such motion picture companies as Warner Brothers had moved into television production. Others soon followed with the result that even an anthology like "Studio One," which originally owed much to its New York location, was produced in Hollywood in its final season, 1957-58. Gotham, Rod Serling wrote, "once the home of live television production, is in the process of being deserted by TV's writers."[38] John Crosby recalled, "Something went out of the game when TV drama, if you can call it that any more, moved to film and Hollywood."[39]

To the critics' dismay, TV series made in California tended to resemble the grade B movie. Common prior to television as the second feature for a double-billing or as a single show for the marginal or neighborhood movie houses, the B picture could be a Western, mystery, or comedy. B pictures were uniformly and cheaply made; an episode of "The Donna Reed Show" (ABC, 1958-66) took three days to shoot. Most Hollywood series had stereotyped characters and situa-

Table 2. Live Programming for All TV Networks, 1953-1962 (percent)

June 1953[a]	81.5
December 1953[a]	83.0
March 1955[a]	86.7
October 1955[a]	77.7
March 1956	76.8
October 1956	72.9
March 1957	73.5
October 1957	74.3
June 1958	69.7
June 1959	49.1
June 1960	35.9
June 1961	26.5
June 1962	27.8

[a]Includes data for the Du Mont Network.

Source: Broadcasting Yearbook 1963. (Washington, D. C., 1963), 20.

tions and lacked "name" performers and production crews. Although not by definition bad, B movies did come closest to Hollywood's version of the assembly-line product. "If something comes out of Warner Brothers," one TV producer complained, "you know just about what it is going to be."[40]

Entertainment programming was undergoing a standardization. Filmed series were overtaking live dramas. Writing in May 1957, Marya Mannes of the *Reporter* found "a growing number of people . . . disturbed" by the transformation of television. Three or five years earlier, she wrote, there had been great expectations: "the air was charged with intent and possibility." But the home screen was "now set in a rigid pattern from which it either cannot or will not break free."[41] The geographic shift, *Fortune's* Richard Austin Smith wrote in December 1958, officially ended TV's golden age. By taking up Hollywood's standards, Smith reasoned, television had lost "its essential individuality" and had become "the me too medium." "Television's exotic economics have reached a stage," Smith determined, "where they cannot be depended upon to improve the product (the program). On the contrary, TV economics tend to establish and perpetuate mediocrity."[42]

Arguments over the schedule soon came to involve news programming at CBS. Between 1956 and 1958, CBS began dismembering its prestigious news division and cancelling public affairs and news programming. Murrow's "See It Now" had been removed from the regular weekly schedule in July 1955. In early 1958, "See It Now" left the air altogether, as CBS cancelled other regular news programs and restricted the growth of its domestic and overseas news organization.[43]

The dropping of Murrow's "See It Now" in particular invited protests. Crosby blamed the cancellation of "See It Now" on the quiz program and attributed the deed to that moment, several years earlier, "when it was discovered that television was far better suited to play parlor games and give away money." "See It Now," he wrote, was "by every criterion television's most brilliant, most decorated, most imaginative, most courageous and most important program. The fact that CBS cannot afford it but can afford 'Beat the Clock' is shocking."[44] Citing the newspaper and magazine criticisms of the dropping of "See It Now," the head of CBS News, Sig Mickelson, remarked that the print media "hopped on the bandwagon to point out the demise of 'See It Now'." The president of CBS Television, Louis Cowan, tried to allay fears by commenting that the report of the "demise of 'See It Now' like [those of] the death of Mark Twain have been greatly exaggerated."[45] Nevertheless, Senators John F. Kennedy of Massachusetts and Warren R. Magnuson of Washington, the latter the chairman of the Senate committee that reviewed broadcast regulation, expressed concern over the fate of Murrow and CBS News.[46]

Murrow made his own attack in October 1958. In a stern lecture to the Radio and Television News Directors' Association, Murrow described evening prime time as consisting of "decadence, escapism, and insulation from the realities of the world." The networks underestimated the mentality of the viewer, he declared. "The American public is more reasonable, restrained, and more mature than most of our industry's program planners believe." Networks and sponsors, Murrow found, possessed a "fear of controversy" and had hence chosen to limit news coverage at a time of "mortal danger" for America. To remedy TV's ailments, Murrow suggested that the FCC consider compelling more individual stations to carry news programs.

And the newscaster asked that "the twenty or thirty big corporations which dominate [by advertising] radio and television" surrender a portion of their sponsored prime time to underwrite news programming without running commercials. "We are currently wealthy, fat, comfortable and complacent," Murrow said. "Our mass media reflect this."[47]

In his October address, Murrow offered what became the basic criticism of the new television. The programming of the late 1950s, by promoting mere amusement, jeopardized the virtue of the republic if not the security of Western democracy. Advertisers and network executives were to be blamed, not the majority of viewers or those involved in creating the less popular fare of the golden age. Finally, intervention by the FCC was recommended as a solution.

The networks largely ignored such attacks until revelations late in 1959 offered the most extraordinary example of the medium's recent corruption. The great hero of "Twenty-One," Charles Van Doren, confessed to a House committee in November 1959 to having been party to a massive fix of the recently popular quiz programs. Like some one hundred other contestants, Van Doren had allowed the program producers to coach his performance and encourage him to lie before a New York grand jury investigating the affair.[48] In Van Doren, academic knowledge, so precious in the age of Sputnik, had not only betrayed the house of intellect by selling itself to the heirs of George Washington Hill, but had done so in an underhanded way.[49] *Broadcasting* commented, "a national hero came tumbling down last week. With him fell the public's opinion of the medium that pushed him into national prominence."[50]

After two years of budding criticism, TV now had to deal with its greatest scandal. Such national commentators as Walter Lippmann, normally concerned only with the great affairs of state, took time to discuss what he termed "the TV Problem."[51] Syndicated columnist Roscoe Drummond decried advertisers for assuming "that the nation is populated by boobs and morons."[52] "Charles Van Doren's abject and humiliating confession of deceit and deliberate untruthfulness is shocking, dismaying and deeply disturbing," the *St. Louis Post-Dispatch* intoned. "It reveals so much that is wrong with our society."[53]

"If there is one poor soul in any of the fifty states," the *New Republic* commented in early November, "who doesn't know by now that the public has been tricked on television, he deserves to be preserved as a national curiosity in the Smithsonian."[54] The *Herald Tribune*'s columnists and editorials were so critical of television that the owner of the newspaper, John Hay Whitney, who ordinarily did not intervene in its day-to-day operations, angrily asked his managing editor to cease running such "fatuous piety" about the scandal.[55]

Many, however, shared the sentiments of Whitney's underlings. Into the White House mailroom came letters lambasting the TV trade. "We cleaned up Italy," one veteran telegraphed the former allied commander. "We cleaned up Germany and all of Europe. How about cleaning up Grand Rapids television station WOOD before you go out of office?" The president of a Greenville, Illinois, bank wrote Eisenhower, "The airwaves are a natural resource and should be used to improve and help our citizens, especially the young, instead of debasing them with violence and sometimes scenes developing the lower sex feelings."[56] "We are going to pay for those mistakes for a long time," one CBS executive remarked early the next year, "and we are paying for them now. All sorts of dissatisfactions about television crystallize as a result of these miserable events."[57]

Eisenhower and other political leaders could not avoid commenting on TV's time of troubles. The president himself had never been a quiz-show viewer; he preferred televised golf tournaments and "This Is Your Life." But in an October 22 press conference, he described the programs' rigging as "a terrible thing to do to the American public." A month later, when asked by James Reston of the *New York Times* to remark on Van Doren's confession, Eisenhower likened the young man to "Shoeless Joe" Jackson, one of the players involved in the fix of the 1919 World Series.[58] The Director of the U. S. Information Agency, George V. Allen, declared that the scandals had hurt America's prestige abroad, where they were being attributed to the nation's "low state of public morals." Governor Nelson A. Rockefeller of New York simply termed the revelations "tragic."[59]

Heard, too, in the wake of the quiz-show revelations, were references to the lost golden age. Analyzing CBS's October plans for greater self-regulation, Jack Gould included a mournful reference to the passing of live dramatic anthologies displaced by the "missing realism by mechanical means" of filmed series.[60] Congressman Peter Mack, Democrat of Illinois, asked Robert Kintner, president of NBC if that network might not have avoided "your problems on rigging and dishonesty, [and] hanky-panky" by originating more programs from Chicago as it had during the golden age.[61] Congressman John Moss, Democrat of California, somewhat incongruously criticized ABC for cancelling "The Voice of Firestone" program popular with an unusually large number of congressmen.[62]

Congressman Moss and others offered the observation that the new television of the late 1950s had become too concerned with the tastes of the majority of viewers. Efforts to maintain a balanced schedule appeared to have been virtually abandoned by 1959. "I have watched other favorites disappear," Moss complained. "This same drive to achieve a larger circulation, a larger exposure for the commercials, has resulted in a deterioration of what I would call balance."[63] An American Civil Liberties Union (ACLU) official testifying before the FCC in December 1959 maintained that the television industry's drive for larger profits had created "a built-in, extremely powerful private censorship which, for the sake of financial gain, has substituted rigged entertainment for straightforward information and . . . has barred controversial discussion of many important subjects."[64] Several months later, a major advertising executive agreed, commenting, "I think the critics are rightly dismayed by the plight of the minority of viewers whose desire for more intellectual stimulation and satisfaction from television is fulfilled all too rarely.[65]

Privately, some industry leaders acknowledged what had happened to their medium. In a November memorandum, Louis Cowan of CBS, who had created "The $64,000 Question," was forced to observe, "Television is presently at a crossroad." Cowan called for a restoration of the golden age, citing "the need for more serious drama, education, discussion, debate, news, and documentary-type programming; serious music; elimination of violence, the development of new forms; the evaluation of the 'specials' concept."[66]

Within weeks, the president of CBS, Frank Stanton, and its chairman of the board, William Paley, fired Cowan. Although he protested his innocence, his close ties to several of the rigged programs made him a public relations problem and cast him as the sacrificial lamb. His successor, James Aubrey, lacked Cowan's interest in the programming of the good old days. Indeed, Aubrey had been among those who had encouraged the use of Hollywood productions at the expense of those less popular series Cowan had been prepared to return to the network's schedule.[67]

By the decade's end, television no longer seemed to offer places for creative energies. In a 1949 essay, the sociologist Paul Goodman had written optimistically about the prospects for mass culture in the postwar world. In *Growing Up Absurd*, published in 1960, Goodman concluded that "popular culture is controlled by hucksters and promoters as though it were a salable commodity, and our society, inundated by cultural commodities remains uncultivated."[68]

During 1960 many of TV's detractors elevated the debate over television to the controversy over "national purpose," or America's lack of one. Television, such social critics maintained, had been betraying standards of excellence—so much more important as the nation discovered the Soviets' skills in satellite and missile construction—by the very coveting of mass audiences and by portraying "average" Americans in situation comedies, to say nothing of amoral or less than heroic heroes in the new adult Westerns. To one writer, TV had helped to breed a "cult of mediocrity" and render Americans, the requisites of the cold war notwithstanding, "confident and complacent."[69] Critics like Robert Lewis Shayon of the *Saturday Review* had watched with horror in early 1958 an episode of "Leave It to Beaver" that portrayed young Theodore Cleaver as traumatized when a school IQ survey accidentally characterized him as a genius. "Beaver" does not want to be a genius or be sent to a "progressive" school. "Do we not desperately need geniuses for survival?" Shayon asked. "President Eisenhower, his Cabinet and Congress may lay heroic plans for producing the brainpower the nation requires," he noted. Yet "before we can mass-produce genius we must respect and honor genius." Such episodes "are certainly not going in the right direction."[70]

Television could instill virtue in the citizen, Dr. Benjamin Spock, the nation's expert on baby care, wrote Senator John F Kennedy in March 1960. "Instead, there is the constant search for the commonest level of taste in passive entertainment . . . used, in turn, to sell goods, in a manner which breeds insincerity and cynicism, and which appeals always to more gratification.[71] Writing in November for the President's Commission on National Goals, August Heckscher decried TV's "diet of mediocrity" and argued that "third— and fourth-rate material seems increasingly to replace the better shows" whereas "what is required is some means of providing standards of excellence."[72]

Finally, television criticism revealed an aspect of American liberalism during the late 1950s. Many liberals felt betrayed by the emerging popular will in the arts; the older faith in the public was perhaps first unsettled by the popular enthusiasm for McCarthy among some ethnic blocs once for the New Deal.[73] It appeared all too ironic that with recovery from the Great Depression, the "great audience" drew upon mass communication systems not to be enlightened but to be entertained. "Universal education, the alleviation of physical misery, the drift of equality," wrote sociologist Edward Shils in 1957, "have not brought with them that deepening and enrichment of the mind to which liberals and revolutionaries alike aspired." Instead, Shils observed, "the silliness of television" satisfied the masses.[74]

In light of this gross disparity between mass prosperity and mass enlightenment, some liberal Democratic party strategists attempted to redirect the Democracy. The Eisenhower landslides of 1952 and 1956 caused some to ponder the future of a party said to be the champion of the worker and underclass; prosperity seemed to be turning the proletariat into Republicans, while all but eliminating poverty from the landscape. This body of Democrats, of course, assumed that the New Deal had resolved what Arthur M. Schlesinger, Jr., termed the "essentially quantitative" problems of the 1930s of providing all Americans with the basic necessities of food, shelter, and employment; the Republicans had won in 1952 and 1956 because the Democrats had "run out of poor people." Now Schlesinger, historian and adviser to Adlai Stevenson and John F. Kennedy, spoke of "qualitative" problems of an affluent America. Shorter workweeks, earlier retirements, and longer life expectancies had, in Schlesinger's mind, brought Americans not the self-fulfillment anticipated but a "spiritual disquietude," a condition worsened by the state's inadequate attention to the "quality" of American life, including its mass culture. Liberalism, he wrote, "must for the moment shift its focus from economics and politics to the general style and quality of our civilization."[75]

Writing about television in the wake of quiz scandals, Schlesinger joined those seeing decline, while advocating governmental intervention. "I cannot repress my feelings that, in the main, television has been a great bust." He recommended that networks free themselves of advertisers, that stations be compelled to share in the burdens of airing less popular programming, with the possibility of the FCC's setting standards and annually renewing licenses on the basis of program practices. The government must act, he found, citing

Richard Austin Smith's 1958 article in *Fortune*, "because there seems no other way to rescue television from the downward spiral of competitive debasement.[76]

What had begun as a fairly specific dissatisfaction blossomed into a wholesale condemnation and, ultimately, a cry for augmented federal regulation. A group of leading critics had not liked what has displaced dramatic anthologies or "See It Now." The sense of television's diminution frustrated those who searched for national purpose and coveted standards of excellence amid a culture seen as championing mediocrity and conformity. Thus, some called for state intervention in broadcasting as a logical step to preserve and enhance the quality of American life. These critics looked to the FCC.

Chapter Three

The Government and the TV Problem, 1952-1960

Could the FCC in the 1950s have prevented the TV programming crisis? The FCC was incapable of regulating television, some argued, because it was the "captive" of the industry it had been mandated to police. According to this view, the FCC's natural sympathies rested with the very constituency—broadcasting—that the commission had to coax or bludgeon into reform. Only rigorous enforcement of the FCC's stated goals for licensees would have enhanced American television. "Broadcasters," Gilbert Seldes wrote after the cancellation of "See It Now," "*alone* have defined the FCC's crucial phrase, 'the public interest.' A social and moral vacuum was created when the FCC refused to provide a definition."[1]

Chairman Doerfer, representing the Eisenhower majority on the FCC, freely denied any interest in programming. This is not to say he was a First Amendment absolutist. He disapproved of subliminal advertising, which attempted to sell goods by subconscious appeals to consumers. He supported the postmaster general's attempt to suppress the distribution of D. H. Lawrence's *Lady Chatterly's Lover*, which Doerfer deemed offensive to society's sexual mores. But the chairman stubbornly held that for the FCC to intervene ever so slightly in scheduling decisions would violate the Bill of Rights and Section 326 of the Communications Act, which forbade the censoring of programming.[2]

Other critics of the commission, many of them economists, have faulted the FCC under Doerfer for not having adequately stimulated technologies that would have provided a greater diversity of programming. Specifically, the commission should have fostered the use of an underutilized portion of the TV band, pay television, and cable TV signal systems. These would have increased the number of both stations and program sources. The diversity that editorial writers and others demanded of TV would have been achieved.[3]

As early as 1949, several types of cable and community antenna relay systems (CATV) were developed in Washington State and Pennsylvania which transmitted signals past natural physical boundaries. But these processes were few and far between in the late fifties. They were designed only to improve reception in isolated communities— not to offer viewers greater choice in programming.[4] Cable and related systems were regarded as crutches for the disabled rather than as common carriers.

If CATV did not offer the dissatisfied viewer solace in the late fifties, a large and unused portion of the television band did. To many, TV's imbalances might have been avoided if the commission had found a way to increase the number of stations on the ultra high frequency (UHF), channels 14 through 83. By the late 1950s, the commission had awarded virtually all of the very high frequency (VHF) channels, 2 through 13, in the larger viewing areas. Most of these went to commercial interests with one or more network affiliations. Unlike VHF stations, few UHF outlets had succeeded. If UHF could be made more attractive both to entrepreneurs and viewers, however, the expansion of new television services might follow.

The strengthening of UHF might have remedied the TV crisis in several ways. Substantially more UHF stations would have divided the "mass" market of TV into various specialized ones, thus assuring greater selection in programming. There would have been ample room for pay TV systems. Finally, a potential noncommercial service would have depended on UHF stations. The commission, in issuing the 1952 master plan, had reserved channels for the use of educational and other nonprofit associations; most of these were in UHF.

No single matter before the commission in the 1950s, however, had been more disappointing than the UHF problem. Until 1952, the commission had awarded licenses on the VHF portion of the spectrum only. When the FCC promulgated a master plan in April 1952 for allocating TV channels throughout the nation, a majority of the commissioners had assumed that UHF stations would be fully competitive with VHF ones. Despite evidence that UHF was a less powerful transmitter of the signal—and more expensive to operate[5]—the commission determined that time and consumer choice would render UHF stations equal to their VHF rivals.[6] Thus many individual viewing areas or markets (such as Providence and Baton Rouge) were in commission jargon "intermixed": the agency set VHF and UHF services against each other. Yet within two years of the 1952 order most of the new UHF stations were in severe financial straits. Some television set manufacturers had refused to produce "all-channel" sets, which could receive both the VHF and UHF signals. Many early UHF tuners were poorly designed and all cost more than the sets providing only VHF. Consumers, in turn, refrained from paying the extra $25 to $50 for all-channel receivers. As a result, the typical UHF station manager found that his outlet enjoyed only 5 to 20 percent of the total audience his VHF competitor commanded. Most advertisers refused to buy time on UHF channels, while all three networks—in seeking affiliate stations—discriminated against outlets in the new frequency.[7]

Many UHF operators met with hardship. By January 1956, 60 of 159 stations on the UHF band had gone off the air. Through 1959 no individual UHF station earned more than $200,000 a year, while in 1957, 117 VHF channels passed that income figure, 43 of them netting more than $1 million each.[8]

Nothing the commission did between 1952 and 1959 corrected the disparity between UHF and VHF operations. In November 1955 the commission voted five to two not to "deintermix" the intermixed markets, or transform them into all-UHF or all-VHF areas, which would have placed stations on an equal footing. That order also put off indefinitely relief for many UHF operators, who had been clamoring for help for well over a year. "What the Commission has done today," Commissioner Rosel Hyde said in dissent, "may deal a death blow to UHF television service."[9]

To the Eisenhower majority on the FCC, however, refusing to aid UHF television was consistent with its advocacy of the free market as broadcast regulator. Through the remainder of the decade, a majority of commissioners, led by Chairmen McConnaughey and Doerfer, contended that UHF's inferiority was such that to impose it in certain areas would deny some viewers in outlying areas basic television service altogether. Moreover, if consumers truly wanted more TV channels, they would pay the additional price for an all-channel set.[10]

Although the FCC refused to untie the UHF allocation knot, Congress, not the commission, shelved still another potential answer to the TV problem: pay or subscription television. Since the early 1950s several film and TV set manufacturing companies had, with the FCC's approval, test marketed several types of pay television broadcast systems. These groups promised much: live Broadway theater, home baseball games, heavyweight championship fights, ballet, and feature films not available to the "free" TV networks and stations. "Subscription television can succeed," one pay TV petitioner told the FCC in September 1955, "only if it offers unique and high quality programs which are beyond the economic reach of the producers of advertising sponsored programs."[11] Subscription TV, wrote a frequent critic of the medium, "is the only answer in the horrid battle existing in our republic today between quality and quantity."[12]

Despite the opposition of the networks, station operators, and motion picture theater owners (who dreaded the loss of even more of their dwindling audience), the FCC decided in December 1955 to permit pay TV tests to continue. "One can wonder whether America's progress in literature or the stage or the arts would have reached its present heights," the commission argued, "had the progress of these arts depended upon the support of advertising sponsors."[13] Writing for *Barron's*, John Chamberlain observed, "The FCC was not set up to protect the moving picture theatres, or to save the broadcasters trouble."[14]

As pay television entrepreneurs continued to experiment, however, "free" TV executives and consumers began to protest more vigorously the prospect of "fee" TV. In 1955, when the FCC held hearings on pay systems, some 24,000 consumers (the most ever to have written the agency on a pending matter) sent letters and postcards objecting to any form of subscription television. By late 1957, the AFL-CIO opposed the experiments.[15] A fear developed, fueled by broadcasters, that pay TV would siphon off the more popular programs and players and eventually wipe out free television. Subscription television, Robert W. Sarnoff, president of NBC, told a Pittsburgh group in October 1957, would ultimately offer "precisely the same types of programs now offered on free television."[16]

Many less well-to-do and older users of TV sets accepted the industry's logic. Although such publications as the *Saturday Review* indicated reader support for pay TV, many more Americans unhesitantly wrote their senators and representatives insisting that no pay TV channels be allowed to operate. In one three-day period early in 1958, an Oklahoma congressman received 1,947 pieces of mail on pay TV, of which only two supported the continuation of the subscription TV tests.[17] "We are an elderly couple and have scraped enough money together to be able to have one [TV]," a Wisconsin woman wrote her senator. "We would not be able to pay the fee for running it if there was a charge."[18] An indignant Bronx man likened pay TV to New York City's new pay toilets. "If you don't have the money to pay for it—your [sic] out of luck and if you do and go inside—its [sic] not any cleaner."[19]

Early in 1958, the House Commerce Committee forced the FCC to put off further pay TV tests. Doerfer and others insisted that the systems warranted a trial.[20] But Oren Harris was equally adamant. Chairing the committee that oversaw FCC operations and policies, Harris could make life unpleasant for Doerfer and his agency, already troubled by conflict-of-interest scandals. Doerfer, though an advocate of the free-market's primacy in broadcast regulation, backed down. The commission postponed indefinitely further pay TV tests in selected markets.[21]

Into the late 1950s, the commission was unable or unwilling to prevent the TV problem. Congress frustrated pay TV tests. Cable TV appeared little more than an aid to people living on the wrong side of a mountain; UHF stations had been left to the mercy of TV set manufacturers and indifferent consumers and advertisers. And the commission itself defined the First Amendment rights of broadcasters so broadly that direct program regulation seemed unlikely.

Any momentum for changing American television in the late 1950s rested within the industry. Early in 1959, as critics increasingly decried the passing of the golden age, two of the three networks began to recognize the need for concessions. Even before the House Commerce Committee revealed the quiz-show fix, both CBS and NBC started rearranging their schedules, apparently to correct some of the imbalances imposed on viewers since the fall of 1957. The president of CBS, Frank Stanton, announced in May 1959 that his network would schedule a biweekly hour-long news program, "CBS Reports," in evening prime time. The network named Fred Friendly, Murrow's old partner on "See It Now," to produce "CBS Reports."[22] Though NBC placed no news programs in evening prime time, it did include two one-hour segments, "Sunday Showcase" and "Star-time," modeled after the golden-age anthologies and spectaculars. Each program consisted of a different variety, dramatic, or musical special. Then NBC scheduled radio's "Bell Telephone Hour" for TV on Friday nights. Stressing renewed diversity, the network termed its fall 1959 offerings, "total television."[23]

The beginnings of the House quiz-show inquiry in October accelerated this trend. Midway through the hearings, Stanton tried to defuse the new and greater criticisms by announcing in New Orleans on October 16 CBS's cancellation of all of its remaining quiz programs. Broadcasters, Stanton said, "have indeed failed fully to meet our duty with regard to quiz shows." The CBS network intended to assert control over the production of programs, with Stanton pledging to end all deceptions in the remaining programming. No longer would the news division rehearse interviews or situation comedies use "canned" laughter.[24] Wags wondered about the implications of Stanton's intentions. Would real bullets rather than blanks be utilized for TV Westerns? Would actors impersonating Santa Claus have to confess to millions of American children.[25] Regardless, Stanton's speech was widely covered and brought forth much praise, notably from Oren Harris, who had chaired the House's inquiry into the fraud. Others, such as Representative Peter Mack, termed Stanton's address a blatant effort "to head off legislation."[26]

Stanton's New Orleans speech did not, in fact, quiet industry detractors; some began to raise the possibility of unprecedented federal involvement in programming. Although doubtful that the government could do anything, President Eisenhower asked Attorney General William P. Rogers to study the question of what the government might have done to prevent the fix.[27] Senator William Langer of North Dakota, senior Republican on the Judiciary Committee, criticized the industry and implied that increased federal authority would follow.[28] In the House, Republican Congressman John Bennett of Michigan reintroduced a bill that empowered the FCC to license networks. Chairman Harris asked his staff to survey the possibility of holding hearing on TV violence and the excessive number of TV Westerns. Congressman Henry Reuss, Democrat of Wisconsin, suggested that Congress require stations to allot 20 percent of their broadcast day to "sustaining" (unsponsored) public affairs programming.[29] "There now is the chilling prospect," *Variety* commented on November 11, "that the Harris quiz hearing may have been only a mild curtain raiser."[30]

Much of this response conveyed a frustration with existing regulation. Among other things, the fix had indicated how unwilling the commission had been to involve itself in programming matters. After many rumors of a fix, the FCC secretary had sent mildly worded letters to the two networks airing the quiz programs. Otherwise, the agency had done nothing to reveal the hoax. Once the affair had been uncovered, Doerfer exasperated many by insisting that the FCC could not have investigated or now punish the transgressors. Although terming the quiz producers' actions "most reprehensible," the chairman argued that the commission could not oversee the networks' programming without raising grave constitutional questions.[31]

For his narrow views, Doerfer and the FCC received the most unrelenting abuse. Several cited the agency's 1958 conflict-of-interest scandals as the real reason for the commission's inability to recognize wrongdoing. "The Commission has been charged in recent years with practices which suggest that Caesar's wife has not always been its model for conduct becoming to officials whose absolute integrity the public is entitled to assume," a former FCC staff member remarked.[32] In the *New Republic*, TRB spoke of the FCC's "implied powers" under the "public interest" criterion as a way of policing the transgressors. But since, over the years, the commission had proved to be "the weakest sister of all of the regulatory commissions," the industry felt free to abuse the airwaves. "That is why the television quiz shows were rigged." The *Chicago American* dismissed Doerfer's early testimony as "sophistry." "The Commission could have inquired into the operation of the quiz shows, and if it had inquired diligently it could have found out" and "warned the public."[33] One of Doerfer's harshest detractors, Congressman Walter Rogers of Texas, accused the chairman of "straining constructions of the laws to avoid doing something."[34] *Consumer Reports* charged in January 1960, "There is not a single item of broadcasting malpractice that the FCC did not have the obligation to know about and, knowing, did not have the power to curb."[35]

Such blasts left Doerfer little choice but to modify his views. A steadfast advocate of the First Amendment's extension to broadcasters, who stubbornly, even bravely, maintained his beliefs before the most hostile interrogators, Doerfer realized that he had to persuade broadcasters to protect their own interest, and freedoms, in a positive fashion. In Chicago on November 20 the chairman warned the trade: Congress, the commission, and the courts "have been very liberal" in granting licensees autonomy, Doerfer said. Unless the industry

better policed itself immediately, it risked "strict government controls" when Congress returned in January. Otherwise, "the American
system of broadcasting will come to a crisis" with "no one to blame
but itself."[36] Les Brown, covering Doerfer's talk for *Variety*, wrote
of a "New" Doerfer, less trusting of his wards, and "resigned to some
governmental corrective action."[37]

Four days after Doerfer's address, the leaders of all three networks
met at New York's St. Regis Hotel after Stanton called for a consensus about industry strategy, especially increasing "public affairs" (news
and cultural) programming to compensate for the good-will spent on
the quiz fix. The problem was that public affairs programs did not
then ordinarily command good ratings or attractive advertising sales.
For CBS Stanton and William Paley suggested that the three networks
commit themselves to a weekly news and public affairs time period
but on an alternating basis to spread the losses incurred. After heated
debates, David and Robert Sarnoff and Robert Kintner of NBC rejected
the CBS plan, and the meeting ended without the direction Stanton
had hoped to give the industry.[38]

The failure of the St. Regis meeting notwithstanding, the networks
already were conceding some prime time to news coverage. In late
October, amid the Harris quiz-show hearing, NBC expanded its
number of five-minute TV news programs by 50 percent and its
special, hour-long "depth" coverage of selected public issues by 100
percent. The number of special network news programs rose sharply
after Van Doren's confession in early November. In December, President Eisenhower went on a world tour, and the networks assigned
crews to follow the chief executive in unprecedented "special
coverage."[39] "Charlie Van Doren," one network executive commented, "did great things for information programming."[40]

Such changes of heart, however, failed to placate Attorney General
Rogers. Late in December 1959, Rogers reported to Eisenhower on
the quiz fixes. Brusquely faulting the FCC, Rogers called for "more
and vigorous action." The attorney general insisted on increasing
federal regulation over networks and suggested that the commission
police individual stations through a spot-check system akin to that
used by the Internal Revenue Service. The FCC would select stations
at random to monitor their program schedules, while looking for any
of the quiz-scandal related excesses. Finally, Rogers dismissed
Doerfer's advocacy of greater self-regulation with the comment, "Industry efforts to clean house should be applauded, but it is unlikely

that such attempts will be successful unless the appropriate regulatory agencies manifest a continued concern in protecting the public interest and exercise their powers directly and promptly."[41]

While Walter Lippmann praised Rogers's findings, *Broadcasting* reported shock within the TV industry. An editorial dubbed Rogers's study, "Blue Book Two."[42] Former president Hoover wrote Doerfer, "I had hoped, like you, that much of his [objectives] could be accomplished within the industry. I still hope this may be done." But the attorney general's analysis "creates an entirely new situation."[43]

Not long after the release of Rogers's report, the industry faced the second session of the 86th Congress and decidedly unfriendly proposed amendments to the Communications Act. In a February 1960 report, Oren Harris's committee called for the direct supervision of the networks by the FCC. The commission's powers over individual licensees would be greatly strengthened. Stations violating the Communications Act or commission regulations would be fined $1,000 a day, ordered off the air until they corrected such violations, or have their license renewed for one, rather than three, years.[44]

As Harris prepared his Communications Act revisions, Doerfer dropped his lingering reluctance about interfering with the networks' programming practices. "Doerfer was the last one you'd expect to try to prescribe programs," Rosel Hyde recalled, "but in the atmosphere of rigged quiz scandals, he did it on his own."[45] In mid-January 1960 the FCC chairman devised a scheme for rotating the airing of public affairs programming. By the "Doerfer Plan," as it became known, the three networks would each schedule a full hour per week of news or "high" cultural fare in evening prime time (8:00-11:00 P.M.). Local stations would produce a similar proportion such that each night one network or network affiliate would air one hour of news and/or cultural programming. The plan would take effect in November 1960. In exchange, the FCC would not, among other pledges, move against network "option time," those periods of the broadcast day that the commission permitted exclusive network-station arrangements. Doerfer secured the approval of his fellow commissioners and of the attorney general, who had to pass on the antitrust proprieties of the three networks' coordination of programming policy. With a letter from Rogers, Doerfer persuaded all three networks to adopt his plan. Considering the inability of Stanton and others in November to agree upon a similar scheme, Doerfer had fashioned what appeared to be an impressive compromise. "This action," Doerfer proclaimed, "demonstrates the ability of the industry to respond promptly to a felt need."[46]

With his intricate negotiations completed, Doerfer went to Florida in late February for fishing and golf, a natural itinerary for a weary regulator. He traveled to and from Miami, however, in the Storer Broadcasting aircraft and spent some six days aboard the yacht of George Storer, president of the company that operated twelve radio and TV licenses. Some two years earlier, Doerfer's enthusiasm for Storer's largesse had been much criticized by Oren Harris and other members of the Legislative Oversight Committee. Doerfer had then promised not to engage again in such intimate, *ex parte* social contracts. Now he had compromised himself.[47]

Doerfer's six days on Storer's cabin cruiser ended his public career. At first the chairman tried to deny spending more than one or two days aboard Storer's ship, but soon thereafter, Doerfer fully detailed how he had spent his time in the sun. Citing this violation of the chairman's 1958 pledge, Harris demanded his ouster. Doerfer defended himself, saying, "I do not think a Commissioner should be a second-rate citizen," and even went to the president to plead his case, made all the more indefensible by his deep tan. But Eisenhower, furious over Doerfer's indiscretion, secured his resignation.[48]

Critics of the commission saw in Doerfer's conduct further, damning evidence of the corruption and biases of the FCC. The hapless chairman received little or no credit for having formulated the Doerfer Plan. Instead, he became the source of many diatribes directed at the administrative agencies under Eisenhower. Murray Kempton of the *New York Post* wrote that if Doerfer "did not exist, the broadcasting networks would have had to invent him."[49]

Doerfer's exit was by no means beneficial to those unhappy with American television in 1960, although this fact was little appreciated at the time. His successor, Frederick W. Ford, possessed an integrity and commitment to regulatory principles alien to Doerfer. On the other hand, Ford did not approve of the Doerfer Plan, which he thought an improper, extralegal response. With the chairman's departure, his voluntary scheme for minority interest programming fell by the wayside.

A West Virginia Republican and career civil servant, Frederick Ford had been a commissioner since August 1957. Previously, he had worked in the Justice Department, after serving as a legal specialist at the commission. He possessed both experience and personal honesty uncommon for an Eisenhower FCC appointee. And unlike Doerfer, Ford had good relations with congressional overseers like Harris.[50]

Not surprisingly, some broadcasters looked apprehensively at the appointment of Ford. Many identified him with Attorney General Rogers, under whom he had served in the Justice Department. One trade journal warned in March, "The FCC will get tougher."[51]

Ford was actually less influenced by William Rogers's "modern Republicanism" than by the FCC's lost regulatory legacies. Like James Lawrence Fly, Ford believed that competition would benefit the medium. Breaking down barriers to the formation of new stations or sources of TV production would bring more balance in programming. Then, too, the new chairman accepted the premise, once identified with Commissioners Paul Porter and Clifford Durr, that the FCC should review the schedules of individual stations. In other words, Ford combined two distinct regulatory approaches: one that relied on the marketplace, the other, a visible hand, to achieve a greater diversity of programming.

Ford set the tone of his new regime in his April 1960 speech to the annual convention of the National Association of Broadcasters. Like Rogers, Ford assumed that government had to regulate broadcasting in a more concerted manner and not leave matters to his capacity for friendly persuasion or to the industry's good-will. Although agreeing that the FCC should not censor specific programs, the chairman insisted that licensees recognize certain obligations to their communities, that they "be responsive to the public interests."[52] In a letter to one dissatisfied viewer, former ambassador Clare Boothe Luce, Eisenhower's press secretary cited Ford's NAB talk with the comment, "I'm sure that he means what he says and will follow up along such lines."[53]

In July, the new chairman persuaded his fellow commissioners to list fourteen different types of programming the airing of which the commission would henceforth regard as serving the public interest. Ford, like nearly everyone else at the agency, did not expect station managers to surrender great blocks of time to such programming. But the commission did ask that programs falling under the rubric of "public service" include not only news, weather, and sports programs but discussions of community issues, religious programs, and other less popular fare. The July policy statement constituted the first clear emunciation of what broadcasters should air since the Blue Book was issued in 1946.[54]

Ford's second major objective as chairman was to foster new television services. In addition to direct regulation, TV's imbalances could be overcome, Ford concluded, with the advent of more TV stations on the UHF band. To that end, Ford sought to compel set manufacturers to make only all-channel sets. As chairman, he called on Congress to allow the FCC to issue receiver standards to manufacturers. To Ford, such legislation afforded the simplest, long-term answer to the UHF issues.[55] But the administration and Congress all but ignored Ford's proposal. Congress did approve in July 1960 a $2 million two-year test of a UHF signal in New York City to see if, after all, the higher frequency was worth the pain of all-channel receivers and deintermixture.[56]

Still, the most immediate effect of Ford's ascension related to the Doerfer Plan. The new chairman did not approve of his predecessor's scheme; Ford regarded mandating such programs and their air time—even as a voluntary arrangement—as an exercise in censoring programs.[57] Network executives accordingly abandoned their voluntary arrangement. The man that they had been dealing to had left the card game. In April 1960, ABC announced that it planned to schedule one of its Doerfer Plan offerings, "Expedition!" between 7:00 and 7:30 P.M. on Thursday, not in prime time, and hence, a violation of the plan. As ABC pulled out, the other networks felt free not to follow the scheme.[58]

Congress offered another reason for the collapse of the Doerfer Plan. Considering Harris's amendments to the Communications Act between February and June 1960, Congress removed those proposals least pleasing to broadcasters. In so doing, industry lost any incentive for adopting Doerfer's scheme: there were to be no new, sharp teeth in the Communications Act. In late June, the House rejected the licensing of networks. Harris himself had come to disapprove of the idea, which he believed might place a network, already an operator of stations, in double jeopardy.[59] But the 1960 articles did prohibit stations from engaging in free "plugs" and from deceptions in the staging of quiz programs unless the licensee acknowledged the staged elements before or after the individual telecast. The Senate, however, weakened a House feature that would have invested the FCC with the power to levy heavy fines. The final bill empowered the commission to punish stations through the issuance of "short-term," or one-year, license renewals. That is, the FCC could renew the license of a negligent station for one year, instead of the standard three years, a punitive act because of the legal and other costs accompanying the renewal process itself.[60] But with the absence of network licensing, heavy fines, or Henry Reuss's proposal for a set amount of nonentertainment fare, broadcasters fared rather well.

Congress probably never intended to deal harshly with the industry. There was of course the historic aversion to anything smacking of interference with a medium of communication. A more powerful FCC would raise the potential of program censorship.[61] A few congressmen who owned shares in local TV or radio stations worried about self-interest. Many more, however, had little idea what had been happening to TV during the late 1950s; most watched little television and apparently relied on constituent mail for the barest information about the medium.[62]

Another factor that no doubt operated to the industry's benefit was that few Americans apparently cared deeply about the quiz producers' improprieties. In late 1959, ministers and magazine editors saw in Van Doren's discomfort a great moral lesson for all Americans.[63] An extraordinarily large number of Americans, some 92 percent according to the Gallup survey, knew of the quiz-show fix—more than were aware of the location of Quemoy and Matsu or the significance of Little Rock. Yet familiarity with a wrong by no means indicated a widespread outrage over the scandal or enthusiasm for changes in the medium. Although such prominent commentators as Walter Lippmann and John Fischer sensed from their circle of friends and correspondence an anger over the industry's ways, that mood apparently prevailed only among the upper-middle-class readers of the stronger editorial pages and *Harper's*.[64] In the Middle West, a *Variety* contributor found in January 1960, "people don't like the idea of two or three New York columnists dictating to the networks what's good for us."[65] Few citizens elsewhere in the country who wrote letters to such popular magazines as *TV Guide* or to their congressmen evinced a deep interest in TV's problems.[66] Viewers continued to buy the products of sponsors implicated in the scandals, and the total number of television watchers increased. "The attitude of viewers toward TV as a whole," *Business Week* reported, "has been affected surprisingly little by the quiz blow-up."[67]

Still, the weightiest reason for Congress's weak response may well have been the proximity of the elections of 1960. Politicians respected the industry's sentiments, since radio and television could help or hurt an incumbent's reelection effort. With their network ties, local stations were likely to be owned or operated by community business leaders or local newspapers. Legislators coveted the loyalties of these hometown "influentials." "Congress in an election year," James Reston had predicted in November 1959, "is not going to want to punish the TV industry too hard."[68]

The relaxing of congressional pressure and shelving of the Doerfer Plan by no means ended the commitment of the three networks to some changes in their schedules. These primarily involved news programming. Although complaining of insufficient demand from sponsors, all three networks nevertheless augmented their public affairs programming for the 1960-61 season. Each substantially covered the great events of 1960: the continued global journeys of Eisenhower, the budding space program, international incidents, and the normal list of disasters. Indeed, compared with the low point of the 1957-58 season, network coverage of news events in 1960-61 increased just over 145 percent.[69] This increase stemmed partly, but not entirely, from the reportage of a presidential campaign. The ABC network committed itself in early 1960 to a special documentary series on Sir Winston Churchill, "The Valiant Years."[70] In mid-1960, the third network agreed to program occasional documentaries, "Close-Up!" along the lines of "CBS Reports."[71] In the fall of 1960, NBC added "The Nation's Future" to focus primarily on the 1960 presidential campaign, while CBS placed "Face the Nation," a news interview program, on Sunday evenings and "Eyewitness to History" on Friday nights.[72]

A wish to placate opinion leaders and subtle congressional pressures combined to force the three networks into airing free presidential debates. Early in 1960, Senator Mike Monroney, Democrat of Oklahoma, recommended that the networks provide eight hours of free time to each of the two national parties' presidential campaigns.[73] No network chief liked that notion, and Robert Sarnoff of NBC hit upon a compromise in April: televised debates. Both Sarnoff and Kintner expected the debates to take up less air time (possibly none, if one of the candidates turned down the opportunity), and they looked forward to controlling or "staging" the event. Moreover, the networks would be able to air commercials.[74] (Stanton and Richard Nixon, the Republican nominee, later rejected the running of ads.)[75] Congress agreed to the proposal in August, and by waiving the "equal time" provision of the 1934 act, freed stations from any legal obligation to provide time for third party candidates.[76]

Perhaps no single action created more good-will for the television

industry than the "Great Debates." Soon after the Republican National Convention, Vice President Nixon, then behind in some polls,
agreed to participate with his rival in the unprecedented, televised
sessions. John F. Kennedy, the Democratic nominee, wired Sarnoff,
"I believe you are performing a notable public service."[77] Signing the
legislation, President Eisenhower remarked in his characteristic syn-
tax, "it is a fine thing in the public service that the networks will
be performing by allowing these people to do this on an equal time
basis and without cost."[78] The debates themselves received high
ratings, with as many as 120 million Americans viewing the first session, and the majority of commentators praised the forum. *Saturday
Review*, long one of the periodicals most critical of the medium, named Stanton "Businessman of the Year" for 1960. Some lions had obviously been tamed.[79]

A few observers suspected the networks' motives. Soon after the
1960 election, industry spokesmen like Stanton hailed TV's Great
Debates and expanded news programming in what one critic, George
Rosen of *Variety*, described in January 1961 as "the most publicized
do good job in communications history." Broadcasting, Rosen wrote,
had needed "to square itself with the government sleuths and slayers
who were breathing down its necks."[80] Similarly, an advertiser observed in March 1961 that "the networks put the public service shows
on this year [1960-61 season] to get the government off their backs."
He anticipated that "in another two years, they'll be entirely out of
prime time."[81]

The industry's self-praise regarding news coverage notwithstanding,
television as a whole did not substantially change with the fall of
Charles Van Doren. The concern with image mirrored in news programming decisions did not filter down to basic scheduling and production determinations. The number of Westerns did decline, but only
from oversaturation: the cowboy rode off into the sunset, to be replaced by the private eye.[82] No serious effort was made to revive forms
from the golden age or to reverse the trend to filmed, action-adventure
drama. The networks did not completely abandon artistic pretense;
NBC continued to air "Hallmark Hall of Fame," for example, occasionally. But by 1960 most teleplays were adaptations of famous
novels and plays, not the original dramas of the old anthology programs.[83]

Some critics simply could not reconcile themselves to what had
happened to television since 1957. Assessing the 1959-60 season, Jack

Gould of the *Times* regretted the standardization of the evening schedule, on which regular weekly series had supplanted the unpredictable anthologies and "spectaculars." "Literally weeks may pass," he wrote in June 1960, "without the occurrence of anything a little special or newsworthy in the prime time evening schedule."[84]

Critics more frequently alluded not to the golden age but to the mere absence of choice in the schedule. *Sponsor* in March 1960 considered the networks' claims of increased public affairs programming to be greatly exaggerated: "There's still more talk than action."[85] In July, Congressman Harris complained, "I don't see how three hours of detective thrillers and westerns in an evening provide any program balance."[86] Even advertisers confessed in a TV trade journal survey that the medium still lacked diversity.[87] The quiz scandals, Gould wrote in October 1960 had had scant effect: "The answer of TV to the supposed crisis has been just business as usual. The volume of tripe has grown."[88]

The impression that nothing had changed on television unfairly implied that the medium's policeman, the FCC, had no new sense of direction under Ford. Yet the commission, with little fanfare, was moving away from the relative lethargy of the Doerfer period. Tests of pay TV systems, which the House had earlier insisted on delaying, quietly resumed.[89] In September, the FCC eliminated thirty minutes from evening network option time; Ford himself had favored its abolition.[90]

Ford's initiatives largely went unnoticed. A career civil servant, he was not especially skilled at (or concerned about) self-promotion. Accordingly, many observers continued to regard the commission as a scandal-infested place, leaderless and without purpose. One consumer group representative described the FCC in November 1960 as "an agency which has been moving slowly downhill ever since the Roosevelt administration."[91] Although Ford remained on the commission after Kennedy's election, he was not retained as chairman.

Nothing better illustrated the FCC's still fallen state than the Landis Report of December 1960. Within days of his victory over Nixon, Kennedy asked James M. Landis, one of the leading experts in administrative law, to prepare an analysis of the independent commissions. Once clerk to Justice Brandeis and a former dean of Harvard Law School, Landis had chaired the Securities and Exchange Commission under Roosevelt and the Civil Aeronautics Board under Truman. In the 1950s, Landis worked as a legal and political adviser to the president-elect's father, a member of both Hoover commissions. Landis's own representations before the FCC on behalf of pay TV systems had made him an impassioned critic of the agencies. Accepting Kennedy's charge, Landis commented, "In a sense, I've been working on this report all my life."[92]

Landis quickly wrote a report that reiterated every harsh assessment made of the commissions during Eisenhower's presidency. Singling out the FCC for special condemnation, the dean castigated the commission for failing to allocate UHF services effectively and engaging in *ex parte* contacts. "The Federal Communications Commission presents a somewhat extraordinary spectacle," Landis wrote. "The Commission has drifted, vacillated and stalled in almost every major area."[93]

The TV problem might be resolved, Landis remarked soon after his report's release, by restoring the standards of the Fly and Porter years—through championing competition and minority rights. Increasing competition within broadcasting by "find[ing] an economic viability for the UHF band" would allow for more stations and "improve the quality" of broadcasting. Nor should the agency ignore programming for minority audiences. Landis asked that the FCC review more searchingly under the criteria of the 1946 Blue Book, license renewal applications. Stations failing such public interest guidelines should suffer. "If these licenses were originally granted to them upon their representation of their proposed program content," he said, "their ability to live up to these promises bears some relationship to their privilege to keep a frequency."[94]

By disregarding Ford's efforts to foster more competition and minority interest programming, Landis had essentially reinforced that perception of the commission that followed the ousters of Mack and Doerfer. An enterprising *Fortune* writer, drawing on Landis's study (and *Guys and Dolls*), referred to all of the commissions collectively as "the oldest established mess in Washington."[95]

Neither the commission nor the industry had, then, satisfied everyone. Of course, given the snobbery of some toward mass culture, this continued unhappiness should have been expected and dismissed. Yet this small band of viewers and critics had influence; their attitudes had far greater weight than their numbers warranted. They not only had become distressed about television but ardently believed that TV could be regulated—and the golden age brought back. The loss of balance or diversity in programming as they defined it spurred them and others to advocate regulation more visible, more punishing than Frederick Ford's. His speeches and the industry's new news programs and specials had not placated them.

Still, these viewers and journalists could have been ignored by the industry but for the great unknown of the winter of 1960-61. TV's Great Debates had helped to elect a new president with pleasant memories of the golden age; more than once after its passing, he had called upon TV to improve itself. And he was expected to name a new FCC chairman and commissioners lacking the quiet demeanor of Ford and far removed from the yacht of George Storer. Broadcasting might, after all, become a truly regulated industry.

Chapter Four

"The Minow Show"
and the Promise of 1961

For the first time since the decline of TV's golden age and the quiz-show scandals, the television industry had to deal with an FCC chaired by an articulate adversary, capable of garnering national publicity. Kennedy's FCC chairman, Newton N. Minow, aroused industry and public opinion with a May 1961 address that vigorously criticized TV in a manner unprecedented for an FCC chairman. With one cleverly phrased speech, Minow emerged as the symbol of all of those who had so long been determined to reshape television.

From the beginning, the new administration showed unmistakable signs of holding an unprecedented interest in FCC and television. Presidential aides like Arthur M. Schlesinger, Jr., worried about TV's role in the "quality" of life in America. To Schlesinger, the state had inadequately attended to the promotion of high culture, a circumstance all the more alarming given the expansion of leisure time. The new administration had to involve itself in the "quality" of American mass culture. "Today," Schlesinger wrote in 1960, "we stand at a critical point in our cultural history. For there hangs over America in the mid-twentieth century a peculiar and ominous threat—the threat of leisure. The imminence of this age of leisure gives the question of how we propose to fill the vacant hours of our lives a high place on our national agenda."[1]

The President himself rather incompletely shared Schlesinger's concern for culture. Although appalled by Eisenhower's pedestrian tastes, Kennedy possessed a mind more open to than full of high culture. He enjoyed reading, especially nineteenth-century English history, as well as contemporary novels and conventional poetry. But Schlesinger confided to one journalist that the president thought attending concerts or exhibitions more as "something he ought to be doing."[2]

Perhaps the most memorable example of the new president's symbolic commitment to culture came on the night of November 13, 1961. In honor of the governor of Puerto Rico, the Kennedys hosted a dinner for two hundred, including Nobel Prize winners from the Western Hemisphere and twenty-one composers, orchestra conductors, and eminent musicians. Cellist Pablo Casals gave a rare recital after dinner in the Blue Room. Washington could not recall any president—certainly not Eisenhower—who so self-consciously courted great minds and great artists. Composer-dramatist Gian-Carlo Menotti described the affair as "one of the most exciting evenings I have spent in my thirty years in America." In culture, he added, "it is the first time Americans have really shown they are above Europe."[3]

The public, of course, could not be there. Television, not a White House banquet, served as the most convenient cultural outlet that night. And in most American homes, the programming had been determined by the three commercial networks, which collectively offered four hours of action programs (two police dramas, one Western, and a crime anthology, "Thriller"); an hour and a half of adult drama, one story set in a hospital, the other in a small town; two hours of situation comedies; two quiz programs; and a half-hour children's program about a horse ("National Velvet").[4]

Although Kennedy had other commitments that evening, he was interested in television. The new president enjoyed good relations with figures from the medium's golden age. Fred Coe, producer of dramatic anthology programs, aided in preparing Kennedy campaign television spots. Edward R. Murrow, the great martyr of the lost epoch, had interviewed Kennedy on the first "Person to Person" telecast and had recommended him to narrate a film at the 1956 Democratic National Convention. The senator, in turn, protested CBS's cancellation of Murrow's "See It Now" program in July 1958. That year, Kennedy had also publicly called for more public affairs telecasts, and otherwise had conveyed regret over the golden age's passing.[5]

Yet Kennedy owed much politically to the "new" television. Although the fates of Murrow and Coe upset him, the president-elect was mindful of the networks' extensive coverage of his presidential campaign. He recognized that his performance in the first of the television debates had given a great boost to his chances of election. He felt especially indebted to Frank Stanton, who had promoted the encounters and had taken the greatest pains in overseeing their production. To return the favor, Kennedy offered the CBS president the directorship of the U. S. Information Agency (USIA). Only after Stanton declined did Kennedy follow his suggestion and call on Murrow to be USIA director.[6] The manager had been asked before the martyr.

Kennedy hoped that Stanton and others would continue their expanded information programming. Public affairs programs, he said in December 1960, "are the things that TV can do best." Extensive news presentations, Kennedy stressed, would help to inform the public about the need to win the cold war. At a time "when freedom is under its greatest attack," the president in May 1961 asked broadcasters "to tell our people of the perils and the challenges and the opportunities that we face," helping "an informed citizenry to make the right choices in response to danger."[7]

In addition to such early declarations, Kennedy committed himself to the rehabilitation of the administrative agencies. He could hardly claim unfamiliarity with their operations. His father had been the first chairman of the Securities and Exchange Commission (SEC) and head of the Maritime Commission. As a senator, Kennedy had closely studied the workings of the National Labor Relations Board (NLRB) and had come to share the Democratic distaste for the conflict-of-interest scandals commonplace under Eisenhower. In his acceptance speech before the 1960 Democratic convention, Kennedy had attacked the FCC by alluding to the Doerfer and Mack scandals with the comment that "blight has descended on our regulatory agencies."[8]

Kennedy intended to rebuild the agencies in three ways. The White House would better direct and coordinate the policies of all of the independent commissions. Legislation would be secured to strengthen the commissions' administrative and adjudicatory mechanisms, seen as weak, slow, and ineffective in the light of Representative Oren Harris's Legislative Oversight Committee hearing in 1958, 1959, and 1960. Finally, the new president deliberately sought out younger, talented people to chair the different agencies as he had done to fill cabinet and foreign service positions. Thus, the New Frontier's youthful vigor would be infused into the heretofore ponderous and bland administrative agencies.[9]

Kennedy's search for able commission appointments mirrored a larger liberal view of the independent panel. Much of the criticism of the FCC and other regulatory agencies had revolved around the matter of who served on the commission. As the agencies came under increasing fire between 1957 and 1960, Bernard Schwartz, James Landis, and other critics maintained that the caliber of Eisenhower's commission appointments had been the greatest problem. That is, had Eisenhower appointed abler individuals to the various agencies, then much of the petty corruption and incompetency might not have ensued.[10]

To chair the FCC, Kennedy selected in January a young and unknown law partner of Adlai Stevenson, Newton N. Minow.[11] After clerking for Chief Justice Fred Vinson in 1951-52, Minow had worked for Stevenson, then governor of Illinois. Although only twenty-six, Minow had established himself quickly with the Stevenson staff, he proved to be altogether devoted to Stevenson, without playing the young sycophant, and displayed an unusually mature and tough-minded approach to politics and policy. Indeed, during Stevenson's presidential campaign in the fall of 1952, Minow stayed behind in Springfield as the unofficial acting governor. After his defeat, Stevenson formed a law firm with Minow and W. Willard Wirtz in Chicago. There Minow came to know members of Chicago's liberal establishment, such as William Benton, publisher of the *Encyclopedia Britannica*.[12]

Minow also cemented loyal ties to the Kennedy family. In 1955, he met Joseph Kennedy, the family patriarch with substantial business interests in Chicago, and R. Sargent Shriver, the future president's brother-in-law, who oversaw them. Shriver became a close friend and introduced him to John Kennedy. During Stevenson's 1956 campaign, Minow favored Kennedy for vice-president and befriended Robert Kennedy, the president's brother traveling on the Stevenson plane. In 1960, Minow tried to persuade Stevenson to endorse Kennedy after the latter appeared to have the nomination sewed up. The Kennedy family appreciated Minow's efforts. Right after the election, Shriver, one of those handling patronage, approached Minow about joining the administration. Although Mayor Richard J. Daley of Chicago may have opposed rewarding Minow, who had not been especially loyal to the Democratic machine, the Kennedy people—especially Bob Kennedy— were determined to find a place for the young Stevensonian.[13]

Minow, though reluctant to leave Chicago, indicated that there was one position he would accept, one indeed he had long considered seeking: the chairmanship of the FCC. As a member of Stevenson's entourage, Minow had been one of the few close aides who had paid heed to the role of television in the 1952 and 1956 presidential campaigns. In 1956, Minow had urged Stevenson to challenge Eisenhower to televised debates and had helped to draft Stevenson's demand to the FCC for equal time following Eisenhower's October Suez Crisis address. Thereafter, Minow followed the FCC's foibles, convinced that as chairman, he could improve the public's estimation of the agency.[14] And the prospect of overseeing television as FCC chairman fascinated him.

Virtually from the medium's beginning, Minow had followed television regularly. His parents had been among the first in his native Milwaukee to own a TV set. At his own home on Sunday afternoons, social obligations notwithstanding, he insisted on watching "Omnibus," the Ford Foundation's educational series. In contrast, Stevenson, among others, simply did not share Minow's enthusiasm for TV. Like many busy public figures, the governor had neither the time nor the respect for television that his protégé did.[15] Minow, though, had regularly watched "See It Now." When Murrow used that program to attack Senator Joseph McCarthy in March 1954, Minow wrote his first TV fan letter. He was among those who saw *Marty* on "The Philco-Goodyear Playhouse." During the televised Army-McCarthy hearings of 1954, Minow took inordinately long lunches to watch the proceedings. A non-drinker, he sat for hours in bars that had the hearings on.[16]

Minow not only had watched TV in the fifties but was among those nostalgic about television's first decade. He closely followed the criticisms of the medium offered by Jack Gould of the *New York Times* and Robert Lewis Shayon of the *Saturday Review*, celebrants of TV's golden age that had been the victim of standardized, filmed, action-adventure series. And Minow himself had most enjoyed those early 1950s programs that had disappeared by the 1960-61 season. Soon after becoming chairman, he told an aide that in his opinion the quality of television had declined.[17]

In seeking the FCC chairmanship, however, Minow possessed more zeal than experience. He had provided legal counsel for a Northwestern University classmate, Sander Vanocur of NBC News, and Burr Tillstrom, who had created the widely praised early TV program for children, "Kukla, Fran and Ollie."[18] Otherwise, Minow's qualifications for the position were meager. He had done little work in broadcast law and had never practiced before the FCC or any other administrative agency.

Nor did Minow appear to recognize how circumscribed his powers as chairman would be. Breakfasting with Frank Stanton the day after the inauguration, Minow unsettled the network official with his ambitious ideas for improving programming. Stanton sensed that Minow scarcely understood what awaited him.[19] Minow told the Senate committee weighing his nomination in February that "I do think that the Commission has a role in elevating and encouraging better programs, and I am determined to do something about it."[20]

Indeed, Minow's confirmation hearings before the Senate Commerce Committee in February 1961 only re-enforced the new chairman's missionary impulse. Republicans and Democrats, southerners and northeasterners, all joined in admonishing Minow to do something about television's "quality." No one on the panel discouraged the chairman from taking some sort of action on programming. Senator Mike Monroney, a liberal, and Senator Strom Thurmond, a conservative, asked that TV ratings be made more reliable. Chairman John Pastore of Rhode Island led a chorus complaining about the overabundance and violence of TV Westerns. Monroney bemoaned the passing of "The Voice of Firestone," long a congressional favorite. For Minow, who shared these sentiments, the hearings proved to be altogether amicable. The committee unanimously approved the nominee. And Minow was left with the impression, he later recalled, that the senators "wanted the FCC to be shaken up."[21]

In one sense, however, Minow posed no great threat to American broadcasting. However unhappy with the golden age's passing, Minow still enjoyed cordial ties to certain industry leaders. Blair Clark, a CBS vice president, was a close friend.[22] Robert Kintner, president of NBC had many ties to Minow's mentor, Stevenson, his child's godfather.[23] Also, Minow had participated in his firm's work for RCA. Engaged in a civil suit against Zenith, RCA had recruited Stevenson's firm in 1955; both Stevenson and Minow worked on the case. Curiously, the name of this client, as opposed to Tillstrom or Vanocur, never came up in the hearings.[24]

The industry itself all but ignored Minow while busily hailing voluntary changes in programming since the scandals of 1959. Although most individual stations had taken few initiatives, trade journals pointed to the increased network news coverage for the 1960 presidential election and miscellaneous cold war crises. The actor Yul Brynner traveled around the world for CBS to report on the global refugee problem; Bob Hope hosted an NBC tribute to Will Rogers; and in March 1961 ABC ran "Adventures on the New Frontier," a documentary on the new Kennedy staff. Such fare counted as "public service" programming. Under the headline "Network TV's Greatest Season," *Sponsor* reported on May 8 that "never before in history, the webs feel, despite criticisms of 'low quality' programming, has there been so much 'high quality' entertainment available to any nation."[25]

It was in this self-congratulatory mood that the National Association of Broadcasters invited Chairman Minow to address its 1961 national convention in Washington. There was little significance in Minow's participation. FCC chairman always spoke to the NAB's annual conclave, though Minow, ignorant of such tradition, had to ask his predecessor for a recommendation regarding attending.[26]

Minow had fairly modest intentions in mind. He wished to praise broadcasters for their recent good deeds while admonishing them to do better yet. The chairman recalled planning a "conciliatory speech," anticipating a mild audience reaction. Then, too, Minow sought to combat the public's ignorance of the commission and its powers. Early 1961 surveys revealed that just under 25 percent of the public understood that by law, radio-TV frequencies belonged to the people. "I want to alert people to their rights," Minow remarked several months after the talk.[27]

Minow, two friends, and an assistant at the commission labored over the speech for several months. John Bartlow Martin, a veteran speech writer of the Stevenson campaign and fellow Chicagoan, and Tedson J. Meyers, an aide to the chairman, drafted most of the address, though Stanley A. Frankel, vice president of McCall's Corporation, offered ideas as well. Meyers and Martin each wrote a draft, and Meyers edited the two into one text. Then Minow revised Meyers's revision, putting in some of his own phrases and restoring some of Martin's. Meyers and the chairman's other aides, Henry Geller and Joel Rosenbloom, unanimously recommended toning down the last draft, but to no avail.[28]

The final copy, then, owed most to Martin. With many liberals, he had acquired very stern views about TV; Murrow's October 1958 attack on television partly inspired him[29] but so did his own observations about the medium. In Chicago, both he and Minow deliberately seated themselves all day and night before their TV sets; they completed the exercise disgusted at the incessant advertisements, soap operas, daytime quiz shows, Westerns, and other commercial fare. The sheer lack of diversity especially dismayed Martin. "Publishers still publish poetry," Martin wrote later. "But in the television industry, as a whole, such sentimentality is rare."[30]

Martin apparently modeled his draft after Stevenson's 1952 talk before the American Legion convention, when the governor, after saluting the group, courageously challenged its ostentatious patriotism.[31] Minow's speech had the requisite Stevensonian self-depreciation: "I was not picked for this job because I regard myself as the fastest draw on the New Frontier." The opening also included the trap of praise, in this instance, for programming of the better sort: "When television is good," Minow said, "nothing—not the theater, not the magazines or newspapers—nothing is better." He recognized broadcasting's economic basis, and disclaimed any radical notions: "I believe in the free enterprise system." Minow went on to deny any plans "to muzzle or censor broadcasting." Then came the Martin blast:

> I invite you to sit down in front of your television set
> when your station goes on the air and stay there without a
> book, magazine, newspaper, profit-and-loss sheet or rating
> book to distract you—and keep your eyes glued to that set
> until the station signs off. I can assure that you will
> observe a vast wasteland . . . .a procession of game shows,
> violence, audience participation shows, formula comedies
> about totally unbelievable families, blood and thunder,
> mayhem, violence, sadism, murder, Western bad men,
> Western good men, private eyes, gangsters, more violence,
> screaming, cajoling, and offending. And most of all,
> boredom. True, you will see a few things you will enjoy.
> But they will be very, very few.[32]

That condemnation owed much to a sense of television in decline. Through various drafts, including the final one, Minow took some pains to note the presence of good programs on the 1960-61 schedule. Yet such efforts appeared forced. An April 28 version included a listing of various golden age programs, including "Playhouse 90," just cancelled by CBS. Then Minow was to note "some wonderfully entertaining" programs, except that phrase was followed by blank spaces, as Martin and Minow apparently groped for current examples. Only at the last moment did the chairman find ones.[33]

Broadcasters, Minow maintained, simply must air more of these types of programs. What television required and, indeed, constituted Minow's definition of the public interest, "is balance." The public interest "is made up of many interests," he said. "You must provide a wider range of choices, more diversity, more alternatives."[34]

That cry for more types of programs formed the core of Minow's talk. Partly because of its wide range and skillful wording many of the chairman's adversaries misunderstood it to be still another postwar indictment of popular culture. In fact, Minow was not assailing certain types of programs so much as he was condemning the absence of other kinds of TV fare. Nowhere in the chairman's address did he argue that "Omnibus" was preferable to "Mr. Lucky" or "Wagon Train." In that regard, he was not so much Matthew Arnold as Arnold's nemesis, John Stuart Mill. Minow "probably does not expect the sudden abandonment of 'adult' westerns and the substitution of a diet of Ibsen and long-hair music," the *Chicago Daily News* observed. Rather, the chairman was decrying the absence of choice, that *Hedda Gabler* and Mahler were not available at all.[35] The terrain of television programming was not just a wasteland, but a "vast" one. Its gardens and fertile valleys had died out. Where in evening prime time were the oases? "The word for success," a Wilmington paper noted, "is 'balance.'"[36]

"Balanced" programming appeared all the more vital a regulatory issue given the warlike assumptions of the young administration. Like Murrow in his October 1958 speech and Kennedy in appearances before publishers and broadcasters in April and May 1961, Minow freely used a crisis rhetoric inspired by the cold war. He went out of his way to forgive the industry for the quiz-show scandals of 1959, episodes he might have evoked to good effect. Instead, Minow asked that broadcasters and regulators not "continue to wrangle over the problems of payola, rigged quiz shows, and other mistakes of the past," but cooperate. "We live together in perilous, uncertain times," he explained. "We must not waste much time now by rehashing the clichés of past controversy." With "Laos and the Congo aflame . . . Communist tyranny on our Caribbean doorstep," Minow said, Americans lived "in a time of peril and opportunity." For broadcasters, that meant the "the old, complacent, unbalanced fare of action-adventure and situation comedies is simply not good enough."[37]

To bring more balance, Minow offered the decidedly capitalist cure of more competition. "Most of television's problems," he said, "stem from [a] lack of competition." There were not enough stations to allow diversity; those facilities that did operate felt bound to seek a mass audience. To provide Americans with additional channels, Minow pledged to resolve the UHF crisis; most viewers lacked access to the channels in the upper spectrum. Here Minow restated an argument from the 1950s. More stations would create "a much wider range of programs," he said. "Programs with a mass-market appeal required by mass-product advertisers certainly will still be available. But other [new] stations will recognize the need to appeal to more limited markets and to special tastes."[38]

Another of the new FCC chairman's solutions to the TV problem stung his audience. With Churchillian embellishment, Minow warned, "I did not come to Washington to idly observe the squandering of the public's airwaves," and asserted, "never have so few owed so much to so many. . . . the people own the air. They own it as much in evening prime time as they do at 6 o'clock Sunday morning. For every hour that the people give you, you owe them something." Under his regime, the renewal of licenses would be reviewed with far greater care, with an eye to balance and, possibly, with local public hearings on the responsibilities of stations. "I understand that many people feel that in the past licenses were often renewed *pro forma*," he noted. "I say to you now: renewal will not be *pro forma* in the future. There is nothing permanent or sacred about a broadcast license."[39]

On what it dubbed "Black Tuesday," *Broadcasting* reported generous applause for the chairman's introduction and sparse clapping at his speech's conclusion. Some managers and owners praised Minow for his eloquence and bravery. Others compared the address to Chairman Fly's likening of the NAB to a dead mackerel in 1941 or the release of the Blue Book in 1946.[40] One operator referred to a "sneaky kind of censorship we can't fight," while another objected to Minow's use of the first person pronoun "I" as "an indication of his authoritarian thinking."[41] Trade publications speculated that the market value of stations would soon drop, that the chairman really intended to use the FCC as a springboard to the White House. Le Roy Collins, president of the NAB, wrote Minow, "It would be an understatement indeed to say that your remarks to the NAB convention were sensational!"[42]

The leadership of NBC and CBS had surprisingly little to say. Robert Sarnoff, board chairman of NBC, and William Paley, his CBS counterpart, offered no comment. Frank Stanton, CBS president, privately pondered Minow's reference to license renewal. Stanton thought the chairman had inadequately emphasized broadcasting's self-improvement from the depths of 1959. "That speech could have been written two or three years earlier and been more valid," Stanton remembered. "I didn't think he was justified in some of the things he said as far as CBS was concerned."[43]

Unlike their rivals at CBS and NBC, ABC's chairman and president complimented Minow on his address, but the third network's own interests came shining through. It had the fewest number of basic or "primary" affiliate stations and stood to gain most if Minow could provide more channels in those markets where ABC needed access. "I was not shocked by the speech," Oliver Treyz, president of ABC, commented. "We welcome more competition on TV, as Mr. Minow suggested it." He added. "We, like him, represent the New Frontier in TV." Chairman Leonard Goldenson described Minow's speech as "very courageous" and argued that "the greater the competition, the greater TV will be." The ABC chairman hoped, of course, that in the wake of Minow's address, "the FCC will speed up the granting of additional TV channels in one or two-channel markets," to most of which ABC lacked access, "to foster this increased competition."[44]

Most industry leaders dreaded both Minow's debut and the new administration's seeming embrace of the chairman's position. Although no one at the White House cleared the speech, Schlesinger had worked on an early draft. Even before the address, Minow was impressing other White House staff members. Frederick G. Dutton, helping to oversee the FCC, wrote on April 13 that "Minnow [sic] is developing into probably the most alert and politically effective of our Commissioners."[45] In the wake of the NAB talk, Minow received private support from the president, who, encountering the chairman at a social function soon thereafter, warmly approved his work. The president's father had already called Minow to offer his congratulations and support.[46]

Still, the greatest praise for Minow came from outside of

government: TV critics in newspapers and magazines, unhappy viewers, and the disenchanted workers in the industry itself. Edward P. Morgan of ABC News termed Minow's talk "the best speech of its kind ever read. I couldn't begin to do it justice."[47] An executive producer for the TV film division of Allied Artists, Jack L. Copeland, similarly hailed Minow's effort. Sponsors, agencies, and network executives, Copeland wrote, "have the habit of thinking in terribly mediocre terms." He was sure that "the only thing which will shock these people into assuming a responsible attitude is the loud, persistent and undying criticism of people like yourself."[48] The creator of the "Dobie Gillis" situation comedy, Max Shulman, praised Minow, and "as a toiler in the television waste land," urged the chairman to compel all of the networks to air more news and public affairs programs and simultaneously."[49]

The most favorable response to Minow's NAB address came from TV's newspaper columnists. Initially, many major newspapers buried or abbreviated reports of Minow's speech.[50] There were exceptions. The *Washington Post*, the *Detroit Free Press*, the *New York Times* and the *New York Herald Tribune* gave Minow's talk front-page treatment. The regular TV critics of the *Times* and the *Post*, Jack Gould and Lawrence Laurent, respectively, provided first-day analyses. Gould called Minow's attack "the most withering, complete and searching ever to emanate from a head of a regulatory agency."[51] Several days later, on May 11, Del Carnes, TV critic for the *Denver Post*, a daily that had originally given little space to the May 9 controversy, virtually repeated Gould.[52] Cecil Smith of the *Los Angeles Times* caught up the following day with the inevitable reference to Minow as "a big fish."[53] For the *Toledo Blade*, an enterprising critic outdid all by taking up Minow's charge and sitting before his TV set watching intently for nineteen hours straight to confirm the chairman's observations.[54]

Syndicated columnists joined in as TV, for the first time since the quiz-show scandals, became the subject of a larger, political opinion leadership. Cartoonist Herbert Block of the *Washington Post* paid Minow the ultimate tribute of a favorable cartoon, one in which everything about TV regulation could be defined by the good and evil dichotomy of a bad Western.[55] Others extravagantly praised Minow. Columnist Doris Fleeson remarked on May 11 that "official Washington, not to mention the TV industry, is only slightly less interested in Minow than in the astronauts, with the honors for nerve

Cartoonist John Fischetti's response to Minow's NAB speech.
Done for the Newspaper Enterprise Association, the cartoon appeared in many smaller dailies and weeklies. Reprinted by permission of Newspaper Enterprise Association.

HERBLOCK'S EDITORIAL CARTOON
"Gentlemen, This Here Town Is Due For Some Changes"

Washington Post, May 11, 1961. From *Straight Herblock* (Simon & Schuster, 1964), 43.

being distributed more or less evenly."[56] Eleanor Roosevelt wrote in her column that the FCC enjoyed new life and as for TV itself, "It certainly looks as though we're going to have to limit our westerns."[57]

Other sources informed an even broader public of Minow and his speech. Whether as a result of the coverage of certain newspapers, or their editors' own intuition, such national weeklies as *Life*, *U. S. News and World Report*, *Time*, and *Newsweek* did features on the new FCC chief. *TV Guide* had run an open letter to the TV viewer by Minow the week prior to his talk. All of this exposure, as well as subsequent appearances on national television interview programs,[58] secured Minow an audience unusually large for the chairman of an independent agency.

Some five thousand people wrote Minow in response to his May 8 address. And even *Broadcasting* grudgingly acknowledged that most were thoughtful criticisms of the medium: "Few were of the crack pot nature."[59] People wrote disclaiming ever having written to a government agency official before; most of them—2,049 of the first 2,542—overwhelmingly endorsed the chairman's sentiments.[60] Many clipped their weekly or daily TV schedule to bolster the chairman's major point about the lack of balanced programming. "If only we could have freedom of choice on T.V. during prime evening time," a Long Island man wrote on May 13. "Let the cowboy and adventure programs remain, but not on every channel at the same time." A California college student simply cried, "I'm sick of the cow country."[61]

Most of those responding to Minow's remarks offered, like the chairman, broad criticisms of the medium rather than specific charges against stations, networks, or particular programs. A few simply thanked Minow, since they were contemplating the purchase of their first TV set.[62] Others worried about TV's effects on children. "They tell me TV is a good baby-sitter," an Oregon housewife wrote. "I would just as soon hire Al Capone to babysit."[63]

The response to Minow's talk showed that some people had not been placated by the industry's own efforts at regulation. Many expressed dissatisfaction with the "sweeping reforms," as one commented, which had been supposed to follow the 1959 scandals. "Instead," a Manhattan woman wrote, "incredible as it seems, television programming became increasingly violent and tasteless. The network people simply gave lip service to Washington then went ahead even more irresponsibly."[64]

Now television faced an FCC chairman willing to the ranks of those disturbed by what Walter Lippmann "the TV problem." For so many years, those fighting for the uplift had numbered some congressmen, a great many critics, and in 1959, a few individual industry leaders. To them, cast regulation had languished during the Eisenhower years. Kennedy new FCC chairman, however, forcefully indicated that the commission would *act*, do things in the "public interest" to transform television.

With Minow's arrival, those despairing over the FCC had cause for exhilaration. Minow's address "comes like a wave of fresh air across a hot and burning desert," wrote Clarence Dill, one of the authors of the Radio and Communications Acts. "I had about given up hope of seeing any reform."[65] The Senate majority whip, Hubert Humphrey, commented to the new chairman, "This is what I have been waiting to hear for years and years . . . .It is about time these boys began to realize television licenses are a public trust and not a license to steal."[66] Such public interest associations as the ACLU, the Parent-Teacher Association (PTA), and the American Association of University Women (AAUW) shared Humphrey's delight. "Minow's forthright utterances," observed a Milwaukee newspaper columnist, "have made him [the] new champion of parent-teacher and other civic and improvement groups who are now sending their complaints to the FCC chairman instead of to their congressman."[67] For the weary critic it had been a long wait, and now it was time for celebration. Doris Fleeson wrote of "the possibly dreamy idealists who really want the regulatory agencies to perform the functions assigned to them [who] are toasting Chairman Minow."[68]

This optimism was to be sorely tested. The NAB speech set off a vigorous debate with the industry over broadcast regulation. Even winning that duel, Minow had to transform his ideas into administrative policy in order to contend successfully with fellow commissioners and a commission bureaucracy that had more often resisted being an agency of decisive change. Congress, too, might balk at an expansive FCC. Finally, Minow had to determine the true depth of public support for his vision of broadcasting.

join if not lead
had dubbed,
medium's
wspaper
broad-
dy's
-s-

Chapter Five

Minow's admirers proved to be of little help in the months immediately following his "vast wasteland" address. He had to reckon with indifferent colleagues and an unsympathetic Congress. Struggling to maintain momentum by still more spirited speech-making, he only encouraged charges of censorship. These he deeply resented, enough to lead him to redefine and narrow his solutions to the TV problem. In the process, he became less a public leader and more a cloistered bureaucrat. And at least one experienced overseer of the FCC, Chairman Oren Harris of the House Commerce Committee, foresaw Minow's transformation. To a nervous home town broadcaster, Harris wrote several days after Minow's speech, "Of course he will not be able to accomplish anything like the proposals he espoused."[1]

The first test of congressional sentiment closely followed Minow's May 9 talk as Congress weighed the administration's proposed reorganization of the FCC and six other regulatory agencies.[2] The president's special assistant for the regulatory agencies, James M. Landis, drafted each of the reorganization plans, which Kennedy announced in April. Under the Executive Reorganization Act of 1949. Congress had sixty days to consider the orders, which would take effect if neither chamber vetoed them.

Landis sought to unravel the procedural maze that Congress had imposed on FCC proceedings under the 1946 Administrative Procedure Act and the 1952 McFarland amendments to the Communications Act. A wish to model commission adjudicatory proceedings after the courts, reflected in the 1946 and 1952 legislation, had fragmented the agencies and had been a source of frustration for Minow's usually hapless predecessors.[3] Under Landis's plan, the provisions in those statutes requiring formal commission hearings would be modified, with the chairman rather than the petitioner setting priorities. Thus, to borrow on Minow's own example, the chairman would decide, not a shrimp boat operator, whether all seven commissioners needed to gather to hear the operator's plea for a radio license.[4]

After the "vast wasteland" address, however, reorganization of the FCC became a referendum not on administrative efficiency but on Minow's well-publicized intentions. No other agency's reconstitution snared so much attention nor engendered so much opposition. The lopsided defeat which followed was immediately regarded as a rebuke of Minow. One critic termed it "the saddest news of the television season."[5]

Yet even before Minow spoke to the National Association of Broadcasters, the FCC plan (number two of the seven) appeared to be in trouble. In fact, there was little enthusiasm on the Hill for any of the seven plans. Nor did recent history give grounds for optimism. Since the New Deal, Congress had been preoccupied with the rights of constituents affected by the regulatory process. Moreover, many congressmen expected the agencies to be free of executive dictation while subservient to congressional sway. At the inauguration, Speaker of the House Sam Rayburn sternly warned Minow, "Don't ever forget that you're an arm *of Congress*."[6]

Landis's conduct prior to the submission of the FCC plan reinforced this congressional jealousy. In his report to Kennedy in December 1960 on the regulatory agencies, Landis had spoken of the need for greater executive guidance of the independent commissions. To Landis, a major problem of the agencies under Eisenhower had been their lack of direction, an unwillingness or inability to plan and coordinate their activities with other areas of the government. "I believe in executive overall leadership," Landis said. "I don't know where it will come from unless it comes from the executive."[7] Such opinions evoked memories of Eisenhower's chief aide, Sherman Adams, and his penchant for interfering with commission decision-making. These fears grew as the White House asked each regulatory agency chairman to submit monthly reports on his agency's activities.[8]

With extraordinary insensitivity to congressional prerogatives,

Landis angered House Democratic leaders. The Republicans stood solidly against the reforms, yet because the Democrats had healthy majorities in both chambers, GOP forensics mattered little if Speaker Sam Rayburn and House Commerce Committee Chairman Oren Harris acquiesced to Landis's proposals.[9] But neither did.

On May 19, Harris testified against the Landis plan. Although he had agreed to Landis's investigation of the commissions in December, relations between the two men became sorely strained in the administration's first months. Landis drafted his plans without consulting with Harris, and Harris appeared bothered by agency "independence" in Kennedy administration. When a White House aide demanded monthly reports from commission chairmen, evoking the impression of executive management of the fourth branch, Harris irately issued the same request. Finally, Harris had a high regard for the very procedures Landis sought to eliminate.[10]

Rayburn abandoned the administration in June. The Speaker's nephew, Robert T. Bartley, had been a commissioner since 1952 and with most of his colleagues resented investing his chairman with new authority. And, Bartley argued, the Landis Plan would transform the FCC into an executive department. No longer, then, would the FCC be an "arm" of Congress. Given his affection for Bartley and proprietary interpretation of the administrative agency, Rayburn soon stood against plan number two. It marked his first break with the young administration he had been laboring for and one of the few times he offered his own opinion on the floor.[11]

Most of Minow's fellow commissioners joined Bartley in speaking against all or most of the plan. Ford had objected to Landis's December 1960 report on the commission and secretly provided Harris with a forty-page memorandum outlining his reservations about plan number two. The former chairman testified vigorously against the scheme in public and executive hearings. The reorganization plan, Ford concluded, would adversely affect the status of the other commissioners. With his increased powers, the chairman could in assigning work reward or punish commissioners for their opinions.[12]

Ford's colleagues, fearful that, as he put it, Minow might order them to Alaska on the day of a critical commission vote, likewise spoke against the plan. Minow's ambitious and well-publicized goals caused some to worry that he might be tempted to play the autocrat. "The FCC plan doesn't shift any more power to the chairman than do the SEC, CAB, or FTC plans," Commissioner Rosel Hyde said. "But none of the other chairmen have indicated a willingness to use that power quite so dramatically as has Mr. Minow." Only two commissioners, John Cross and T. A. M. Craven, gave the plan even tepid endorsement.[13]

They did not need to worry. On June 15 the House vetoed plan number two in a 323-to-77 roll-call vote. The plan's supporters were younger, liberal Democrats from the East and West coasts. Most of their colleagues from outside the Confederacy as well as nearly all southern Democrats joined every Republican colleague in lining up against the measure. Although two of the president's other regulatory agency reform plans also suffered rejection, none did by quite so lopsided a margin. The vote was commonly seen as the administration's first significant legislative defeat and a rebuke to Minow for his NAB discourse.[14]

What had gone wrong? Why had Minow, having earned public favor so unprecedented for an FCC chairman, suffered such a humiliation? Much of the blame had to be placed on the White House staff, whose members had offended people like Ford, Rayburn, and Harris. Ailing, Landis had often acted undiplomatically and irrationally.[15] Moreover, as in amending the Communications Act after the quiz-show scandals, Congress had indicated an unwillingness to invest the FCC with much authority. Whatever the perception of the TV "problem" by Minow's friends and new found allies, Congress did not believe its solution necessitated a strengthening of the chairman's powers.

Congress remained outwardly far more concerned about the slightest possibility of arbitrary broadcast regulation. Congressman James Wright, a moderate Democrat of Texas, voted against plan number two without denying the merits of Minow's NAB speech. Congress's action, he wrote his constituents, "reflects a healthy concern against centralization of power in the sensitive field of television and radio broadcasting." Minow himself posed no danger, he explained. "Still, because of the latent although wholly unexercised power inherent in the Commission's right to revoke licenses . . ., Congress instinctively and rightly reacts with extreme caution against anything which even remotely smacks of increased power which could conceivably result in even the subtlest censorship."[16] Although he praised Minow, Wright worried about potential abuses. He and other critics of plan number two asked what a different FCC chairman might do with excessive authority. Broadcasters had to be protected against a Minow successor disrespectful of freedom of expression.[17]

Many observers held that the broadcasting industry's lobbying—intensified by Minow's talk—killed plan number two. "The actual murderer of the proposal is the TV industry," *Newsday* claimed.[18] Other sources restated this melodramatic thesis of conspiracy. A California columnist wrote of America's "three superpowerful lobbies": the United States Bank in the age of Jackson, the Power Trust during the New Deal, and for Kennedy, "the Radio-Television lobby, whose tentacles reach into every city, town and hamlet in the country, successfully frustrating Minow and FCC reform."[19]

Indeed, the trade had little difficulty commanding attention on the Hill. Worried station managers in particular could exercise a subtle pressure. Radio and television outlets, each with the enormous power to report—or ignore—the activities of the congressman, dotted each district. Only in the most densely populated urban districts, served by so many stations that individual operators could be snubbed, did broadcasters apparently have little leverage.[20] About 3 percent of the legislators, including, briefly, Oren Harris, actually held a financial interest in stations,[21] and an unspecified number owned stock in a broadcast-related industry.[22] Many more had good friends in broadcasting, whose interests they naturally sought to guard.[23] Frank Stanton was regularly approached by congressmen seeking CBS affiliations for constituents, and a senior Republican on the House Commerce Committee personally interceded to secure an ABC contract for a station in his district.[24] A disheartened Minow muttered in July, "I have no illusions about the influence the industry wields in this town.[25]

Industry lobbying played a role in the dimensions of the commission's defeat if only because of the absence of other forms of persuasion. In seeking to reform administrative agencies, the Kennedy administration discovered what Presidents Roosevelt and Truman had unhappily found: the public, or much of it, took absolutely no interest in a reorganization battle.[26] In the absence of much organized constituent involvement, congressmen were more likely to accept the entreaties of local station managers who had been helpful in reelection campaigns.[27]

That summer, Minow salvaged some of the reorganization proposal. After berating White House assistants for their clumsy efforts on plan number two, Minow took it upon himself to fashion a bill with Oren Harris and which both Houses approved in August.[28] The measure repealed several of the 1952 McFarland amendments and modified some provisions of the Administrative Procedure Act that had fragmented the FCC staff organization. "We are now consulting with the Chief Engineer and General Counsel on matters where we were cut off from their expert judgments before," Minow wrote Senator Pastore after the Harris bill became law. "Our Hearings Examiners now can discuss matters of law with each other." The final bill also allowed certain cases to be decided by staff as opposed to the full commission. But it did not grant Minow rights over other commissioners, which the chairman could have used to gain power and authority.[29]

The Administrative Procedure Act still provided that Minow and the other commissioners attend to many of those petitioning for redress. "Until we get beyond the day-to-day administrative problems," Minow warned, "there won't be much time for contemplation." One Wednesday, he noted, "we voted 100 times. . . . We vote thousands of times each week on the most trivial matters."[30] That emphasis on each case left Minow and his colleagues with little time to weigh the larger question of the TV problem. "Our greatest hope," Minow cracked in December, "is that Russia will adopt the Administrative Procedure Act."[31]

The defeat of plan number two foreshadowed Minow's difficulties with his fellow commissioners. On the one hand, nearly all of the commissioners liked their new chief; pleasure rather than jealousy greeted the attention Minow (and the commission) received because of his NAB speech.[32] But few if any of Minow's brethren, as he liked to call them, shared many of his notions about TV or the role of the FCC. Four of his six colleagues had openly parted with Minow on the Landis proposal. And, though Minow enjoyed a four-to-three Democratic majority on the panel, partisan affiliation did not predict identification with his regulatory philosophy.[33]

Even in viewing habits, Minow stood apart. In the 1950s, while Minow had watched "Omnibus" and "Studio One," Ford viewed "77 Sunset Strip" and Westerns (like Eisenhower, Ford read Western novels avidly). Robert E. Lee, too, liked horse operas; he told *Television Digest* in mid-1959, "I'm not very eggheady." John Cross and Robert Bartley spoke only of sports programming, while T. A. M. Craven, another sports enthusiast, went further than Lee in his sentiments toward "serious" programming: "I'll tell you what I don't like—opera and discussion programs with a bunch of longhairs all talking at the same time about something they don't know anything about."[34]

There were other sharper contrasts between Minow and his colleagues, especially the Republicans. As chairman, Ford had in many ways tried out for the regulatory role Minow started playing in May. But Ford would not go so far as the regulation of programming.[35] Nor would Rosel Hyde, another Republican. Hyde offered experience stretching back to his days with the FRC, when he served as a staff lawyer. A commissioner since 1944, Hyde had been chairman for one year, 1953-54, under Eisenhower. Although more than willing to advise Minow on procedure, he held an even more constricted view of the FCC's role in policing television than Ford. Hyde objected to the spontaneous wave of support for Minow's NAB address. In July he told Idaho broadcasters, "It is unfortunate that the public is being led to look to the FCC for fulfillment of its program interest."[36]

Robert E. Lee, the third Republican, hailed like Minow from Chicago. A former aide to FBI director J. Edgar Hoover and congressional Republicans, Lee had been closely connected to Senator Joseph R. McCarthy of Wisconsin. In drafting his notorious Wheeling, West Virginia, speech of February 1950, McCarthy had relied—carelessly— on a confidential report Lee had written earlier for a congressional committee. The two Irish Catholics became close friends. Lee's wife campaigned for the Senator's allies in Maryland and served as matron of honor at McCarthy's 1953 wedding. Lee himself helped to arrange the ceremony.[37]

As a member of the FCC since 1953, however, Lee, like Ford, proved no Old Guardsman. He had occasionally nettled segments of the broadcasting trade. With Hyde and Ford, Lee had differed with Doerfer and his ilk in the late 1950s by seeking some forceful means of strengthening UHF telecasting. Lee had by then separated himself from well nigh all his brethren, to say nothing of Republican regulatory principles, by advocating limits to the amount of time TV and radio stations sold to advertisers. Commissioner Lee "remains an enigma to friends and foes alike," a trade journal had remarked in 1959. "His record has been a series of self-contradictions."[38]

The three Democratic commissioners proved to be only slightly more predictable. Craven, an engineer, had been a commissioner from 1937 to 1944, when Fly arranged his ouster partly because of his conservative views. Reappointed in 1956, Craven well fitted the Eisenhower regulatory equilibrium. He took no unusual stances. However, like Hyde, Craven did offer experience to Minow, in this case, technical expertise.[39] Bartley, like Lee, held a contradictory set of positions. His background projected a dualism: by upbringing he was a mild Texas Populist, yet he had also labored as a broadcast lobbyist for the Yankee network, a regional radio chain, between 1939 and 1949. Bartley had an aversion for national networks, but a healthy regard for the rights of individual licensees, which Minow wanted to scrutinize.[40] Similarly unreliable was John Cross, dubbed "Oren Harris's boy" by one wag. Cross often voted against Minow and rarely kept up with the workload.[41]

As a body, Minow's colleagues exhibited a deadening caution. They were not the corrupt or kept men of legend. Those fitting that stereotype of regulators as captives of the industry—John Doerfer and Richard Mack—had disgraced themselves off the panel. The remaining commissioners deferred not to the captains of the industry they oversaw but to a bureaucratic tradition of the 1950s, a tendency toward circumspection. Four of the six began their service in the fifties. Only Hyde and Craven had any recollection of the agency during the late New Deal "activist" period, from which both stood aside. The others, whether Democrat or Republican, were used to construing the commission's role in the narrowest manner.[42]

The extent to which Minow was outnumbered by conservative regulators could be seen in key commission actions early in his chairmanship. The TV market in Rochester, New York, consisted of two VHF and three UHF assignments. With UHF still the poor relation, viewers in the Rochester area and ABC sought a third VHF service. Rochester's two VHF channels carried CBS and NBC fare, leaving ABC with the problem of access to the country's forty-ninth largest TV market. The Joint Committee for Educational Television (JCET) also wanted a VHF channel for Rochester. On July 27, 1961, the commission met, assigned a third VHF to Rochester, and elected not to reserve it for educational use. Despite the pleas of JCET and a few viewers versed in administrative procedure, the commission did not even hold hearings on the question. The American Broadcasting Company now had a primary VHF affiliate in George Eastman's town. Minow alone dissented.[43]

In February 1962 came another instance, not quite so striking, of Minow's isolation. Westinghouse Electric Company owned TV stations in such major markets as Cleveland and Pittsburgh, operated by a subsidiary, Westinghouse Broadcasting Company (WBC). A year earlier, the Justice Department had successfully prosecuted Westinghouse on nineteen counts of price fixing and antitrust law violation.[44] The Communications Act empowered the FCC to move against licensees tied to such practices. Minow accordingly wanted to chasten WBC. He proposed that the Westinghouse licenses up for renewal be extended for one year rather than the usual three years. Such a move, though not nearly so dreaded as revocation, nevertheless constituted a legal expense and administrative burden for stations and station chains.

Minow insisted that WBC be punished for its parent firm's transgressions, even though WBC had an unusually good record in public affairs programming and was led by Donald McGannon, a good Democrat and reform leader of the NAB. This time, Ford joined Minow in support of a one-year renewal. Bartley dissented because of the absence of evidentiary hearings. The other four commissioners, Hyde, Lee, Cross and Craven, voted to renew for three years.[45]

As in the Rochester case, the anti-Minow philosophy held sway. The majority preferred the reality of commercial service to the possibilities of a different course.

Thus, for Minow, one serious frustration was collegial. Kennedy could not remove a commissioner. And until the president named his own commissioners at the expiration of each one's term, initiatives Minow took would be at best limited in scope. Cross's term was due to end on June 30, 1962, but the Arkansawyer had married a former House chairman's daughter and had powerful allies on his home state's delegation. He could count on the support of not only Harris but both of Arkansas's senators, McClellan and Fulbright, who chaired the important Government Operations and Foreign Relations committees.[46] Craven turned seventy in January 1963, and could be forced out; two other seats remained Eisenhower's legacy until 1964 and 1966.

While waiting for new and sympathetic colleagues, Minow returned to the rostrum. Unable to institute reforms, he could still speak out, urging stations and networks to improve programming. Who would object to his ministerial pleas? Norris Cotton, who like most congressional figures dreaded the slightest hint of censorship, told a correspondent that Minow's "best course seems to be one of encouraging the industry to police itself with the aid of an informed public."[47]

Yet speech-making had its perils. Many in and outside the trade were unaccustomed to an FCC chairman commenting on programming. The critics of scheduling practices in the 1950s did not include FCC chairmen, only a few congressmen and many television critics. Now came a critic with official status, which prompted the question. Is Minow to be the censor?

Some had praised him in May, but others—defining freedom of speech most broadly—regarded his NAB debut with alarm. The *Wall Street Journal* found "grave implications in Mr. Minow's [NAB] speech."[48] David Lawrence, a widely syndicated conservative columnist and editor of *U.S. News and World Report,* launched a virtual one-man crusade against Minow and his attempts to " 'take over' the radio and television stations of the country, and make them obey the Government's dictations."[49] Governor Jack R. Gage, Republican of Wyoming, complained in June of the "pseudo-police tactics" of the FCC under Minow.[50] Another station operator spoke of Minow's intentions as "the very essence of censorship."[51] The *Chicago Tribune,* Minow moaned, had dubbed him "the cultural Khrushchev."[52]

In his NAB talk, Minow had attempted to forestall such charges by declaring his aversion to censoring specific programs. The chairman had asked only that stations present more types of programming in the public interest and had suggested that during his chairmanship the FCC would expect such behavior from stations. For years the commission had asked that licensees pledge to air some measure of public service programming. Minow simply proposed to review licensee's pledges more carefully and revoke the franchises of those failing to fulfill the promises made.

Many remained unpersuaded. Bill Monroe, a New Orleans broadcaster, dismissed any FCC role in the name of "balance," which, he argued, "represents, if not censorship in the usual sense, at least a step toward censorship. There is no clear-cut difference between government control of specific programs and government control of what over-all types of programs can be scheduled." Carried to another medium, "the government might just as well suggest that newspapers be required to carry a certain proportion of actual news material."[53]

At a broadcast regulation forum at Northwestern University in August, Minow's defense of the FCC's programming role came under greater attack. W. Theodore Pierson, a prominent Washington communications lawyer, accused Minow of being unable to reconcile his aversion for censorship with his quest for balance. Pierson dismissed the criterion of diversity as beyond definition, a way of foisting unpopular religious or educational fare on the viewer. He added,

"The balanced programming guideline is but an instrument of conformity and censorship." More damningly, he accused Minow of advocating "prior restraint" by threatening broadcasters with nonrenewal if they did not agree to his definitions of diversity in submitting to the FCC—as all did—their future program schedules.[54]

Such charges appeared all the more serious when echoed in Evanston by Professor Louis L. Jaffe of Harvard Law School. With his old mentors, Landis and Frankfurter, Jaffe ranked as one of the nation's leading authorities in administrative law. Highly critical of the FCC under Eisenhower, Jaffe shared many of Minow's goals for television. Yet, he berated the chairman for dangling revocation before operators failing to promise to schedule certain categories of programs. "you can't censor anything regardless of whether it's a privilege [use of the radio spectrum] or it's before or after."[55]

Soon after the Evanston meeting, even friends deserted the chairman over the censorship issue. Janet Kern, TV critic for the *Chicago American* and a Minow supporter in the spring, wrote a series of columns sympathetic to the contentions of Jaffe and Pierson. "Few of us would—or do—disagree, as private citizens, that TV oftimes resembles that 'vast wasteland,' " Kern wrote. But a powerful FCC bothered Kern. "Whatever precedent you might establish," she wrote Minow, "remains for any of your successors to use for even the most nefarious of ends."[56]

That argument frustrated Minow. The chairman considered his civil liberties record spotless; he had long belonged to the American Civil Liberties Union, which had warmly embraced his program.[57] Minow's law firm had represented the publisher of D. H. Lawrence's *Lady Chatterly's Lover* against Eisenhower's postmaster general, who had refused to deliver copies of the novel.[58] Responding to Jaffe's remarks at Evanston, the chairman had trouble controlling his temper. Jack Gould, who attended the conference, observed that "Minow's display of sensitivity" to what the critic deemed "a little criticism, immediately caused the industry to raise an eyebrow."[59]

"Those broadcasters," the chairman complained, "who would clothe themselves with the arguments of John Milton should also be prepared to serve the public interest."[60] To those like Jaffe, fearful of an expansive FCC, Minow pointed out that the courts would protect the broadcasters' liberties. He wrote Kern, "You know me. I would hope you agree that I am as opposed to censorship as any broadcaster and as long as I have anything to do about it, there will be no censorship by the FCC."[61]

Nevertheless, after the Evanston conference, Minow labored to elude the allegation of censorship. Asked to recommend a CBS children's television program soon after the Northwestern meeting, Minow declined. In a letter to a CBS executive he wrote, "Unfortunately I feel it inappropriate for me ever to comment specifically about particular programs—I am called censor enough without justifying the charge."[62]

After August, Minow spoke less of what he disapproved of (too many Westerns, too many situation comedies) and more of what could be *added* to the schedule. In May, for example, he had praised broadcast news services while deriding an oversupply of non-news. After his summer bouts with Pierson and Jaffe, the chairman emphasized the need for more news programming, without criticizing the trade for airing so much else.

In a September 1961 address, Minow championed the news as a specific, "positive" standard in his speech-making advocacy of the public interest. He asked the networks to lead the trade by expanding their evening news programs from fifteen to thirty minutes. The chairman called for more special affairs news programs, as well as more regularly scheduled weekly news programs. Local stations were encouraged to upgrade their news services. "News, information and public affairs programs," he said, "are the heart of broadcasting in the public interest."[63]

Championing the cause of more news programming held a special appeal for New Frontiersmen. Television news programs tended in the early 1960s to concentrate on political leaders, especially the president.[64] And this served Kennedy all the more given the commonplace assumption that he was the first chief executive to master the medium. In battle with occasionally hostile newspaper columnists and editorial writers, the administration eyed broadcasting as an instrument of direct communication with the people. "We couldn't survive without TV," Kennedy confessed.[65] His aides and other staff went out of their way to cooperate with the networks, encouraging them to telecast the president's news conferences live (a first)[66] and to produce documentaries about the administration. For CBS in February 1962, Mrs. Kennedy gave a televised tour of the White House.[67]

Although newspaper columnists and the *New York Herald Tribune* could infuriate Kennedy, television rarely gave him cause for concern. Television newsmen stood well within the bounds of the genteel consensus. For various reasons, the TV networks rarely rewarded the contentious or highly opinionated reporter.[68] TV newsmen treated the president and his office with a respect that bordered on sycophancy. When infrequently not doing so, they left Kennedy baffled. On an April night amid the 1962 steel price crisis, the president called Minow at home to criticize the antiadministration tone of that evening's "Huntley-Brinkley Report." The president screamed at Minow, "I thought *they* were our friends."[69]

Aside from news, Minow held to another "positive" standard— better children's programming. Again Minow hoped to persuade network leaders to air more educational programs for children. Minow all but ignored the inquiry chaired by Senator Thomas Dodd, who sought to connect TV violence directly with child deviance. Instead, drawing on recent social science studies of the effects of television, Minow maintained that TV should be regarded less as a cause of juvenile delinquency than as a basis for preadult development. He had, in other words, great faith in the medium's educational possiblities for children. And, increasingly mindful of censorship charges, Minow by the late summer of 1961 assumed that few would argue over the need for some government influence in children's programming.[70]

In September, Minow proposed a daily "children's hour." Each network would air for one hour twice weekly in the late afternoon programming designed to enlighten as well as entertain the young viewer. He announced that Attorney General Robert Kennedy endorsed his plan and waived antitrust enforcement. To his earlier critics, Minow said that giving the viewers what they wanted made business sense for adults but was wrong for setting the children's program agenda. The children he polled overwhelmingly "preferred candy to spinach . . . , movies to Sunday school." Paternalism here was easily justified. "There is nothing wrong with giving children some candy in the form of television escape, but there is something wrong in not giving them some spinach in the form of enrichment."[71]

The American Broadcasting Company sabotaged the plan. Although CBS and NBC appeared willing, ABC in early October refused to associate with the children's hour scheme. It had already planned a new daily children's program, *Discovery*, but some seventy-six ABC affiliates, ten of which were in the largest twenty-five markets, would not accept it. As a result, potential revenues from toy and candy company sponsors fell below already modest forecasts. President Treyz postponed scheduling the program.[72] Without ABC's cooperation, CBS and NBC each produced "quality" children's programming, but they telecast them simultaneously and only once a week. A writer for United Press International later sadly observed, "The overall response to pleas for good new [children's] programs of an educational nature had been farcically inadequate."[73]

Despite the collapse of his children's hour plan Minow could not resist claiming much for his rhetorical labors He acknowledged, of course, that it took time for his pleas to have an effect; the 1961-62 schedule had been set and in production well before his May address. But he maintained in September and December that TV networks and stations "are doing a better job" by airing more news and public affairs programming.[74]

In the wake of Minow's NAB speech, program production and network officials did apparently weigh changing their ways. Minow's sudden and forceful appearance reinforced the arguments of those at all levels of the industry already pleading for more public affairs programming. A few stations unexpectedly began to carry or "clear" the less popular network news or cultural programs they had heretofore eschewed. Everywhere, one executive commented in June, "Mr. Minow has caused everyone to pause."[75]

At the very least, Minow prevented a retrenchment in the area of news programming. Indeed, the number of network specials and documentaries actually rose slightly in 1962. All three networks kept such prime-time news programs as "CBS Reports" and "Chet Huntley Reporting" on the air despite low ratings. As a percentage of the night's schedule, however, informational programming did not increase. If anything, the new FCC chairman had simply delayed any reversal of the trend to more informational programming that had begun prior to his arrival in Washington.[76]

The bulk of the schedule remained unaffected by Minow's presence. Production notes for "The Untouchables" following Minow's NAB address showed no lessened interest in infusing violence into scripts.[77] One producer, Quinn Martin, tried to create a thinking man's detective series, one bereft of violence; "The New Breed," however, proved to be another action-adventure melodrama. "I'm begging the FCC's pardon," Martin said. "But we had hoped to come out with an antiviolence show first."[78] Most of those previewing the whole 1961-62 season saw little reason to hail Minow. A Milwaukee critic warned that if Minow "considered last season's network offerings a 'vast wasteland,' he's not out of the desert yet."[79] If Minow had hoped through his speeches to arouse the industry's conscience, all he had shown in late 1961 was—as Freud once complained of an American client's subconscious—that the trade lacked one.

Minow kept insisting that he *was* having an effect on programming. In a *Variety* interview in December, Minow alluded to the "very substantial improvement" of TV programming. Minow then cited an example of all three networks airing different special programming at the same hour: a dramatic special, "Victoria Regina," starring Julie Harris; a variety special starring Yves Montand; and a "CBS Reports" feature on bookie joints.[80]

The chairman had rather innocently loaded his adversaries' weapons. A senior Republican congressman described Minow as "a very impulsive young man [who] tends to be a bureaucrat in the broadest sense."[81] Network officials, in turn, abandoned their relative silence regarding Minow's admonitions. Furiously, they now assailed him for commenting, even affirmatively, on specific programs. Robert Sarnoff of NBC asked, "When criticism comes—pointedly and suggestively—from the voice of governmental authority, speaking softly but carrying a big hint—at what point does criticism become coercion?" Stanton remarked, "If government is going to set standards" for program "balance" or quality, "whose standards are they going to be? The chairman of a commission?"[82]

In a December address, Minow angrily defended his *Variety* interview. He asked his antagonists to cite actual examples of FCC censorship. Demanding that stations fulfill pledges regarding public service programming made when they applied for the franchise, he insisted, was not the same as calling for the removal or change of individual programs. If stations promised to air a set amount of public service programs, the FCC had every right to see that they did. "Freedom of speech should not be confused with freedom to make promises in order to secure a television license and then freedom to break those promises in order to exploit that license," he said.[83]

Amid this conflict, Minow had to reckon with one other argument: that what he really objected to was the public taste. If television had changed for the worse in the late 1950s, or lacked the balance the chairman held to be necessary in 1961, was not the majority of viewers, who preferred stolid cowboys and wacky housewives, at fault? Stanton of CBS had called broadcasting "cultural democracy." What went over the air most of the time was what audience ratings indicated most viewers preferred. He complained to Minow in February 1962, "The more sophisticated who are restless with the type of entertainment that appeals to others may need a rededication of faith in that hopeful experiment that is our democracy."[84]

Minow and his allies had ready rejoinders to such logic: audiences, they wrote, responded favorably to those stimuli *offered*. Without a true choice of programming, viewers took what remained. Sociologist Bernard Berelson denied that the public taste equaled the public interest. "A two-way process [is] at work." he remarked in 1961. "The public tastes reflect a preference for what is made *available* and familiar by the media."[85] Schlesinger, writing Minow in December, agreed that "cultural democracy" only partly determined TV programming. "The act of accepting or rejecting what is offered is one way" of establishing viewers' preferences. "But this way is obviously limited by the limitations of what is offered."[86] Minow simply cited Bernard Shaw, observing that the reason Chinese ate rice was that they had never tried steak.[87]

The Columbia Broadcasting System challenged the contention that viewers lacked a choice in early 1962 by promoting a televised memoir of the Eisenhower presidency. Scheduled to compete with ABC's popular series about prohibition agents, "The Untouchables," the program garnered relatively few viewers. Indeed, Elliot Ness could do what Adlai Stevenson had only dreamed of, overwhelm Eisenhower in popularity. Against Ness and NBC's "Sing Along with Mitch," Eisenhower obtained a miserable 11 percent rating.[88]

Minow did not dispute the mathematics of audience calculation. Soon after he became chairman, an aide assured him that the rating services were essentially accurate indexes,[89] and Minow never joined those critics haphazardly attacking the statistical utility of measurements of audiences. Rather, Minow simply spoke of the rights of minorities, the perennial losers of the Nielsen and Arbitron "sweeps." To Stanton, Minow again quoted Shaw, "liberty means responsibility. That is why most men dread it."[90]

At this point, the administration acted to bolster Minow's position. The Budget Bureau, after reducing the appropriations requests of all agencies, agreed to restore Minow's original amount.[91] The president, in turn, met with reporters off the record in late December and described Minow's performance as among those aspects of his first year that had most pleased him.[92] At a January press conference, Kennedy willingly defended his FCC chairman against charges of "censorship." "Mr. Minow," Kennedy commented, "has attempted not to use force, but to use encouragement, in persuading the networks to put on better children's programs, more public service programs."[93]

Nevertheless, Minow emerged from the renewed debate over broadcasters' freedom of expression all too mindful of his detractors' cries of censorship. The chairman ceased listing specific programs of which he approved.[94] And he pondered alternatives to setting both his positive and negative standards.

Only in mid-1962, when Cross's term would expire, could Minow hope to begin to fashion a majority of like-minded commissioners able to bite as he had tried to bark. A year later, Craven's term would be up. Until then, Minow could expect to accomplish little, given the FCC's already limited powers and his colleagues' restraint.

Despite the attention focused on Minow's "vast wasteland" speech and all the hopes raised, Minow remained the prisoner of a weak agency, one restrained by strict interpreters of the First Amendment and a suspicious House. Each circumstance led him to more narrow objectives, any one of which still might provoke heated criticisms. By late 1961, he had limited his once encompassing criteria for balanced programming. He had shifted from seeking, so to speak, both "CBS Reports" and "Playhouse 90" to advocating only "CBS Reports." Furthermore, voluntary efforts, in this instance, to improve children's programming, had not worked. Taken as a whole, these setbacks and obstacles did more than limit Minow's freedom of action. They demonstrated how difficult it was to be for this New Frontiersman to alter matters significantly.

Chapter Six

Competition as Regulation
1962

As 1962 began, an FCC chairman who was uncommonly well known was nevertheless forced to lower his expectations for his agency. Newton Minow drew upon a less controversial and less direct proposal to improve programming: encourage the establishment of more stations. Such a strategy invited neither the furor nor the frustrations of 1961, though it still entangled him in a complex web of interests—those of Congress, the industry, and one network.

Minow labored for a competition that he anticipated would afford viewers greater choice. Three commercial networks nationally and three or fewer stations within most large markets coveted one mass audience. They perpetuated a limited cycle of program "types" or genres that he had derided in his NAB talk. "One of the principal problems in television now," Minow said in March 1962, "is that unless a program appeals to so many millions of people, it has very little chance."[1]

That oligopolistic structure—one that only rewarded the purveyors of mass culture—could be broken by stimulating the use of UHF television. The UHF portion of the radio band could double or triple the number of stations in individual viewing area, if a means could be found to promote the founding of UHF stations and selling TV sets with UHF tuners. Otherwise, UHF remained the "sick man" of broadcast regulation.

By 1961, the plight of UHF television had become most severe.[2] Some one hundred UHF stations established after the 1952 *Report and*

Order had left the air; thirty-nine others remained operating—at a $20 million loss. Of all American TV sets, 94 percent were unequipped to receive UHF signals, nor would their owners pay the thirty-five dollars necessary to "convert" their receivers to obtain the UHF channels, 14 through 83.[3]

The commission bore much of the blame for the problem. It had assigned UHF frequencies prematurely, before adequate transmitters and receivers could be perfected. Additionally, the FCC had placed many UHF operations at a disadvantage by "intermixing" or placing them in direct competition with VHF channels, 2 through 13.[4] As a result, new UHF facilities came and went. "The FCC, with its dilatory and discriminating policies,"a Florida newspaper observed, "effectively killed all hope of putting the 70 UHF channels to good use."[5]

In 1956, the Senate Commerce Committee insisted that the FCC "deintermix" certain medium-sized television markets to ensure three channel services in the same frequency band.[6] That meant either creating a third VHF service in some areas or transforming others to all-UHF. But between 1956 and 1961, the commission, many of its members skeptical of UHF, hesitated and refrained from exposing some communities only to UHF.[7]

The entanglements of UHF and deintermixture mattered enormously to one of the national networks, American Broadcasting. Of the three chains, ABC faced the greatest trouble winning affiliates and clearing programs in intermixed markets that had only one or two VHF stations. In such areas, ABC most likely had to share an affiliation or rely on UHF outlets for local affiliates. ABC had twice as many UHF affiliates as either CBS or NBC. These stations served such smaller cities as Madison, Wisconsin; Erie, Pennsylvania; and Rockford, Illinois. Yet they were of sufficient size to drag down ABC's earnings. Normally, advertisers discriminated against ABC because its weaker group of affiliates denied it the comparative "coverage" of CBS and NBC. That is, despite some popular evening programming, the network could not "deliver" as many TV homes and therefore could not charge as much to time buyers.[8]

Since 1955, ABC had fought unsuccessfully for a substantial revision of the Table of Assignments.[9] Then in July, 1961, Minow and the FCC voted four to three to consider changes in the allocation of frequencies. In February 1962, ABC submitted petitions requesting the creation or "dropping-in" of third VHF services in eight markets. In addition, the network called for the deintermixture (transforming to all-UHF service) of eight markets. Of these sixteen areas, ABC lacked basic affiliates in nine, to CBS's four and NBC's three. Robert Coe, a vice president of ABC, termed the reallocation of these areas "vital to our development." Coe complained, "ABC has been the principal victim of the shortage of competitive facilities in these important markets."[10]

Coe and others at American included in their appeals promises of better meeting the "public interest" in network programming. Allocation policies, ABC representatives argued, hindered the network's capacity to schedule news and public affairs programs.[11] Had the third network the same access to markets that CBS and NBC enjoyed, then it would earn more and, like its rivals, be more able financially to air the costly and less watched fare that Minow termed valuable.[12]

Furthermore, if the commission provided equal access in their intermixed markets, ABC's spokesmen contended, American would have less of a problem clearing programs with those stations sharing affiliation with ABC; such stations tended to take only the network's entertainment offerings. Fewer of NBC's larger grouping of stations were likely to share affiliation, which meant, for example, that 132 stations carried the news program, "David Brinkley's Journal." A similar ABC offering, "Howard K. Smith and the News," was accepted by 87 stations. Oliver Treyz, president of ABC, argued that because so many areas "still have less than three competitive channel services, we find ourselves hampered in scheduling top quality, hour-long live dramas or live variety shows." Without selective deintermixture, "we can neither satisfactorily clear, nor reasonably expect to enlist advertiser support for programming in the live drama and variety fields."[13]

As part of its calculated courtship of the FCC chairman, ABC cited recent changes in programming. In May 1961, only Treyz and Chairman Leonard Goldenson of the network executives had praised Minow's NAB address (with its plea for more competition).[14] They also noted how even before that speech, their network, long the laggard in news coverage, had begun expanding its news division. Between the 1959-60 and 1960-61 seasons, ABC's budget for news and informational programming virtually doubled.[15] As part of that offensive, one week after Minow's NAB message, ABC gave Adlai Stevenson, the FCC chairman's mentor and Kennedy's United Nations ambassador, his own biweekly TV series, "Adlai Stevenson Reports."

The program went on the air without a sponsor.[16]

If not directly because of ABC's overtures, Minow did favor deintermixture. The Chairman believed that the commission had to respect the Senate Commerce Committee's 1956 recommendation that some areas had to be converted to all-UHF. A key adviser to the chairman, Kenneth A. Cox, chief of the FCC's Broadcast Bureau, had been counsel to that Senate panel and continually stressed to Minow the need for deintermixture. The principle of equal access for all networks, the chairman concluded, should be followed. Asked later the number of stations reach large community might optimally have, Minow replied, "As a matter of general national policy," there should be "room for all the three network services," and each network should have "an outlet in a city."[17]

The dilemma of too few VHF channels, however, particularly hampered noncommercial and educational television (ETV). Although ABC felt cheated out of VHF stations in a few markets, ETV groups had to settle for UHF outlets in most communities. Of the channels reserved by the FCC educational and other non-profit agencies in the 1952 Table of Assignments, 182 of 274, or 66 percent, lay in the UHF band.

For ETV to be available to large numbers of Americans, UHF had to be rendered effective. In Columbus, Ohio, WOSU, an UHF ETV channel, went on the air in 1956, yet four years later only 15 percent of that market's sets could even receive the signal. Los Angeles ETV forces had been even less fortunate. On the UHF band in 1954, that community's ETV outlet went out after one year of operation.[18]

Educational broadcasting remained a struggling enterprise in 1961. The weaknesses of UHF posed one problem, but so did a lack of broad support for the very premise of ETV. Many states and localities rejected educational broadcasting as too expensive.[19] Starting and maintaining an ETV outlet proved to be an onerous financial burden, despite some $60 million poured into the system between 1955 and 1961 by the Ford Foundation. In January 1961 twenty-two states and most TV markets, including New York and Los Angeles, lacked ETV service.[20] "Large areas of our country still do not enjoy the benefits of educational television," Secretary of Education and Welfare Abraham Ribicoff said in May 1961. "Many who have a real interest in starting educational television programs are frustrated by a lack of equipment and funds."[21]

Much of the momentum for educational television came from adult education and public school groups, both of which defined ETV's mission narrowly. None proposed that the federal government create a network modeled after the British Broadcasting Corporation. A few of the critics of TV in the late 1950s, however, including Walter Lippmann, had begun for the first time to suggest a modest nonprofit system of broadcasting as the most obvious alternative to majority television.[22]

What educational outlets did present contrasted sharply with commercial television. Daytime schedules were given over to instruction. In the South, ETV channels substituted for crowded classrooms; Chicagoans could receive college credits by taking courses telecast over WTTW. Evenings tended to be used for inexpensive, adult educational offerings that the commercial networks had by the late 1950s relegated to Sunday morning. Eleanor Roosevelt hosted a discussion show over Boston's WGBH. Other ETV units offered yoga, dance classes, and lectures and conversational programs that featured college professors.[23]

Although such fare commanded minuscule ratings—educator Robert Hutchins once observed that "that the trouble with educational television is that the shows are not good"[24]—Minow took solace in some studies of viewer responses to ETV programming. In 1960 and 1961, several surveys indicated that in those markets having a VHF ETV channel, up to 25 percent watched one ETV program at least once a month. Such findings (challenged by some as exaggerated) inspired Minow to aid educational broadcasting.[25]

The test of Minow's commitment to ETV came early. New York City, by far the nation's largest TV market, had been assigned seven VHF channels, one of them ostensibly to Newark, New Jersey, just a few miles away. The FCC had reserved an ETV frequency for New York, but in the UHF band. In March 1961, however, the independent Newark VHF station, WNTA, was up for sale. Through a complex and controversial administrative maneuver, Minow forced WNTA's owners to sell their station (at a price 30 percent lower than that tendered by a commercial party) to educational TV interests. And the country's most populous area had an educational outlet that all viewers could receive on their sets.[26]

Elsewhere, ETV groups remained stuck on the UHF band. But Minow could not similarly shift VHF assignments to ETV organizations: there were not enough VHF frequencies available. Because most large communities lacked a fourth VHF assignment, under the FCC's 1952 Table of Assignments, one-half of the country's thirty-six largest cities had their ETV channel reservations in the ultra high frequency. These included Philadelphia, Los Angeles, Detroit, Baltimore, Cleveland, Washington, Buffalo, Cincinnati, Kansas City, Indianapolis, and Atlanta. As noted earlier, ABC's skillful lobbying had stripped Rochester, too, of an ETV VHF channel reservation.[27] The chairman planned to rerun his WNTA show in Los Angeles and snatch VHF station there for ETV interests. But the leaders of the Los Angeles ETV committee elected to try again with their UHF assignment,[28] a brave move, considering that few Angelenos (about 10 percent) had all-channel sets.

In the capital itself, educational broadcasters began to operate over channel 26 in September 1961, only to find that few Washingtonians had sets that could obtain the signal. No Washington TV set dealers or wholesalers had all-channel converters in stock. In his FCC office, Minow himself had trouble receiving the channel on his own all-channel set.[29]

The plight of ETV led Minow to a solution first offered by his predecessors. Commissioner Ford had been urging his successor to fight for an all-channel set law. On Ford's initiative, the commission had in February 1960 recommended to Congress and the Bureau of the Budget that the FCC be empowered to direct TV set manufacturers to make only receivers capable of obtaining both UHF and VHF signals. Under Ford's bill, buyers of new sets would have to purchase an all-channel receiver. As new sets replaced old, the percentage of homes receiving both frequencies would rise. This diffusion would encourage the founding of UHF outlets and advertisers to buy time on them. Although agreeing to resubmit the proposal early in 1961, Minow at first questioned Ford's confidence that all-channel sets provided the best solution to the UHF problems. In September 1961, however, National Educational Television leaders endorsed Ford's bill. Their confidence and that of the Los Angeles ETV group finally persuaded the chairman to begin to lobby hard for the all-channel receiver bill.[30]

By the end of 1961, other circumstances combined to make the all-channel set bill Minow's sole option. The chairman had been unable to fashion a voluntary arrangement whereby set makers would agree to produce only all-channel receivers.[31] As for reallocating channel assignments, the commission would continue to attempt to deintermix the mixed markets. The ideal and least painful solution would be simply to create new VHF services in others. Again, however, the propagation problem loomed. Because of the great reach of VHF signals, the FCC could authorize only a finite number of new VHF channels in the relatively contiguous northeastern and Great Lakes cities. The few VHF channels available for allocation there limited each community to a few channels free of interference. Nor would the Defense Department and other government agencies surrender the six VHF frequencies they had been given in the 1940s.[32]

As chairman, Ford had helped to lay the foundation for an all-channel set policy. Part of the argument against the upper frequency stations had involved the signal's inferiority. Late in his chairmanship, Ford had persuaded the commission and Congress to fund a $2 million test of UHF propagation in New York City, whose tall buildings had been thought to hinder UHF telecasts. Even before the FCC completed this experiment in 1962, Minow and others somewhat exaggeratedly declared the UHF tests to be a success. In March 1962, Congressman Emanuel Celler of New York termed the commission's Manhattan project unqualified proof that "UHF broadcasting has come of age from a technical point of view." He added that "good UHF reception has also been reported from the Holland Tunnel in the event that anyone wishes to set up housekeeping there."[33]

Celler and Minow did not consider a third possible cure for the medium's imbalances; community antenna television or cable transmission systems. In use in less populated Appalachia and Rocky Mountain areas far from TV transmitters, the process relied on large antennas and direct wiring into the home. It afforded consumers an even greater potential range of channels—both local and distant— than a fully utilized VHF-UHF service. With CATV, the number of choices available to a consumer might run to twelve or more outlets. The most a viewer could hope for with a revitalized UHF was an increase from three to six services. Cognizant of that difference, Frank Stanton of CBS and a few other industry leaders had suggested to Minow that CATV, and not UHF, might represent the true future of television technology. But the chairman ignored such counsel, gambling that to correct the errors of the 1950s would suffice. Few disagreed with him.[34]

The idea of championing competition through UHF appealed to

Minow for another reason. Contemplating the allocation problem in the latter half of 1961, he was being accused of promoting government censorship, an allegation that stung sharply. A means might be found, however, to achieve the ideal of diversity without confrontations. Creating new stations rather than meddling with existing ones would rescue Minow from a civil liberties tempest. "The broadcasters can't have it both ways," Minow said in February 1962. "Either you will have [a] limited [number of] channels and government regulation, or unlimited channels and no control. The ills of television, unlike many problems which face the world today, can be cured, and opening up UHF channels 14 through 83 for more television stations is a solution."[35]

The need for the FCC to review programming would all but disappear with all-channel television. Howard J. Trienens, like Minow, a Chicago attorney and former Supreme Court clerk, advised the chairman in a November 1961, memorandum that "broadcasters have a clear choice: They can either favor increased competition with the resulting reduction in the F.C.C.'s concern over programming; or they can choose restricted entry which carries with it F.C.C. review of programming at the time of application and renewal."[36] "If we gradually replace VHF sets," Minow wrote in March 1962, "we will also act to loosen, rather than tighten, the bands of regulation, because we will move toward a promised land with many television services and choices."[37] Later he termed his principle, "Minow's law": "the extent of government regulation should vary with the number of competitors in each community."[38]

Minow admitted that his strategy held risks. "Many thoughtful people," he told *Theatre Arts* in December 1961, "say the broadcasters, by competing more actively for the fragmented audience, under UHF, will hit ever-lower levels of programming—instead of rising higher." Yet he foresaw a possibly cheerier outcome.

> A TV broadcaster trying to reach a minority audience will have to compete on ever higher levels. Just as, in the magazine field, we have mass magazines and highly specialized periodicals—so, in television, we could also have such diversity: stations serving smaller, special groups—but groups that are, in *toto*, significant both in numbers and taste.[39]

Minow's advocacy of competition was all the more compelling

given the views of his brethren. One of Minow's first-year frustrations had been his colleagues' resistance to his positions. A habit of
caution, born of the fifties' nonactivism, conditioned most to avoiding
anything smacking of controversy. For Minow, coalition-building was
not easy. Virtually all of the commissioners, however, accepted the
alternative of competition as regulation. Ford had offered the all-
channel receiver bill as a solution, and Commissioners T.A.M. Craven
and Robert Bartley tended to go along with it. Bartley, especially, was
committed to the small-scale entrepreneur likely to enter UHF television.

Even one of Minow's most conservative colleagues, Rosel Hyde,
had long favored greater competition. Hyde had been concerned with
the plight of UHF since the middle 1950s. In a February 1962 interview, Dwight Macdonald of the *New Yorker* recorded Hyde as saying, "I'd rather accept a few programs I don't like than risk government censorship." Hyde, Macdonald wrote in his notes, "has
principles—free market, free speech, free enterprise. His solution:
wider area of competition."[40]

Commissioner Robert E. Lee offered the most extreme case. A
Republican commissioner identified with the Old Guard, Lee nevertheless had been advocating since the mid-1950s the fairly radical solution of converting all of television to the UHF band.[41] Such a policy,
most experts agreed, would cost telecasters and consumers millions
of dollars. In September 1955, CBS had calculated that the expense
of converting all stations and sets to UHF would run between $1.1
billion and $2.6 billion.[42] Yet Lee continued to call for an all-UHF
television into late 1961. Short of that cure, he would support the
all-channel receiver proposal.[43]

Minow thus enjoyed the luxury of virtual unanimity among the
commissioners. The brethren had divided over the administration's
June 1961 reform of the commission's procedure, but only one commissioner, John Cross, failed to endorse the all-channel receiver bill.
He alone remained so convinced of the inferiority of UHF that he
would not back the measure.[44] With that exception, Minow promoted
the all-channel receiver bill with a united commission behind him.

The all-channel set proposal became Kennedy administration policy
in early 1962. Secretary of Commerce Luther Hodges originally opposed the measure as too severe, and the administration deferred to
Hodges[45] until early January 1962, when Minow finally won over the
commerce secretary. Two months later, the president included the

all-channel receiver bill in his consumer protection message. "I strongly urge its passage," Kennedy said, "as the most economical and practical method of broadening the range of programs available.[46]

Minow and others acknowledged one drawback to the all-channel set solution: it would be some time before the medium felt its effects. TV sets lasted from four to six years, depending on the consumer's care and use. Therefore, the chairman calculated in March 1962, most American homes would be equipped with all-channel sets by 1970, assuming the FCC could act by 1964 to force the diffusion of UHF tuners. Commissioner Lee, though long a champion of UHF, disagreed; Lee had testified one month earlier that rather than Minow's estimate of six, conversion would take ten to fifteen years, or not until 1974 or 1979, before being realized.[47]

The negative connotations to any lag, however, were partly offset by the assumption of many that consumers' cultural preferences in the early 1960s were rising. The public would surely welcome the specialized programming UHF television might bring. One advertising analyst forecast that TV would steadily improve as Americans adjusted to the medium's presence in their homes: "TV has passed the gigglebox stage and can no longer attract audiences by its sheer novelty . . . a more sophisticated public [is demanding] more variety in its programming.[48] Similarly, a Michigan State University political scientist observed, "A nation like ours, with its ever-rising levels of public education and public taste, is simply not going to tolerate our kind of TV forever."[49] An NBC News producer maintained in December 1961 that "the dramatic mill in Hollywood has run dry" and that the TV documentary would begin to command larger audiences: People are beginning to watch. They're conscious of television's voids.[50]

Others encouraged the chairman's UHF policy. Prior to taking office, Minow met with representatives of the ACLU, who restated their support for more channels as TV's cure.[51] Fairfax Cone of the Foote, Cone and Belding advertising agency insisted in October, 1961 that "our real difficulty is that we have no little television stations. We have only giants fighting each other."[52] The *Washington Post*, commenting on Minow's all-channel conversion, agreed that, "the country could benefit from expansion, increased competition, and greater diversity of programming in television."[53]

Some appeared to be simply resigned to the idea of all-channel television. Senator Cotton, a member of the Commerce Committee, admitted that "it may well that there is no other solution to the problem."[54] *New York Post* columnist James Wechsler remarked that "not many people can afford to establish and run a TV station, and most of them will be conservative Republicans." Wechsler added, "Expansion is no guarantee of anything. But the premise of a free society is that many voices are preferable to a few."[55]

No reaction to the all-channel receiver proposal, however, proved to be more surprising than that of the television industry. If an all-channel receiver law eventually caused new UHF stations to commence operations, those stations already established stood to lose shares of their markets to the upstart telecasters. Yet the response to Minow's bill was anything but hostile. Although most television set manufacturers opposed the measure as an unwarranted burden,[56] many powerful elements of the trade actually endorsed the bill. "This legislation," wrote a prominent Kansas broadcaster, "has the backing of most of the responsible people in the television broadcast industry."[57]

Most trade leaders apparently realized that the all-channel receiver law represented the least unpleasant solution to the allocation crisis. Conversion to an all-UHF system, for example, would have cost VHF channels millions of dollars in new transmitters and other equipment. Those particular VHF outlets faced through deintermixture with a compulsory conversion to UHF especially dreaded the prospect of the additional outlays. The all-channel receiver idea would not only pose no great financial burden but meant that UHF would not be fully competitive for years. Jack Gould of the *New York Times* commented, "Present TV broadcasters are assured of no more significant competition for years to come."[58]

Part of that reaction, however, owed something to Minow's relationship to the leaders of the industry. Against the sentiment of many members of the NAB board, its president, Le Roy Collins, testified on behalf of the bill. Stanton of CBS, too, spoke for the bill before congressional committees in March.[59] Deals with others were struck. Over lunch, David Sarnoff of RCA agreed to have NBC endorse the all-channel receiver bill in return for a favor; Minow personally asked Attorney General Kennedy to drop an antitrust investigation into RCA's color television manufacturing operations. Kennedy did.[60]

Leonard Goldenson of ABC similarly went along with the all-channel receiver bill if Minow promised to stand by his earlier pledge to deintermix those markets in which ABC lacked affiliates.[61] Yet while favoring the all-channel receiver bill, ABC jeopardized the proposal by coupling that endorsement with renewed pleas for deintermixture. ABC representatives insisted on immediate as well as long-term relief: eight mixed markets should be converted to all-UHF.[62]

The pleas of ABC for deintermixture *and* all-channel receivers fueled a powerful opposition among affected VHF station owners, their viewers, and congressional representatives to *any* deintermixture. Although significant portions of the broadcasting industry accepted the all-channel receiver bill, virtually all of the trade opposed deintermixture. Collins and Stanton, for example, expressly denied supporting deintermixture in addition to the all-channel receiver proposal.[63] Their influence, in turn, was soon felt at congressional offices. Senators and Congressmen forgot any "mandate" of 1956 for deintermixture.

Unaware of deintermixture's sudden ill will, Minow continued to insist on both all-channel and deintermixture as a "short-term solution in certain particular communities." His resolve flowed in part from counsel he received from the Senate's earlier call for action on the problem. Since 1956, Minow noted, Congress "has been telling us to solve the allocations problem."[64] He was also honorbound. Although less than sympathetic to ABC's plight, Minow has committed himself to the third network.

Meanwhile, viewers in the affected communities began protesting the prospect of losing their VHF signals. Deintermixture would have left areas heretofore served by at least one VHF channel with only UHF service. And people living on the fringes of such markets worried about the loss of TV signals altogether. These viewers' sets, even with a converter, could likely obtain only a VHF signal: forced conversion to UHF would place them in what FCC engineers called "white areas," forty or more miles from the transmitter and where UHF signals were thought too weak to substitute for the VHF channel. A few sparsely populated areas, ABC did admit, would be affected. But others grossly distorted the consequences of nothing but UHF television (though it was worth noting that the two commissioners known to be adamantly opposed to deintermixture were also the only engineers of the seven). Many more viewers, ignorant of radio physics, simply resented having to pay for an all-channel converter.[65]

As a result, managers of VHF stations in the markets that ABC sought to deintermix had little difficulty enlisting masses of viewers to protest a possible loss of service. From the Madison, Wisconsin,

area alone, the commission received thirty volumes of letters and petitions opposing the loss of channel 3.[66] One committee mailed 523
petitions signed by citizens in central Illinois and western Indiana
protesting the possible end of Champaign's VHF.[67] That wave of indignation, in turn, reached the offices of congressional leaders.[68]
"Deintermixture? If you think that's painless," commented a Minow
ally in the Senate, "I suggest you talk with a Congressman from an
area where the Commission has proposed to take out the VHF channel and substitute a UHF."[69]

Location also figured in the debate over deintermixture. The eight
markets listed by ABC included four state capitals, communities with
unusual access to their states' political leadership. Particularly active was Illinois's delegation. Both the state attorney general and
senate sent formal protests of the proceeding.[70] The Senate minority
leader, Everett Dirksen, the House minority whip, and a prominent
member of the House Commerce Committee, all hailed from Illinois.
And as the all-channel receiver bill came up for a hearing, nearly all
testified to demand that the commission not deintermix the Champaign and Rockford areas.[71]

The odds still should have been on Minow's side. Although the constituents of some prominent members of Congress would be affected
by the shift, those eight congressional districts and seven states hardly
made for a majority. Moreover, a good number of deintermixture's
most noteworthy opponents were Republicans in an overwhelmingly Democratic Congress.

The intensity of opposition against deintermixture was sufficiently intense, however, for that minority of congressmen to win their
colleagues' sympathy. Few representatives and senators had any enthusiasm for deintermixture. Others, such as Senator Prescott Bush
of Connecticut, indicated that although in favor of deintermixture,
they did not wish it for cities in their states.[72] It was a small matter,
then, and simple congressional courtesy, for members of the
Democratic majority, including Oren Harris, chairman of the House
committee, to join the ranks of deintermixture's foes. There was more
important legislation to draw blood over.

Legislators accordingly acted to blackmail the commission. A coalition of congressional leaders threatened to kill the all-channel receiver
bill unless the commission pledged not to proceed with deintermixture. Although Minow continually insisted that deintermixture and
all-channel television were separate issues, those congressmen repre-

senting the affected viewing areas disagreed. To discourage the commission from acting affirmatively on ABC's memorials, House and Senate members, including Dirksen, indicated that they would forestall the all-channel set bill without an express deal about deintermixture. Dirksen complained that the FCC sought both all-channel television and "to destroy valuable and effective VHF channels." Any effort to remove Champaign's VHF frequency would constitute an "appalling" exercise of the "sacred trust of licensing."[73]

Urged on by Ford, Minow then compromised. Orally and in writing, he promised the chairmen of the House and Senate commerce committees that the commission would not pursue the deintermixture proceedings. And with that pledge, the all-channel receiver bill passed both houses in July while ABC struggled to keep the deintermixture issue alive.[74]

As in the struggle for regulatory reform in 1961, Minow had encountered a congressional opposition of no little sway. The all-channel receiver bill did bring about a long-term solution to the UHF crisis, a problem Minow's predecessors had been unable in a decade to end. Yet, to win the bill's passage, Minow has been compelled to abandon deintermixture. Congress effectively closed eight adjudicatory proceedings. And Gould dubbed that concession "a severe blow" to the commission's prestige.[75] With the all-channel receiver bill, Minow had not asked for much from Congress. He received even less.

Chapter Seven

To Omaha and Back:
The FCC and Local Stations,
1961-1963

Congress refused to expand the FCC chairman's prerogatives and limited the agency's reallocation of TV frequencies, but the FCC's basic power remained. No one disputed the commission's right to regulate individual radio and television stations. In exercising this authority, Minow followed two approaches. The first involved the largely unnoticed, bureaucratic, or internal, method of using the FCC's potentially vast licensing and renewal powers as a lever against irresponsible franchise holders. A second tactic was public, or external: holding hearings in different localities to ascertain their stations' performance.

The chairman's intentions, as so often, related to his antipathy for the unrelenting "mass" appeal of television and his nostalgia for the medium's early days. He insisted that stations surrender some portion of their more coveted evening air time to the perennial losers in the audience rating wars: racial, religious, and educational "minority" interests. Minow also hoped that networking itself would be decentralized; perhaps the networks would again, as in the 1950s, utilize their Chicago stations, and not just New York and Los Angeles production groups, for national programming.

Chicago's role in TV's golden age constituted the one constant reference in Minow's advocacy of more local programming. As in his encouragement of news and cultural fare, Minow looked to the television of the early 1950s to justify regulatory policy in the early 1960s. In this instance, Minow recalled Chicago's contributions to national networking: the children's program of his former client, Burr Tillstrom, starring Kukla, Fran, and Ollie, as well as such series as "Stud's Place," "Zoo Parade" and "Garroway at Large." Despite artistic successes, the programs of the "Chicago School" of television had all but disappeared, along with so many other forms of the golden age. The time had now come for a revival. Chicago "did it before," he said, "and Chicago can do it again."[1]

Then, too, regulatory precedent inspired Minow. From the days of the Radio Commission, licensees had been asked to allot time for "local expression," under the category, "local, live." That meant, quite simply, community news and weather reports; information programs; discussion forums featuring political, social, and religious leaders; and locally produced entertainment programs. A station, in other words, could not schedule just from the networks, and its own offerings had to strike a balance between entertainment and news. The commission had reaffirmed its commitment to this licensee responsibility policy in the 1946 Blue Book and 1960 local programming report.[2]

Past admonishments notwithstanding, the amount of initiative by stations had varied. Local programming constituted about 12 percent, on the average, of the entire schedule, with regular news, weather, and sports reports taking by far the largest share. Less frequently aired religious, educational, or community discussion telecasts tended to be presented at odd hours: Sunday mornings or before seven on weekday mornings.[3] Some outlets offered original local, live talent programs, though; in the 1950s, a Fort Smith, Arkansas, station had its own version of NBC's "This Is Your Life." In Huntington, West Virginia, WSAZ produced a children's program, "Steamboat Willie," as well as "TV Handyman," "Farmer Bill Click," "Let's Doodle," and a country music show, "Parson's Study."[4]

Stations relied most, however, on filmed productions created in New York or Hollywood. Old cartoons, originally made for motion picture houses, absorbed most of the time on children's shows, while syndicated series took up most of the local adult entertainment time during hours a network did not seek. Syndicated programs were either reruns of such network series as CBS's "I Love Lucy" or cheaply made entries rented to stations by such independent producers as ZIV Films (which created "Highway Patrol" among other non-network efforts). Of the near addiction to the syndicated product, *Variety* observed in February 1963, "The old film shows never die; they don't even fade away."[5]

In the early sixties, virtually all stations depended on the networks for programming. In fact, so many outlets actively sought network association that the overwhelming majority—in 1961, 503 of 527 stations, or 95 percent—had one or more affiliations.⁶ During the "most watched" hours, between 7:00 and 11:00 P.M., the networks were responsible for almost everything that outlets scheduled. By June 1960, network fare consumed 63 percent of an affiliate's total schedule and about 95 percent in evening prime time.⁷

This extraordinary dependence on networks and syndicators underscored a critical limitation to the FCC's long-running doctrines of localism: the economies of scale in television. Compared with single stations, networks and independent producers spent more on individual programs. They could afford to do so, both because they were larger enterprises and because they offered larger audiences to advertisers than did the single outlets. For example, one episode of NBC's "Bonanza" cost $120,000 in late 1961, or roughly ten times more than one production of WSAZ's "Parson's Study." Yet the audience for one NBC program, carried by 150 stations, dwarfed that for a WSAZ series, which was broadcast only in Huntington.⁸ Thus for the individual outlets, the real or relative expense of developing much of their own programming was enormous, especially when outside sources presented a ready-made and reasonably priced alternative.

Affiliates sometimes rejected those few network programs Minow regarded as serving the public interest. A Cincinnati doctor complained to the chairman in May 1961 that his area's CBS outlet bumped "CBS Reports," a documentary series, for "Sea Hunt," a ZIV sea adventure program.⁹ In December 1961, when twenty-five ABC affiliates declined to accept a violent episode of "Bus Stop," Minow praised such independence from the network yoke by remarking that "progress is being made when twenty-odd stations refused to clear a network program they believed to be objectionable."¹⁰ But even more ABC stations had rejected "Discovery," the educational children's program the network had hoped to air for the fall season.¹¹

Minow and his supporters wondered whether the individual licensee, and not the octopuslike networks, should be cast as the villain. He and others felt uneasy about the low acceptances by stations of network news and educational children's fare, a problem especially acute in areas with only one or two stations.¹² Many NBC affiliates refused to clear a critically well-received production of *Macbeth* in November 1960, causing a *Saturday Review* writer to comment, "The fact that 'Macbeth' even won half a dozen top TV awards would cut no ice with these local Caesars."[13] The adversary, then, did not necessarily work on Madison or Sixth Avenue. "[T]he culprit is not always 'big business'—the networks," a Cornell economics professor, Alfred E. Kahn, wrote Minow in May 1961, but "the local franchise owner who rejects the public service programs that the networks make available to him."[14]

Into the early 1960s stations' managers had found the temptations of larger profit margins greater than their fear of federal regulation. Through the fifties, licensees' scheduling practices had not commanded the FCC's attention, and by the decade's end, most stations, particularly in the bigger markets, were accruing vast earnings, with rates of return more impressive than those for the networks themselves. "Stations are run like grocery stores," one producer commented later, "a raking-in-the-money kind of business."[15] Thus, TV station executives took exception to FCC imperatives for less popular programming, not because such programs threatened insolvency but because of opportunities for far greater receipts. TV men, Minow complained in November 1961, "think this [industry] is an oil well. Unless they're making 30 percent a year, they consider it a failure."[16]

Ironically, the commission's own licensing forms tended to strengthen the hand of those broadcasters wishing to eschew less popular, public interest programming. Upon application for a license, parties pledged to air a specified percentage of news, religious, and other minority interest programming. They could forfeit their license renewal if they failed, within reasonable limits, to broadcast those percentages of public service fare. At renewal time, the Broadcast Bureau scrutinized three sample weeks of the station's schedules to determine if the promised proportion of nonentertainment fare had been aired. This procedure, however, failed to have much effect, because the commission asked for data so broadly categorized under rubrics like "local, live" that an operator could count a high school football game as the moral equivalent of a city council debate.

This looseness of definition rendered the calculations virtually worthless. In 1962, one legal analyst of the application process described the forms' "various ambiguities" which encouraged " 'paper' " compliance.[17] A very different observer of the commission, conservative columnist and broadcast licensee William F. Buckley, Jr., wrote more harshly: "The FCC encourages a rank hypocrisy offensive to honest men." Buckley likened the forms' request for pledges of amounts of types of programming to guarantees of civil rights in the Soviet Constitution: "one promises in one's career as a broadcaster to be guided by heavenly motives of public service and universal enlightenment which have nothing whatever to do with the sordid business."[18]

So apparently trivial a matter as revision of the license form, then, offered Minow one possible avenue for change. Under Ford, the commission had revised the application in July 1960 suggesting fourteen bases of defining local service.[19] Minow favored such a detailed listing of information, but he also wanted the form to include a request for data on the quantity of network news programs carried by the stations. He expected the commission to look with disfavor on those outlets that refrained from accepting such efforts as "CBS Reports" or "Chet Huntley Reporting." The other commissioners, however, refused to add such a question to the form, and they delayed approval of other possible alterations.[20]

The chairman did achieve with the KORD decision a consensus among his colleagues about gross violations by licensees. A Pasco, Washington, radio station, KORD, had failed to schedule any educational or discussion programs, despite having pledged in its original application in 1956 to allot 7.5 percent of its total schedule to such fare. Moreover, between 1956 and 1960, KORD had aired 1,600 spot commercial announcements per week, 900 more than it had agreed to limit itself to in its 1956 application. Needless to say, the commission did not find these excesses and shortchanges permissible. In July 1961, the brethren extended KORD's license for one year only, and in messages to all stations, enunciated the KORD "doctrine." Henceforth, the FCC warned, public service programming plans would be checked more stringently. "By issuing this opinion," the commission declared, "we immediately make clear to broadcasters the seriousness of the proposals made by them in the application form."[21] Hailing the KORD edict, a Virginia TV columnist wrote, "The FCC is moving at long last toward the correction of abuses the public . . . has suffered for a long time."[22]

The KORD doctrine took on added import when Minow named Kenneth A. Cox head of the Broadcast Bureau soon after becoming chairman. The bureau staff—called Cox's army—first screened the applications of all radio and television stations. A Seattle attorney and special counsel to the Senate Commerce Committee's investigations of television during the late 1950s, Cox had earned a reputation as an advocate of vigorous regulation. He was especially committed to local, live fare, and aired in evening prime time, not just at odd, or less popular, hours. Furthermore, Cox held to a "magic number," a percentage that stations should allot for local, live productions.

Under Cox, the bureau placed discreet pressures on stations. Except for the most flagrant violators, bureau officials did not recommend many license revocations to the commission. Cox did, however, believe in using the "regulatory lag" as an instrument of regulation. If a station's intentions on the form regarding local, live productions failed to impress the bureau chief, he could and often forcefully did convey his disapprobation. And rather than renew licenses automatically, as had traditionally been done, or ask the commissioners to suspend a franchise, Cox strode a middle path. He deliberately postponed action, pending the receipt of more information. Affected operators received from Cox "letters of inquiry," which cited the KORD doctrine and requested more detailed data on public service programming. Word quickly spread that Cox was really asking for "improvements" in the form of increases in the amount of such programming or better time slots for it. Under ths system his staff delayed some 500 (out of 2,000) renewal petitions by late 1961. "No longer," *Broadcasting* reported, "is a regular three-year renewal considered pro-forma by either the industry or the FCC."[23]

For all the mail exchanged, Cox's army secured only a little ground in its battle with the broadcasters. To be sure, Cox's raised eyebrows moved some station managers. *Broadcasting* reported instances of Cox's letters causing licensees, anxious for speedy renewal, to shift one or two public service programs into evening prime time or to increase the percentage of religious or discussion shows. By such a manipulation of the schedule, station operators obtained an automatic approval from the bureau. "Broadcasters get the hint," Robert Kintner of NBC said of the exercise.[24] Yet the bureau chief later denied that his approach had much influence on most licensees. Rather, Cox recalled "a continuous reduction in the level of public affairs [program] proposals" by stations large and small despite his many letters.[25]

A far more effective action might have been the revocation of a license whose holders had failed to honor the KORD edict. Such a suspension might have shaken all the trade into better observing the commission's commandments about public service obligations. But significantly, the commission revoked no licenses under the KORD doctrine.[26] Those who did lose their franchise in the early 1960s were the small-time operators whose practices bore little relationship to those of most broadcasters.

During Minow's chairmanship, the FCC initiated revocation proceedings against twenty-three stations, fourteen of which lost their licenses. Most of them were small radio stations in small markets. Nine outlets received short-term renewals, an administrative and legal burden for the unlucky broadcaster but an outcome obviously preferred to revocation, the dreaded "death sentence." Few of these cases won much attention, even in *Broadcasting*, because they involved such narrow technical violations as the misdirecting of an antenna.[27]

Minow had hoped for one severe action. Early in 1962, the chairman directed his staff and Broadcast Bureau members to select a station in a major television market that had failed to fulfill its public service obligations pledged on the form. Minow sought the revocation of a TV license in a large city. To kill a goose laying golden eggs would set a far more telling precedent than to fell a lame duck. In seeking a fitting victim, the chairman's aides decided upon a Los Angeles VHF channel.[28]

Having selected this Los Angeles lamb for slaughter, Minow found, however, that his fellow commissioners so ardently opposed the strategy that he could not bring the issue up for a formal vote. The evidence in the Los Angeles station case did not compare with that assembled in earlier revocation proceedings. The station in question had not, for example, broadcast obscene country humor programs or aired thirty minutes of nothing but used-car advertisements. It had simply not fulfilled relatively minor obligations promised when the license had been previously renewed. That difference proved to be critical. Minow's colleagues, with the possible exception of Robert Bartley, would not broadly enforce the KORD doctrine and would suspend a license only if a station's practices were blatantly antisocial. Thus, the brethren refused to sign the California station's death sentence.[29]

The reasons most commissioners abhorred revocation and its symbolic uses are murky. The Los Angeles license never came to a vote, and other, related, majority opinions went unsigned. Furthermore, because most commissioners, operating case by case, tended to look narrowly at each proceeding, certain basic assumptions about the inviolability of licenses often went unrecorded.

Nevertheless, certain generalizations are possible. Most commis-

sioners regarded a license, once awarded, with the requisite invest-
ment in equipment and programming, to be private property rather
than a public utility subject to public regulation. More significantly,
Minow's colleagues preferred to hope a transgressor station would
mend its ways rather than to despair over its past failures. In the 1962
Westinghouse order,[30] noted earlier, the majority hailed improvements
in those stations' public service records just prior to the vote; in
KORD, the brethren put off revocation because the station's managers
took the FCC's very interest in their programming as a warning and
had begun to institute changes. In subsequent proceedings, too,
hopefulness defined and delimited the commission. "One of the tenets
of our society," Commissioner Lee wrote in a 1964 opinion, "is that
even a criminal should have a second chance."[31]

As Minow's colleagues groped for reasons not to act, the chairman
resolved to go outside the commission to find support and add to the
pressures on individual broadcasters. Besides revocation, the FCC
possessed another, though less dramatic, device to police licensees:
local open forums to determine citizen opinion regarding area broadcasters' service to the public. During the mid-1940s, Commissioner
Clifford J. Durr had held such sessions for radio station renewals.
Minow seized upon the idea. In his May 1961 speech he suggested
that "when a renewal is set down for hearing, I intend wherever possible to hold a well-advertised public hearing, right in the community
you have promised to serve."[32]

For Minow the appeal of local hearings mirrored his idealism about
citizen participation in the governmental process. "I am sure the
public does care about TV," Minow remarked in late 1961.[33] He accordingly sought to involve the great audience in the process of determining the social responsibilities of licensees. "I want to alert the
public to their own rights," he said. "I doubt that very many people
really know the power they have over broadcasting."[34] The industry
itself might protest, because local hearings had been so long avoided
and they portended nothing but trouble. But, he told broadcasters in
Chicago in April 1962, "The public must have its say in your planning and building."[35]

The chairman decided to try Durr's exercise in the Second City,
where local service had clearly declined since the early 1950s.
Although the three national networks owned stations in the city, none
had attempted to revive an earlier practice of originating series for

national audiences in Chicago. For example, NBC, refused comedian Bob Newhart's request to film his series in Chicago, and instead had the program shot in California. In addition, all three network stations in Chicago had cut back on local, live shows intended for area audiences only.³⁶ The worst offender, NBC's station, WNBQ, had actually discontinued a local show despite sponsor objections. And for many working at WNBQ, effects were disastrous: in 1957, WNBQ employed 130 engineers; that figure had dropped to 7 within five years.³⁷ A spokesman for the American Federation of Television and Radio Artists (AFTRA) had asked in October 1961, "Is Chicago to get all of its culture, all of its thinking, from New York and Hollywood? Can't the second largest city contribute anything to the United States besides money?"³⁸

In Chicago, Minow had the two elements he needed to initiate an area-based proceeding. The Chicago stations had undeniably decreased their local, live programming, and the chairman could point to dissatisfied local groups. Since 1958, Chicago groups led by the AFTRA chapter had been filing complaints about the stations' programming practices and had been demanding revocation of their licenses.³⁹ In 1959, the FCC had disregarded these petitions and renewed the Chicago licenses.⁴⁰ But three years later, with the licenses up for renewal again and complaints still being voiced by AFTRA, Minow raised the matter in a stunning fashion at a commission meeting on February 21, 1962. Minow wished to grant AFTRA's petitions; he asked that the three network stations' requests for renewals—or at the very least, that of NBC's WNBQ—be denied completely or renewed for one year only. Rather horrified, his colleagues compromised. With only Rosel Hyde objecting, the commission agreed to send Commissioner Lee to conduct hearings in Chicago on the issue.⁴¹

Held in March and April 1962, the Chicago proceedings all but confirmed AFTRA's charges. As expected, AFTRA leaders and other television talent groups cited the loss of jobs that followed the curtailment of local operations. That the networks exploited Chicago, as opposed to New York or Los Angeles, by investing relatively less there than in the coastal cities, proved to be indisputable.⁴²

Network station representatives, however, made some telling points. National programs originating from Chicago had never comprised more than 5 percent of the total schedule. Most of Chicago's network programs had been intended merely to fill the temporary gap created by the lack of a national coaxial cable, which the American

Telephone and Telegraph Company was in the process of laying, to connect eastern and midwestern stations; most programs had therefore initially been viewed in only one region of the country. Chicago programs that were continued nationwide, including "Kukla, Fran and Ollie," suffered low ratings. Moreover, the networks needed the high earnings gained from their Chicago operations to compensate for the lower profits (and occasional losses) experienced in national programming. The benefits were traditionally larger and more certain in running a station than a network. Finally, in a shrewd bit of programming revenge, WNBQ aired portions of the hearings by delaying broadcast of "The Jack Paar Show," a network feature. Poor ratings and a flood of angry phone calls from Paar fans followed.[43] The public, over whose interest Minow watched, were not very interested in this exercise of "public interest" regulation.

Non-network representatives offered Minow no solace: few present spoke for the viewer at large or the whole community; "public" witnesses, those outside the trade, quickly equated the public interest in Chicago TV with their own interest.[44] The Catholic church representatives protested the poor studio facilities and less desirable air time available to them, and AFTRA sought not more local programs, per se, but shows that would require the employment of more union members.[45] Italian-Americans disliked the characterizations of their ethnic group and Chicago on ABC's "The Untouchables."[46] Civil rights associations objected to the invisibility of blacks on television.[47]

Such criticisms, however justifiable, did not necessarily represent "Chicagoland." They certainly evaded broader matters of mass culture for the whole of the community. The hoped-for town meeting about a mass medium often lapsed into a faction-ridden ritual. Commissioner Lee may not have been Pericles, but the Chicagoans bothering to testify before him made poor Athenians too.

At best the proceedings had a muted effect on Chicago television. In his report, Lee recommended renewal but did attack the stations for reducing programs of local origin; he also called for similar hearings elsewhere.[48] In response, WNBQ and the other stations slightly augmented their local coverage. *Variety's* Chicago correspondent, Les Brown, reported a few more hours of religious discussion and other local fare but no substantial changes.[49]

However mixed the results in Chicago, Minow sought to hold additional local proceedings and asked the Broadcast Bureau to scour for another city. Under Cox's direction, the staff looked for a medium-sized community with three stations, each affiliated with, but not owned by, a national network and with mixed records in public service. The choice narrowed to Buffalo or Omaha. The Nebraska city, despite the renewal of its stations' licenses in mid-1962, was selected.[50]

Minow could not have another local proceeding without support from his colleagues. Chicago had been a special case, with local petitioners, clear evidence of the abandonment of local, live programming, and the licenses due for renewal anyway. In Omaha, the justification appeared less obvious; only two other commissioners, Lee and Bartley, would agree to the Nebraska inquiry, and Minow needed one more vote. Cross, Craven, and Ford would not accept what they construed to be an arbitrary hearing, while Hyde opposed the procedure altogether, with or without local petitioners.[51]

Minow could fashion a new majority coalition   one needed for an Omaha proceeding—by ridding himself of fellow Democrat Cross, whose term expired on June 30, 1962, and whom he regarded as not only lazy but disloyal. Cross, however, would not be easily removed. For months, the commissioner from Arkansas had been assiduously mobilizing support from his native state's powerful congressional delegation, led by Senators J. William Fulbright and John J. McClellan and the House Commerce Committee chairman, Oren Harris. At one point, Harris telephoned the White House to say about Cross's reappointment, "BY GOD I'm interested in this one."[52] Such sponsors caused Kennedy and his assistants to hesitate over Minow's demand for the Arkansawyer's ouster in favor of Cox, who could claim support from Senator Warren Magnuson.[53] And Kennedy's decision could determine the extent to which Minow actually led the agency. "The FCC chairman needs a majority of the commission" Shayon observed in August 1962, "which he has not had."[54]

In the resulting melee, neither Cox nor Cross won appointment. Kennedy played off Cox, Cross, and their angels by naming E. William Henry, a young Tennessee attorney who had supported him in 1960. Henry qualified mainly because of his friendship with Robert Kennedy.[55] Like Minow in 1961, he lacked experience in administrative law, having never practiced before a regulatory commission; nor did he know much about broadcasting (he did a stint on Yale's radio station, while an undergraduate).[56] But Minow at last had another sympathetic commissioner; Henry shared most if not all of his notions regarding the public service obligations of local stations. In late

November, Henry agreed to support another local hearing in Omaha and joined with Minow, Lee, and Bartley, to affirm the motion.[57] Minow then selected Henry to chair the session.

When announced, the decision aroused only resentment among the Omaha citizenry. Most of the mail the FCC received from area viewers defended the stations and questioned the propriety of the hearing. One resident wrote the commission that "to my knowledge, there has been no indication of widespread local dissatisfaction with the programming offered"[58] Even Henry noted in his opening statement that the commission had no record of complaints about the service of the Omaha stations.[59]

Henry made the skeptical scornful by remarking on arriving in the city that he and the FCC better understood the public interest in broadcasting than did Omahans. "They may not like the fact that we are established to regulate their interest," he said.[60] Henry later qualified his statement to the editor of the *Omaha World-Herald* by writing, "What I meant to say if I was quoted correctly—was that we are established to regulate *in* their interst."[61] The first day of the hearings, observed the *World-Herald's* TV critic, "it was hard to tell the hunter from, the hunted."[62]

Henry was already in trouble with the state's political leaders. Well before his arrival, Nebraska's legislature and congressional delegation joined in condemning the commission's inquiry. The Democratic governor, Frank Morrison, decried "opening the door to anything which could be construed as Federal censorship" and declared that Nebraskans resented "a paternalistic inflow from the outside."[63]

Such criticisms distinguished the Omaha from the Chicago proceedings. In the Second City, political leaders, whether because of the strength of the local party machine or the then small audiences for TV news programs, had ignored their stations' confrontation with the FCC. But in Nebraska, political leaders felt obligated to Omaha's stations. They benefited from exposure on the channels, one of which even telecast a program hosted by Governor Morrison's wife, Maxine.[64]

In other ways, however, the Omaha affair could be likened to that in Chicago: similar preoccupations predominated at the sessions. Only 20 of the 125 scheduled witnesses did not represent a special group. Of these 20 unaffiliated participants, at least 10 were public officials and not the common man wandering into the assembly hall to speak his piece.[65] As before, the AFTRA local chapter and talent agencies protested the dearth of programs originating at home; the Omaha Musicians' Union asked for a local version of Jack Paar's variety-talk shows.[66] Religious leaders sought better time slots. Once again, area television managers defended their service; one of them, in airing Henry's opening statement rather than the NBC quiz show, "The Price Is Right," only raised viewer ire.[67]

Altogether, the Omaha proceedings had less than clear-cut results. In October 1963, Henry submitted a report critical of Omaha's TV service. He concluded that the stations limited local productions to news, weather, farm market, and sports reports.[68] Such observations, as with Lee's in Chicago, did not go unnoted. Soon after the hearings the local stations began producing some relatively costly, local public affairs shows. But these, too, proved few and short-lived.[69]

The most striking aspect of the hearings in Omaha and Chicago was what had not occurred. Minow had hoped that the public—en masse, or in more organized fashion—would participate. "I intend to find out whether the people really care," Minow said in May 1961 of his designs for local hearings.[70] Although certain groups indeed expressed their opinions, the chairman could not justifiably claim that a significant portion of citizens of either city followed or engaged in the proceedings.

Indeed, public indifference all but mocked the administrative process. Those who did join in usually represented small, special interests, with program complaints particular to their race or ethnic heritage. Media coverage or stereotyping engrossed them, causing an Omahan to cite testimony there as an "exhibition [of] the failure of American community leaders to evaluate television by standards other than 'exposure' given their own organizations and projects."[71] Labor representatives complained not of the almost total lack of series mirroring working-class culture and aspirations[72] but of the adverse effect on some AFTRA members of reliance on national programming.

Particularly in the smaller communities, too, many regarded the licensee as a hometown entity worth protecting against outside intervention. An American Bar Association analyst of the FCC observed, "The commission lacks grass-roots support when it seeks to challenge the manner in which a broadcaster has been using its license; the contest is seen as one between a local citizen, the broadcaster, and a distant Washington bureaucrat."[73]

Furthermore, broadcasting's exercise of majoritarianism—cultivating public satisfaction with the scheduling practices—checked the FCC chairman. No evidence exists that local expression could compete with the national, standardized entertainment of the networks. Viewers not only repeatedly preferred Jack Benny or Hoss Cartwright (of NBC's "Bonanza") to a local wit or community program forum but often held the hometown production in contempt. "If any of your members watched one of these local, live television programs," an Omaha woman wrote in January 1963, "you would readily acknowledge that such programs are so poorly planned and ineptly done that we certainly need no more of them cluttering up the T.V. channels!"[74] Thus the very element Minow sought most to contain, the incessant supply of a mass-produced product, generated enough popular support to deny him any substantial following for the reform of programming practices.

Dismissing the Omaha and Chicago proceedings as meaningless regulatory rituals, however, ignores their tie to other liberal activities in the sixties. Through the decade, planners of social programs—like Minow at the FCC—assumed that community participation could be achieved and incorporated into their efforts. But instead of town hall democracy, they found a great indifference, even from those affected by their labors. Only those few with the most direct interest in such programs availed themselves of the process.[75]

For Minow and his allies at the commission and elsewhere, the Omaha and Chicago hearings strongly suggested that the chairman commanded a very small constituency. He uncovered no great grassroots movement sharing his regard for balanced programming. Rather, it became all too apparent that Minow and others labored under what Henry Fairlie dubbed an "elite consensus" of the Kennedy years.[76] A small body of opinion leaders—in this instance, TV columnists and regulators—had common concerns uncommon to the great majority of Americans.

Evidence of the elite consensus about television extended to personal habit. In 1961 the average American watched four hours of television per day. Few of Minow's admirers could claim such attentiveness. William Benton, a prominent liberal critic of TV and friend of Minow, had boasted, a mutual friend told Minow in August 1961, of never having watched more than one hour of television in his life.[77] When, in 1962, the New York newspaper columnist Marie Torre polled fifty members of the intellectual minority of viewers, twenty-nine confessed to watching an hour or less of television per week.[78] "The ideal standard," complained an Omaha TV critic, "is upheld by those who have no set at all."[79]

There had been inklings of the shallowness of support. Some 5,000 people had sent supportive letters, postcards, and telegrams after Minow's NAB address of May 1961. Minow and his allies had pointed to such mail as an expression of mass dissatisfaction with the medium.[80] Yet, some 24,000 communications had been sent to the FCC in 1955 to protest the prospect of pay television. And proportionally more viewers wrote or petitioned the commission whenever it pondered removing the powerful VHF channels (in favor of UHF ones) in particular markets.[81] Still, the possibility that a majority of Americans did not follow or even agree with the chairman's remarks was not entertained by Minow and his followers.

Minow, of course, had gone to the public partly because a majority of his colleagues refused to take more drastic steps, including the revocation of a major television station license. Few disputed the FCC's right to regulate licensees, but to exercise that power the commissioners first had to agree among themselves about the problems of license forms and those who violated the pledges made thereon. This area of agreement could not be found.

Nor would a commission majority contemplate suspending the license of a large station. That symbolic gesture would have compelled five hundred other television stations and several thousand radio stations to take their FCC forms more seriously. "[The] FCC had but to take away a single license for the right reasons," *Variety's* Les Brown observed later, "to shock every station from coast to coast into a more responsible . . . service."[82]

The chairman had, indeed, been left to rely on the indirect, or marginally effective, devices. In the end, Minow could point to only the smallest gains. The percentage of all local programming on stations affiliated with networks rose only 2 percent between 1960 and 1962, or from 12 to 14 percent of the total schedule.[83] It is by no means clear that this increase, which tapered off soon thereafter, had very much to do with Kennedy's FCC chair. On the whole, station managers continued to schedule as before, as if Minow and the New Frontier had never come to the federal city. Only slightly, if at all, did broadcasters augment the amount of "public service" programming that Minow and others defined as being in the public interest.

Those who wrote later on the commission's local station regulation often described Kennedy's chairman contemptuously. Viewing an all-too-obvious gap between the promise and the performance, they berated the chairman for too much style and too little substance. A former aide, Hyman Goldin, referred to Minow as one "famed for his literary allusions" and then noted how the FCC during his tenure failed to suspend the license of a large station.[84] With a like regret, Les Brown found Minow "overrated" and his reputation "still a myth" in 1971 because of his "vast wasteland" talk ten years earlier.[85]

Minow's lack of success, however, should not have invited such rancor. Defending minority interest programming, Minow found himself the member of two minorities. Most of his colleagues resisted his more forceful proposals to regulate local stations, and the chairman could not remove recalcitrant commissioners but only await their terms' end, and then hope the White House would force their retirement. Until then, he had to rely on public opinion in those communities where the commission held hearings on the performance of stations. Yet those exercises revealed only apathy, not sentiment for vigorous FCC action on programming. The chairman could not find his public in Chicago or Omaha. And this lack of broad support rendered the agency all the more vulnerable to any future confrontation with the House and a new president.

Chapter Eight

The Association,
the Chairmen, and the House
1963-1964

By mid-1963, after a series of frustrations with intransigent congressmen and apathetic viewers, Newton Minow had something to look forward to: a New Frontier majority on the FCC. The opposing majority had begun to disintegrate in mid-1962, when President Kennedy appointed E. William Henry to replace John Cross. Another New Frontiersman entered the picture in early 1963 when Kenneth Cox succeeded T.A.M. Craven. With three votes, Minow's actual influence over the agency grew, as did his designs for regulating the industry.

The shift in the balance of power within the commission was reflected in the FCC's attitude toward the National Association of Broadcasters. In his first years as chairman, Minow could only hope for the best in the industry's trade group and its new president, former governor Le Roy Collins of Florida. Minow encouraged Collins's ambitious plans for a strong, self-policing organization. By early 1963, however, Minow, had lost patience with the NAB and, with his new majority on the commission, elected to take matters into his own hands. In mid-1963, the commission prepared to adopt as regulation what had been the NAB's voluntary code for stations.

Yet the long-awaited arrival of a New Frontier in broadcast regulation only provoked the House of Representatives. In late 1963 and early 1964, the House acted to curb the commission's powers. Although many congressmen meant only to rap the agency's knuckles, the skirmish left the commission with a broken hand, and it soon backed down in disgrace. The *Nation*, which had championed so many of Minow's endeavors, unhappily dubbed his commission the "Sad Sack Agency."[1]

Founded in 1922 by station operators and radio receiver manufacturers, the NAB was soon serving stations, most were on its membership roles, almost exclusively. Traditionally, the NAB had operated to check government regulation in favor of a mild self-regulation[2] and to host pleasurable annual conventions. In the wake of the 1959 quiz-show scandals, some voices demanded that the NAB assume a more vigorous role in the trade. Industry and governmental leaders from Robert Sarnoff of NBC to Senator Eugene J. McCarthy argued that the NAB should become more actively involved in encouraging higher program and professional standards.[3]

An enthusiasm for greater self-regulation led the association's board of directors in December 1960 to name Governor Le Roy Collins of Florida as NAB president. A moderate Democrat and symbol of the "New South" of the 1950s, Collins had prestige and a sense of mission.[4] To Collins, only more self-regulation, and not mere lobbying, could forestall greater federal regulation. In May 1963, he told a South Dakota group, "All our NAB efforts are designed to make the individual broadcaster stronger; keep him from being imposed upon from any quarter, government or otherwise."[5]

To offet the possibility of a larger federal role, Collins upon assuming office called on NAB members for more news and cultural programming. In January 1961 he said, "I believe broadcasting is in serious trouble, that its public favor is dangerously low." But the industry could save itself through "improving the kind and quality of programming, the diversity of programming in prime time." Repeating these themes frequently[6] he even called for a revival of the moribund 1960 Doerfer Plan, under which each network would agree to schedule two hours a week of news and public affairs programming in prime time.[7]

Collins's intentions as NAB president delighted Minow. Encouraging greater self-regulation, Minow reasoned, would allay charges of "censorship" casually issued against the FCC. Moreover, a powerful NAB championing individual stations could act as a counterweight to the national networks. Minow, though not close to Collins in the 1950s, nevertheless sensed that they shared similar views toward TV's impact on society and the broadcasters' responsibility to their communities. Consequently, he went out of his way to hail the NAB president. In a March 1961 letter to Oren Harris, Minow wrote that "dedicated and enlightened leadership for the broadcasting industry—as exemplified by Governor Collins—is a prime source of improvement in program quality."[8] In calling for more news and public affairs programming, Minow frequently began by citing Governor Collins's addresses and referring to his "great leadership,"[9] and in Washington the two men kept in constant touch with one another. It was a congeniality much removed from the time when James Lawrence Fly compared the NAB to a dead mackerel.

Collins could be expected to aid Minow most by shoring up the NAB codes. The association, first for radio in 1929, then for TV in 1951, had formulated the Code of Good Practice for stations. These mostly enumerated what a station should *not* air, such as nudity and hard liquor advertisements. But they also set higher and broader criteria for programming that suited Minow's purposes. For example, the codes spoke of "the special needs of children," of giving them "a sense of the world at large."[10] Furthermore, the code stated, "program materials should enlarge the horizons of the viewer, provide him with wholesome entertainment, afford helpful stimulation, and remind him of the responsibilities which the citizen has towards his society." Minow had incorporated this excerpt into his first NAB address.[11] An adviser to Minow commented in August 1961 that if spirit of the NAB television code "were observed by the industry, the imbalance in television programming would be corrected."[12] When the NAB Code Authority reviewed children's advertising for the 1962 Christmas season, Minow described the screening process as "exactly what this Commission seeks to encourage."[13]

Collins soon set out to have the code further strengthened[14] with Minow helping as best he could. The chairman arranged and participated in a meeting with Collins and Attorney General Robert F. Kennedy in June 1961. Collins needed assurance that the NAB's efforts would not violate antitrust rules. The governor had little cause for concern; the attorney general quickly approved of the NAB's efforts. In October, the chief of the Antitrust Division, Lee Loevinger, all but waived enforcement of the Sherman and Clayton acts by reporting that his branch was "sympathetic" to the NAB code's revision.[15] Collins thereupon enlarged the Code Authority's budget and capacity to monitor subscribers.

Still, Collins faced serious obstacles in using the codes, not the least of which was the reluctance of many stations to subscribe to them. Stations did not have to belong to the NAB to display the organization's seal, yet they did have to pay a fee, graduated on the basis of their charges to advertisers.[16] And whereas most station managers belonged to the NAB, about 60 percent of all American radio outlets and 30 percent of all U. S. TV facilities refused to participate in the code process.[17]

The NAB Code Authority had even more difficulty enforcing the guidelines among member stations. There was virtually no way the NAB code's goals of more educational programming could be imposed. Petty transgressions, such as excessive advertising or ribald copy, could be policed, but only superficially.[18] In effect, then, adherence to the code remained largely voluntary. One NAB attorney later termed obedience to be a goal "to be lived by," one akin to a minister's wish "to have everybody in church on Sunday."[19]

The worst punishment that the NAB Code Authority could mete out hardly constituted the stuff of depression-era prison films. As a last resort, the NAB empowered the Review Authority to withdraw the station's seal of good practice, an action meant to arouse public opinion. Such revocations occurred on occasion, but to little notable outcry. In June 1959, for example, nineteen stations lost their seals for having aired commercials for a hemorrhoid remedy.[20] Yet there is no evidence listeners or advertisers boycotted any of these outlets. All told, station managers found that if they violated some code stricture, they had little to fear.

Furthermore, the effectiveness of the codes—if not of Collins's presidency—rested in large part with the cooperativeness of the national networks.[21] And almost from the outset, neither Collins' nor the Code Authority could count on the heads of the national chains. If anything, the networks resented Collins: and summarily rejected his resurrection of the Doerfer Plan.[22] Such cavalier attitudes surfaced even as the Omaha and Chicago hearings confirmed the predominance of network programming during the popular evening hours. Each network, though a code subscriber, successfully resisted having the NAB pass on its product. None would allow Code Authority officers to prescreen network programs, except in the two extraordinary circumstances. Even then, Collins's staff could not "reject" a program by advising members not to carry it.[23]

Collins's problems with the networks underscored the overwhelming problem he faced as NAB chief: his selection as president had not, after all, signaled a widespread change of heart within the trade. His calls for self-policing fell on deaf ears, as did his pleas for the adoption

of new, professional values, Indeed, Collins met with a constant com-
placency among his constituency. Most industry spokesmen appeared
quite pleased with scheduling changes effectuated between the 1959
scandals and 1961. With more news and public affairs programming,
notably the televised 1960 presidential debates, many concluded that
the industry had done enough. Any broadcasting "crisis" and need
for a trade "czar" like Collins had passed.[24] Broadcasters accordingly
sought praise, not pleading, from their trade leader.

Ironically, Minow himself helped to undermine Collins's position
as NAB president. Minow's early, unexpected and well-reported attacks on television not only upstaged Collins's own plans to
"jawbone" the trade but placed the governor on the defensive. Anti-
Collins factions within the industry regarded the governor as Minow's
man. Collins's criticisms seemed only a variation on a theme by
Minow. *Variety* merged Minow and Collins in May 1961 into "the
hottest and most daring act in broadcasting."[25] And this perception
of Minow and Collins as Elmer Gantry and Sister Sharon Falconer
seriously hurt Collins's standing among NAB members almost from
the outset of his tenure.

Collins eventually had scant choice but to separate himself from
the chairman. The governor faced severe criticism from *Broadcasting*,
the major trade organ. There were hints of rebellion within the NAB;
stations in Texas and Colorado contemplated quitting the NAB en
masse in protest against Collins's leadership.[26] To preserve his position, the governor became one more shrill foe of the FCC. In his NAB
presidential address of April 1962, he severely attacked the commission's Chicago hearing. The FCC, he said, typified the "federal government wasteland."[27] *Variety* reported the formal "break-up" of the
Minow-Collins "act."[28]

With Collins only another adversary and not an ally, Minow slowly came to a grim realization. The governor could not be relied upon
to do the commission's bidding; both he and his association were pro-
ving to be insincere self-regulators. And accordingly, Collins's role
in Minow's plans for television's uplift all but ended.

Minow's references to Collins, the NAB and the code at successive
NAB national conventions evinced this enveloping gloom about the
trade association's possibilities. In May 1961 the chairman struck a
note of hope by reciting portions of the NAB code and commenting,
"I urge you to respect them as I do." The following year, however,
Minow lamented the large number of stations that either did not

subscribe to or did not observe the code. Then came a hint of retribu-
tion. "If you are unable to achieve self-discipline," Minow warned,
"we may have to adopt a rule on commercials which does apply to
everyone." A year later, in April 1963, Minow observed, "The trouble with that Code provision [on commercials] is that it is not com-
plied with and is not adequately enforced."[29]

Minow prepared to strengthen the NAB by investing the association with semiofficial status. The chairman wished to transform the
NAB into a policing agency of the commission, just as the Securities
and Exchange Commission had converted the National Association
of Securities Dealers (NASD) in 1938. Minow's former law professor,
William L. Cary, then Kennedy's SEC chairman, had encouraged his
former pupil.[30] After meetings with Cary and Minow's aides, the
FCC's Office of Network Study recommended late in 1962 that all
broadcast licenses be compelled to join the NAB and subscribe to the
NAB code; in addition, the association would be invested with quasi-
governmental authority similar to the NASD. Minow promoted this
scheme in his April 1963 NAB convention address.[31] Under the plan,
the NAB would have the power to police all stations violating the
codes, just as the NASD oversaw security dealer transactions and was
empowered to suspend individual operators after review by the SEC.
The NAB would in effect inform on those stations disobeying the
many guidelines expressed in the code. In this instance the FCC
would retain the right to revoke licenses, but in considering license
renewals, it would nonetheless look upon the NAB's code board as
an extension of the Broadcast Bureau, the formal investigator of station performance.

Nothing came of the NASD concept. Congressman Oren Harris,
chairman of the House committee that oversaw the FCC, opposed the
idea; *Broadcasting* editor Sol Taishoff angrily resented the comparison
of station managers to the "swindlers and stock manipulators" of the
1920s.[32] Most important, Minow found little enthusiasm among his
colleagues for submitting to Congress the enabling legislation. His
trade association concept, *Business Week* reported in April, "isn't
taken seriously within the Commission."[33] Here, as in the FCC's actions on stations—when the chairman sought the symbolic revocation of a large station's license—Minow found his brethren unen-
thusiastic about an unfamiliar approach to broadcast regulation.

The Commission could still seize upon the NAB code to combat a single problem, "overcommercialization," the airing of too many advertisements. The NAB code specified that a station could allot to commercials up to 17.2 percent of an hour in regular time and 27.2 percent of an hour in evening prime time.[34] Minow and others proposed to set these quotas as FCC policy. The NAB's percentages could then be used by the Broadcast Bureau to assure uniformity in considering each application for a new license or renewal.

Additionally, by adopting the measure of the trade association, the commission would be extending its own powers without seeming unduly harsh or arbitrary. What station owner could argue against his own trade association's criterion? It was all very neat. "The Code was written by this industry," Minow said of the commercial limits in April 1963, "and represents the thinking of responsible broadcasters about advertising practices."[35]

Minow's soothing logic notwithstanding, some saw a dangerous tendency in his emphasis on the NAB code. On the one hand, by backing off from the NASD idea, Minow seemed to be settling for only one of the NAB's guidelines. But might not the FCC soon add other code strictures, specifically ones with programming criteria in mind? The same *Business Week* feature that had sarcastically noted the commission's lack of enthusiasm for the NASD idea, warned ominously: "The commercial time limitation is important as a foot in the door. . . it gets into an area of where [the FCC] can establish major precedents. Once federal standards are adopted to determine how many commercial stations can broadcast, the FCC majority could easily go further and apportion time among types of programs."[36]

The task of initiating a limitation of commercials fell to Commissioner Robert E. Lee. Although the intimate of Old Guard Republicans and otherwise a champion of free enterprise, Lee had long favored some sort of restriction. Unbridled broadcast advertising, Lee maintained, added to the costs of goods and services; he assumed too that TV's consumers, like himself, overwhelmingly disapproved of the number of commercials and the ever-increasing interruption of programs.[37] (He was also annoyed at the loudness of many commercial messages, which invariably interrupted his occasional naps in front of the TV.) In November 1962, Lee mistakenly thought he had the votes to have the NAB's regulation placed on the agenda for consideration as an FCC rule. But by a vote of four to three, the commission voted not to commence a rule-making procedure on the commercial limits proposal.[38] Only Minow and E. William Henry, the two New

Frontiersmen on the panel, stood with Lee.

In early 1963, then, Lee and Minow still needed the vote of another commissioner to begin the process of restricting commercial time by means of the NAB code. Frederick W. Ford stood unalterably opposed to the proposal, as did Rosel Hyde. Bartley and T.A.M. Craven, both moderate Democrats, had also spurned Lee. Craven's days, however, were numbered. He agreed to leave the commission in January 1963, several months before his term expired. In his place, Minow finally secured the appointment of Kenneth Cox.[39] Because his regulatory enthusiasm knew no bounds, Lee's proposal fared well when it next came before the commission.[40]

At a March meeting, Cox joined Lee, Minow, and Henry in support of a rule-making procedure to restrict commercials. Accordingly, the FCC was to hold hearings and receive communications regarding the idea, after which it would vote on the matter. If Lee's motion carried, the NAB code's article on commercialization would become a fixed FCC standard. TV stations would be restricted to 10.33 commercial minutes, radio stations to 18 minutes, per hour.[41]

In Cox, Minow thus had not just the needed support for a single proceeding but a fourth, majority, vote for other initiatives. Lee, Bartley, or even Ford might go with the New Frontier commissioners on a given matter. "Despite all his talk, Minow hasn't done much to alter the structure of broadcasting," *Business Week* observed in April 1963. But the elevation of Cox changed the odds, and Minow had a winning alignment: "The New Frontier appointees are beginning to move beyond the traditional 'raised eyebrow' style of regulation towards significantly tougher rules."[42]

At the threshold of a new era in broadcasting regulation, the chairman did the unexpected by resigning from the commission in June. Minow found himself missing Chicago and the good life too much to remain in Washington earning $21,500 a year. Nor did other positions in government interest him. As a young and impressionable aide to Stevenson in the 1950s, Minow had seen enough of the public life and its tolls to want too much of it himself. Instead, he accepted William Benton's lucrative offer to work for Encyclopedia Britannica in the Second City.[43]

At first, Minow's leaving portended only a more severe regulatory attitude. Kennedy filled his vacancy on the commission by appointing Lee Loevinger, chief of the Antitrust Division of the Justice Department. Briefly a judge on the Minnesota Supreme Court,

Loevinger had joined the division in January 1961. He did not get along well with his superior, Robert Kennedy, and in May 1963 the FCC appeared the most convenient dumping ground. After some flattery, then a few threats, Loevinger acquiesced. Trade journals, unaware of the Kennedy-Loevinger feud, looked dourly upon Loevinger's designation and predicted harder days to come.[44]

With Minow's encouragement, Kennedy promoted Commissioner Henry to the chairmanship. To broadcasters, Henry appeared to be another Minow, if not worse. Henry, after all, had presided over the controversial Omaha hearings on licensees' responsibilities. He had regularly voted with Minow on important policy questions. Like Minow, Henry believed in an "ideal type" station manager, the executive as public steward or trustee of the airwaves. The broadcaster, he wrote of his Omaha proceedings, "is not free to maximize profits at the expense of the public interest" and "the essence of the Communication Act's public interest mandate is that broadcasting must be more than a business."[45] With Henry adhering to such views, *Variety* alluded to a popular chocolate bar with the headline, "OH HENRY! THAT AIN'T CANDY!"[46]

Already on record in favor of Lee's proposal, the new chairman had come to share his predecessor's disillusionment with the trade association's capacity for self-regulation. Like Minow, Henry had undergone, in a shorter time span, a metamorphosis concerning the desirability of imposing—rather than encouraging—NAB standards. In December 1962, Henry had declared, "It is the broadcasters' primary responsibility—not the government's—to police their industry."[47] But soon he began to echo Minow's disgust with the NAB's self-policing. In September 1963 the new chairman stated, "Anyone who has placed his hand on the Bible, looked solemnly at the judge and sworn to represent the interests of the viewing public, must sooner or later question whether industry codes are, in and of themselves, a sufficient answer to the problem of overcommercialization."[48]

Henry might have chosen his first major cause as chairman more carefully, for a string of setbacks and one tragedy accompanied the fight over commercial time, and left the FCC's reputation greatly damaged. Even before the commission voted on Lee's original motion, members of the House prepared to endorse overwhelmingly an amendment vetoing the rule. Commissioner Loevinger, thought to be tied to the Minow-Henry regulatory philosophy, surprised all by indicating late in 1963 that he would probably not vote for the Lee proposal. Finally, the death of President Kennedy proved to be an especially hard blow for the commission. The wife of the new chief executive, Lyndon Johnson, owned broadcast properties in Texas, and Johnson himself possessed decidedly relaxed views on government regulation.

The commission's problems began in September 1963, when Congressman Walter Rogers, Democrat of Texas and a member of the Commerce Committee's Communications Subcommittee, offered an amendment to the Communications Act that forbade the commission from limiting the amount of advertising on stations. The fight over Rogers's amendment, in turn, proved to be the touchstone to opposition to the FCC's attempted extension of power.

In late November, before any vote on Rogers's amendment, John Kennedy, was assassinated in Dallas; any notion that the FCC enjoyed a White House mandate to save American television died with him. It had been widely held that Minow and Henry had been intimates of the president, doing his bidding in broadcast regulation. Much of this interpretation had been grossly overstated; *Broadcasting*, for example, in a characteristic attempt to engender paranoia among subscribing station managers, had noted in mid-1963 that William Henry's daughter attended the same day school as Caroline Kennedy.[49] In truth, since the defeat in June 1961 of the reform bill, Kennedy had distanced himself from the regulatory bodies. Rarely if ever had Henry or Minow consulted with him or his aides in formulating policies.[50] Nevertheless, the perceived close association of the FCC with the New Frontier continued until Dallas.

Lyndon Johnson's immediate effect on the commission was similarly overestimated. The new president played no role in the debate over the Rogers amendment, which, the *Wall Street Journal* noted on November 22, the day Kennedy died, already appeared sure of passage.[51] Nevertheless, a superficial connection was drawn between the House's budding revolt against the FCC and Johnson's coming to power.[52]

Johnson's arrival may have changed one vote on the commission and thereby doomed Lee's proposal. Under Kennedy, Loevinger was apparently prepared to accept some of the Minow-Henry agenda. But he wanted a federal judgeship, and after Dallas, he needed to placate a president not sympathetic to Kennedy's men. Thus, the newest commissioner began to separate himself from his fellow New Frontiersmen.[53]

Although agreeing with his colleagues that the FCC had the right to force a limitation, he could not support the restriction itself. Loevinger accepted the tenets of those who hailed television as "cultural democracy"; the majority of consumers, and not the commission, must determine the matter of overcommercialization. In December 1963, Loevinger sarcastically told the National Association for Better Radio and Television (NAFBRAT) and other petitioners that viewers aggravated by aspirin advertisements could always shut off their sets: "I wonder why people insist upon this masochistic exercise of subjecting themselves to that which they find objectionable."[54]

As if Loevinger's doubts were not bad enough, on December 17, the House Commerce Committee passed favorably on Rogers's bill by a vote of twenty-five to eight. Henry had urged Oren Harris to delay acting, since the commission had yet to decide the issue of limiting commercials. But Harris refused the new chairman's request. For the first time since the fight over the reorganization of the FCC in June 1961, Harris openly broke with the commission.[55]

On January 15, 1964, Henry, Lee, and Cox surrendered to the mathematics of the House Commerce Committee, the Commission, and Loevinger; the brethren voted seven to zero to end the proceeding and possible adoption of the rule.[56] The rule, the commission determined, "would not be appropriate at this time." More information would be required before the agency would adopt "definite standards."[57]

Such language hardly veiled the immediate cause for the panel's retreat: Loevinger would not side with Henry, Cox, and Lee, and agree to a set limitation. "I'd like to see the code adopted as a guide," Henry told the *Washington Star*, "but it was obvious that the majority of the commissioners, in this proceeding anyway, were not going to get tough. I could have gone off on my white charger, but to what purpose?"[58]

One month after the commission's vote, on February 27, the House approved the Rogers amendment by a vote of 317 to 43. No southern Democrat and only five Republican congressmen voted against the amendment. The commission had actually fared better two and a half years earlier, when seventy-seven House members endorsed the Kennedy administration's controversial reorganization of the FCC. Twenty-six of those who voted against the Rogers amendment had also served in the Eighty-Seventh Congress and had favored the

Kennedy administration's reorganization plan for the FCC. Fifteen of them came from two states, California and New York. (The commission's friends were not only few but geographically far between.) Nearly all were easily categorized as liberal Democrats: Morris Udall of Arizona; John Moss of California; Torbert Macdonald of Massachusetts; John Dingell, Jr., of Michigan; Otis Pike, William Ryan, and Emanuel Celler of New York; Henry Reuss and Robert Kastenmeier of Wisconsin.[59]

Cox and Henry later bravely held that, the House tally notwithstanding, Loevinger alone warranted blame for the FCC's surrender.[60] The Senate, they contended, would not have gone with Rogers and Harris. Senator John O. Pastore of Rhode Island, who chaired the subcommittee which oversaw the FCC, believed that the commission had the right to decide the commercialization issue without congressional interference. He could have saved Henry's face in the upper chamber.[61]

Others, however, including a financial analyst for International Telephone and Telegraph (ITT) looking for broadcast properties, maintained that the very size of the House vote rendered Senate action superfluous. An aide to a member of the Senate Commerce Committee wrote a station manager, "this was a substantial slap at the Commission."[62] A longtime FCC staff member recalled, "The Commission knew the jig was up."[63]

It was difficult to escape the conclusion that the House had all but destroyed the premise of the FCC as an independent agency. Whereas in the 1950s critics of the commission maintained that the agency badly needed a sense of direction, and the FCC wallowed in procedural minutiae, the commission under Minow and Henry needed no street signs. Regulatory actions between 1961 and 1962 originated within the agency itself. With the Rogers vote, however, Congess reasserted its earlier sway, causing Henry Steele Commager, professor of history at Amherst College, to write, "If the Congess is to dictate specific controls to the supposedly independent regulatory commissions, they will in a short time destroy the effectiveness of these commissions."[64]

The House's action offered striking evidence of just who the captive of regulated industries was. In the 1950s political scientists had concluded that the agencies eventually became the willing tools of the enterprises they were supposed to be regulating. In the case of the commercial time proposal, however, no commissioner apparently considered Lee's proposal except as a matter of regulatory principle or political advancement. None was the kept man of broadcasters or the NAB. Yet members of Congress appear to have been all too attentive to radio and television industry interests and to have dutifully humiliated the FCC.[65]

The House tally followed an intense lobbying offensive. Over the summer of 1963, the NAB mobilized an impressive campaign meant to convince House members that their self-interest rested with that of the broadcasters.[66] Those stations earning less money would, with the Lee proposal, be less likely to run public affairs programs with congressmen as invited guests. A radio station in the red could ill afford to air a free, five-minute report congressmen made available to stations.[67] Smaller outlets, notably those in rural areas, one small broadcast company representative said in July, would suffer enormously. With less revenue, such outlets would have to curtail local news and informational programming and in effect "become repeaters for the major networks."[68] Among other effects of Lee's idea, a Minneapolis advertising agent predicted in October, "no political candidate could buy broadcast time to speak in his own behalf."[69] A special horror, no doubt, with an election in the offing.

Such lobbying did not necessarily assure the success of the Rogers amendment. Losers in congressional tallies could always conveniently blame an insidious interest group for their failures, and they did so without always citing the exceptions.[70] Well-managed letter-writing campaigns did not always determine matters. In the eighty-ninth Congress, an aggressive American Medical Association could not block enactment of federal health insurance for the elderly; the Senate withstood in 1967 a vigorous offensive via the mails against a consular treaty with the Soviet Union.

Regarding the Rogers amendment, however, the cards and letters did have influence. Which constituents championed the bill mattered to many representatives. That many unsympathetic to the industry did not take a position undercut the commission's position. Citizens did not ordinarily follow congressional proceedings closely, and the debate over the Rogers bill was no exception. "Pressure groups," one political scientist observed of communication lawmaking later, "are most effective on specialized legislation where there is little or no public opinion or awareness."[71]

In the face of entreaties by station managers to support the bill, congressman heard surprisingly little from either private citizens or self-proclaimed public interest groups. Although surveys showed widespread dissatisfaction with the number (and quality) of commercials,[72] few viewers wrote the FCC or their congressmen in support of restricting commercial advertisement. Not one Oklahoman, that state's delegation informed the commission, had written to complain to his congressmen about overcommercialization. Even Senator Monroney, a champion of Minow in 1961, joined his fellow Sooners in opposing the "illegal extension of the Commission's operation."[73]

Those who did write included leaders of religious and voluntary organizations. Two special associations representing viewers joined the fray: NAFBRAT and a specially formed League Against Obnoxious Commercials, which claimed between 2,000 and 6,300 members in every state but Alaska.[74] These groups, however, could not match the organizational prowess of the industry. Indeed, one congressman sympathetic to the antiadvertising lobby wrote of "the poor benighted listener, who seems to be the only person without a lobby on Capitol Hill."[75] Without that consumer activism, one observer wrote, "the right to assail the general public with radio and television commercials is apparently inviolable."[76]

In the absence of a measurable public outcry, congressmen looked to their self-interest. Within individual disticts, radio and television stations offered an efficient source of exposure, a reminder to voters of a representative's name and positions. In some communities, such publicity was vital if the local newspaper opposed the congressman. Stations aired tapes produced in special studios on the Hill. A South Carolina congressman confessed: "Any person in politics benefits, ordinarily, by any radio or television interview. The honest politician will tell you that he knows the value of being placed before the public in the off season, when there is no political contest involved. It is advertisement at its best insofar as his ambitions are concerned."[77] It was no coincidence, then, that those favoring the FCC's limitation on commercials tended to come from the more densely populated viewing areas served by many stations, any group of which might still offer a liberal representative exposure.[78]

Others, even liberal or moderate Democrats, could not resist, especially on realizing that the FCC could not win. John E. Fogarty of Rhode Island, upon learning of his state's broadcasters' strong views, asked an aide to check the prospects for the Rogers amendment. When told that things looked bleak for the commission, Fogarty voted for the Rogers bill.[79]

Some representatives proved attentive to broadcasters for more complex reasons. Southern and border state Democrats, like Oren Harris, were among those least likely to support a strong FCC. Most served in politically less competitive areas and had less cause to worry about media exposure than their northern colleagues. But they often identified with those small-town entrepreneurs likely to own or operate a TV or radio outlet.[80]

Economic interest was not apparent. Although data on representatives' stock in broadcast-related industries are incomplete, 12 of 435 congressmen (2.8 percent) owned an interest in a radio or television station. Of these 12, 2 Republicans James Battin (Montana) and Robert Taft, Jr. (Ohio) did not vote; 8 supported the Rogers amendment; and 2, Udall of Arizona and James Roosevelt of California, opposed it.[81]

Those who complained about the commission's shortcomings often failed to note how often Congress had deliberately acted to limit the agency's freedom of action. In the aftermath of the 1959 quiz-show scandals, Congress had watered down amendments to the Communications Act that would have increased the FCC's powers over stations. In the debate over the distribution of television services in early 1962, both chambers had effectively suspended moving on an all-channel set bill until Minow had promised not to upset the prevailing imbalances within certain viewing areas.

As Minow and then Henry finally assembled a majority coalition willing to implement their approaches to the policing of the airwaves, they discovered a rebellious House ready to disassemble their proposals. That a bureaucratic body should occasionally be constrained by elected representatives seemed reasonable. But those members of the House overwhelmingly behind the Rogers bill were not responding to a broad public dissatisfaction with the commission. Rather, the 317 congressmen voted on behalf of an interest group threatened by the FCC. The House served as a last and comfortable resort of broadcasters. It, not the commission, had been captured by the regulated entities; the lower chamber, not the FCC, prepared to do their bidding if the Commission pursued the limitation on commercials.

The promise in the spring of 1963 of an expansive FCC had been forgotten by the winter of 1963-64. The House's decision left the commission demoralized, with little in store to provide solace. One consumer group representative wrote of a visit to FCC office in

February 1964: "I was depressed by a general climate of hopelessness which seems to prevail."[82]

The New Frontier commissioners had one further frustration awaiting them. Kennedy's death had brought into office a political leader with no enthusiasm for regulation in general and of broadcasting in particular. Mainly through his power to appoint commissioners, Lyndon Johnson made certain the mood at the FCC officers continued to be grim.

Chapter Nine

Resignations, 1964-1966

For a president fighting a land war in Asia and warring against poverty at home, Lyndon Johnson spent an inordinate amount of time deciding whom to name to the Federal Communications Commission. The FBI checked and rechecked names of people that the president then resolved not to nominate. One commissioner, planning to retire, was brought to the White House and admonished by Johnson to stay. After some spirited language in the Rose Garden, the commissioner elected to remain.[1]

Johnson's intimate involvement in designating commissioners did nothing for the agency's reputation during his presidency. In fact, between 1964 and 1966, the Federal Communications Commission went from being an industry nuisance to a regulatory nonentity. Chairman E. William Henry, the talented and purposeful Kennedy appointee, found himself philosophically outnumbered by colleagues and out of sympathy with the White House. A conservative faction of commissioners reversed most of the policies begun during the New Frontier years. Johnson might have rescued Henry by adding to the ranks of liberal commissioners. Instead, Johnson chose to spurn the regulators and court rather than confront broadcasters.

The FCC swiftly and with a striking completeness abandoned almost every vestige of the Minow era. Between 1964 and 1966, the agency all but ended attempts to encourage more public affairs programming. The commissioners ordered the Broadcast Bureau to cease utilizing the NAB code to determine if certain stations presented an excessive number of commercial announcements. Similarly, the bureau ended efforts to foster more local programs. Gone altogether was the prospect that the brethren might revoke the license of a large station that ignored agency guidelines.

The commission's collapse began as a retreat on overcommercialization, when Henry, lacking the four votes necessary to win Lee's advertising time limit proposal, withdrew the proposal in January 1964. None objected. Any lingering hopes that the NAB might become an instrument of policy vanished with the departure of Le Roy Collins in July to assume a subcabinet position in the Johnson administration. The NAB's board of directors, in turn, avoided selecting another prominent political leader for the NAB presidency. Indeed, early in 1965 the NAB board eliminated Collins's position by dividing his duties between two functionaries of the association.[2]

With Collins out, the NAB offered no realistic promise as a self-regulatory authority. Henry continued, as Minow had done, to endorse efforts by the NAB to encourage the airing of less popular, public service programming.[3] But individual outlets evinced no more interest in the code than they had earlier in the decade. In fact, any sense of urgency born of a desire to forestall greater regulation in 1960, or to please an FCC chairman one year later, had passed by 1964 and 1965.

Although two of the three networks did informally adhere to the code's suggested levels of advertising time and violence, ABC ignored both strictures. With "Batman" in January 1966, ABC increased sponsored time from three to four minutes per hour, despite the code's prohibition against such an expansion.[4] Later studies indicated that ABC during this period violated other NAB guidelines on the extent and treatment of violence in such programs as "The FBI."[5]

With self-regulation obviously unfeasible, the FCC tried to enforce on a case-by-case basis the NAB code's suggested limits on the number of commercials per hour. With Henry's quiet but firm encouragement, the Broadcast Bureau closely checked individual renewal applications for the number of commercial messages pledged on the license form versus those actually aired.[6] Henry had in December 1963 warned Harris that his agency would do so "whether or not the Commission has a rule on this subject," for the FCC "must inevitably be concerned with the extent of commercialization when [passing] upon applications for new broadcast licensees or renewal."[7]

The Broadcast Bureau had also been encouraging local presentations. In accord with FCC precedent, the bureau had since 1961 been sending "letters of inquiry" to stations that had failed in applying for renewal to promise an adequate percentage of local programming (not including news, weather, and sports) or to schedule enough of it in evening prime time. This informal practice of reviewing stations' schedules had continued on a case-by-case basis well into 1965.

Henry's reliance on the FCC's bureaucracy might have worked but for a powerful, countervailing tendency within the commission itself. The composition of the "brethren" was changing. Votes for tough regulation were not to be found in the middle 1960s. Instead, an anti-Henry alliance forcefully led by Commissioner Lee Loevinger emerged and effectively set the direction of the agency in 1964, 1965, and 1966.

The first showdown concerned overcommercialization. In mid-1964, the Broadcast Bureau accused stations in Louisiana, Mississippi, and Arkansas of running too many commercials and recommended that each be granted a short-term license renewal pending a lengthy investigation into their advertising practices. But in July, Loevinger's faction of Rosel Hyde, Frederick W. Ford, and Robert T. Bartley vetoed the bureau's recommendation and renewed all of the licenses.[8] That month also, the four horsemen ignored Henry's motion not to extend the licenses of some South Carolina stations guilty of airing too many advertisements.[9]

As in the matter of overcommercialization, the full commission ordered the bureau to stop harassing licensees over their levels of local programming. At a June 1965 meeting, a coalition led by Loevinger voted five to two (Henry and Cox dissenting) for the renewal of four stations' licenses whose extension the bureau had held up pending responses to letters of inquiry. In addition, Henry was ordered to instruct the bureau to cease sending such communications. Cox noted bitterly, "If we don't believe licensees should do more local, live, we shouldn't write letters."[10]

These votes on overcommercialization and local, live programming left the bureau with little leverage and stations with great independence. The discreet, but ever-present bureaucratic pressures of the early 1960s had essentially disappeared by the decade's final years. Some FCC staff members monitored stations' activities occasionally, but only after charges of obscene or off-color remarks.[11] Otherwise, the commission offered less regulation and stations less program "balance." As shown in table 3 the percentage of productions by stations remained at levels achieved preceding Minow's or Henry's coming to Washington. Of those channels earning more than $2.5

Table 3. Live and Taped Programs Produced by Network-Affiliated
Stations, June 1958-June 1968 (percent)

June	Live	Tape or film	Total
June 1958	13.1	—	13.1
June 1959	12.1	—	12.1
June 1960	10.6	0.8	11.4
June 1961	10.4	1.5	11.9
June 1962	11.6	2.1	13.7
June 1963	11.4	1.9	13.3
June 1964	11.0	3.0	14.0
June 1965	10.3	2.8	13.1
June 1966	10.0	3.0	13.0
June 1967	10.3	4.7	15.0
June 1968	10.0	2.0	12.0

Note: Dashes indicate that data were unavailable. Most stations—in 1961, 95
percent—were affiliated with a network, while few taped their own programs
until the late 1960s.

Source: Broadcasting Yearbook 1963 (Washington, D.C., 1963), 18; *Broadcasting Yearbook 1968* (Washington, D.C., 1968), D36; *Broadcasting Yearbook 1971* (Washington, D.C., 1971), A119.

million in 1964, just under 15 percent originated any local, live programming in evening prime time.[12] A check of Oklahoma stations four years later confirmed what everyone thought: networks continued to dominate the programming of individual stations, which in turn, offered little local programming other than news, weather, and sports reports.[13] The FCC's lessening emphasis on the obligations of stations led Louis Jaffe to conclude in 1969, "In the last few years, the Commission seems to have given up any control whatsoever."[14]

Needless to say, the threat of license revocation in the middle 1960s lay dormant. Henry, like Minow, saw the symbolic advantages of suspending the license of a TV channel in a major market. Only by such an extreme measure might all telecasters heed the FCC regarding standards on overcommercialization or local, live programming. Henry had sought to revoke the license of one of these larger stations, just as Minow had; Henry, too, could never bring his colleagues to consider the idea.[15] *Variety's* Les Brown observed bitterly,

"The net effect was that an individual could be awarded a radio or television license for promising to serve the public interest, convenience and necessity, but would not lose it for really failing to do so."[16]

There was no more striking example of the brethren's high regard for the license holder than the WLBT case. A Jackson, Mississippi, TV station, WLBT had indisputably violated the FCC's Fairness Doctrine of affording time to viewers wishing to express opinions in conflict with the station's editorial stances. Moreover, WLBT had, like so many southern institutions, grossly discriminated against black viewers. Few Negroes ever appeared on the channel; its managers commonly censored or refused to carry network programs favorable to blacks. These manifold violations first came to the FCC's attention in 1962, when Eleanor Roosevelt called Minow to protest the station's denial of advertising time to a black congressional candidate.[17] Minow, Henry, and Cox all called for swift and severe punishment. Yet the brethren would not act. Rather, the majority took to heart the promises of WLBT's operators to end blatant broadcast racism; the FCC renewed the license.[18]

Eventually, a federal circuit court ordered the commission to revoke WLBT's license. For the majority, Judge Warren Burger wrote, "After nearly five decades of operation, the broadcast industry does not seem to have grasped the simple fact that a broadcast license is a public trust subject to termination for breach of duty."[19] Burger berated not only broadcasters but the Loevinger-led commissioners, who had refused to act against WLBT in the first place. "A pious hope on the Commission's part for better things," Burger found, "is not a substitute for evidence and findings."[20]

The WLBT and related decisions by these commissioners underscored how little leverage Henry had. The composition of the commission during his chairmanship determined its attitudes. The fragile coalition of votes Minow assembled, which appeared permanent as he left office, gave way soon after Henry assumed the leadership.

Henry plainly found Loevinger, of any colleague, the most exasperating. In a flurry of speeches and writing, Loevinger declared himself the great applier of the First Amendment to broadcasting. In his newfound mission, he broke with recent custom. Most commissioners, notably during the Minow years, avoided airing in public fundamental disagreements with their chairman. Those who did, like Commissioner Hyde, had done so in a rather mild manner. Not

Loevinger. Before the NAB national convention in March 1965 Henry described a "working program . . . . that has the support of a working consensus" of commissioners; the next day, Loevinger brutally dismissed almost every element in Henry's plan. He gibed, "We're not the moral proctor of the public, or the den mother of the audience."[21]

Loevinger attacked virtually every element of Henry's regulatory philosophy. In a March 1965 law review article, he protested that the FCC's listing of religious programming as part of stations' public service obligation violated constitutional separations of church and state. That month, before the NAB, Loevinger lambasted local, live broadcasts with the remark, "As far as I'm concerned, a lot of local, live ought to be dead." Network programs, he found, were both better and more popular than stations' originations, and network informational programs far superior to local efforts.[22] As to the FCC enforcers' call for some local, live and religious programs, Loevinger commented in a July 1965 *TV Guide* interview, "I've seen pig pens better run than the Broadcast Bureau."[23]

Loevinger did not go unanswered. At the March 1965 NAB meeting, Cox argued that a station should try to serve as well as amuse and not worry about matching the higher production values of the networks. "It's not important whether your stuff is better than the networks'," Cox declared, "but whether you do the job you were put there to do to help solve the problems of your community." Henry simply dismissed Loevinger's barbs as a "mish mash of erudite irrelevancies."[24]

Yet Loevinger's positions were significant in light of the composition of the commission. Cox and Henry were the agency's hardcore New Frontiersmen. To draft new regulations or to act against certain stations, the Henry faction required two more votes. Past positions suggested that Commissioner Lee or Bartley might join them on a given matter. But a fourth vote from Commissioner Ford or Hyde was by no means certain, since each adhered to a fairly narrow philosophy of broadcast regulation. Hopes for a potential fourth vote rested with Loevinger, the third Kennedy appointee who, unfortunately for the chairman and Cox, talked and voted like one named by Dwight Eisenhower.

If Cox and Henry were to succeed in securing more local programming or less commercialization from stations, President Johnson had to replace at least some of their brethren. The president, however, used his power of appointment to maintain the conservative advantage on the commission. He ordinarily retained old hands or designated new ones who did not share Henry or Cox's opinions. Nor did the president confer with Henry about upcoming nominations, as Kennedy had with Minow, or agree to remove hostile commissioners, as JFK had done with John Cross in 1962. Instead, Johnson reappointed all four members of the anti-Henry faction—Ford, Bartley, Hyde, and Lee—between 1964 and 1967.[25] Loevinger, leader of the four horsemen, repeatedly asked to be named to the federal judiciary, but Johnson denied that request.[26]

In March 1965, Johnson chose James J. Wadsworth, scion of a distinguished, upstate New York Republican family, and considered a "safe" replacement for Ford, who had resigned. Although Wadsworth had impressive credentials as a diplomat, he knew nothing of broadcasting.[27] Nor was he willing to compensate for his ignorance; instead the former ambassador complained of overdetailed memoranda. "I don't understand the technical jargon," Wadsworth confessed. "Anything over two or three pages, I can't handle it."[28] Furthermore, a penchant for martinis at lunch often led to naps at afternoon meetings. Although Wadsworth occasionally sided with Henry and Cox on such matters as overcommercialization,[29] he otherwise belonged to the Loevinger coalition.

Johnson's appointments to the commission well conveyed his contempt for the two Kennedy chairmen. In May 1961 Vice President Johnson had, unlike Kennedy, disapproved of the chairman's "vast wasteland" NAB talk. Johnson shared with his mentor, Sam Rayburn, a dislike for Minow's proclivity for publicity and regulatory zealotry[30] Regulators, Johnson believed, should be hardly seen and never heard, particularly those overseeing American broadcasting. Henry recalled being brought to the White House in December 1963 to hear Johnson tell him and the other independent agency chairmen, "I want you to approach your job in the spirit of cooperation, not confrontation."[31] *Broadcasting* reported "a clear indication the President was out of sympathy with the generally 'hard' regulatory line the FCC has taken under Henry."[32]

Then, too, broadcasters enjoyed a unique fellowship with Johnson. The president's wife, Lady Bird, owned several radio and television stations worth some $7 million.[33] These properties Johnson refused to sell upon assuming the presidency, although he turned over their operation to trust officers after November 1963. In contrast, both Eisenhower and Kennedy had placed their financial holdings in "blind trusts"; neither man knew how his monies were being invested. Throughout his presidency, Johnson understood where his family's nongovernment income originated.[34]

Because of his wife's holdings, broadcasters assumed Johnson would handcuff the FCC. *Broadcasting,* after Dallas, spoke of "a new tone of regulation."[35] With scant evidence, many construed the FCC's January 1964 vote to drop the limitation on commercials, for example, as proof of Johnson's moderating influence over the FCC. Johnson's presidency, *Barron's* reported, "brought an appreciable softening in the Federal Communications Commission's previous truculent attitude toward the industry."[36]

Too much, however, can be made of Johnson's own stake in weak broadcast regulation. Although the editors of *Broadcasting,* the *Wall Street Journal,* and Republican National Committee newsletters quickly pointed to a conflict of interest, the president's attitudes are better understood in light of his philosophy toward business generally. Regarding the FCC, then, it would not have mattered if Lady Bird had owned an airline rather than a TV outlet. Johnson simply did not believe in an adversarial relationship between business and government. His address to all of the regulatory agency chairmen served as one example, as did his assurance to a group of business leaders in December 1963 that "we will not harass or persecute you."[37]

Part of the explanation for the new president's behavior relates to his own experience in Texas politics. Although Johnson had been touched by the Texas Populist tradition, by the time he entered state politics, he discovered that most successful Texas Democrats looked after the needs of the state's business oligarchs. In a one-party state, Democratic primary contests decided the winner and financial support from at least one financial kingfish was vital for victory. By the 1940s, the Populist enthusiasm for state regulation of enterprise had been spent. In 1949, Johnson was among those in the Senate opposing the renomination of Leland Olds to the Federal Power Commission. Closely tied to the New Deal ideal of public power, Olds had advocated strict regulation of natural gas, contrary to the wishes of Texas vested interests. For Johnson, a biographer noted, "the task was to dispel any doubts among the oil and gas barons that he was their agent."[38]

Johnson not only disdained the regulatory agencies' activists but in Congress, perfected a political style that avoided public confrontation whenever possible. He ridiculed Senate orators, especially liberal ones. His strong, obscene language came in cloakrooms, not on the floor. It is not surprising, then, that Johnson cringed at Minow's open declarations of dissatisfaction. "Johnson's career," wrote political scientist Doris Kearns, "was marked by a continuing effort to avoid confrontation and choice, to prevent passionate and emotional discussions over issues."[39]

As president, Johnson strove mightily to overcome the business community's habitual opposition to liberal administration. He wanted to make social welfare programs palatable to those long opposed to excessive government spending. Thus, early in his presidency, Johnson engaged in much-publicized budget cutting, characterized by his switching off some of the White House lights at night.[40]

Johnson's style of leadership, moreover, called for a "consensus," a sharing of goals among organized groups in and outside of government for social action. That harmony, of course, necessitated some measure of support from free enterprisers. And in contrast to the New Frontier and New Deal, the Great Society strenuously avoided even the appearance of tension between business and government; corporate leaders formed an integral part of Johnson's system of governing. "The consensus he had cultivated for the Great Society," wrote a Johnson biographer, "enlisted industrialism and its corporate managers in the quest for a better quality of life."[41]

Yet governance by consensus in effect gave over power to the unelected components of the "broker state." The president wanted the FCC to surrender authority that Henry and others wished to exercise, but not because Johnson believed with University of Chicago economists and Eisenhower administration refugees that a free marketplace would solve the TV problem. To Johnson, that "problem" and the FCC's mission were irrelevant, the Communications Act and *Saturday Review* notwithstanding. Far more important was an industry's cooperation in creating the Great Society. An agency supposed to oversee broadcasting was expected to do less, regardless of any legal mandate. In the broker state Lyndon Johnson led, not only were broadcasters more influential allies than minorities of viewers, but that power defined regulatory action. "Having granted exclusive privileges to private groups in the public domain without laying down practical conditions for perpetual retention of the domain itself," wrote political scientist Theodore Lowi in 1967, "the FCC had actually given over sovereignty."[42]

The application of Johnson's consensus on broadcast regulation was nowhere more painfully evident to Henry than at the March 1965 NAB convention. The chairman used the forum, just as Minow had four years earlier, to bemoan the state of television programming. Yet the station manager from Memphis or Manchester listened not only to Henry and the caustic Commissioner Loevinger but also to Vice President Humphrey and the president's family attorney, Leonard Marks. Humphrey and Marks hailed the trade and, in effect, blunted any possible "jawboning" effect from Henry's speech. Such divisions within the administration had not occurred four years earlier, when Kennedy and other administration figures said nothing to undermine Minow.

Addressing the NAB four years after Minow's famous talk, Henry found no greater diversity in programming. Like his predecessor, Henry saw redeeming characteristics, but "at best, it is a mixed bag, with some changes for the better—some for the worse—most of the movement is horizontal, not vertical." Violent Western and detective series had not given way to a restoration of live drama or spectaculars. Instead, "situation comedies have taken over from action-adventure shows." The amount of informational series fell as broadcasters increasingly scheduled news programs on an irregular or "special" basis. In a move Minow had long urged, CBS and NBC expanded their evening newscasts from fifteen to thirty minutes in September 1963. But at the same time, they cancelled such regularly scheduled evening news programs as "David Brinkley's Journal." "The overall size of the network public service effort has remained static or declined," Henry declared. He went on to cite data (see Tables 4 and 5) indicating a reduction in the number of hours such that the 1960-61 season, he pointed out, had "had 22 percent *more* network public service hours, and 15 percent *more* network public service programs than the season [1963-64] just past."[43]

After Henry's systematic indictment, broadcast conventioneers heard the vice president lavish praise. Humphrey, who had once aided Minow during the FCC's legislative battles and had saluted the FCC chairman with his characteristic exuberance,[44] now saw nothing but lilies in the wasteland. "I'm no snob, I like television," he said, calling American TV "the greatest single achievement in communication that anybody or any area of the world has ever known."[45]

Humphrey assured listeners of both his and the president's devo-

Table 4. Network Public Affairs Programming, October-April 1959-1960 to October-April 1963-1964

Season	No. Shows	Total Hrs.	%Aired Evenings
1959-60	39	189	25
1960-61	68	271	51
1961-62	78	269	51
1962-63	71	270	47
1963-64	58	210	46

Source: Sponsor (16 Sept., 1963), 13, and A. C. Nielsen Co., memo 057917, copy in box 70, E. William Henry Papers, State Historical Society of Wisconsin.

Table 5. Network News Programs, 6:00 to 11:00 P.M., Eastern Time, Third Week in January, 1958-1967

Year	Hours	Percent
1958	8.2	9
1961	13.5	15
1964	12.5	13
1967	13.0	13

Source: Lawrence W. Lichty and Malachi C. Topping, eds., *American Broadcasting: A Source Book on the History of Radio and Television* (New York, 1975), 436.

tion to the First Amendment and free enterprise. "Government doesn't own you, Government is not your master," he declared. "Government is here to help you and serve." Furthermore, "President Johnson made it clear," the vice president said, that "he does not believe in Government by scare or threat."[46]

In exchange for such assurances, however, Humphrey asked that NAB members join in building the Great Society. That social vision required a "creative federalism," the vice president noted, a spirit of cooperation, not confrontation, in which government, business, and other organized groups operated in concert. "There is ample meeting ground for Government and industry to work together as a team."[47]

Marks spoke in a similar vein, offering himself, in fact, as the Great Society's alternative to Newton N. Minow. "You do not operate in a 'vast wasteland,' " Marks told an NAB group on the eve of the meeting. "This clever catch phrase uttered several years ago obscured the contributions of many talented broadcasters." Rather, television in the mid-sixties should be praised. "Instead of living in a 'vast wasteland,' " he declared, "we live in a cultural oasis."[48]

Although there was every indication that Johnson shared the views of Marks and Humphrey, the president refrained from registering publicly his opinions of television or its regulation. Sensitive to charges involving his wife's broadcast holdings, Johnson left to others the task of presenting his soft regulatory line. Invitations to address the annual NAB convention were ignored until after the president had decided not to seek reelection in 1968.[49]

Johnson not only avoided meetings of the NAB but ones with Chairman Henry as well. On at least one occasion, the president turned down the chairman's request for an appointment to meet with him.[50] Henry, in turn, regarded himself as so isolated that, he later jested, if he had suspended the licenses of all of America's five thousand broadcast stations Johnson's secretary, Bill Moyers, would have replied calmly, "Well, whatever you feel is in the public interest, I'm sure you'll do."[51]

Johnson had to treat Henry gingerly. In the wake of Kennedy's murder, the new president had pledged to retain all of those named by his predecessor. He could therefore neither remove Henry as chairman nor risk his resignation by asking him to perform in a manner outside of the New Frontier pattern. He could only ignore Henry and hope for his voluntary retirement.[52]

The president separated himself from the FCC for another, more apparent reason: the first lady's radio and television stations. Although determined not to sell the properties that his wife had labored long and hard to render profitable, he also dreaded the thought that these holdings might suggest a conflict of interest. Any "instructions" to Henry or Cox might become public, and reporters and Republicans would be quick to smell scandal. "Johnson obviously was somewhat circumspect [toward the FCC] because of his own family interests and broadcast properties," recalled one commissioner. "There was never a single instance of any interference whatsoever by him."[53]

Still, Johnson could not resist lecturing the non-Kennedy appointees. When named or reappointed, individual commissioners came to the White House to meet Johnson. The president then used this formality to deliver colorfully worded interpretations of the Communications Act. He usually echoed those comments made to Henry in December 1963. Meeting Rosel Hyde in May 1966, for example, Johnson said he wanted "no harassment" of broadcasters. "Don't be a public scold," Johnson said, alluding to Minow's chairmanship. Such encounters, it should be noted, during which the president even began to proffer regulatory policy, had not occurred under Presidents Eisenhower and Kennedy.[54]

Finally, Henry and those sharing his view of broadcast regulation had to recognize Johnson's close ties to the leaders of the two leading networks. Through the Johnson radio properties, the president had developed friendships at CBS. Frank Stanton, CBS president, had loyally supported Johnson since Lady Bird purchased her first radio station in 1942 and affiliated it with Columbia. When as a senator Johnson appeared on CBS's "Face the Nation," Stanton personally called some CBS affiliates in Texas to urge them to carry the telecasts.[55] Stanton met with Johnson immediately after the latter assumed office, indeed, even before the new president moved into the White House. The CBS president advised Johnson about his TV appearances and their ratings. Moreover, he personally repaired the president's desk in the Oval Office and supervised installation of a special TV unit designed to receive all three networks' signals simultaneously.[56]

Nor had Johnson neglected NBC over the years. He once termed NBC's parent corporation, RCA, "a key element in our defense structure."[57] When Robert Sarnoff assumed the presidency of RCA in September 1965, Johnson phoned his congratulations.[58] But to no one at NBC was Johnson closer than NBC President Robert Kintner. Johnson had known Kintner from his days as a Washington journalist in the 1930s. Like Stanton, Kintner consulted regularly with the president about his TV appearances and "audience share." His wife worked in Johnson's 1964 campaign. In August 1965 Kintner called Johnson "America's greatest patriot."[59] Soon after quitting NBC in February 1966, Kintner became a special assistant to Johnson and secretary to the cabinet.[60] His duties had nothing ostensibly to do with broadcasting, though he occasionally advised the president about his TV performances and nominations to the FCC.[61]

Johnson's intimacy with Kintner and Stanton hardly aided Henry's cause. Whereas Johnson never regularly contacted his FCC chairman, he did meet or telephone the CBS and NBC presidents constantly. And there is no evidence the president ever called his friends to plead for more diverse programming, to ask that they air more news or educational children's series. Instead, Johnson asked about his TV image or protested "biased" coverage of the Vietnam War. The content, not the quantity, of such informational programming preoccupied the president.[62]

Why did Johnson not share the concern of Henry and Minow over television's imbalance? Personal taste may have accounted for much of Johnson's inattentiveness. Unlike Kennedy, who genuinely enjoyed public affairs programs (along with golf and boxing matches), Johnson and his wife were "Gunsmoke" fans.[63] Then, too, both Johnsons understood the broadcast trade well enough perhaps to recognize the futility of appealing to Kintner's or Stanton's altruism. Finally, the president may have seen no point in antagonizing friends. The administration was better off eschewing confrontation with the powers that be.

The president damaged Henry in one more way. Like a competing carnival barker, Johnson had lured Henry's audience away from him. Quickly after taking office, Johnson firmly established the agenda of Democratic liberalism. Earlier, Democrats had divided over whether the party should emphasize "quality of life" issues, such as the environment and culture, or "quantitative" problems, such as the persistence of rural and urban poverty. Minow's labors—so warmly endorsed by many within his party—had been part of the liberal preoccupation with the quality of leisure time. They had reflected the qualitative liberalism of Democrats who regarded such things as television's reformation as important. Soon after becoming president, however, Johnson put off for the time being concerns with the quality of life. He declared war on poverty and racial injustice. Under him, Democrats discovered the presence of Appalachia and Harlem and forgot the cancellation of "Omnibus" and "See It Now." "We had only just learned," Marcus Cunliffe wrote early in 1965, "that the nation's economic problems had to do with affluence, when we were told the real worry was poverty."[64]

The effects on the chairman were clear. No speech he gave ever received the attention or generated the correspondence that Minow's 1961 "vast wasteland" indictment had—even when he borrowed from the language of the Great Society in December 1964, terming television programming "our electronic Appalachia." After 1963, the commission received far less mail. A great many people had seemingly misplaced the commission's address. To liberal faddists, the "television problem" had become passé.[65]

If gains under Kennedy had been at best marginal, they were absent under Johnson. Laissez-faire did not bring out the best in chain broadcasting of the middle 1960s. Instead, the networks abandoned any attention to Minow's earlier pleas to grant more autonomy to the stations that they owned and to add more news, informational, and educational children's programming. Even plans for a series about the Department of Health, Education, and Welfare, to star Robert Taylor, were mysteriously dropped after the Johnson succession. In September 1965, a bitter Jack Gould observed, "TV has disintegrated into the rumpus room of the Great Society, a baby sitter for the underdeveloped segment of the population."[66]

In operating their Chicago stations, the networks now freely disregarded the public service ideals of Minow and Henry. After the FCC hearings in Chicago in early 1962, the Chicago stations' general managers had altered their practices slightly to fit better the commission's goals for more local programming. But in February 1964, ABC fired its free-wheeling Chicago general manager, Sterling H. Quinlan, who had displayed too much of an appreciation for local, as opposed to network, productions. Chicago TV critics construed Quinlan's ouster as a blow to the Second City stations' independence. "Quinlan has been a leader in Chicago television," a *Sun-Times* columnist wrote. "He believed that local television could be creative and that a local station could and should come to grips with the issues of the community in which it operated."[67] In so acting, however, the leaders of ABC, like their rivals along Sixth Avenue, saw no need to worry about reprisals from the commission. Indeed, those network executives still fretting over the FCC, said one trade wag, were the inconsequential types "with too few tasks to occupy their minds."[68]

The networks again organized their schedules with less concern for balance and more for the Nielsen audience ratings. Whereas after the 1960 presidential campaign the networks slightly increased their news and related programming, the number of news and documentary programs fell after the 1964 election (see table 6).[69] In October 1965, *Variety* found "definitely less pressure from Washington in the Johnson administration." The reduction in the amount of informational series commenced when "Newton Minow went West" and "old buddy broadcaster LBJ changed the D.C. climate."[70]

Of course, decisions by the networks to air news programs had always been partly influenced by economics, but with a moribund FCC they were more so. Earlier, networks ran news programs in the

Table 6. Network Documentary Programs, 1958-1968

Year	Number
1958	178
1959	223
1960	297
1961	336
1962	447
1963	396
1964	321
1965	296
1966	290
1967	270
1968	251

Source: Raymond L. Carroll, "Economic Influences on Commercial Network Television Documentary Scheduling," *Journal of Broadcasting* 23 (Fall 1979), 415.

absence of demand from advertisers for entertainment shows or because such series were unavailable. Moreover, all three networks appreciated the good-will earned with the commission by increasing their informational programming. By the middle sixties, however, network executives could dismiss the commission altogether.[71]

A much-publicized controversy surrounding the airing of Senate hearings exemplified this new attitude. The rate of growth in CBS's earnings had fallen in 1965. In February 1966, CBS's Television Division president, John A Schneider, cancelled live telecasts of the Senate Foreign Relations Commission's hearings on the Vietnam War, despite NBC's continued presentation of the sessions.[72] The hearings included testimony hostile to the administration's Asian policies. But Schneider believed above all else that CBS had to consider the revenue lost by not airing reruns of "I Love Lucy" and other situation comedies (popular old series that NBC's daytime schedule lacked). Defending Schneider's decision, Stanton noted on February 25 that CBS had lost $2 million already in covering the hearings, half of that in advertising monies.[73] The president of CBS News, Fred W. Friendly, resigned in protest. Suddenly he emerged from the relative obscurity of the control room to become a hero of the antiwar movement. And to many skeptics of the war, CBS was now regarded as Johnson's goat.

When asked by CBS News to appear, as he had before the incident, in a special interview program, Walter Lippmann declined for fear that his negative views on Vietnam would be censored.[74] Senator Albert Gore of the Foreign Relations Committee complained of a "television network using the wave lengths that belong to the whole people to advertise soap when we should be having critical examination of the issue of war and peace. . . . Government has been very profligate in allowing the wave lengths to be monopolized by commercial organizations."[75]

Friendly's quitting conveyed the extent to which the regulatory atmosphere had reverted to that of the late 1950s. Friendly, in effect, had joined his former partner, Edward R. Murrow, in video's oblivion. Murrow's fall from grace in 1958 had also come when the FCC was uninvolved and disregarded. When CBS cancelled his news program, "See It Now," he lambasted the industry for thinking too much of advertisers and audiences. Friendly had at that time remained with the network, silently obeying its leadership, and was named executive producer of "CBS Reports" in 1959 and president of CBS News in 1964. Yet after eight years, he, too, came to the same conclusion Murrow had and left CBS.

Even Robert Kintner—friend of Johnson and no foe of his venture in Vietnam—left his network post in February 1966 in a dispute over the direction of NBC's programming. Kintner, in contrast to Friendly, had, between 1958 and 1966, presided over both the NBC network as a whole and the news division and had enjoyed far more success in increasing his network's news budget and air time. And he had sought even more. Kintner wanted to expand "The Huntley-Brinkley Report" from thirty to sixty minutes and maintain or increase other evening prime-time news programming. But he found this and other suggestions increasingly unpopular with NBC's chairman, Robert Sarnoff.[76] In his letter of resignation, Kintner called for "greater experimentation in regular programming." He asked that NBC preempt more of the entertainment schedule for news and public affairs programming and offer "an increasing number of dramatic entertainment programs dealing with controversial social, economic, and political problems." The networks, he insisted, "must be prepared from time to time to sacrifice over-all rating leadership."[77] But he was ignored. By October 1965, NBC had dropped 50 percent of its news and public affairs programming.[78]

Chairman Henry left the FCC in the spring of 1966. President Johnson, keeping to his pledge to retain the Kennedy people, had done nothing to encourage Henry's retirement—except to ignore him. But the chairman had served three years by mid-1966 and had grown tired of weekly forensics with Loevinger. Ironically, when a White House spokesman announced Henry's resignation in April 1966, Loevinger was in Switzerland for an international communications meeting. Henry noted, "With Loevinger in Geneva, I've never had more fun." Still, more than Loevinger's verbal abuse moved Henry to depart; he simply found the satisfactions of being FCC chairman limited. He was still young enough, at thirty-seven, to take on other challenges. An excuse came when an old friend, John Jay Hooker, asked Henry to return to Tennessee to aid his campaign for the Democratic gubernatorial nomination against, interestingly enough, Buford Ellington, an old Johnson ally. Like Minow, Henry seized his chance to go home.[79]

In naming Henry's successor, Johnson, against the advice of some White House advisers,[80] elevated Rosel Hyde to the chairmanship. Perhaps the most conservative member of the commission, Hyde had ardently opposed virtually every initiative of the Minow-Henry years. *Business Week* dubbed him "the reluctant regulator" while the *New York Times* observed, "Hyde has been noted more for his amiability than vigor."[81] Stanton and Kintner, however, had recommended his selection. "He would not," Kintner wrote, "engage in public speeches such as Newt Minnow [sic] and Bill Henry."[82]

If the FCC had been growing weaker under Henry, the situation gave signs of worsening with Hyde. In September 1966 Hyde proposed that broadcast licenses be extended from three to five years.[83] Secondline appointments supplied more compelling evidence of the FCC's changing state. One of Minow's and Henry's few opportunities to instill purpose within the commission had been the naming of bureau chiefs. Hyde, however, appointed George A. Smith as Broadcast Bureau chief. This key position of overseeing the radio and TV licenses of the nation, once held by Kenneth Cox, now fell to a man totally out of sympathy with the rigorous regulators. Even the ages of the two new major figures in the FCC—Smith was sixty-five, Hyde sixty-seven—contrasted sharply with the New Frontier's image. Jokesters mindful of the "Batman" TV series fad had sardonically dubbed them the "dynamic duo."[84]

Henry's departure still left Johnson with an FCC vacancy to fill. In

June 1966 the president chose Nicholas Johnson, former assistant professor of law at the University of California at Berkeley. The younger
Johnson, not related to the president, possessed impressive credentials. In the tradition of Minow and Henry, he was, at age thirty-three,
ten to twenty years younger than his colleagues. Minow's career had,
in fact, inspired Johnson to enter public service in the early 1960s.[85]
As Maritime Administrator between 1964 and 1966, he played no
favorites, to the annoyance of both the powerful shipbuilding concerns and the maritime union leaders. Together they joined with
Senator Warren Magnuson, chairman of the Commerce Committee,
to insist that Johnson, be removed. Johnson, however, had intended
to leave anyway, even before the president tapped him for the FCC
in June.[86] Broadcast industry representatives, so pleased with Hyde's
selection as chairman, hardly noticed the newcomer.[87]

To President Johnson's dismay, Nicholas Johnson proved to be an
aggressive regulator. He quickly sided with Cox on almost every question, assuming stances even more anti-industry than Henry's. The
president soon asked Stanton to see the newest commissioner and
tutor him on points of administrative restraint. But Nicholas Johnson
instead asked Stanton if he had any evidence he could use to stop
the proposed ABC-ITT merger, which the administration quietly
favored.[88]

Nicholas Johnson distanced himself from the other Johnson appointees all the more by publicly expressing concern over both broadcasting and the FCC itself—by being, in other words, both seen and
heard. By 1967 and 1968, Johnson found himself speaking to public
interest groups and writing extensively for upper-brow magazines.[89]
If Minow's tenure early in the sixties had signalled a new faith in
the FCC, Johnson's actions half a decade later revealed a disillusionment. The commission's ineffectiveness frustrated him enormously. He urged viewers to organize themselves into consumer groups;
they should not rely on the commission.[90] "Each day," he wrote, "the
Commission churns out innumerable memoranda, orders, decisions,
letters, and rulemaking proposals which in effect preserve the status
quo and the profitable stability of the industries involved."[91]

Nicholas Johnson and Kenneth Cox divided over the stridency of
the newest commissioner. Although sharing most of Johnson's
idealism about broadcasting and regulation, Cox disapproved of public
statements critical of the commission. His young colleague, Cox held,
should maintain a low profile, defer to his brethren and use the

FCC's procedures to effect change. But Johnson disagreed. Cox, Henry, and Minow had sought to use the commission to transform television but to no avail, and of Cox's pleas to keep silent and cooperate with his colleagues, Johnson said, "That's been tried and it doesn't work."[92]

Nicholas Johnson proved the one exception to Johnson's FCC nominations. He, unlike the others, was an unquiet, ambitious regulator. "Lyndon Johnson only apppointed one Nick Johnson to the FCC," commented two scholars of the process of nominating commissioners.[93] "I don't think it was ever in Lyndon Johnson's mind," recalled Henry, "that Nick Johnson would regulate the industry the way he did."[94]

President Johnson, disapproving of the young commissioner's positions, asked intermediaries to persuade him to leave the FCC. The president tendered him the chair of the Administrative Conference of the United States, a quasi-governmental body of scant consequence. The younger Johnson chose to stay and fight in his own way.[95]

Nicholas Johnson notwithstanding, the new president and his majority of FCC commissioners left broadcasters with the impression that they were free agents. The trade had made few efforts to placate Minow with more balanced programming, but it sacrificed even less to Henry and simply ignored Rosel Hyde. Amounts of news and children's programming leveled off. Broadcasters, one survey of station managers found, "had to pretend that the regulators were frighteningly powerful while recognizing that they were little or no threat except in the most extreme circumstances."[96]

Chapter Ten

The Public Broadcasting Act of 1967 and the Failure of Commercial Television

By the middle 1960s, one policy identified with Minow remained. More stations, he and his allies believed, would lead to more choice in programming. And the FCC should do everything in its power to create a climate favorable to the starting of new TV stations. Although little noticed, the commission's advocacy of competition continued well after Minow and Henry had left Washington.

To Minow and the commission, achieving this competition meant promoting UHF stations. On that portion of the spectrum rested most potential new commercial outlets which could offer alternatives to the relentlessly majority-oriented television of the national networks and their affiliates. Budding subscription or pay TV systems were expected to rely on the ultra high frequency, and any hope of a non-commercial, educational television system depended on UHF. "On the success or failure of UHF," commented one Senate supporter of the FCC's UHF policy in April 1964,"rests the future of educational television, the desires of developing local outlets for many substantial communities and the potential of additional commercial programming services."[1] That same year, the historian David Potter declared that expansion of UHF television "might even destroy the monolithic bulk of the mass audience and lead to a situation where the viewing public, like the reading public, forms a variety of audiences, and chooses from a considerable range of offerings that are really different, rather than between two situation comedies or two crime thrillers that might as well be one."[2]

The benefits of UHF proved so marginal, however, that for the first time other answers to the television problem received serious attention. The most radical of these—given the historically commercial assumptions of the American system of broadcasting—became an actuality in 1967, when Congress created the Public Broadcasting System (PBS). Although PBS's birth might be regarded as a great victory for TV's long-suffering critics, in many ways the advent of the system offered the most compelling evidence of the shortcomings of the FCC and the failure of commercial television.

In early 1962, Minow had won congressional support for the All-Channel Television Receiver Act, which invested the FCC with the power to specify that all TV sets be equipped to receive UHF signals. Up to this point, four out of every five set owners had lacked the choice of watching UHF stations. This circumstance, in turn, had greatly discouraged the founding of both commercial and noncommercial UHF outlets.

In the years following Minow's departure, his arguments enjoyed support even among those commissioners, like Lee Loevinger, determined to undo the greater part of Minow's designs. Although cast as the Black Prince of the anti-Minow coalition, Loevinger nevertheless favored infusing competition into broadcasting by means of UHF. Ideally, a new form of competition would emerge, one along the lines of radio rivalries in certain large listening areas. In radio broadcasting, a specialization in program "format" had occurred with some stations focusing on a particular program form, such as classical music or local discussion. "The net effect," wrote Loevinger in 1966, "is that the listening public has a choice among diverse kinds of programs presented by different stations."[3]

Such unanimity—rare at the commission—nonetheless underscored the ever-present weaknesses of Minow's and Henry's positions. Both chairmen had found their colleagues to be unsympathetic to the more direct and dramatic steps for policing the airwaves. But competition—and expecting that step alone to bring balanced programming—inflicted no punishment on stations already operating and therefore avoided questions of the propriety of regulation. Such a course, indeed, had been Minow and Henry's sole alternative.

For this approach to succed, however, required moving against all possible rivals of UHF. Individuals or corporations were likely to invest in UHF operations only if they were assured that the frequency would not be, as during the 1950s, at a competitive disadvantage. Then, the commission had greatly overestimated the technical qualities of and consumer demand for UHF by encouraging UHF outlets to compete directly with VHF channels. As a result, some one hundred UHF stations had failed. And between 1963 and 1967, the commission took a variety of seemingly unrelated positions, all reflecting a determination not to see history repeat itself. The upper band had to be given an opportunity to succeed. The FCC, Henry told the NAB in March 1965, had achieved a "working consensus" and "has stuck to its guns. As a result, UHF is on the road toward being a truly competitive service."[4]

Sometimes the commission contradicted itself outright in the name of UHF. In June 1965 the commission proposed to limit the number of stations owned by one corporation or individual. No group or person could own more than three VHF and two UHF stations in the fifty largest viewing areas. While still pondering that edict in late 1967, the agency permitted the Aviation Corporation (AVCO) to operate six UHF outlets in the top fifty markets. A four to three majority justified the decision because the channels were in the UHF band.[5]

The American Broadcasting Company's disproportionate reliance on UHF proved helpful during deliberations over the network's pending sale to ITT. In early 1966 the network petitioned the commission to permit a takeover by ITT.[6] The FCC had to approve the combination because the transaction involved the transfer of radio and television licenses. Through the initial stages of this proceeding, ABC representatives stressed the network's relative dependency on UHF stations for affiliates in such markets as Louisville and Dayton. Among ABC's stations in September 1966, 24 of 137 were in the UHF band.[7] With ITT's technical and managerial aid, ABC could stimulate research into UHF itself while being able, with ITT's financial assistance, to offer programming likely to stimulate viewers to use the frequency in those regions where ABC had been left with the UHF station. In July 1966 the commission hearing examiner accepted such arguments and recommended the ABC-ITT combination as a boost to UHF television.[8]

In December 1966 the Commission voted four to three to approve the ABC-ITT merger. The majority concluded that ITT would help to expand the network's dormant news and special program division. Such "positive" competition from ABC, the commission majority reasoned, would encourage ABC and NBC to redouble their efforts in news and other minority interest fare. Moreover, UHF, as the frequency band so important to ABC, would gain. If ABC's programming improved, the commission argued, more viewers in places like Louisville would turn to ABC's UHF affiliates. Finally, ITT pledged to invest heavily in improving the technology of UHF to upgrade the transmission and reception of the upper-band stations. Only later did the commission learn that ITT had been less than forthright about the acquisition and its own corporate character. Yet a giant international corporation nearly acquired one of the country's three networks because it promised to enhance UHF television.[9]

The FCC's defense of UHF extended to a new and perceived threat to the upper-band stations: cable and community antenna television systems. Such processes sent signals through direct cable connection into the home or relayed them via microwaves to the home antenna. Manmade or natural barriers, often hindering UHF reception, were overcome. But most commissioners and trade experts determined that cable operators jeopardized UHF television. By carrying the telecasts of distant stations into communities (such as a New York or Chicago channel into central Pennsylvania or western Massachusetts), cable placed local UHF stations in small localities in direct competition with established operations from large communities. Demand for UHF service might shrivel, as viewers in Scranton, for example, opted for New York's channel 9 rather than the hometown channel 44. And the whole premise of the 1962 all-channel receiver law might be undone. "The development of additional sources of free, local television service has been, and continues to be," one UHF manager wrote a White House aide, "blunted by the unrestricted and unregulated growth of CATVs."[10] Said another UHF chain executive of cable television, "It's going to splinter the audience to such a degree that it might well be economically unsound for me to operate."[11]

Readily accepting such entreaties, the commission restricted the diffusion of cable systems. In separate orders issued in 1962, 1965, and 1966, the FCC first asserted its jurisdiction over CATV processes and then imposed the most restrictive rules on their operation in the one hundred largest television markets. In disallowing the unimpeded growth of CATV in the late 1960s, the agency acted to protect UHF facilities. The FCC commented in its 1966 cable rule, "We cannot sit back and let CATV move signals about as it wishes, and then if the answer some years from now is that CATV can and does undermine the development of UHF, simply say, 'Oh well, so sorry that we didn't look into the matter.'"[12] Community Antenna Television, the commission stated in 1966, could not be allowed to expand "at the expense of healthy maintenance of UHF operations."[13]

Such protectiveness by the agency nurtured demand for UHF licenses and all-channel TV sets. The number of of UHF stations rose from 76 in 1961 to 118 in 1967; large corporations like Time-Life and Kaiser Industries secured their first UHF franchises.[14] With the All-Channel Television Receiver Act, the number of TV receivers that obtained both UHF and VHF signals also increased. Consumers, many participating in a boom for color TV sets, eagerly replaced older, black-and-white receivers, most of which could only get VHF. In 1961, the commission estimated that 6 percent of all TV sets could receive UHF signals; four years later, 33 percent were capable of obtaining stations in the upper band. In 1967, 42 percent of all sets had UHF tuners.[15]

Yet despite the frequency's greater availability to consumers, UHF was not affording them the hoped for specialization in programming. Those attempting to establish fourth commercial networks met with disaster without raising expectations about program uplift in the process. These budding systems relied heavily on network reruns, old motion pictures, or bad imitations of NBC's "The Tonight Show."[16] Nor did individual UHF station managers, competing against four or five, rather than two or three, channels, schedule more "quality" or public affairs programming. Careful analyses of programming in the late sixties showed that most new UHF stations offered little other than reruns of network series and occasionally more sports. "Up to now it's been that same ball game with the UHF's," Robert Lewis Shayon wrote, "comparable not even to minor league teams, merely bush league and semi-pro."[17]

Nor did local service—news and entertainment produced by the individual station—increase with the added relief for UHF operators. Indeed, UHF managers ranked below their counterparts running established VHF facilities; UHF stations originated less programming.[18] Anxious to recover their initial investments, most new UHF station executives kept operating costs to a minimum. Accordingly, the UHF manager was less likely to seek expensive programming.[19]

Still, attempts by other UHF outlets to offer programming appealing to racial or ethnic minorities brought some positive results. Except at the less popular, Sunday morning hours, established VHF stations had normally refrained from presenting programs designed for blacks or foreign-speaking viewers. But with the all-channel receiver policy of the FCC, Spanish-language stations commenced operations in San Antonio and New York City by late 1965, and Washington's black majority finally had a TV channel.[20]

Elsewhere, the evidence was less consoling to the champions of cultural pluralism. The operators of a Milwaukee UHF outlet airing German films discovered that most of the area's many viewers of Teutonic descent had either forgotten their native tongue or preferred American TV series. In Los Angeles, a UHF station offering evening entertainment for blacks found that an insufficient number tuned in to justify program specialization by race.[21]

Most UHF television programming closely followed VHF practices. Minow and others had hoped that doubling of channels would encourage some managers to offer specialized programming—in other words, to divide up the mass market in ways that increased consumer choice. In practice, however, the size of each viewing region still proved sufficiently large for each station executive and all advertisers to struggle for the largest possible audience share. A divisor of six no more guaranteed balanced programming than had one of three. "Serious questions are raised," wrote an economist surveying the question of UHF and diversity, "about the efficacy of new commercial entry as the sole or major instrument of widening viewer choices."[22]

Finally, despite the greater availability of UHF channels, pay television systems using the upper-band frequencies fared poorly in the middle 1960s. Since the late 1950s critics of the commission had maintained that subscription telecasting could provide disgruntled viewers with the choices they otherwise expected the FCC to force on mass-minded station managers. But fee television tests in Hartford, Connecticut (which Chairmen Ford and Minow had quietly encouraged), failed in the early 1960s to demonstrate an audience large enough to support the more expensive programming identified with the golden age.[23] Elsewhere, opposition to the construction of an elaborate pay system proved too great. Former NBC president Sylvester L. Weaver's ambitious pay TV project for California was undone in November 1964, when voters overwhelmingly supported a referendum outlawing any pay processes. As in the fifties, pay TV proponents could not overcome the fears of those who depended on "free" TV.[24]

Still, there had been a noncommercial element in the original plea for more stations through UHF. Much of the momentum for FCC decisions protecting the upper-band frequencies related to educational television. More than any other broadcast system, ETV relied on UHF. Since 1952, the FCC had reserved most of the stations for noncommercial or educational institutions in the UHF band, including the ETV allocations for Los Angeles, Cleveland, Washington, D.C., and Buffalo. If many Americans were to sample the fare of educational TV, UHF had to be available to them.

The FCC and Congress had much encouraged the growth of ETV. In 1962, Congress passed the ETV Facilities Act—warmly endorsed by Minow—which offered matching grants to communities willing to form an ETV outlet. Thus the government partially subsidized the start-up costs of station construction and equipment procurement. As a result, educational television expanded greatly in the mid-1960s. Such cities as New York, Cleveland, Washington, and Los Angeles finally used their ETV reservations, most of them in UHF. The total number of ETV stations had by 1966 risen to 127.[25]

Yet the founding of more ETV stations by no means assured their success. Most educational outlets found the early going rough. The federal government covered only the initial costs of a station and not the ever-burgeoning expenses of running one. As a result, stations curtailed productions to such an extent that in late 1964 Chairman Henry estimated that three fourths of the ninety-three ETV stations were on the air for five days or less. An informal ETV "network," the National Educational Television Center (NET), could not afford to produce many series. Nor could it pay for the cable interconnection that could link all NET-affiliated stations for simultaneous transmission, despite contributions from individuals, corporations, and foundations. The president of NET complained, "The good Lord has never created anything than can gobble up money the way television can."[26]

The flagship station of NET , WNET, in many ways typified the problems of most ETV outlets. The New York City station, for which Minow had helped in 1961 to secure a VHF allocation, found itself in constant financial turmoil. Like smaller ETV outlets elsewhere, WNET could not raise the operating monies necessary for more than a pathetic, barebones effort.[27] By 1966 and 1967, it had become obvious that without additional government support, the New York and many other ETV units would simply go dark.[28]

Slowly, the federal government moved toward saving noncommercial television. In late 1964, after several crises over WNET's finances, NET leaders began meeting with Henry and White House aide Eric Goldman. In early 1965, another White House staff member, Douglass

Cater, entered these negotiations.[29] While Cater, Goldman, and Henry mulled over ETV's fate, Senator Warren Magnuson, chairman of the Commerce Committee, asked the president about extending the Facilities Act, due to expire in 1967. On the recommendation of Cater, President Johnson, as was his custom in problem-solving, agreed in November 1965, to appoint a commission, sponsored by the Carnegie Foundation, to study the matter.[30]

In January 1967 the Carnegie Commission on Educational TV completed its study and called for a much expanded federal role in noncommercial television. A tax on the sale of television sets was recommended to subsidize a corporation for public television, which in turn would loosely oversee all noncommercial outlets. To avoid an overcentralization of power, most monies would go directly to the stations, not the public "network," to produce more series. Federal aid for the building of new stations would be extended.[31]

President Johnson adopted most of the Carnegie Commission's recommendations by endorsing a public broadcasting bill in a February 1967 message to Congress. Johnson rejected the Carnegie panel's call for a TV set excise tax, which he feared might endanger the bill's chances of passing. Instead, the president asked that a long-term financing plan—one meant to insulate the system from excessive political pressures—be put off until 1968. Until then, he requested that Congress appropriate a modest $9 million from general revenues for the first year's operation of the new corporation.[32]

To Johnson, support for a new, public, network made great political sense. By using his appointment power, he could continue to check the power of the Henry-Cox faction of commissioners, much to the relief of the commercial broadcasters Johnson courted. With a public broadcast authority, however, he could also please that group of liberals and intellectuals once the champions of Newton Minow.

The president handled the issue with the formal distance characteristic of his earlier dealings with broadcasters. To avoid charges of conflict of interest stemming from his family's broadcast properties, he asked Cater to select members for the ETV panel and had the Carnegie Foundation pay for its operations.[33] But Johnson continued to convey his disdain for TV's past critics. He refused to call on Minow, who volunteered to lobby for the bill. When Cater, in planning the signing of the bill into law, drafted a statement for the president that included a quote from Murrow's famous 1958 attack on TV, Johnson, ever the friend of the newscaster's nemesis at CBS,

Frank Stanton, commented, "No Murrow for me."[34]

Congress passed the administration's bill in October 1967 with little opposition. No hostile lobbying campaign developed, as virtually all major trade leaders and associations, normally hesitant about a federal role in broadcasting, backed the bill.[35] The Senate approved the measure in May by voice vote. In the House, however, Republicans and southern Democrats held up passage. Most suspected that the corporation (renamed the Corporation for Public Broadcasting [CPB] to include radio) might develop into an instrument of federal propaganda; in October the "conservative coalition" nearly struck the CPB from the measure by a 167 to 194 tally. After the administration agreed to some minor modifications of the proposal, the House passed the Public Broadcasting Act by 265 votes to 91. Included were the extension of the Facilities Act and the $9 million initial appropriation.[36]

In passing the bill, Congress followed earlier patterns in broadcast legislation. Not that many members interested themselves in the legislation; Cater, in search of votes, had to break up one congressman's sexual liaison in a district hotel.[37] Those who did participate in the debate on the bill, as during that on the 1962 all-channel receiver act, took the route least threatening to the status quo of broadcasting. By appropriating a modest initial fund for PBS and not resolving the issue of permanent financing, House and Senate members did not create a very powerful rival to the established networks and stations of the private sector.

Johnson immediately associated the Public Broadcasting Act with the Great Society. His presidency would not only attack economic inequalities—the persistent "quantitative" problems of postwar America—but improve the "quality" of life for all Americans, he said. In the same spirit, the administration had championed federal highway beautification legislation. To subsidize creative impulses, the president had sponsored the National Arts Foundation. And on signing the Public Broadcasting Act in November 1967, Johnson spoke of public TV as one more qualitative component of the Great Society. "While we work everyday to produce new goods and create new wealth," he said, "we want most of all to enrich man's spirit."[38]

Johnson's stated reasons for the Public Broadcasting Act notwithstanding, the decision to start a federal network owed more to the failure of commercial broadcasting and its regulation. By 1967, the FCC could no longer be expected to bring more diversity to TV.

Indeed, as early as the fall of 1965, a *Columbia Journalism Review* contributor saw so little achieved at the agency that he suggesed Congress abolish it.[39] The resignation of Henry in June 1966 added to the view that the FCC was a regulator's Lost Cause. The new chairman, Rosel Hyde, was an honest but unimaginative career bureaucrat twice his predecessor's age. He hardly fit the dynamic Henry or Minow mold; nor did he seek to. He disliked jawboning and generally limited his role in any debate about broadcasting. A year into Hyde's chairmanship, journalist Elizabeth Drew, writing for the *Atlantic*, recounted the trivial preoccupations of the commissioners, contrasting them sharply to the exciting days of the early New Frontier. Drew did not advocate the FCC's elimination; she pronounced it already dead.[40] After reading Drew's article, a New York congressman wrote, "Backbone: jellyfish," and scrawled on the margin, "It is unthinkable that you, the regulatory body, remain arms folded and stolid and silent in the face of ever enlarged profits of the TV chains whose main asset is public property."[41]

The relationship between the commissions's decline and the rise of public television can be seen in the administration's bill. The public system was expected to provide what the FCC had been unable to obtain from commercial television. One frequent complaint about commercial stations had been that they avoided local in favor of syndicated and network productions. Earlier, Minow and the FCC had encouraged licensees to originate more programming, and in May 1963 the commission even ordered an end to "option time" contracts, which the networks had used to command from their affiliates as many broadcast hours as possible. Yet none of these and related steps had checked the tendency of stations to turn over huge blocks of time to the national chains or West Coast film companies.[42] The Public Broadcasting Act, however, specified that individual PBS stations, and not the new public network, receive most of the money appropriated for the system, and that each station assume a share of the responsibility for producing series.[43]

Those contemplating a public network also frequently referred to children's series, which earlier in the 1960s, the commission had asked the industry to upgrade. But by 1967 the special children's programs that all three networks had experimented with at Minow's urging had left the air. With one exception—CBS's "Captain Kangaroo," which predated Minow's regime—parents had little choice for their offspring but rounds of cartoons, violent, silly, or pun-filled.[44] The absence of selection did not escape the congressional debate. The majority of children's programs, contended Congressman Claude Pepper of Florida, "are merely a device to keep them quiet rather than stimulate their curiosity and learning."[45] Public TV, to Pepper and others, offered alternatives. An ETV station manager noted how a Pittsburgh NET outlet had successfully started an educational children's program, "Mister Rogers."[46] To a New York Democrat, such series might rescue offspring from—borrowing Minow's terminology—the "mini-wasteland" of commercial television's programming for the child.[47]

Heard too during the debate over the bill were familiar cries for more minority interest programming. The biases of commercial networks and stations toward majority tastes had been consistently condemned by Minow and Henry. Ignoring such jawboning, broadcasters scheduled as before, with evening prime time awarded ordinarily to those who ran fastest in the Nielsen and Arbitron marathons. Thus the Minow-Henry chairmanships saw no appreciable gain in the small amount of minority interest fare.[48] The lack of choice upset many who were discussing public television, even Republicans out of sympathy with Minow. "Why isn't television," asked Senator Hugh Scott in April 1967, "applying that principle that what serves the cultural interest of the minority tends ultimately to serve the majority?" Senator Norris Cotton of New Hampshire called TV "perfectly sickening. It is far below the standard of my mind."[49] Wrote one ETV enthusiast, "For the large majority, TV is a medium of entertainment. Anything that the viewers acquire by way of information or culture is incidental and almost accidental."[50]

By the time of the Public Broadcasting Act, then, a consensus had emerged among those disenchanted with American TV. Little or nothing the FCC could do would transform television. Louis Jaffe, administrative law scholar and among those critical of the agency during the Eisenhower years, commented in February 1964, "I'm afraid in this country, quality by ukase will not work. We must look to other factors for improvement . . . . The greater hope, I think, is educational TV."[51] An ETV spokesman commented the next year, "It simply doesn't make sense any more for the government to wage the perennial, on-going battle against commercial television."[52] With ETV, the *Columbia Journalism Review*'s advocate of the FCC's abolition argued, "we could then be in sight of achieving what the FCC never could: the program balance that is what 'service in the public interest' should be."[53] Gore Vidal, novelist and playwright of TV's golden age, wrote of the Public Broadcasting Act's realization: "The fact that so many dominions and powers (among them the owners of KTBC-TV [the Johnson family]) agree that such a network is needed is proof that nothing can be done about commercial television. There is no way to improve it, nor has there been since the 1950s."[54]

Indeed, for many who had long been unhappy with television and who had once looked to the FCC for TV's reform, educational broadcasting now promised salvation. Vance Packard, who had bewailed and exaggerated advertisers' influence over TV, and Marya Mannes, who had attacked almost everything about the medium since 1957, both praised ETV. Former Senator William Benton, a Minow friend and frequent TV detractor, also turned to noncommercial television. In March 1964, Benton wrote that educational TV would bring "the superlative potential of television to broaden man's knowledge, deepen his understanding and enrich his life."[55] Seven months later, Cecil Smith of the *Los Angeles Times* found that only Los Angeles's newly formed ETV station, KCET Channel 28, gave relief from the commercial networks' diet. That station, he noted, presented Robert Flaherty's classic documentary *Nanook of the North* and jazz music. Furthermore, there were no commercials or plugs to jar him. When Julia Child hosted "French Chef," a cooking program, she "never tells you to dash out to Safeway [the food store chain] to get eggs for your hollandaise." Commercial television, in contast, offered "not a single show that one looks forward to with excitement." An Angeleno, Smith suggested, "could do worse than to lock his television set at Channel 28 and forget the other channels."[56]

Others hailing the Public Broadcasting Act symbolized this change of heart. In the 1950s, *Saturday Review* had periodically hailed the commercial programming of the golden age and had even granted annual awards for the best TV productions. But by the middle 1960s, its editor, Norman Cousins, had ended that exercise because the medium no longer warranted such attention. Thanking Johnson in November 1967 for sponsoring the Public Broadcasting Act, Cousins now saw promise only in noncommercial television. "Your support of this immensely meaningful bill," Cousins wrote, "heartened greatly all those who, with you, see television as an agency of cultural and educational advance."[57]

Finally, the fate of Fred Friendly characterized this change from commercial to noncommercial expectations. A knight of the golden age, Friendly had coproduced "See It Now" and had served as executive producer of "CBS Reports." Friendly, a good company man, defended his employer while hailing the FCC chairman.[58] Minow, he wrote in May 1963, "wasn't only the best Chairman of the Federal Communications Commission—and still is—but the first."[59] To Friendly in mid-1963, an equilibrium existed between a "responsible" network like CBS and a reasonable FCC chairman like Minow. Within three years, however, Friendly had resigned in protest from the corporate broadcast world and he immediately dedicated himself to the Ford Foundation's efforts to secure federal funding for ETV.[60] He had given up. No longer could Friendly regard the "American" system of "free" broadcasting regulated by the FCC to be adequate to achieve a measure of diversity. In fact, he dismissed the FCC as "a tower of jello on the Potomac."[61]

By late 1967, the country had something totally different: a public broadcasting authority. But the balance between public and commercial television was not exactly equal. The country had made what seemed like a reasonable compromise except that PBS was left short of the money and stations it needed to compete with its established, commercial rivals.[62] The hegemony of majority television remained undiminished.

Chapter Eleven

Conclusion

Why had the FCC been unable to change American television? The commonplace explanation, nurtured by studies of the independent commission in the early 1950s and transformed into conventional wisdom by histories of the regulatory agencies in the 1960s, was that none of the agencies could function properly because they had been "captured" by the industries they had been intended to regulate.[1] By the end of the sixties, this view gained new popularity with the work of consumer organizations led by Ralph Nader. If the commissions did not operate in a more and more vaguely defined "public interest," it was because the commissioners were corporate pawns—or lobbyists' lackeys.[2]

Champions of "captive" thesis, however, often fail to take into account the inherent limitations of the independent agency. In this regard the commissions have been fundamentally misunderstood. Proponents of regulation—notably modern liberals and "consumer advocates"—have believed in the efficacy of government by independent commission. When an agency has not worked in the public interest, simple-minded causes, such as a commission's closeness to the enterprises regulated, have been offered in the way of analysis. But it would seem that their "failure" or shortcoming had less to do with their susceptibility to lobbying than with the jealousy and designs of the formal three branches of government.[3] The commissions have not ordinarily been free agents. Although dubbed the fourth branch of government, the regulatory commission could, in truth, succeed only with the cooperation of the other three wings, notably the presidency and the Congress. Any one of these branches of government might handcuff the agency.

In contrast to some of their predecessors, Minow, Henry, Cox, and other commissioners were not the servants of the industry they policed; nor apparently were those commissioners who disagreed with them and other liberal exponents of regulation. The chairmen and commissioners of the sixties, unlike some of their predecessors, were not treated to elaborate lunches by individuals applying for a TV channel. They did not fish off the pleasure craft of a licensee. "If he were a professional," John Crosby wrote of Minow in May 1961, "he'd go yachting with the broadcasters whose affairs he regulates."[4] But Minow refrained from such outings. He would not even accept a dollar won from the president of NBC in a bet over the ratings of Jackie Kennedy's CBS special.[5] For Minow and others, policy was not shaped by a conflict of interest.

Those naming the commissioners, and not the commission itself, helped to chart its direction. Kennedy had carefully selected commissioners sympathetic to Minow. Only one of Kennedy's four appointments, Lee Loevinger, named in June 1963, joined the anti-Minow group, and that affiliation had been unexpected. In contrast, Johnson deliberately designated commissioners disinclined toward the Minow-Henry philosophy of regulation. He was determined not to see the commission upset his "consensus" with American broadcasters. With one exception, the president's six nominees and his choice for chairman, Rosel Hyde, usually identified with Loevinger and a soft position. As a result, after 1963, the composition of the commission shifted away from the Minow-Henry axis. The agency relaxed enforcement of regulations encouraging public service programming. The Broadcast Bureau spent less time monitoring licensees' performance.

The liberal commissioners of the 1960s were confined by the president's appointment prerogative. Had Henry not been left with so many commissioners who were unwilling to take his counsel, the agency could have been expected to take up the proposals that he and Cox brought up at weekly meetings. But without the power of a majority, Henry posed no threat. He could be ignored by stations and networks programming anything other than the outrageous.

Even as a majority coalition, however, the Minow-Henry faction often saw its freedom of action curtailed by procedures imposed on the agency by Congress. In 1946 and 1952, Congress had approved legislation protecting the rights of parties directly involved in the commission's determinations and limiting the role of third parties or consumer organizations. The 1946 Administrative Procedure Act and the 1952 McFarland amendments to the Communications Act provided broadcasters with so many guarantees against swift and arbitrary justice that the commission had difficulty deciding anything quickly, if at all. The resulting regulatory lag normally served the status quo, while weakening the resolve of those favoring punitive measures against a violator-licensee. Regulatory initiatives took months or years to decide. Minow complained later of the FCC's "archaic procedure" and about allocating "enormous time on unimportant matters."[6]

During the sixties, Congress continued to affirm its sway over ambitious commissioners. In 1961, both houses frustrated the Kennedy administration's efforts to unleash the agency from some of the impediments of the APA and McFarland amendments. Three years later, the House overwhelmingly endorsed a resolution rebuking the FCC for seeking to limit the number of commercials on the air. Although the Senate failed to act on the bill, the size of the House vote much embarrassed the agency.

Successive Congresses sent clear messages. Although no representatives sought a return to the commission's lethargic, scandal-ridden past, only a minority, mainly liberal Democrats of the East and West coasts, wished to see the FCC operate against the interests of the established broadcaster. The agency was expected to perform a narrow range of duties honestly and well.

The FCC's essential weaknesses thus resulted from a dependency on congressional and presidential support. It was not enough for Minow or Henry to build coalitions among the commissioners. New regulations had to be endorsed by Congress and the White House as well. Without such backing, the agency's liberal faction suffered legislative setbacks and new, unsympathetic colleagues.

Within Congress, a natural jealousy of the fourth branch of government partly explained the fate of the Minow and Henry policies.[7] Some congressmen, particularly members of the House from southern and western states, who, because of the seniority system, were most likely to chair the key communication committees, were especially sensitive about an FCC promulgating rules out of line with their own regulatory philosophies. Many, like Speaker Sam Rayburn, regarded the agency as an "arm of Congress."

In other cases, political advantage directed both congressional and presidential antagonism toward Henry and his type of regulator. For the representative always faced with reelection, good-will with broadcasters was prized above the FCC's claims to the public interest. President Johnson was equally anxious to court broadcasters. In exchange for a consensus favorable to the Great Society, the president sought to ease businesses' regulatory burdens. The last thing Johnson welcomed was confrontation or jawboning.

It was not a matter of a captive agency but a weak one, crippled, indeed, at the start of the race. Congress and the president could not abide a strong FCC, not when its wards, local and network television, could deliver more votes than the TV editor of an opinion-leading newspaper or magazine. The commission was a small, toothless dog kept on a very short leash.

The FCC was not the only independent commission to lack congressional and presidential sanction for new policies inimical to an established industry; the Federal Trade Commission encountered a similar fate while battling the tobacco trade. In January 1964 the U. S. Surgeon General reported a link between cigarette smoking and cancer. That June, the FTC announced that after January 1, 1965, all cigarette packages and cartons, and after July 1, 1965, all cigarette advertising, including radio and TV commercials, were to include the admonition: "Smoking is dangerous to health and may cause death from cancer and other diseases." Dismayed members of Congress, notably those from tobacco-growing states, and others, like Congressman Walter Rogers, who had led the fight to check the FCC's power over air time for commercials, now favored legislation designed to roll back the Trade Commission's order. Again, those supporting the FTC included the same minority of liberal Democrats who earlier had stood with the FCC in key 1961 and 1964 votes. The House Commerce Committee chairman, Oren Harris, and President Johnson forced the FTC to put off the order until July 1965. Then, both houses agreed to a different, more mildly worded label: cigarette smoking "May Be Hazardous to Your Health." In addition, the Federal Cigarette Labeling and Advertising Act specified that the inscription need only be used on cigarette packages and cartons; under the law, the FTC was forbidden to interfere with any form of tobacco advertising for four years.[8] A group of Senate and House liberals complained to President Johnson that the law, "instead of protecting the health of the American people, protects only the cigarette industry."[9]

Still, Congress and even Lyndon Johnson could have been prodded by public opinion. Had large numbers of viewers organized and embraced the FCC, the executive and legislative branches might have held more respect for Minow's and Henry's intentions. But the public never rallied to the champions of the public interest. True, several thousand wrote Minow after his first NAB address. Yet few unhappy TV viewers contacted their elected representatives. When contemplating voting on the FCC in 1961 and 1964, congressmen heard only from broadcast interests.

On at least one major issue facing the FCC in the 1960s, excessive TV advertising, an American majority was unorganized and unheeded. If anything annoyed TV users in the sixties, it was television commercials, and the commission's effort to curb excessive advertising commanded more popular backing than congressional action against the agency indicated. But those favoring the overcommercialization proceeding were not well mobilized or connected to individual congressmen. Power clustered around those with easy access to the Hill.

On most regulatory issues, however, the size and composition of Minow's supporters presented difficulties. Those sharing most of his concerns tended to be among the least representative Americans: the well-educated, well-heeled upper-middle-class liberals. Although expert at mobilizing a PTA chapter, they made for a minor constituency, an elite. Absent were members of the working class or racial and ethnic minorities who, while arguably victimized by television programming, evinced little displeasure with the medium. Indeed, one study found that even most of those of the upper and upper-middle classes—Americans with more than one university degree and drawing a handsome salary—preferred majoritarian television to the "balanced" programming championed by TV's critics and regulators.[10]

The thinness of Minow's ranks can be shown in his efforts to rally public opinion. When Minow held FCC hearings in Omaha and Chicago, they generated little local interest. Few watched the televised proceedings. Most witnesses represented not consumers but religious or television production groups adversely affected by the stations' scheduling practices. "There were," Henry recalled, "far fewer straight public interest groups devoted solely to the performance of television stations."[11] And the effect of such inattention from the public or organized segments of it undermined the capacity of the regulatory agency to serve a public interest. Remarked one historian in 1975, "The system had degenerated from an original dream of constitutional democracy and the general welfare, to a hopelessly fragmented melange of small, autonomous constituencies sensitive only to self-interest."[12]

Of course Americans should not have been expected to fight for the rights of minorities of viewers, even if that was what was ultimately required for the success of the FCC's initiatives. The commission was trying to force stations and networks to telecast precisely those programs least popular with the American TV consumer. Citizens could hardly be counted upon to rally for programming they normally avoided.

For their part, broadcasters had satisfied enough large and important elements to forestall potential support for the FCC. By serving the tastes of the majority each night, broadcasters not only pleased advertisers but limited the number of would-be dissenters. Audience sizes for TV remained constant through the 1960s, with the average American watching TV for four hours a day [13]

Members of Congress and President Johnson proved to be far more selective consumers of television. Few elected officials had time for viewing any commercial programming.[14] Lyndon Johnson watched only "Gunsmoke" (sometimes) and his own prerecorded appearances.[15] Yet the industry willingly served their specialized needs as well. The networks and individual stations donated to congressmen and the president that most precious of commodities in the age of television: air time.

The TV industry also benefited from the ever-present questions of civil liberties in broadcast regulation. Whenever the commission contemplated new edicts, trade leaders always remembered the rank order of the Bill of Rights. "We shake the finger and lift the eyebrow," Henry remarked in October 1964 to a group of broadcasters. "You holler 'censorship' and wave the Constitution."[16] And that reaction to the most modest of designs on programming practices of stations added to the industry's ranks. After voting against the administration's first FCC reform plan, Congressman James Wright, Democrat of Texas, explained to his constituents:

> Administrative powers once granted are seldom relinquished, and the ultimate test of executive authority is not how it can be exercised by good men possessed of wisdom and restraint, but how it could be abused in the hands of bad men. No person could desire a more direct vehicle for the

opinions expressed on radio and television. And it is this realization which underlies the great Congressional caution.[17]

Even among those viewers unhappy with the product of American television, divisions often emerged over the propriety of many of the FCC's tactics. Some who disliked the medium and welcomed Minow's rhetorical assaults nevertheless worried that certain FCC measures endangered the free expression of licensees. His hometown ACLU chapter condemned the chairman's policies toward local stations, with one member complaining of "the potential civil liberties dangers implicit in the Minow proposals."[18] Gilbert Seldes, long *Saturday Review's* TV critic, objected to holding local hearings, the mere act of which constituted a "grand jury indictment, with only a faint chance of [the licensee] being acquitted."[19] Equally unhappy was Irving Kristol, like Minow a liberal of the 1950s bothered by the quality of mass culture. Kristol likened the hometown FCC exercises to the notorious House Un-American Activities Committee. "If anything," Kristol commented, the FCC's proceedings "are even more arbitrary."[20]

In the modern American state this reluctance to see the FCC do too much made sense. Through the second and third quarters of this century, the central government extended its powers and means of enforcing the intentions of its leaders. Nearly always, it did so to redress some perceived or indisputable injustice. But with each addition to the American Leviathan came the risk that one day men and women not concerned with social betterment but with their own petty and foul ends would use the new instrumentalities of a strong state to destroy liberty. "We have built up new instruments of public power," Franklin Roosevelt declared in January 1936. "In the hands of a people's Government this power is wholesome and proper. But in the hands of political puppets of an economic autocracy such power would provide shackles for the liberties of the people."[21]

In that sense, then, not only were the nation's broadcasters more free but society better off with the FCC circumscribed. There was always the danger, so alive in the Nixon presidency, that a powerful FCC could act against political "enemies" or censor individual programs displeasing to some guardians of republican virtue. Aides to President Nixon planned to use the FCC as a means of humbling their adversaries in broadcasting or journalism who also operated stations.

The commission, however, effectively ignored such Florentine plotting—most of the time.[22]

It must be noted, however, that neither Minow nor Henry ever attempted to punish the opponents of the New Frontier. When, in a fit of pique, President Kennedy ordered Minow to do something about NBC's unfavorable coverage of the April 1962 steel-price crisis, his FCC chairman quietly ignored him. The next day, Minow telephoned the White House to inform an aide, "Tell the President that he's very lucky that he has an old friend at the FCC, who knows enough not to do what the President tells him to do when the President is angry."[23]

Minow and Henry never advocated censoring specific programs or redrawing the schedules to please only subscribers of the *Saturday Review*. "I have never suggested that television should concentrate on 'cultural' or 'highbrow' programs to the exclusion of those with mass audience appeal," Henry remarked in March 1965. "I expect broadcasters to program for the masses most of the time. All I ask is that the minority who want something better than horse opera or soap opera be taken into account some of the time."[24]

Rather than calling for the state to intervene into areas of free expression, Minow and Henry revealed their idealism about the possibilities of the "American system" of broadcasting. They expected America's capitalist leaders to serve both a mass market and a higher calling or mission, to be good entrepreneurs and good citizens. Minow and others shared the vision of all Americans using the new and exciting technology of television—to be amused and made aware. The ideal had been that one people, would use one, commercial, medium.

For a moment in the 1950s, some had held that television might indeed be capable of realizing Pat Weaver's vision of a medium serving as an "enlightenment machine" for "an all-people elite."[25] Television could include some programming that commanded large audiences and some that satisfied smaller, more demanding ones. Even as the medium's early, experimental elements began to leave the home screen, men like Minow still saw "a promised land"[26] and believed that TV's rush to standardization would prove only temporary.

They were all wrong and there was little the Communications Commission could do about it. John Kennedy's FCC chairmen could not make their agency a means of achieving more minority interest programming. They could not bring about a restoration of the golden age. Where there had been hope for the commission and the medium in 1961, there was resignation six years later. Institutional solutions were no more easily found for the "TV problem" than for a host of other items on the liberal agenda in the 1960s.[27]

In the 1970s, the FCC enjoyed another revival. The commission took new initiatives on children's programming, curbing the networks' power and encouraging UHF television. Local hearings were even tried again.[28] The extent of the FCC's activism was extraordinary. During Minow's and Henry's chairmenships, the commission issued fourteen volumes of *Reports and Orders*; in the ten-year period 1969-79, the agency published fifty-two volumes.

Several factors accounted for the FCC's newfound aggressiveness. Not among them were changes in presidential administration: the agency's boldest steps in the seventies occurred during Nixon's presidency, when a conservative majority of commissioners predominated. But these reticent regulators found themselves prodded by a larger, more ambitious commission bureaucracy, one that drew inspiration from Cox and Nicholas Johnson. Then, too, consumer groups, not so well mobilized in the previous decade, formed from the ranks of diisgruntled viewers and worried parents.[29] Finally, the Congress, especially the House, became a more liberal place. The abolition of the seniority system as the means of selecting chairmen cost many proindustry, southern Democrats their leverage over the agency. In contrast to the 1960s, regulators were hectored if they did *not* promulgate new rules.[30]

In this atmosphere so conducive to regulation for its own sake, the FCC *still* had trouble tempering American television. The courts judged unconstitutional major efforts to regulate cable television and children's programming.[31] Moreover, some policies that the judiciary left untouched had unintended effects. For example, the FCC found itself encouraging religious fundamentalism. As the commission continued to urge stations to air religious programs as part of their public service obligation, an increasing number of outlets sold (rather than gave) time to those churches willing to pay for air time. And evangelical Protestant sects bought TV half hours with the fervor of a Procter and Gamble account executive. Older, more traditional denominations, which had relied on free air time, lost out to the high priests of a new "electronic church."[32] Efforts to restrict the networks' access in the evening hours and reward local programming initiatives only enriched producers of cheap and even degrading syndicated game programs (some of which, ironically, were created by figures involved deeply in the 1950s quiz scandals).[33]

The commission's greatest error was one of omission. With many broadcasters, the FCC had concluded that cable television would spell the end of smaller television stations and much local programming. Some preliminary evidence did suggest that CATV would hurt UHF stations by cutting into their audiences. Committed to UHF and fearful of repeating the earlier error of neglecting that portion of the spectrum, the agency promulgated layers of rules and restrictions, all designed to slow CATV's diffusion and make all-channel television succeed. Yet by the 1970s, CATV and not UHF appeared the best means through which viewers could enjoy the greater choice in programming that Minow and others had deemed so vital. And the FCC stood accused of limiting audiences' cultural options. One student of the commission declared, "An agency created to protect the spectrum resource now seems a primary cause of its pollution; an agency charged with the responsibility of encouraging communications service now seems a primary cause of its restriction."[34]

All told, the FCC's new purposefulness mattered little. Except for promoting UHF, the commission could not much assist Public Broadcasting. The upper-band stations did become more profitable, but not because they offered viewers the more specialized programming for which Minow and others had hoped. Most new stations relied on older series and films first run on the networks.[35] Among the networks in the 1970s, CBS experimented with more realistic situation comedies, but most observers of the medum regarded the decade as no new golden age of mass entertainment.[36] Minow indicated in March 1977 that if he were FCC chairman again, he would give the same speech he had delivered sixteen years earlier.[37]

Networks and stations did expand their news division, but only after advertiser demand for informational programming grew. In the process, compromises were made, especially on the local level, in the form of shorter individual segments and banter or "happy talk" between news readers that effectively reduced the actual amount of serious news and discussion available.[38] The sixty-minute documentary virtually disappeared in favor of news "magazines," which normally gave ten minutes to an issue or light feature. News directors took on the attitude of entertainers, dreading the prospect of "boring" the viewer. In the fall 1980 campaign, the three commercial networks failed to telecast a single prime-time documentary on the presidential campaign; coverage was restricted to the thirty-minute newscast and late-night specials.[39]

By the late 1970s, the shortcomings of American television left many resigned to the abandonment of regulation. Nothing seemed to work.[40] Only the ineffectiveness or counterproductiveness of agency activities was being demonstrated. Neoconservatives, disillusioned old school liberals, offered a negativism about regulation as an article of faith.[41] Lifelong conservatives rediscovered Adam Smith and spoke euphorically of the marketplace's magical role as the unseen regulator. And the promise of new technologies, telecasting devices beyond cable, seemed to portend a rich range of choices never imagined. Real competition for audiences appeared in the offing. In the early eighties, the FCC steadily eliminated a host of rules.[42] Twenty years earlier, only the most intoxicated station manager attending an NAB meeting where the young FCC chairman had just spoken could have dreamt of such a turn of events.

Appendix

Members of the Federal Communications Commission, 1948-1968

CHAIRMEN: Wayne Coy (D), 1947-52; Paul A. Walker (D), 1952-53; Rosel H. Hyde (R), 1954-54; George C. McConnaughey (R), 1954-57; John C. Doerfer (R), 1957-60; Frederick W. Ford (R), 1960-61; Newton N. Minow (D), 1961-63; E. William Henry (D), 1963-66; Rosel H. Hyde (R), 1966-69.

COMMISSIONERS:

Paul A. Walker (D) 1934-53	Rosel H. Hyde (R) 1944-69[a]	Robert F. Jones (R) 1947-52	Frieda Hennock (D) 1948-55	George Sterling (R) 1948-54	Edward M. Webster (I) 1947-56	Wayne C. Coy (D) 1947-52
John C. Doerfer (R) 1953-60	Eugene H. Merrill (D) 1952-53		Richard A. Mack (D) 1955-58	George C. McConnaughey (R) 1954-57	T.A.M. Craven (D) 1956-63	Robert T. Bartley (D) 1952-72
Charles R. King (R) 1960-61	Robert E. Lee (R) 1953-		John Cross (D) 1958-62	Frederick W. Ford (R) 1957-65	Kenneth A. Cox (D) 1963-70	
Newton N. Minow (D) 1961-63			E. William Henry (D) 1963-66	James J. Wadsworth (R) 1965-69		
Lee Loevinger (D) 1963-68			Rosel H. Hyde (R) 1966-69[a]			
Nicholas Johnson (D) 1966-73[a]						

[a]Hyde, when up for reappointment in 1966, took the remaining three years of Henry's term. Turning seventy in 1969, Hyde was to have to surrender his seat. Nicholas Johnson accepted Hyde's six-year term in 1966.

Abbreviations

ABAJ	*American Bar Association Journal*
AB-UP	American Broadcasting Co.-United Paramount Theatres
CF	Confidential File
COHC	Oral History Collection, Columbia University
EX	Executive File
FDRL	Franklin D. Roosevelt Library, Hyde Park, N.Y.
FG	Federal Government-Organizations
FLOHC	James Lawrence Fly Oral History Project, Oral History Collection, Columbia University
Gen	General File
GSA	General Services Administration, Suitland, Md.
INSPIRE	Institute for Public Interest Representation, Broadcast Pioneers Library, Washington, D.C.
JFKL	John F. Kennedy Library, Boston, Mass.
KSHS	Kansas State Historical Society, Topeka, Kans.
LBJL	Lyndon B. Johnson Library, Austin, Tex.
LC	Library of Congress, Washington, D.C.
LE/ED	Legislation: Education
NA	National Archives, Suitland, Md.
NAEB	National Association of Educational Broadcasters
NETRC	National Educational Television and Radio Center
OF	Official File
RR	Pike and Fischer, *Radio Regulation*
SHSW	State Historical Society of Wisconsin, Madison, Wis.
UT	Utilities
WCCET	Wisconsin Citizens' Committee for Educational Television
WHCF	White House Central Files
WHOF	White House Official Files
WHSF	White House Subject Files

Notes

INTRODUCTION

1   Lester Chester, Godfrey Hodgson, and Bruce Page, *An American Melodrama: The Presidential Campaign of 1968* New York, 1969), 40-47; Norman Macrae, *The Neurotic Trillionaire: A Survey of Mr. Nixon's America* (New York, 1970), passim; Alonzo L. Hamby, *The Imperial Years: The United States since 1939* (New York, 1976), 303-5, 308-11, 322; Eli Ginzberg and Robert M. Solow, eds., "The Great Society: Lessons for the Future," *Public Interest* 34 (Winter 1974). See also Warren I. Susman, "The Persistence of American Reform," in Daniel Walden, ed., *American Reform: The Ambiguous Legacy* (Yellow Springs, Ohio, 1967), 94-108; Irving Kristol, *On the Democratic Idea in America* (New York, 1972), ix.

2   Jim F. Heath, *Decade of Disillusionment: The Kennedy-Johnson Years* (Bloomington, 1975), 299.

3   Kariel, *The Decline of American Pluralism*, 96; Schubert, *The Public Interest*, 223; "National Policy and the 'Public Interest'—A Marriage of Necessity in the Communications Act of 1934," *University of Pennsylvania Law Review* 114 (Jan. 1966), 387.

4   A.J.P. Taylor, *New Statesman* 65 (1963), 238-40, cited in John W. Boyer, "A.J.P. Taylor and the Art of Modern

History 49 (March 1966), 66.

5 See Bernard Rossiter, *The Mythmakers* (New York, 1964), 121, for criticisms of this view, easily located in such works on the FCC as Kohlmeier, *The Regulators*, and Cole and Oettinger, *Reluctant Regulators*.

6 McCraw, "Regulation in America," 159-83, ably summarizes the state of the literature and the popularity of the "capture" thesis.

7 Marver H. Bernstein, "Independent Regulatory Agencies: A Perspective on Their Reform," *Annals of the American Academy of Political and Social Science* 400 (March 1972), 21.

8 William Gillette, *Retreat from Reconstruction, 1869-1879* (Baton Rouge, 1979), xii-xiii.

CHAPTER 1

1 *Television Age* (9 March 1959), 112; *New York Times*, 16 Nov. 1958.

2 Hoogenboom and Hoogenboom, *A History of the ICC*; Skowronek, *Building a New American State*, 121-50.

3 Elihu Root, "Address of the President," *ABAJ* (Oct. 1916), 735-55; Rexford G. Tugwell, "The Economic Basis of the Public Interest" (Ph.D. diss. Univ. of Pennsylvania, 1922), esp. 1-11; Cushman, *The Problem of the Independent Regulatory Commission*, 10; Landis, *The Administrative Process*, 24; Lindley, *The Constitution Faces Technology*, 253, 262; Carl Grafton, "The Creation of Federal Agencies," *Administration and Society* 7 (Nov. 1975), 328-65.

4 Commissioner Henry A. Bellows, quoted in FRC, *Annual Report* (1927), 7. See also David P. Thelen, *Robert M. La Follette and the Insurgent Spirit* (Boston, 1976), 117; Charles McCarthy, *The Wisconsin Idea* (New York, 1912), 15 and passim; Robert M. La Follette, *La Follette's Autobiography* (Madison, 1913; reprinted ed., 1960), 145, 145, 149-50, 1953; Henry Steele Commager, *The American Mind* (New Haven, 1950), 339.

5 See, e.g., Kolko, *The Triumph of Conservatism*, idem, *Railroads and Regulation*; Robert H. Wiebe, *Businessmen and Reform: A Study of the Progressive Movement* (Cam-

bridge, Mass., 1961); George J. Stigler, "The Theory of Economic Regulation," *Bell Journal of Economics and Management* 2 (Spring 1971), 3-21. Rarely did the architects of the administrative state challenge the basic, capitalistic foundations of the regulated enterprise or construe the interests of business as invariably antithetical to the public interest. (J. Joseph Huthmacher, "A Critique of the Kolko Thesis," in Otis L. Graham, Jr., ed., *From Roosevelt to Roosevelt: American Politics and Diplomacy, 1901-1941* [New York, 1971], 101-3; Unofficial Observer [John Franklin Carter], *The New Dealers* (New York, 1934), 323.

6   U.S. Department of Justice (hereafter Justice Dept.) Attorney General's Committee on Administrative Procedure, *Federal Communications Commission*, II: 173-74.

7   Herbert Hoover, *The Memoirs of Herbert Hoover: The Cabinet and the Presidency 1920-1933* (New York, 1952), 140-43; idem, "Radio Gets a Policeman," 73-76.

8   Justice Dept., *Opinions of the Attorneys General of the United States* 35 (Washington, D.C., 1926), 126, 129; *Hoover v. City Intercity Radio Co.*, 52 App. D.C. 339, 28 F. 1003 (D.C. Cir., 1923); *U.S.* v. *Zenith Radio Corp.*, 12 F.2d 614 (N.D. Ill., 1926). See also U.S. Congress, Senate, Committee on Interstate and Foreign Commerce (hereafter Senate Commerce Committee), *Regulation of Radio Transmission*, 1.

9   Statement before the First National Radio Conference, 27 Feb. 1922, p. 3, Radio File, Herbert Hoover Papers, Stanford University; Hoover, *Memoirs*, 139; David R. Mackey, "The National Association of Broadcasters—Its First Twenty Years," (Ph.D. diss. Northwestern Univ., 1956), 326, 334-35; Hoover, interview with Harry A. Mount, *Cleveland Plain Dealer*, n.d., p. 3, transcript in Commerce Dept. Files, box 490, Hoover Papers, HHL.

10   See, e.g., Herring, "Politics and Radio Regulation," 167-78; Cushman, *The Independent Regulatory Commissions*, 297. For a more balanced approach to radio regulation's evolution, see Rosen, *The Modern Stentors*.

11   Warren Lester Lewis to Wallace White, 7 Feb. 1925, box 42, White Papers; See also William Pinckney White, Jr., to William Cabell Bruce, 1 Nov. 1926, Daniel Nelson Clark to Hoover, 19 Jan. 1925, H.J. Kail to White, 3 Dec. 1926, box

51, ibid.; *Congressional Record*, 69th Cong. 1st sess., vol. 68, pt. 3, 29 Jan. 1927, p. 2570; ibid., 2d sess., vol. 68, pt. 3, 6 Feb. 1927, p. 3257; Pusateri, *Enterprise in Radio*, 29, 31; W. C. Geer to Hoover, 3 Jan. 1923, Commerce Dept. Files, box 501, Hoover Papers, HHL.

12 Corporate anarchy had, one historian contends, similarly led to the ICC Act. See Lee Benson, *Merchants, Farmers, and Railroads: Railroad Regulation and New York Politics 1850-1887* (Cambridge, Mass., 1955), 228ff.

13 On Hoover's objectives in radio regulation, see Ellis W. Hawley, "Herbert Hoover"; idem, "Three Facets of Hooverian Associationalism: Lumber, Aviation, and Movies 1921-1930," in McCraw, *Regulation in Perspective*, 99, 115; idem, *The Great War and the Search for Modern Order: A History of the American People and Their Institutions, 1917-1933* (New York, 1979), 103; Joan Hoff Wilson, *Herbert Hoover: Forgotten Progressive* (Boston, 1975), 112-13.

14 Hoover to George B. Lockwood, 8 May 1926, Commerce Dept. Files, box 501, Hoover Papers, HHL; Garvey, "Secretary Hoover," 66-70; Godfrey, "The 1927 Radio Act," 73; McKerns, "Industry Skeptics," 128-31; Godfrey, "Senator Dill," 477-89; *Congressional Record*, 69th Cong., 1st sess., vol. 67, pt. 5, 13 March 1926, p. 5558; Rosen, *The Modern Stentors*, 74, 82ff, 95-98.

15 Robert M. Hurt, "FCC: Free Speech, 'Public Needs,' and Mr. Minow," *New Individualist Review* 2 (Spring 1963), 25,36; Barnouw, *A History of Broadcasting*, I:195-96; Caldwell, "Standard of Public Interest," 300-1; Holt, "Origin of 'Public Interest,'" 15-19; "The Reminiscences of Clarence C. Dill" (1971), Broadcast Pioneers Library, Washington, D.C., pp. 7-8.

16 Minow, *Equal Time*, 8-9, includes remarks Dill made to Minow in 1961 concerning radio rate regulation.

17 Caldwell, "Standard of Public Interest," 313-14; address by Hoover, 16 Aug. 1924, p. 7, Commerce Dept. Files, box 490, Hoover Papers, HHL.

18 White to Frederick William Wile, 13 March 1926, box 51, White Papers; Hoover, interview, *St. Louis Post-Dispatch*, Nov. 1924, transcript in Commerce Dept. Files, box 490, Hoover Papers, HHL.

19 Fainsod and Gordon, *Government and the American*

Economy, 387; Caldwell, "Standard of Public Interest," 326; FRC, *Annual Report* (1927), 2, *Annual Report* (1928), 2, 8, 11-13, 17-18.

20 Hoogenboom and Hoogenboom, *A History of the ICC, 188*.

21 FRC, *Annual Report* (1929), 32-35.

22 *Columbia Law Review* 47 (Sept. 1947), 1045; FRC, *Annual Report* (1931), 67-78 (1933), 11; Gerald Carson, *The Roguish World of Doctor Brinkley* (New York, 1960), 93, 135, 143-47, 266; Donald R. McCoy, *Landon of Kansas* (Lincoln, 1966), 91-92; telegram, George S. Sexton to FDR, 17 July 1933, WHOF, box 136, Roosevelt Papers.

23 See, e.g., *Congressional Record*, 73d Cong., 2d sess., vol. 78, pt. 8, 15 May 1934, pp 8828ff; *Yale Law Journal* 40 (April 1931), 969; Goldberg and Couzens, " 'Peculiar Characteristics,' " 3-4.

24 Statement by Hoover, 27 Feb. 1922, and Hoover, interview, *St. Louis Post-Dispatch*, Nov. 1924, transcript, Commerce Dept. Files, box 490, Hoover Papers, HHL; Herman H. Hohenstein to FDR, 11 May 1934, WHOF, box 859, Roosevelt Papers; Koppes, "Social Destiny of Radio," 368-72, 374.

25 Quoted in Pusateri, "Stormy Career," 404-5. See also Barnouw, *A History of Broadcasting*, I:189-95, 203-7, 219-24, 249-51, 272-83; FRC, *Annual Report* (1928), 21, 52; Paley, *As It Happened*, 41-51; address by Hoover, 16 Aug. 1924, pp. 8, 13, Commerce Dept. Files, box 490, Hoover Papers, HHL.

26 *The Public Papers and Addresses of Franklin D. Roosevelt*, 5 vols., (New York, 1938), III:107-8; *Congressional Record*, 73d Cong. 2d sess., vol. 78, pt. 10, 2 June 1934, pp. 10312-13, 10317; copy of report, with cover letter, Roper to FDR, 23 Jan. 1934, WHOF, box 859A, Roosevelt Papers; *Washington Post*, 27 and 28 Feb. 1934; *New York Times*, 28 Feb. 1934; *Chicago Tribune*, 28 Feb. 1934.

27 Mackey, "The National Association of Broadcasters," 443-45; Barnouw, *A History of Broadcasting*, II:33; Lawrence Laurent, "Commercial Television: What Are Its Educational Possibilities?" in Elliott, *Television's Impact*, 133; *Congressional Record*, 73d Cong., 2d sess., vol. 78, pt. 10, 9 June 1934, p. 10989.

28 Marvin H. McIntyre to Wetmore Hodges, 23 July 1937, WHOF, box 1049, Roosevelt Papers; Marver H. Bernstein, *Reg-*

lating Business, 86; Lichty, "The Impact of FRC and FCC
Commissioners' Background, 97-110.

29 William O. Douglas, *Go East, Young Man: The Early Years:
The Autobiography of William O. Douglas* (New York,
1974), 463.

30 Thomas K. McCraw, *TVA and the Power Fight* (Philadelphia,
1971), 110-11; *New York Times*, 7 Jan. 1966; Mackey, "The
National Association of Broadcasters," 556-78; Lyons, *David
Sarnoff*, 258-59; Barnouw, *A History of Broadcasting*,
II:169-70.

31 "The Reminiscences of Neville Miller" (1967), FLOHC, 1-2;
"The Reminiscences of Edward Brecher" (1967). FLOHC,
23-24; "The Reminiscences of Marcus Cohn" (1967), FLOHC,
37; Chafee, *Government and Mass Communications*, II;474.

32 FCC, *Report on Chain Broadcasting*, Commission Order 37,
5060 (May 1941); "The Reminiscences of Joseph Rauh"
(1967) FLOHC, 12-13; Robinson, *Radio Networks*, ch. 16,
210-12; *Yale Law Journal* 60 (Jan. 1951), 79-87; "FCC Regulation of Competition among Networks," 448-65; Herman S.
Hettinger, "The Economic Factor in Radio Regulation," *Air
Law Review* 9 (April 1938), 115-16.

33 The other networks were NBC, CBS, and the Mutual Broad-
casting System (MBS). "The Reminiscences of Harry Plotkin"
FLOHC, 10: "The Reminiscences of Telford Taylor" (1967),
FLOHC, 31; memorandum, "Washington D.C.—November 25
and 26, 1941," G.M.B. to Joseph Pulitzer II, box 108, Pulitzer
Papers; FCC, *Reports and Orders* 10 (1943), 212-14; *Chicago
Tribune*, 5 Jan. 1944

34 *NBC* v. *U.S.* 319, U.S. (1943), 190, 212, 215-16; memoran-
dum, Chain Broadcasting Cases, n.d., box 4-8, Frankfurter
Papers. Murphy and Roberts dissented; Black and Rutledge
did not participate. The draft of materials relating to Murphy's dissent is in box 66, Murphy Papers. See also, *Scripps-
Howard Radio, Inc.* v. *FCC*, 316 U.S. (1942), 4, 14; Avard
Brinton, "The Regulation of Broadcasting by the FCC: A Case
Study in Regulation by Independent Commission" (Ph.D.
diss., Harvard Univ., 1962), 40; *Christian Science Monitor*, 9
July 1943; editorial, *Saturday Evening Post* (17 July 1943),
100.

35 Memorandum and letter, Fly to FDR, 17 June 1944, FDR to

Fly, 22 June 1944, President's Secretary File, box 149, Roosevelt Papers; *Washington Post*, 27 Nov. 1975.

36   Paul F. Lazarsfeld, "An Episode in the History of Social Research: A Memoir," *Perspectives in American History* 2 (1968), 316; *New York Times*, 2 May 1948.

37   FCC, *Public Service Responsibilities of Broadcast Licenses* (1946); Edelman, *The Licensing of Radio Services*, 76-79; Gale Eugene Peterson, "President Harry S. Truman and the Independent Commissions, 1945-1952," (Ph.D. diss. Univ. of Maryland, 1973), 34, 159, 161-62; Rosenberg, "Program Content," 375-401.

38   Siepmann, *Radio's Second Chance*, esp. ch. 6; idem, *Radio, Television, and Society*, 37-40.

39   Peterson, "President Harry S. Truman," 161; Rosenberg, "Program Content," 392-93; Paul C. Fowler, "The Policy of the Federal Communications Commission with Respect to Programming," *Journal of Broadcasting* 2 (Spring 1958), 100-4; Richard J. Meyer, "Reaction to the 'Blue Book,' " 295-312.

40   Commission on Orgnization of the Executive Branch of the Government, Committee on Independent Regulatory Commissions, *Staff Report on the Federal Communications Commission*, (Nov. 1948), copy in Hoover Commission Files, box 26, pt. 3, p. 52, Hoover Papers, HHL.

41   FCC, *Annual Report*, 1946-52, inclusive, list network data for ABC, CBS, NBC, MBS, and the Du Mont television network. See also Peterson, "President Harry S. Truman," 474; Lessing, "The Television Freeze," 126.

42   *Washington Post*, 15 and 23 April 1948; John Michael Kittross, "Television Frequency Allocation Policy in the United States" (Ph.D. diss., Univ. of Illinois, 1960), 182; *Broadcasting* (23 Feb. 1958), 200.

43   *New York Herald Tribune*, 16 March 1958; "The Reminiscences of James M. Landis" (1963), COHC, 573, 638; Alonzo L. Hamby, *Beyond the New Deal: Harry S. Truman and American Liberalism* (New York, 1973), 213, 229; R. Franklin Smith, "Madame Commissioner," *Journal of Broadcasting* 12 (Winter 1967-68), 69-81.

44   Martin Codel to Charles G. Ross, 26 July 1947, OF 112, box 1121, Truman Papers; Fly to Truman, 9 May 1947, OF 112,

box 529, ibid.; Peterson, "President Harry S. Truman," 145, 311-12.

45 Gilbert Seldes, "Bad Manners and Good Rules," *Saturday Review* (16 March 1957), 28.

46 Memorandum c. 1952-53, Robert Cutler to Sherman Adams, 12 Feb. 1953, OF 16, box 187, Eisenhower Papers.

47 *Broadcasting* (9 Jan. 1961), 42,44; Frank Stanton, interview with author.

48 Paul Douglas to E.F. McDonald, Jr., 16 July 1956, box 84, Paul Douglas Papers. See also Anne Langman, "Television: Magnuson Committee Report," *Nation* (20 July 1957), 40; David C. Delanis, interview with Martin Mayer, n.d., notes in box 65, Mayer Papers; *Broadcasting* (9 May 1955), 27; Lichty, "An Analysis of the FCC Membership," 828-33.

49 Charles F. Willis to Sherman Adams, 22 Sept. 1954, Ilene [?] to Willis, 18 June 1955, OF 16, box 187, Eisenhower Papers. On the president's distaste for patronage matters, see Robert H. Ferrell, ed., *The Eisenhower Diaries* (New York, 1981), 218, 220, 221, 249-50; Willis, interview with James M. Graham and Victor H. Kramer, 6 July 1973, notes in INSPIRE Papers.

50 Quoted in Quinlan, *The Hundred Million Dollar Lunch*, 4-5.

51 Huntington, "The Marasmus of the ICC," 467-509; Marver H. Bernstein, *Regulating Business*, passim; Kariel, *The Decline of American Pluralism*, 96.

52 Ritchie, *James M. Landis* 174-75.

53 Jaffe, "Independent Agency," 1073. See also Alan F. Westin, "Inquiry into Our Watchdog Agencies," *New York Times Magazine* (23 Oct. 1960), 21.

54 Between 1948 and 1952, the typical station lost money in its first two to three years of operations. By 1954, however, stations averaged an annual profit margin of between 35 to 40 percent before taxes. See Richard P. Doherty, "Is the Television Industry Still in the Growth Stage?" *Analysts Journal* (10 Nov. 1954), 35-36; Stephen David Buell, "The History and Development of WSAZ-TV, Channel 3, Huntington, West Virginia" (Ph.D. diss., Ohio State Univ., 1962), pp. 36-53.

55 Henry J. Friendly, *The Federal Administrative Agencies*, 57-67; William K. Jones, *Licensing of Major Broadcast Facilities by the Federal Communications Commission*,

prepared for the Administrative Conference of the United
States by the Committee on Licenses and Authorizations,
Columbia Univ. Law School, Sept. 1962, pp. 192, 206-7;
Schwartz, "Comparative Television," 665 and passim; U.S.
Congress, House of Representatives, Committee on Interstate
and Foreign Commerce (hereafter, House Commerce Com-
mittee), *Network Broadcasting* [Barrow Report], report 1297,
85th Cong., 2d sess., 27 Jan. 1958, ch. 3; Anthony Lewis,
New York Times, 2 March 1958.

56 Jaffe, "The Scandal in TV Licensing," 77-79, 82, 84; Bendiner,
"The FCC," 26-30; Emanuel Celler to Ruth M. Davis, 25
Sept. 1957, box 3, Bendiner Papers; Henry Geller, interview
with author, U.S. Congress, House of Representatives,
Judiciary Committee (hereafter House Judiciary Committee),
Monopoly Problems in Regulated Industries, pt. 2: *Televi-
sion*, 453-55, includes testimony suggesting that some com-
missioners were on the take.

57 "*Ex Parte* Contacts," 1178-199; Frank T. Colon, "The Court
and the Commission: *Ex Parte* Contacts and the Sangamon
Valley Case," *Federal Communications Bar Journal* 19
(1964-65), 67-86; Bernard Schwartz, interview with author; *St.
Louis Post-Dispatch*, 11 May 1961.

58 *Broadcasting* (11 Feb. 1957), 74; *Congressional Quarterly
Weekly Report* 15 (Jan. 1958), 84; memorandum, Oren Harris
to subcommittee staff, 12 Feb. 1958, group 12, box 10-4-40,
Harris Papers; Harris, "Improving the Regulatory Process,"
19-23; Scher, "Conditions for Legislative Control," 538-39,
541.

59 Frederick W. Ford, interview with author, 19 June 1978;
New York Times, 14 Feb. 1958; Rosel Hyde, interview with
Sterling H. Quinlan, 5 Dec. 1972, tape in box 13, Quinlan
Papers.

60 *Broadcasting* (10 Feb. 1958), 27-32, 35-36 (24 Feb. 1958), 8,
42ff. (3 March 1958), 27-32 (10 March 1958), 64, 66, 71-72;
Schwartz, *The Professor*, 100-2, 111-12, 194-203; Rosenblum,
"How to Get into TV," 173-228; Frier, *Conflict of Interest*,
151-52, 160-73; Goodman, *All Honorable Men*, 163-75; House
Commerce Committee, *Investigation of Regulatory Commis-
sions*, 463, 1287; *Life* (24 Feb. 1958), 28-29; Mack to
Eisenhower, 3 March 1958, OF 16, box 188, Eisenhower

Papers. The vote on channel 10 was also said to relate to the winning applicant's financial contributions to the Republican party. Memorandum to files, Herbert M. Wachtell, 6 Feb. 1958, Morison Burson to Peter Mack, 7 March 1958, box 30, Mack Papers. Richard Mack died in a Miami flophouse five and a half years after his ouster (*New York Times*, 27 Nov. 1963).

61 *Congressional Quarterly Weekly Report* 16 (31 Jan. 1958), 129; House Commerce Committee, *Investigation of Regulatory Commissions*, 219-57, 266-68, 271, 275-76, 320-23, 394-98, 539-45, 2202, 2350; Goodman, *All Honorable Men*, 191; Frier, *Conflict of Interest*, 152-53; Schwartz, *The Professor*, 91-95, 177-82; Hyde, interview with Quinlan, 5 Dec. 1972, box 13, Quinlan Papers.

62 *Broadcasting* (17 July 1958), 5; Edward R. Murrow to David Lawrence, 16 Jan. 1959, box 2-B-7, Murrow Papers; memorandum, "Conflict of Interest," n.d., box 195, Democratic National Committee Records. Many members of Congress disapproved of Adams's interference in the FTC's deliberations, to say nothing of Goldfine's rewards to Adams for having done so. Adams had frequently asked the FCC about pending decisions (Tex McCrary to Adams, 27 Oct. 1953, General Files 41-A(1), box 380, Charles F. Willis, Jr., to Adams, 22 April 1955, General Files 129-A-2, box 1003, and Oakley Hunter to Adams, 24 May 1957, General Files 41 (2), box 379, Eisenhower Papers).

63 *Broadcasting* (10 March 1958), 73.

64 Jaffe, "Independent Agency," 1068; Cushman, *The Problem of the Independent Regulatory Commission*, 16, 32, and passim; Roscoe Pound, "For the Minority Report," *ABAJ* 27 (Nov. 1941), 664-67; "Government by Commission," *Fortune* (May 1943), 205-9; Polenberg, *Reorganizing Roosevelt's Government*, 21, 25-26.

65 Pritchett, *The Roosevelt Court*, ch. 7, p. 173; Nathanson, "Mr. Justice Frankfurter," 240-65, esp. 252-55, 2265; William H. Nicholls, "Federal Regulatory Agencies and the Courts," *American Economic Review* 34 (March 1944), 56-75, esp. 73, 75.

66 House Commerce Committee, *Regulation of Broadcasting*, 77-78; Nathanson, "Mr. Justice Frankfurter," 255.

67   Marver H. Bernstein, *Regulating Business*, 194-95; Heady, "The New Reform Movement," 91; Woll, *American Bureaucracy*, 101-3; Brinton, "The Regulation of Broadcasting," 49, 54-56; address by Landis, 10 Nov. 1961, box 148, Landis Papers, LC; Freedman, *Crisis and Legitimacy*, ch. 12.

68   Frederick F. Blachly and Miriam E. Oatman, "Sabotage of the Administrative Process," *Public Administration Review* 6 (Summer 1946), 226; U.S. Congress, Senate, Committee on Governmental Affairs (hereafter Senate Governmental Affairs Committee), *Study on Federal Regulation*, vol. 4: *Delay in the Regulatory Process*, doc. 95-72, 95th Cong., 1st sess., 1977, p. xiii.

69   Quoted in House Commerce Committee, *Regulation of Broadcasting*, 82-83. See also Bookman, "Regulation by Elephant," 232; James M. Landis, interview, *U.S. News and World Report* (27 March 1961), 83; Kenneth Culp Davis, *Administrative Law Text* (St. Paul, 1959), 172-73, 206; McCoy, "Communication Act Amendments," 8-21.

70   Ford, interview with author, 15 June 1978; *Television Magazine* (Sept. 1957), 111.

71   House Commerce Committee, *Investigation of Regulatory Commissions*, 557, 560, 562; *New York Times*, 2 March 1958; Hyde, interview with Sterling Quinlan, 5 Dec. 1972, box 13, Quinlan Papers; Kittross, "Television Frequency Allocation," 441.

72   Kittross, "Television Frequency Allocation," 449.

73   Fisher, "Communication Acts Amendments," 676.

74   *Television Magazine* (June 1953), 22; Frank Zeidler to Norman Thomas, 19 March 1953, 1 June 1953, box 73, Norman Thomas Papers, New York Public Library.

75   House Commerce Committee, *Investigation of Regulatory Commissions*, 702-94, 2420; *Broadcasting* (10 March 1958), 74; *Television Digest* (27 July 1959), 2, 4-5; Scher, "Congressional Committee Members as Independent Agency Overseers," 919-20; Hyde, interview with Sterling Quinlan, 5 Dec. 1972, box 13, Quinlan Papers. A few congressmen refrained from interfering (F. Gibson Darrison, Jr., to G. William Criswell, 7 May 1958, box 21, William E. Miller Papers).

76 Press release, Dept. of Commerce, 6 March 1927, *Buffalo Evening News*, 8 March 1927, clipping in Commerce Dept. Files, box 490, Hoover Papers, HHL; FRC, *Annual Report* (1927), 2.

77 Hoover Commission, *Staff Report on the Federal Communications Commission* (1949), Washington, D.C., pt. 3, p. 36; FCC, *Annual Report* (1955), 107; House Judiciary Committee, *Monopoly Problems*, 3505. See also V.O. Key, Jr., "Legislative Control," in Fritz Morstein Marx, ed., *Elements of Public Administration*, 2d ed. (Englewood Cliffs, N.J., 1959), 312-37, and James W. Fesler, "Independent Regulatory Agencies," in ibid., 194; Richard F. Fenno, *The Power of the Purse* (Boston, 1966).

78 Kirshner, "The Color Television Controversy," 74, 77; Ed Johnson to Elbert Thomas, 3 Aug. 1950, Elbert Thomas Papers, FDRL, box 321.

79 Barrow, "The Attainment of Balanced Program Service," 656-66; Guimary, *Citizens' Groups*, 23ff.

80 Suggestive is Louis Galambos, *The Public Image of Big Business in America, 1880-1940* (Baltimore, 1976), 47.

81 Schwartz, "Antitrust and the FCC"; Durr, "The Forgotten Client," 9.

82 1-10 April 1952.

83 Pulse, Inc., survey reported in *Broadcasting* (16 May 1959), 84.

CHAPTER 2

1 Marias, *America*, 181-86; Edward C. McDonagh, "Television and the Family," *Sociology and Social Research* 35 (Nov.-Dec. 1950), 113-122; William Zinsser, "Out Where the Tall Antennas Grow," *Harper's* (April 1956), 36-37; *Historical Statistics of the United States, from Colonial Times to 1970*, 2 vols. (Washington, D.C. 1975), II:796; *Statistical Abstract of the United States, 1959* (Washington, D.C., 1959), 590; Hugh M. Beville to Fred Horton, 19 May 1954, box 142, NBC Records; Schramm, Lyle, and Parker, *Television in the Lives of Our Children*, 11-15.

2 The best sources on the three networks are "His Masters'

Voice," *Forbes* (1 Oct. 1956), 15-19; *Business Week* (21 Aug. 1954), 40-44; Mayer, "Television's Lords of Creation"; *Printer's Ink* (20 June 1958); 51ff Robert Cunniff, "Mediocrity's Mahatma," *Show Business Illustrated* (19 Sep. 1961), 43, 48, 96-97; "CBS Steals the Show," *Fortune* (July 1953), 79; "The Money Tree and Madison Avenue," *Forbes* (15 Jan. 1964), 20-25. A fourth network, Du Mont, was badly underfinanced and left the air in Sept. 1955.

3   Harvey J. Levin, "Workable Competition," 434; House Commerce Committee, *Network Broadcasting*, report 1297, 85th Cong., 2nd sess., 1958, pp. 196-98.

4   Ray Stewart to FCC, 11 Nov. 1955, docket 11532, vol. 4, FCC Records, NA.

5   *Broadcasting* (16 Nov. 1959), 56.

6   Daniel Bell, *The Cultural Contradictions of Capitalism* (New York, 1976), 43-45; Macdonald, "A Theory of Mass Culture."

7   Frederic Wertham, *Seduction of the Innocent* (New York, 1954); Senate Judiciary Committee, *Juvenile Delinquency*, hearings, 83d Cong., 2d sess., 1954, pp. 124-30, 288-90; *U.S. News and World Report* (2 Sept. 1955), 75-76; Al Toffler, "Crime in Your Parlor," *Nation* 181 (15 Oct. 1955), 323-24; Don Wharton, "Let's Get Rid of Tele-Violence," *Reader's Digest* (April 1956), 93-96; Goodman, *The Clowns of Commerce*, 208-17.

8   Unpublished study of newspaper TV columnists by Patrick McGrady for the Fund for the Republic, Oct. 1958, copy in box 63, Fund for the Republic Papers. Gould's and John Crosby's columns were widely syndicated. See also *New York Times*, 29 Jan. 1959; "Group Profile: The Critics," *Television Magazine* (Dec. 1954), 44; Leon Morse, "Inside Jack Gould," ibid. (Nov. 1958), 49-50, 94-95; *Newsweek* (9 May 1966), 92; Young, "One Medium: Two Critics"; memorandum, Robert Kintner to Lyndon Johnson, 21 June 1966, WHCF, FG 228, Johnson Papers.

9   Dominick and Pearce, "Trends in Network Prime-Time Programming," 70-80, is the most systematic of these studies and, with the others, argues that there was no golden age even when evidence suggests otherwise.

10 Barnouw, *A History of Broadcasting*, III:25-40; *Washington Star*, 1 May 1955. Tim Brooks and Earle Marsh, *The Com-*

plete Directory of Prime Time Network TV Shows (New York, 1979), is the source for the length of individual anthologies. See also docket 12782, vol. 14, *Proceedings*, vol. 38, p. 5846, vol. 15, vol. 41, p. 6238, FCC Records, Dockets Room, FCC; Chayefsky, *Television Plays*; Robert Lewis Shayon, "The Efficient Murder," *Saturday Review* (26 Feb. 1955), 23-24; J.P. Shanky, "He Celebrates the Bronx," (16 April 1955), 13-14; Britton, *Best Television Plays*; Wilk, *The Golden Age*, 23-42, 106-12, 125-38; Cone, *With All Its Faults*, 210, 212-15. See Kenneth Hey, "*Marty*: Aesthetics vs. Medium in Early Television Drama," in O'Connor, *American History/American Television*, 95-133, for a provocative, critical analysis of the anthologies.

11 Draft of memorandum of meeting with Weaver, 5-6 Jan. 1956, pp. 8, 15-16, Office of Network Study, invoice 72-A-1986, box 13, FCC Records, GSA; Wilk, *The Golden Age*, 113-24; TV notebook, n.d., box 63, Mayer Papers, includes material on *Peter Pan*; *Variety* (17 March 1954), 1, 35 (10 Aug. 1955), 21.

12 Wilk, *The Golden Age*, 95-105, 236-45.

13 *Cue* (21 Feb. 1953), 10; *New York Daily Mirror*, 27 Feb. 1953; *Time* (30 Sept. 1957), 50; Murray Russell Yaeger, "An Analysis of Edward R. Murrow's 'See It Now' Television Program" (Ph.D. diss., State Univ. of Iowa, 1956), 49, 51-52; Fred W. Friendly, *Due to Circumstances beyond Our Control*, xv, 77; Baughman, "*See It Now*," 106-15; Daniel J. Leab, "*See It Now*: A Legend Reassessed," in O'Connor, *American History/American Television*, 1-32.

14 *Variety* (17 March 1954), 25, 35; Seldes, *The Public Arts*, chs. 24-25.

15 See, e.g., "Comments of Columbia Broadcasting System" [May 1966], app. B, docket 12782, vol. 25, FCC Records, Dockets Room, FCC; Gould, *New York Times*, 19 Oct. 1952; Janet Kern in *Television Magazine* (Dec. 1954), 44. Robert Lewis Shayon, "The Critics and the Emperors' Clothes," *Saturday Review* (27 April 1957), 26, criticizes the spectaculars' warm critical reception.

16 Docket 12782, vol. 14, *Proceedings*, vol. 38, pp. 5742, 5749, 5760-61, FCC Records, Dockets Room, FCC.

17 *New York Times*, 8 April 1956; *New York Post*, 11 April

1956; David Manning White, "What's Happening?" 11-13.

18 *New York Times*, 19 May 1955. See also Senate Commerce Committee, *The Television Inquiry*, hearings, 84th Cong., 2d sess., 1956, p. 2143; Langman, "Television," 39-40; Saul Carson, "Reason for Hope," *New Republic*, (30 Jan. 1950), 29.

19 Davis, *Yearning for Yesterday*, 10-12, 20.

20 James Kent Anderson, "Fraudulence in Television: The History and Implications of the Quiz Show Scandals, 1955-1960" (Ph.D. diss., Univ. of Washington, 1975), 45.

21 *Broadcasting* (20 April 1959), 20 (27 April 1959), 9. The cancellation of "The Voice of Firestone" drew so many congressional protests that the FCC took the unusual step of asking the network about the program's fate. (John Ellis Fick to Paul H. Douglas, 15 May 1959, box 85, Douglas Papers; Mary Jane Morris to ABC, 30 April 1959, Mortimer Weinbach to Morris, 20 May 1959, invoice 72-A-1986, box 22, FCC Records, GSA).

22 Anderson, "Fraudulence in Television," 7, 21-22, 50, 34-37, 108-9, 119-21, 627, 634; Foreman, *The Hot Half Hour*, 26, 67-68, 82, 127; Dan Wakefield, "The Fabulous Seat Box," *Nation* (30 March 1957), 269-72; *Time* (11 Feb. 1958), 44-46, 49; Edward Kletter to Thomas McAvity, 25 Oct. 1956, and memorandum, Richard A.R. Pinkham to George Matson, 20 Feb. 1957, box 141, NBC Records; *New York Times*, 17 Feb. 1957; *Television Magazine* (Nov. 1955), 50; Tedlow, "Intellect on Television," 483-87; Andrew Tobias, *Fire and Ice: The Story of Charles Revson* (New York, 1976), ch. 11. Transcripts of telecasts of two programs, "Dotto" and "Twenty-One," are reprinted in House Commerce Committee, *Investigation of Television Quiz Shows*, 16-22, 37-43, 65-71, 78-84, 264-67, 280-82, 290-96.

23 House Commerce Committee, *Investigation of Television Quiz Shows*, 902; Gordon Cotler, "The Question about the Quiz Shows," *New York Times Magazine* (1 Dec. 1957), 90; address by Emanuel Celler, 24 Sept. 1957, box 487, Celler Papers.

24 Vidal, "See It Later," 27; Goodman Ace, "The $64,000 Answer," *Saturday Review* (13 Aug. 1955), 23.

25 Fred Silverman, "An Analysis of ABC Television Network Programming: February, 1953 to October, 1959" (M.A.

thesis, Ohio State Univ., 1959), 150-53; *Sponsor* (3 Nov. 1956), 11; docket 12782, vol. 9, *Proceedings*, vol. 19, p. 3765, FCC Records, Dockets Room, FCC.

26 Adult Westerns also tended to be longer, averaging 30 to 60 minutes rather than 15 to 30. Charles W. Day, "The Television Adult Western: A Pilot Study" (M.A. thesis, Univ. of Chicago, 1958), ch. 1; "The Reminiscences of Richard Boone" (1959), COHC, 591.

27 *San Francisco Chronicle*, 1 Oct. 1957.

28 *Time* (30 March 1959), 60.

29 Ibid., 52-53. See also Cunningham and Walsh, Inc., *The First Decade of Television in Videotown, 1948-1957* (New York, 1957), 2; *Columbus Dispatch*, 29 Sept. 1955; "The Reminiscences of Richard Boone," COHC, 586-88.

30 Groucho Marx to Bergen Evans, 27 Feb. 1959, box 1, Marx Papers.

31 *San Francisco Chronicle*, 6 Oct. 1959.

32 *Business Week* (29 June 1957), 108, 114; *Variety* (7 Nov. 1962), 20; docket 12782, vol. 2, *Proceedings*, vol. 6, pp. 855-56, FCC Records, Dockets Room, FCC; Senate Judiciary Committee, *Juvenile Delinquency*, hearings, 87th Cong., 1st sess., 1961, p. 2305; memorandum re interview with representatives of S.C. Johnson and Son, Inc., 6 Sept. 1961, Office of Network Study, invoice 72-A-1986, box 4, FCC Records, GSA; *New York Times*, 1 March 1957; Bob Stahl, "Five Who Are Taking a Giant Step at NBC," *TV Guide* (10 Oct. 1959), 10; U.S. Congress, House of Representatives, Select Committee on Small Business, *Activities of Regulatory and Enforcement Agencies Relating to Small Business*, 496-98, 505, 596-97. The mercurial attitudes of NBC's president, Robert Kintner, toward the public taste are displayed in *The Chameleons*, a novel by David Levy, a fired underling, esp. 11, 40-41, 48.

33 Memorandum to files, Louis G. Cowan, c. Nov. 1959, Cowan Papers. The ratio of such action programming from NBC was 47 percent, from ABC, 61 percent.

34 *New York Times*, 14 July 1957; *Broadcasting Yearbook 1963* (Washington, D.C., 1963), 20; *Variety* (15 June 1960), 23.

35 *San Francisco Chronicle*, 1 Oct. 1958.

36 *New York Herald Tribune*, 16 Feb. 1959. See also Frank

Pierson, "The Dying TV Drama," *New Republic* (2 Feb. 1959), 22; Rod Serling, "TV in the Can vs. TV in the Flesh," *New York Times Magazine* (24 Nov. 1957), p 54; docket 12782, vol. 14, *Proceedings*, vol. 37, p. 5465, vol. 38, p. 5832, vol. 16, *Proceedings*, vol. 43. pp. 6499-500, FCC Records, Dockets Room, FCC; Kay Gardella, *New York Daily News*, 20 Aug. 1980.

37   Tino Balio, ed., *The American Film Industry* (Madison, 1976), 320-22.

38   Serling, "TV in the Can," 47.

39   "It Was New and We Were Very Innocent," *TV Guide* (22 Sept. 1973), 7.

40   Docket 12782, vol. 14, *Proceedings*, vol. 37, pp. 5660-661, 5671, vol. 15, *Proceedings*, vol. 42, pp. 6418, 6558, FCC Records, Dockets Room, FCC. See also Alexander King, "Paradise Mislaid," *Show Business Illustrated* (5 Sept. 1961), 68; *Los Angeles Times*, 4 Oct. 1960.

41   Mannes, "The TV Pattern," 19; "Exit Mr. Murrow," *Commonweal* (13 March 1959), 613-14.

42   Smith, "TV: The Light That Failed," 78-81. For reactions to Smith's article, see *Sponsor* (29 Nov. 1958), 33-35, 77; Gilbert Seldes, "Is Luce for Light?" *Saturday Review* (20 Dec. 1958), 33; CBS, *Annual Report* (1958), 20.

43   Memorandum re interview with representatives of Alcoa, 23 Aug. 1961, Office of Network Study, invoice 72-A-1986, box 5, FCC Records, GSA; *Variety* (27 July 1955), 23 (9 July 1958), 23; Eric Sevareid to Edwin P. Hoyt, 2 June 1958, box A-3, Sevareid Papers; *Broadcasting* (3 Feb. 1958), 54.

44   *New York Herald Tribune*, 11 July 1958; *Variety* (27 July 1955), 23; Marquis Childs, "Crisis in Communication," *Nieman Reports* 10 (July 1956), 3-5.

45   Handwritten notes of meeting, 7 Oct. 1958, Office of Network Study, invoice 72-A-1986, box 15, FCC Records, GSA.

46   Frank Stanton to Magnuson, 3 Dec. 1958, ibid., box 13; John F. Kennedy to Louis Cowan, 16 July 1958, box 3, Theodore Sorensen Papers.

47   Text of address in box 7-B-25, Murrow Papers. The speech was reprinted in *The Reporter* (13 Nov. 1958), 32-36, and *TV Guide* (13 Dec. 1958), 22-27.

48   House Commerce Committee, *Investigation of Television*

Quiz Shows, 624-30; *Washington Star*, 3 Nov. 1959; *Newsweek* (9 Nov. 1959), 69-70; *New York Herald Tribune*, 5 Nov. 1959; *Columbus Dispatch*, 8 Nov. 1959; George Sokolsky, *Columbus Dispatch*, 2 Nov. 1959.

49 Robert Lewis Shayon, "What Would You Do?" *Saturday Review* (8 June 1957), 24; Hans J. Morgenthau, "Reaction to the Van Doren Reaction," *New York Times Magazine* (22 Nov. 1959), 106.

50 *Broadcasting* (9 Nov. 1959), 37. Samples of editorial reaction are reprinted in the *Washington Star*, 8 Nov. 1959. See also the *Chicago American*, 12 Oct. 1959; Dalton Trumbo, "Hail, Blithe Spirit," *Nation* (24 Oct. 1959), 243-46; *Washington Star*, 3 Nov. 1959, 6 Nov. 1959; *Columbus Dispatch*, 3 Nov. 1959; *Christian Science Monitor*, 7 Nov. 1959; Ralph McGill, *Atlanta Constitution*, 8 Nov. 1959; *Life* (16 Nov. 1959), 36, 106; *Television Digest* (9 Nov. 1959), 7, (16 Nov. 1959), 8; Paul H. Douglas to Earl II. Hill, 17 Nov. 1959, box 434, Douglas Papers; Chester Bowles to Roscoe Drummond, 24 Nov. 1959, pt. 5, ser. 2, box 232, Bowles Papers; speech by Adlai E. Stevenson, 8 Dec. 1959, box 775, Stevenson Papers; Renata Adler, "Reflections on Political Scandal," *New York Review of Books* (8 Dec. 1977), 20.

51 *New York Herald Tribune*, 27 Oct. 1959.

52 Ibid., 21 Oct. 1959.

53 *St. Louis Post-Dispatch*, 3 Nov. 1959.

54 *New Republic* (9 Nov. 1959), 6; *Sponsor* (17 Oct. 1959), 77; Morris L. Ernst to Philip Cortney, 5 Jan. 1960, box 542, Ernst Papers; *Television Digest* (19 Oct. 1959), 5; *Television Age* (16 Nov. 1959), 4; *Variety* (18 Nov. 1959), 46; *Broadcasting* (9 Nov. 1959), 60; Crosby, "What You Can Do," 75; *Newsweek* (19 Oct. 1959), 29; *Life* (26 Oct. 1959), 32; address by Robert E. Lee, 22 Nov. 1959, copy in General Files 41-A(2), box 380, pp. 2-3, Eisenhower Papers.

55 E.J. Kahn, Jr., *Jock: The Life and Times of John Hay Whitney* (New York, 1981), 269-70.

56 Telegram, Boy Wood to Eisenhower, 19 Nov. 1959, W.A. Joy to Eisenhower, 29 Dec. 1959, General Files 129-A-2, box 1003, Eisenhower Papers.

57 Speech by Richard A. Salant, 15 March 1960, copy in file 12-VI-A, Broadcast Pioneers Library, Washington, D.C.

58   *The Public Papers of the President; Dwight D. Eisenhower
     1959* (Washington, D.C., 1960), 738, 769, 771; *New York
     Herald Tribune,* 23 Oct. 1959; *Broadcasting* (26 Oct. 1959),
     36; *Christian Science Monitor,* 5 Nov. 1959. Privately,
     Eisenhower regarded Van Doren as the "goat" of the in-
     dustry (Ann C. Whitman Diary, 7 Nov. 1959, box 11, Whit-
     man Papers).

59   *Television Digest* (2 Nov. 1959),4 (16 Nov. 1959), 8.

60   *Christian Science Monitor,* 6 Nov. 1959.

61   House Commerce Committee, *Investigation of Television
     Quiz Shows,* 1046.

62   Ibid., 1127.

63   Ibid.

64   Docket 12782, vol. 4, *Proceedings,* vol. 3, p. 693, FCC
     Records, Dockets Room, FCC.

65   Address by Fairfax M. Cone, 16 Feb. 1960, p. 11, box 133,
     Cone Papers.

66   Memorandum to files, Cowan, 14 Nov. 1959, Cowan Papers.

67   *Broadcasting,* 14 Dec. 1959, 46-47. The House committee
     counsel and a historian who later investigated Cowan's role
     both supported his claim that the fix occurred after he left as
     producer of "The $64,000 Question." See ibid., 90; *Television
     Digest* (19 Oct. 1959), 5; Anderson, "Fraudulence in Televi-
     sion," 220. On Aubrey, see *Forbes* (15 Jan. 1964), 22-23;
     Miller and Rhodes, *Only You, Dick Darling!;* Keefe Brasselle,
     The Cannibals (New York, 1968).

68   Paul Goodman, *Growing Up Absurd: Problems of Youth in
     the Organized Society* (New York, 1960), 224. Compare his
     "The Chance for Popular Culture," *Poetry* (June 1949),
     157-65.

69   Fuess, "Retreat from Excellence," 21-23. See also Jeffries,
     "The 'Quest for National Purpose' of 1960."

70   Robert Lewis Shayon, "Beaver's Booboo," *Saturday Review*
     (1 Feb. 1958), 26.

71   Spock to Kennedy, 4 March 1960, Pre-Presidential Papers,
     box 748, Kennedy Papers. Like sentiments are expressed in
     an address by William Benton, "Television—A Prescription,"
     11 April 1960, copy in box 3-C-2, Murrow Papers.

72   "The Quality of American Culture," in *Goals for Americans,*
     127, 132, 133, 146.

73   Eric F. Goldman, "What Is Prosperity Doing to Our Political
     Parties?" 10; Goldman interview with author; Sternsher,
     "Liberalism in the Fifties"; Oscar Handlin, "Payroll Prosperi-
     ty," *Atlantic* (Feb. 1953), 29-33.
74   Shils, "Daydreams and Nightmares."
75   Schlesinger, "Where Does the Liberal Go from Here?" *New
     York Times Magazine* (4 Aug. 1957), 36-37. See also his
     "Challenge of Abundance"; *The Vital Center*, xiv-xv;
     Neuchterlein, "Arthur M. Schlesinger, Jr.," 18-19; John
     Bartlow Martin, *Adlai Stevenson and the World* (Garden Ci-
     ty, N.Y, 1978), 197-98.
76   Arthur M. Schlesinger, Jr., "Notes on a National Cultural
     Policy," *Daedalus* 89 (Spring 1960), 394-400; idem, "How
     Television Can Meet Its Responsibilities," *TV Guide* (12
     Dec. 1959), 24-27.

CHAPTER 3

1   Gilbert Seldes, "Indignation Is Not Enough," *Saturday
    Review* (16 Aug. 1958), 25; idem, "Bad Manners," 28; James
    M. Landis, "Pressures Tend to Develop," *New York Herald
    Tribune*, 16 March 1958; Schwartz, "Antitrust and the FCC,"
    754; Westin, "Inquiry into Our Watchdog Agencies," 21,
    119-20, 124.
2   Sec Doerfer's remarks on the 40th anniversary of the FCC,
    Federal Communications Bar Journal 27, no. 2 (1974),
    142-45; Speech by Doerfer, "Community Antenna Systems,"
    10 June 1954, Doerfer Papers; House Commerce Committee,
    Subscription Television, 84, 97, 114; ibid., *Investigation of
    Television Quiz Shows*, 523; Excerpts from Doerfer's ad-
    dresses, undated memorandum, c. Nov. 1959, box 8, Avery
    Papers; *New York Herald Tribune*, 6 Nov. 1957.
3   Coase, "Evaluation of Public Policy"; *Broadcasting* (4 Jan.
    1965), 37; Levin, *Fact and Fancy*; Noll, Peck, and McGowan,
    Economic Aspects; Stanley M. Besen, "Deregulating
    Telecommunications," *Regulation* 2 (March/April 1978),
    30-36; Ronald H. Coase, "Should the Federal Communica-
    tions Commission Be Abolished?" in Bernard H. Siegan, ed.,
    Regulation, Economics, and the Law (Lexington, Mass.,
    1979), 46.

4   Le Duc, *Cable Television*, chs. 4-5.
5   Summaries of Allocation Proceedings, 19, 25, 26 Oct. 1950, box 114, Du Mont Laboratories Records; Speeches by Robert F. Jones, 1 May 1952 and 22 May 1952, box 122, ibid.; Robert Lewis Shayon to William Benton, 14 April 1951, box 10, Shayon Papers.
6   Address by George E. Sterling, 13 June 1952, copy in box 122, Du Mont Laboratories Records; Senate Commerce Committee, *Status of UHF and Multiple Ownership of TV Stations*, 13, 230-31, 321; Wayne Coy to Ed Johnson, c. Feb. 1949, reprinted in *RR* 2 (1949), 125-38; FCC, *Reports and Orders* 41 (1948), 208; Douglas William Webbink, "The All-Channel Receiver Law and the Future of Ultra-High Frequency Television" (Ph.D. diss., Duke Univ., 1968), 21.
7   Senate Commerce Committee, *Television Network Regulation and the UHF Problem*, memorandum prepared by Harry M. Plotkin, special counsel, 84th Cong., 1st sess., 1955, p. 22; House Commerce Committee, *Investigation of Regulatory Commissions*, 2401; Senate Commerce Committees, *Status of UHF*, 449-50, 639, 924; John Floyd Wellman, "Storer Broadcasting Company—Its History, Organization, and Operation" (Ph.D. diss., Univ. of Michigan, 1973), 40-42; Julian F. Skinnel to Richard B. Rawls, 11 Nov. 1953, "exhibit" by John Curtis, ABC research department, 11 May 1954; memorandum, Malcolm B. Laing to Ernest Lee Jahncke, 18 May 1955; Mortimer Weinbach to Mary Jane Morris, 28 Jan. 1958, invoice 72-A-1986, box 21, FCC Records, GSA; Magnuson to Kennedy, 16 July 1956, Pre-Presidential Papers, box 526, Kennedy Papers. In addition, set manufacturers were accused of doing nothing to improve UHF tuners. Norwood J. Patterson to Andrew F. Schoeppel, 16 March 1956, Schoeppel Papers, KSHS.
8   Robert B. Glynn, "Public Policy and Broadcasting," in Elliott, *Television's Impact*, 77; "The Reminiscences of Joseph Rauh, Jr." (1967), FLOHC, 3; Webbink, "The All-Channel Receiver Law," 36, 45, 50.
9   Senate Commerce Committee, *The Television Inquiry*, hearings, 27-28, FCC, *Reports and Orders* 41 (1955), 739, 745n, 748; docket 11333, *Proceedings*, vol. 2, pp. 358, 362, 924, FCC Records, NA; FCC, *Annual Report* (1955), 96; Glynn "Public

Policy," 86.

10 Communications Act, section 307(b); transcript of Report and Order, 26 June 1956, p. 6, and Doerfer dissent, "Report and Order," 26 June 1956, docket 11532, vol. 13, invoice 173-75-9, FCC Records, GSA; *Broadcasting* (10 Oct. 1955), 27, (14 Nov. 1955), 27, (26 Feb. 1979), 78; House Judiciary Committee, *Monopoly Problems in Regulated Industries*, 3110, 5034.

11 Reply comments, Zenith and Teco., Inc., 9 Sept. 1955, docket 11279, p. 30, FCC Records, NA; Ted Leetzell to Paul H. Douglas, 2 July 1953, box 82, Douglas Papers; House Commerce Committees, *Subscription Television*, 199ff, 272, 277; *Newsweek* (11 Jan. 1954), 74-75.

12 Morris Ernst to Emanuel Celler, 13 Jan. 1958, box 512, Celler Papers. Pay television's advocates included former President Truman and William L. White, son of the famous Kansas publisher. Truman to Clayton Fritchey, 21 May 1958, Post-Presidential Files, box 23, Truman Papers; W.L. White, "Why Can't We Have Pay TV?" *Reader's Digest* (Nov. 1958), 57-61.

13 FCC, report and order, 14 Dec. 1955, docket 11279; George McConnaughey to Andrew W. Schoeppel, 28 Jan. 1955, Schoeppel Papers, KSHS; *Washington Star*, 13 March 1955.

14 John Chamberlain, "Pay-As-You-See-TV?" *Barron's* (2 May 1955), 24.

15 *Television Digest* (18 Jan. 1958), 1-2; Robert E. Lee, "Let's Give the Public a Chance at Paid TV," *Look* (20 March 1956), 104.

16 Address by Robert W. Sarnoff, 23 Oct. 1957, and transcript of telecast of "See It Now," 14 June 1955, copies in box 487, Celler Papers; *Newsweek* (28 Feb. 1955), 74; House Commerce Committee, *Subscription Television*, 56-57. On the industry's anti-pay TV efforts, see E.F. McDonald to John S. Knight, 21 March 1958, copy in box 488, Celler Papers; press release, Zenith, Inc., 20 Feb. 1958, copy in box 29, Belcher Papers; *Charlotte Observer*, 5 Feb. 1958, clipping in Schoeppel Papers, KSHS; Simmons, *The Fairness Doctrine*, 45-46.

17 Undated worksheet, c. Feb. 1958, box 29, Belcher Papers; William Langer to Norris Cotton, 3 Dec. 1957, box 42, Cotton Papers; Irving Kolodin, "Subscription TV? Yes: 74%

Saturday Review (28 May 1955), 38-39.

18   Mrs. P. Thibeault to Alexander H. Wiley, 26 Jan. 1958, Mrs. K. LaPointe to Wiley, 25 Jan. 1958, box 3-91-8, Wiley Papers; Harold L. Walker to John F. Kennedy, 27 July 1957, Pre-Presidential Papers, box 682, Kennedy Papers.

19   Martin Schneider to CBS Television, 2 Feb. 1958, copy in group 12, folder 4-2-45, Harris Papers; Ralph E. Pokriefke to Paul H. Douglas, 1 June 1955, box 83, Douglas Papers.

20   House Commerce Committee, *Subscription Television*, 84; editorial, *Cleveland Plain Dealer*, 24 Jan. 1958.

21   *Broadcasting* (3 March 1958), 62; Horton, *To Pay or Not To Pay*, 10ff; *New York Times*, 2 March 1958. Senator Cotton reported a nearly unanimous opposition to further pay television experiments (Cotton to Mr. and Mrs. William H. Bradford, 4 April 1958, box 42, Cotton Papers).

22   Baughman, " 'The Strange Birth of *CBS Reports*,' " 27-38.

23   Outline for advertising campaign, n.d., ser. B-13, box 10, NBC Records; Stahl, "Five Who Are Taking a Giant Step"; *TV Guide* (21 Nov. 1959), 21-23.

24   Address by Stanton, "A New Freedom—A New Responsibility," 16 Oct. 1959, copies of text in Stanton File, Murrow Papers; *Broadcasting* (19 Oct. 1959), 33 (26 Oct. 1959), 44.

25   *Washington Star*, 17 Oct. 1959; *Business Week* (7 Nov. 1959), 29; House Commerce Committee, *Investigation of Television Quiz Shows*, 1058.

26   *New York Herald Tribune*, 17 Oct. 1959; House Commerce Committee, *Investigation of Television Quiz Shows*, 1091, 1111; George Sokolsky, *Columbus Dispatch*, 2 Nov. 1959.

27   *The Public Papers of the President; Dwight D. Eisenhower 1959* (Washington, D.C., 1960), 738, 769, 771; Eisenhower to William D. Kerr, 9 Nov. 1959, OF 250-D, box 915, Eisenhower Papers; *New York Herald Tribune*, 23 Oct. 1959; *Broadcasting* (26 Oct. 1959), 36; *Christian Science Monitor*, 5 Nov. 1959.

28   *Columbus Dispatch*, 8 Nov. 1959.

29   *Christian Science Monitor*, 3 Nov. 1959; *Broadcasting* (9 Nov. 1959), 60.

30   *Variety* (11 Nov. 1959), 30. See also *New York Journal-American*, 9 Nov. 1959; *St. Louis Post-Dispatch* (8 Nov. 1959), B-1; *Wall Street Journal*, 10 Nov. 1959.

31 House Commerce Committee, *Investigation of Television Quiz Shows*, 510-12, 520, 522, 524-25, 538-39; *U.S. News and World Report* (26 Oct. 199), 47; House Commerce Committee, Subcommittee on Legislative Oversight, *Responsibilities of Broadcast Licensees*, 671, 677-79, 713, 714; Doerfer to Henry McPhee, 22 Oct. 1959, General Files, 129-A-2, box 1003, Eisenhower Papers; Thomas, "The Federal Communications Commission"; memorandum, "re. possible courses of action resulting from quiz inquiry," 15 Nov. 1959, box 542, Ernst Papers; *FCC v. ABC, Inc.*, 347 U.S. (1954), 284.

32 Docket 12782, vol. 4, *Proceedings*, vol. 3, p. 627, FCC Records, Dockets Room, FCC.

33 *New Republic*, (19 Oct. 1959), 2. See also Jack Gould, "Forgotten Clues to the TV Crisis," *New York Times Magazine* (13 Dec. 1959), 89; *Chicago American*, 12 Oct. 1959.

34 Jack C. O'Brian, "Networks Must Clean House, or Congress Will," *TV Guide* (7 Nov. 1959), 7; House Commerce Committee, *Investigation of Television Quiz Shows*, 570; docket 12782, vol. 4, *Proceedings*, vol. 3, pp. 627, 630, FCC Records, Dockets Room, FCC.

35 *Consumer Reports* (Jan. 1960) 9.

36 Address by Doerfer, 20 Nov. 1959, Doerfer Papers.

37 *Variety* (25 Nov. 1959), 32.

38 Ibid. (2 Dec. 1959), 1, and (9 Dec. 1959), 26, 48; *Broadcasting* (30 Nov. 1959), 26; Groucho Marx to Norman Krasna, 7 Dec. 1959, Marx Papers.

39 Jim [Thomson] to [Chester Bowles], [25? Oct. 1959], box 232, Bowles Papers. Robert Lee Bailey, "Examination of Prime Time Network Television Special Programs" (Ph.D. diss., Univ. of Wisconsin, 1967), 29-30, 42, 55, 75, carefully measures the number of news programs—scheduled and unscheduled—aired over the three networks. See also advertisements for TV coverage of Eisenhower's India trip in *New York Times*, 12 Dec. 1959; Mannes, *Who Owns the Air?* foreword; Mehling, *The Great Time Killer*, 37; docket 12782, vol. 9, *Proceedings*, vol. 19, pp. 3704-706, FCC Records, Dockets Room, FCC; Small, *To Kill a Messenger*, 19; Carroll, "Economic Influences," 422.

40   Quoted in Thomas B. Morgan, "Crisis, Conflict, and Change in TV News," *Look* (7 Nov. 1961), 51. See also Mott, "A Twentieth Century Monster," 60; Torre, *Don't Quote Me,* 180.

41   Justice Dept., *Report to the President by the Attorney General on Deceptive Practices in Broadcasting Media,* esp. iv-v, 11-12, 25-27, 30, 31; Eisenhower to Rogers, 31 Dec. 1959, OF, 250-D, Box 915, Eisenhower Papers; *New York Herald Tribune,* 1 Jan. 1960; *Television Digest* (2 Nov. 1959), 2-3; *Advertising Age* (11 Jan. 1960), 38.

42   Rogers's study also had a powder blue cover. *Broadcasting* (11 Jan. 1960), 46.

43   Hoover to Doerfer, 4 Jan. 1960, Post-Presidential Subject File, box 138, Hoover Papers, HHL.

44   House Commerce Committee, Subcommittee on Legislative Oversight, *Interim Report,* esp. 38-39; *New York Times,* 24 March 1960.

45   Rosel Hyde, interview with Martin Mayer, c. 1969, notes in box 65, Mayer Papers.

46   *Broadcasting* (18 Jan. 1960), 9, 46, 130, and (25 Jan. 1960), 70-71; *New York Times,* 15, 20, 21, 22, and 23 Jan. 1960; address by Fairfax M. Cone, 16 Feb. 1960, p. 13, box 133, Cone Papers; Kintner, "Television and the World of Politics," 130-31; Martin Mayer, "Keep Out. This Means You!" *TV Guide* (26 Nov. 1966), 18; docket 12782, vol. 4, *Proceedings,* vol. 3, pp. 598, 609; ibid., vol. 9, *Proceedings,* vol. 18, pp. 3488ff, vol. 19, p. 3706; ibid., vol. 19, *Proceedings,* vol. 56, pp. 8589-90, 8630.

47   *New York Herald Tribune,* 3 and 4 March 1960; Rivers, *The Opinionmakers,* 148.

48   Doerfer to INSPIRE, 22 June 1973; Doerfer; notes of interview with Paul Porter, 10 May 1973, INSPIRE Papers; Ann C. Whitman Diary, 9 March 1960, box 11, Whitman Papers; *Broadcasting* (7 March 1960), 60-61; *New York Herald Tribune,* 6 March 1960; *Television Digest* (7 March 1960), 7-8 (14 March 1960), 2-3; *Sponsor* (5 March 1960), 63; Rosel Hyde, interview with Sterling Quinlan, Dec. 1972, box 12, Quinlan Papers; *Broadcasting* (14 March 1960), 31-34; Goodman, *All Honorable Men,* 188-89, 192-93; Frier, *Conflict of Interest,* 183-86; Senate Commerce Committee, *Appointments to the*

Regulatory Agencies, 137-39; House Commerce Committee, *Investigation of Regulatory Commissions* 720-23.

49 *New York Post,* 3 March 1958. See also *Baltimore Sun,* 4, 5, and 8 March 1960; transcript of editorial, WTOP, copy in group 12, box 10-4-33, Harris Papers; Paul N. Pfeiffer, "The Regulatory Agencies," manuscript, box 97, Democratic National Committee Records.

50 Senate Commerce Committee, *Appointments to the Regulatory Agencies,* 95-98, 140; *Television Digest* (14 March 1960), 2-3; *Television Magazine* (July 1960), 82.

51 *Sponsor* (19 March 1960), 55; *Advertising Age* (14 March 1960), 1, 123.

52 "Some Current Problems in Broadcast Regulation," *Federal Communications Bar Journal* 17, no. 2 (1960), 76-82.

53 James C. Hagerty to Clare Boothe Luce, 17 March 1960, General Files 129-A-2, box 1005, Eisenhower Papers.

54 *RR* 20 (1960), 1901; Ford, "The Meaning of the 'Public Interest.' "

55 Robert Lewis Shayon, "The Coming Breakthrough in TV Channels," *Saturday Review* (10 Dec. 1960), 41, 50; Ford, interview with author, 19 June 1978.

56 Ford, interview with author, 19 June 1978; *Television Digest* (7 March 1960), 10; *Variety* (28 Sept. 1960), 32; memorandum, Cowgill to Commission, 16 Jan. 1961, invoice 67-A-433, box 226, FCC Records, GSA; *TV Guide* (11 March 1961), A-7.

57 Ford, interview with author, 19 June 1978; Ford to author, 20 Feb. 1980.

58 *Broadcasting* (11 April 1960), 5.

59 *New York Times,* 28 and 29 June 1960; Oren Harris to author, 23 April 1979, Alexander Wiley to Sprague Vonier, 17 April 1960, Leonard Goldenson to Wiley, 3 March 1960, box 2-25, Wiley Papers.

60 *Congressional Quarterly Almanac, 1960* (Washington, D.C., 1961), 356, 360-61; Charles J. McKerns and Charles J. Robertson, "Disciplinary Powers under the Communications Act Amendments of 1960," 5-9; John Pastore to Norris Cotton, 11 Aug. 1960, Patrick Malin to Cotton, 9 Aug. 1960, box 45, Cotton Papers; *Washington Post,* 29 June 1960; *Providence Journal,* 13 Aug. 1960, clipping, Pastore Papers.

61   Norris Cotton to Harry H. Gilmanton, 3 March 1960, Cotton to Mrs. Philip Guyotte, 4 April 1960, box 45, Cotton Papers; *Congressional Record*, vol. 106, pt. 11, 86th Cong., 2d sess., 27 June 1960, pp. 14596, 14603.

62   *Broadcasting* (7 Jan. 1957), 46, 48; Norris Cotton to Harry H. Gilmanton; John Taber to John V. Beamer, 20 Aug. 1958, box 3, Taber Papers, Cornell University. Speaker Rayburn would not dine with the Lyndon Johnsons unless they promised not to turn on their TV set. Alfred Steinberg, *Sam Rayburn: A Biography* (New York, 1975), 297.

63   Whitfield, "The 1950's."

64   Postcard, Mrs. R.B. Simons to John Fischer, Dec. 1959, 1968 addition, box 1, Fischer Papers; Lippmann to Fischer, 15 Dec. 1959, box 70, Lippmann Papers. Few viewers had moral objections to the deceits, and subsequently many listed popular quiz programs like "Twenty-One" as among those they missed most. Steiner, *The People Look at Television*, 380; Sultzer and Johnson, "Attitudes towards Deception."

65   Jack Hellman, *Variety*, 28 Jan. 1960, clipping in box 2, Max Wylie Papers.

66   Letters to *TV Guide* (21 Nov. 1959), A-29; Lang, "Van Doren as Victim"; *Congressional Record*, vol. 106, pt. 11, 86th Cong. 2d sess., 24 June 1960, p. 14311; docket 12782, vol. 4, *Proceedings*, vol. 3, p. 5353, FCC Records, Dockets Room, FCC. Of the collections sampled from members of Congress, in almost every case, few letters protesting the quiz fix could be located, although there were many regarding pay TV and other matters.

67   *Business Week* (7 Nov. 1959), 29; *New York Times*, 23 Oct. 1960; Torre, *Don't Quote Me*, 191-92; *Historical Statistics of the United States, Colonial Times to 1970*, 2 vols. (Washington, D.C. 1975), II:796; Constituent newsletter, 3 Feb. 1960, box 241, Bowles Papers.

68   *New York Times*, 11 Nov. 1959. See also the interview with Oren Harris in *Television Digest* (30 Nov. 1959), 3.

69   *Sponsor* (8 May 1960), 34-35 (25 April 1960), 30-31; Bailey, "Examination of Prime Time," 77; *Printer's Ink* (13 Jan. 1961), 63; Senate Commerce Committee, *Presidential Broadcasting Act*, 289-90.

70   AB-UP, *Annual Report* (1959), 13; *Television Digest* (20 Feb.

1961), 4; Edgar Peterson to Robert Lewis Shayon, 15 and 26 July 1960, box 10, Shayon Papers.

71 *Broadcasting* (18 Sept. 1961), 34; *Cleveland Press*, 29 Sept. 1960; Robert Lewis Shayon, "Mr. Percy's Touch for Television," *Saturday Review* (8 Oct. 1960), 61-62.

72 *Variety* (22 March 1961), 43; docket 12782, vol. 19, *Proceedings*, vol. 56, pp. 8630, FCC Records, Dockets Room, FCC. Albert R. Kroeger, "You Needn't Go Broke on Public Affairs," *Television Magazine* (Jan. 1961), 86-88; *Printer's Ink* (10 March 1961), 21-23, 53.

73 Adlai Stevenson receives much of the credit for Monroney's proposal; apparently, Monroney and Stevenson coordinated their campaign for forcing free air time. Marquis Childs, *Washington Post*, 29 April 1960; Monroney to Stevenson, 2 Jan. 1961, box 8, Monroney Papers; Senate Commerce Committee, *Presidential Broadcasting Act*, 2-26; John Bartlow Martin, *Stevenson and the World*, 498; address by Richard Salant, 15 March 1960, file 12-VI-A, Broadcast Pioneers Library, Washington, D.C.

74 Address by Robert W. Sarnoff, 21 April 1960, copy in box 394, Democratic National Committee Records; Senate Commerce Committee, *Presidential Broadcasting Act*, 182, 229ff, 285-89.

75 *Broadcasting* (8 Aug. 1961), 70; *TV Guide* (3 Sept. 1960), A-1; Douglass Cater, *Power in Washington: A Critical Look at Today's Struggle to Govern in the Nation's Capital*, paper ed. (New York, 1964), 56-57; "The Reminiscences of J. Leonard Reinsch" (1966), Oral History, JFKL, 35; statement by Reinsch, 31 Aug. 1960, box 1051, Democractic National Committee Records.

76 *Television Magazine* (Jan. 1961), 75; *Congressional Quarterly Almanac, 1960*, 291.

77 Kennedy to Robert Sarnoff, 29 July 1960, Pre-Presidential Papers, box 1051, Kennedy Papers; Sarnoff to Kennedy, 11 Aug. 1960, box 1051, Democratic National Committee Records; Diamond, *The Tin Kazoo*, 232-34.

78 *Public Papers of Dwight D. Eisenhower 1959*, 648.

79 William D. Patterson, "SR's Businessman of the Year," *Saturday Review* (21 Jan. 1961), 46, 101; Speech by Stanton, 3 Dec. 1960, box 1051, Pre-Presidential Papers, Kennedy

Papers. See also the editorials in *Des Moines Register*, 27 Sept. 1960, and *Baltimore Sun*, 28 Sept. 1960; Gilbert Harrison to Joseph Harsch, 13 Oct. 1960, 1968 addition, box 2, Harsch Papers; Small, *To Kill A Messenger*, 178-88; *Los Angeles Times*, 5 Oct. 1960.

80   *Variety* (4 Jan. 1961), p 87. See also John Crosby, *New York Herald Tribune*, 4 Jan. 1960.

81   *Time* (31 March 1961), 36.

82   Robert Larka, "Television's Private Eye: An Examination of Twenty Years of a Particular Genre, 1949-1969" (Ph.D. diss., Ohio Univ., 1973), 130, 137; Cecil Smith, *Los Angeles Times*, 3 Oct. 1960; *Television Age* (8 Feb. 1960), 26-29, 72; Oscar Katz, interview with Martin Mayer, CBS-TV, n.d., notes in box 68, Mayer Papers.

83   *TV Guide* (7 Nov. 1959), A-2; *Variety* (15 June 1960), p 23.

84   *New York Times*, 26 June 1960; *Variety* (15 June 1960), p 23.

85   *Sponsor* (12 March 1960), 35.

86   *Television Magazine* (July 1960), 50.

87   *Broadcasting* (25 July 1960), 27-38.

88   *New York Times*, 23 Oct. 1960; *Variety* (Jan. 1961), p 87.

89   Order, 23 Feb. 1961, docket 13814, vol. 5, FCC Records, NA; Emanuel Celler to Ford, 26 Oct. 1960, box 513, Celler Papers.

90   *RR* 20 (1960), 1568; *Broadcasting* (19 Sept. 1960), 29-30 (3 July 1961), 46; Emanuel Celler to Robert A. Bicks, 3 June 1960, Bicks to Celler, 17 Aug. 1960, file 60-211-62, sec. 6, Justice Dept. Records; *Variety* (28 Sept. 1960), 32.

91   Clara S. Logan to James M. Landis, 25 Nov. 1960, box 2, Landis Papers, JFKL; *New York Times*, 1 April 1962.

92   Ritchie, *James M. Landis*, 176-77; Louis L. Jaffe, "James Landis and the Administrative Process"; Landis to Herbert Hoover, 24 Jan. 1949, box 101, Landis Papers, LC; Victor S. Navasky, *Kennedy Justice* (New York, 1971), 378-80; Richard E. Neustadt, "Memorandum on Staffing the President-Elect," 30 Oct. 1960, Transition Files, box 1072, Kennedy Papers; "The Reminiscences of James M. Landis" (1963-64), COHC, 252-55, 587, 591, 604.

93   Senate Judiciary Committee, Subcommittee on Administrative Practice and Procedure, *Report on Regulatory Agencies to the President-Elect*, 8, 53-54; *Broadcasting* (9 Jan.

1961), 44; Harriet Van Horne, "Television Faces Tighter Controls," *Printer's Ink* (6 Jan. 1961), 41; "The Reminiscences of James M. Landis" (1963), COHC, 637-38; *U.S. News and World Report* (27 March 1961), 83-84; *Chicago Sun-Times*, 1 Jan. 1961; Marver H. Bernstein, "Independent Regulatory Agencies," 18-19.

94 *U.S. News and World Report* (27 March 1961), 85-86; *Television Digest* (8 Feb. 1961), 4; Interview with James M. Landis, *Meet the Press* 5 (22 Jan. 1961); *Television Digest* (16 Jan. 1961), 3.

95 Bookman, "Regulation by Elephant," 137.

CHAPTER 4

1 Schlesinger, "Government and the Arts," 74, 101; idem, "Notes on a National Cultural Policy," 394-400; Cater, "The Kennedy Look."

2 Schlesinger, interview with Richard Rovere, 27 June 1962, box 12, Rovere Papers; *Variety* (9 Jan. 1963), 1, 52; Paul B. Fay, Jr., *The Pleasure of His Company* (New York, 1966), 89-90; Walter T. Ridder, "Presidential Preferences," *Show Business Illustrated* (20 Sept. 1961), 26, 86.

3 *Des Moines Register*, 14 Nov. 1961.

4 Ibid., 13 Nov. 1961. The other programs were "Pete and Gladys," "Window on Main Street," "The Danny Thomas Show," "The Andy Griffith Show," "Hennesey," "I've Got a Secret," "87th Precinct," "Cheyenne," "Ben Casey," and "Surfside 6."

5 Kendrick, *Prime Time*, 365; *New York Times*, 2 and 6 July 1978; Fred Coe to Robert F. Kennedy, 23 Aug. 1960, Pre-Presidential Papers, box 993, John F. Kennedy Papers; remarks by John F. Kennedy, Westinghouse Broadcasting Co., 2d Conference on Public Service Programming, 6 March 1958, box 900, ibid.; Kennedy to Louis Cowan, 16 July 1958, box 3, Sorensen Papers.

6 Interview with Frank Stanton, 10 Nov. 1978; Sig Mickelson, *The Electric Mirror*, 204, 206-7; Kendrick, *Prime Time*, 450, 452-53. Many in and outside the Kennedy compound regarded the first TV debate as decisive in winning the election for JFK (*Television Digest* [6 Feb. 1961], 6; Salinger, *With Ken-*

nedy, 47).

7   *Variety* (28 Dec. 1960) 32; *Public Papers of John F. Kennedy, 1961* (Washington, D.C., 1962) 304-6, 367-70, 376-78. On such "crisis" rhetoric, see Fairlie, *The Kennedy Promise*, ch. 12; Miroff, *Pragmatic Illusions*; Kenneth S. Lynn, review of Garry Wills, *The Kennedy Imprisonment*, in *American Spectator* (June 1982), 34.

8   Quoted in Schlesinger, *A Thousand Days*, 64. See also the Democratic party's 1960 platform, reprinted in *Congressional Quarterly Almanac, 1960*, 786, for more specific regulatory reforms (an end to ex parte contacts, more efficient procedures, and clear delineation of the public interest); and address by James M. Landis, 9 Nov. 1961, box 148, Landis Papers, LC.

9   Schlesinger, *A Thousand Days*, 145; *New York Herald Tribune*, 25 Dec. 1960.

10   Schwartz, "Comparative Television," 664-65; James M. Landis, *New York Herald Tribune*, 16 March 1958.

11   Kennedy was under pressure to name three others: Commissioner Robert Bartley, nephew of Speaker Rayburn; Kenneth A. Cox, a Seattle attorney and former aide to Senator Warren Magnuson; and Commissioner Cross, favorite of the Arkansas congressional delegation (Kenneth M. Cox, interview with author, 14 June 1978; John S. Cross to Kennedy, 15 Aug. 1960 and 12 Jan. 1961, copies in box 10, Minow Papers; Senate Commerce Committee, *Appointments to the Regulatory Agencies*, 156, 158).

12   Minow to Carl McGowan, 9 Jan. 1952, Minow to Stevenson, 26 Jan. 1952, box 267, Stevenson Papers; John Bartlow Martin, *Adlai Stevenson of Illinois* (Garden City, N.Y., 1976), 525, 629, 662, 717; "The Reminiscences of Newton N. Minow" (1967), Adlai E. Stevenson Project, COHC, 6, 9, 10, 12; Parmet, *Jack*, 339, 362.

13   Minow to Stevenson, 12 Nov. 1954, box 401, Stevenson Papers; "The Reminiscences of Newton N. Minow" (1967), Stevenson Project, COHC, 20-23, 34, 36-37, 41, 44, 60-61, 65, 66, 81, 82, 102-3; Minow to Kennedy, n.d., Sorensen to Minow, 23 Aug. 1956, Pre-Presidential Papers, box 934, Kennedy Papers; John Bartlow Martin, *Stevenson and the World*, 139, 153-57, 195, 208, 234, 268, 306, 329, 343, 349, 480, 493,

496, 506, 554, 599; "The Reminiscences of Newton N. Minow" (1971), Oral History, LBJL, 9; Senate Commerce Committee, *Appointments to Regulatory Agencies*, 158; Kenneth P. O'Donnell, interview with Graham and Kramer, (1973), Newton N. Minow, interview with Graham and Kramer, 29 April 1973, tapes in INSPIRE Papers.

14 John Bartlow Martin, *Stevenson and the World*, 328, 354-55, 386; Minow, interview with author, 22 May 1978.

15 "The Reminiscences of Newton N. Minow" (1967), Stevenson Project, COHC, 7; Minow, interview with author, 22 May 1978.

16 Minow, interview with author, 22 May 1978.

17 Ibid.; Tedson J. Meyers, interview with author; Minow to Robert Lewis Shayon, 23 May 1961, box 10, Shayon Papers; Minow to George Geibner, 15 March 1965, box 1, ibid.

18 *Current Biography 1961* (New York, 1962), 317; Burr Tillstrom to Minow, 25 May 1962, box 43, Minow Papers; Senate Commerce Committee, *Nomination of Newton N. Minow to be Chairman of the Federal Communications Commission*, 10; Minow interview with Graham and Kramer, tape in INSPIRE Papers.

19 Stanton, interview with author; *Chicago Sun-Times*, 10 Jan. 1961.

20 Senate Commerce Committee, *Nomination of Minow*, 7, 10.

21 Ibid.; Norris Cotton to Sterling Campbell Conn, 1 March 1961, box 47, Cotton Papers; Minow, *Equal Time*, 4-5; Minow, interview with Graham and Kramer, tape in INSPIRE Papers.

22 Bill Blair to Minow, 30 March 1961, box 11, Minow Papers.

23 Kintner to Stevenson, c Feb. 1955, box 414, Stevenson Papers.

24 Minow, interview with author, 22 May 1978; John Bartlow Martin, *Stevenson and the World*, 153, 155-56, 165. The matter of Stevenson's RCA work arose during his 1956 fight for the Democratic presidential nomination. See Facts on File, *Yearbook 1956* (New York, 1957), 185.

25 *Printer's Ink* (7 Jan. 1961), 41, (10 March 1961), 21-24; *New York Times* 29 March 1961.

26 Frederick W. Ford, interview with author, 15 June 1978.

27 Notes by Minow c. 1964, box 1, Laurent Papers; *Sponsor* (29

May 1961), 9; *NAFBRAT Quarterly* 1 (Summer 1961), 1, copy in box 31, Minow Papers.

28 Stanley A. Frankel to Minow, 23 March 1961, box 28, Minow Papers; Meyers, interview with author; Meyers, interview with Joel Rosenbloom, 25 June 1981.

29 *Washington Star*, 28 April 1965; Robert Lewis Shayon, "Murrow's Lost Flight," *Saturday Review* (22 May 1965), 94.

30 John Bartlow Martin, "Television, U.S.A.," *Saturday Evening Post* (21 Oct. 1961), 20-21 (28 Oct. 1961), 56; Albert P. Weisman to Minow, 12 April 1961, box 26, Minow Papers.

31 John Bartlow Martin, *Stevenson of Illinois*, 653-55.

32 Minow, *Equal Time*, 48-52, 56, 64.

33 April 28 draft, box 28, Minow Papers.

34 Minow, *Equal Time*, 51-55, 58, 63.

35 *Chicago Daily News*, 16 May 1961.

36 *Wilmington Journal*, 11 May 1961, clipping in box 53. Minow Papers.

37 Minow, *Equal Time*, 48-52, 55-57, 64; *Wall Street Journal*, 10 May 1961.

38 Minow, *Equal Time*, 61.

39 Ibid., 53, 56ff.

40 Editorial, *St. Louis Post-Dispatch*, 10 May 1961; *Broadcasting* (15 May 1961), 5, 36-37; *Sponsor* (28 Aug. 1961), 16; *Printer's Ink* (19 May 1961), 12-14; W.N. McKinney to Oren Harris, 16 May 1961, box 4-5-17, Harris Papers.

41 *Broadcasting* (15 May 1961), 37; W. Richard Carlson to Norris Cotton, 20 May 1961, box 47, Cotton Papers.

42 Collins to Minow, 18 May 1961, box 28, Minow Papers; *Newsweek* (22 May 1961), 87; *Variety* (10 May 1961), 1 (17 May 1961), 33.

43 Stanton, interview with author; *New York Herald Tribune*, 10 May 1961; George A. Heinemann to Minow, 11 May 1961, box 31, Minow Papers.

44 *Washington Star*, 9 May 1961; *New York Post*, 10 May 1961; *Christian Science Monitor*, 11 May 1961; *Television Digest* (15 May 1961), 2.

45 Memorandum, Frederick Dutton to Kenneth P. O'Donnell, 12 April 1961, White House Secretary's File, box 170, Kennedy Papers

46 Minow, interview with Sterling Quinlan, Quinlan Papers;

Minow interview; Schlesinger, *A Thousand Days*, 675-76; Minow, interview, CBS News, "Washington Conversation," 14 May 1961, copy of transcript in box 46, Minow Papers; Minow to Robert F. Kennedy, 21 May 1961, box 24, ibid.

47 Morgan to Minow, 11 May 1961, with ABC News radio commentary, in box 27, Minow Papers.

48 Copeland to Minow, 11 May 1961, invoice 63A83, box 240, FCC Records, GSA. See also Robert Saudek to Minow, 10 May 1961, Jack L. Warner, Jr., to Minow, 20 May 1961, box 29, Minow Papers.

49 Shulman to Minow, 12 May 1961, invoice 63A83, box 240, FCC Records, GSA.

50 *Los Angeles Times*, 1 May 1961; *St. Louis Post-Dispatch*, 10 May 1961; *Denver Post*, 9 May 1961.

51 *Washington Post*, 10 May 1961; *Detroit Free Press*, 10 May 1961; *New York Times*, 10 May 1961; *New York Herald Tribune*, 10 May 1961; Jack O'Brian, *New York Journal-American*, 10 May 1961; *Editor and Publisher* (13 May 1961), 13, 74.

52 *Denver Post*, 9 and 11 May 1961; on may 21, the *Post* reprinted parts of Minow's speech.

53 *Los Angeles Times*, 11 and 12 May 1961. See also *St. Louis Post-Dispatch*, 10 and 14 May 1961; *San Francisco Chronicle*, 23 May 1961.

54 Ray Oviatt, "Report on 19 Hours in 'Wasteland,' " *Toledo Blade*, 21 May 1961, clipping in box 26, Minow Papers.

55 *Washington Post*, 11 May 1961.

56 *New York Post*, 11 May 1961.

57 Ibid., 14 May 1961.

58 *Time* (19 May 1961), 53ff; Minow letter to *TV Guide* (13 May 1961), A-2-A-3; *Life* (16 June 1961), 83-84; *Television Digest* (22 May 1961), 22. The 5,125 letters, cards, and telegrams Minow received in response to the NAB speech and subsequent attention were examined by the author; most are in invoice 63A83, boxes 239-244, FCC Records, GSA.

59 *Broadcasting* (22 May 1961), 60.

60 Minow, interview, ABC, "Issues and Answers," 18 June 1961, copy of transcript in box 46, Minow Papers; Jack D. Warren, "Analysis of Letters Received in Response to Chairman Minow's Address," n.d., copy in box 29, ibid.

61 Nathan Trokie to Minow, 13 May 1961, invoice 63A83, box 239, FCC Records, GSA; Carl G. Thompson to Minow, 15 May 1961, Lilian Eisenberg to Minow, 18 May 1961, box 240, ibid.; Andre Leferriere to Minow, 22 May 1961, Roger J. Graham to Minow, 23 May 1961, box 241, ibid.

62 Helen A. Watkins to Minow, 23 May 1961, box 240, ibid.; Mrs. William B. Lloyd, Jr., to Minow, 21 May 1961, box 243, ibid.

63 Mrs. Teivo Sober to Minow, 24 June 1961, box 243, ibid.; Harry T. Thomas to Minow, 12 May 1961, box 239, ibid.

64 Mrs. L.L. Robinson to Minow, 13 May 1961, box 239, ibid.

65 Dill to Minow, 21 May 1961, box 4, Minow Papers.

66 Humphrey to Minow, 10 May 1961, Control Files, 1961, Senatorial Files, Humphrey Papers.

67 *Milwaukee Journal*, 4 June 1961, clipping in box 53, Minow Papers.

68 *St. Louis Post-Dispatch*, 15 May 1961.

CHAPTER 5

1 Oren Harris to W.N. McKinney, 19 May 1961, group 3, box 4-5-17, Harris Papers.

2 The others were the Federal Trade Commission, Securities and Exchange Commission, National Labor Relations Board, Civil Aeronautics Board, Federal Home Loan Bank Board, and Federal Maritime Board.

3 See chapter 1, pp.16-17.

4 U.S. Congress, House of Representatives, Committee on Government Operations (hereafter House Government Operations Committee), *Reorganization Plans*, 27; address by James M. Landis, 9 Sept. 1961, box 148, Landis Papers, LC; Landis to Mike Feldman, 21 April 1961, Landis to Lawrence F. O'Brien and Michael Manatos, 24 June 1961, box 19, Landis Papers, JFKL; Landis to Frederick W. Ford, 24 April 1961, box 29, ibid.; remarks by Minow, 7 Aug. 1961, box 47, Minow Papers; *Washington Post*, 23 June 1961.

5 *San Francisco Chronicle*, 22 June 1961.

6 Quoted in Minow, *Equal Time*, 6. See also *Variety* (19 April 1961), 43 (3 May 1961), 47 (10 May 1961), 70; *New Republic* (26 June 1961), 6; *Television Digest* (15 May 1961), 1, 12;

Tedson J. Meyers to Saul Carson, 24 Sept. 1961, box 4, Minow Papers.

7 Address by Landis, 9 Sept. 1961, box 148, Landis Papers, LC; idem, "Remarks," 49; *Congressional Quarterly Almanac, 1961* 354; Carl McFarland, "Landis' Report: The Voice of One Crying in the Wilderness," 386, 394-401, 430-34.

8 *Wall Street Journal*, 14 March 1961; *Congressional Quarterly Almanac, 1961*, 356; *U.S. News and World Report* (27 March 1961), 86; Alan S. Boyd to Ralph Dungan, 28 Feb. 1961, box 5, Boyd Papers; Andrew F. Schoeppel to Warren Magnuson, 17 and 24 March 1961, Magnuson to Schoeppel, 23 March 1961, copies in box 47, Cotton Papers; Landis to Frederick Dutton, 30 March 1961, box 19, Landis Papers, JFKL; Scher, "Conditions for Legislative Control," 545-48.

9 *Broadcasting* (22 May 1961), 5; William Cary in "Regulatory Agencies Panel" (1964), Oral History, JFKL, 15; Cecil Bolton-Smith to James M. Landis, 13 July 1961, box 19, pp 359-60, Landis Papers, JFKL; *Grand Rapids Press*, 25 June 1961, clipping in box 52, Minow Papers.

10 Harris to E. Barrett Prettyman, 20 Nov. 1960, group 3, box 10-4-30, Harris Papers; memorandum, Frederick Dutton to Landis, 16 March 1961, WHCF, Name File, box 2283, Kennedy Papers; memorandum, Dutton to Lawrence F. O'Brien, 21 April 1961, box 7, O'Brien Papers; *Television Digest* (22 May 1961), 1; House Government Operations Committee, *Reorganization Plans*, 76-78.

11 Cecil Bolton-Smith to Landis, [9 May 1961], box 29, Landis Papers, JFKL; Duscha, "New Voices for Consumers," 19; House Government Operations Committee, *Reorganization Plans*, 86; *Congressional Quarterly Almanac, 1961*, 359; *Milwaukee Sentinel*, 16 June 1961, clipping in box 53, Minow Papers.

12 Ford, interviews with author, 15 and 19 June 1978; *Television Digest* (13 Feb. 1961), 7; House Government Operations Committee, *Reorganization Plans*, [executive session], 248-50, copy box 16, Minow Papers; House Government Operations Committee, *Reorganization Plans*, 144, 152; U.S. Congress, Senate, Committee on Government Operations (hereafter Senate Government Operations Committee), *Reorganization Plans*, 57; Ford to Landis, 27 April 1961, box

2, Landis Papers, JFKL

13 Senate Government Operations Committee, *Reorganization Plans* 57, 70-72, 125, 129-33; House Government Operations Committee, *Reorganization Plans*, [executive session], 202-3, 211, 215, 237-38, 240-45, 257-65; House Government Operations Committee, *Reorganization Plans*, 159-61; Cross to Minow, 20 April 1961, Cross to John McClellan, 8 May 1961, box 16, Minow Papers; *Broadcasting* (22 May 1961), 57; Ford, interview with author, 19 June 1978; address by Landis, 9 Sept. 1961, p. 10, box 148, Landis Papers, LC.

14 *New York Times*, 18 June 1961; Minow to Harris, 5 June 1961, group 3, box 4-5-18, Harris Papers; Minow to Sam Stratton et al., 20 June 1961, box 10, Minow Papers; Bolton-Smith to Landis, 13 July 1961, Landis to O'Brien et al., 13 July 1961, box 19, Landis Papers, JFKL, *Congressional Quarterly Almanac, 1961*, 358-60; *New Republic* (26 June 1961), 5.

15 "The Reminiscences of Oren Harris" (1965), Oral History, JFKL, 35-36; "Regulatory Agencies Panel" (1964), Oral History, JFKL, 6-8; Cary, *Politics and the Regulatory Agencies*, 30-31; Landis to O'Brien and to Manatos, 24 June 1961, box 19, Landis Papers, JFKL; Landis to Harris, 24 June 1961, box 16-1-37, Harris Papers; Duscha, "New Voices for Consumers," 19.

16 Jim Wright, newsletter, 12 June 1961, copy in box 10, Minow Papers.

17 Ibid.; House Government Operations Committee, *Reorganization Plans*, 101.

18 *Newsday*, 26 May 1961, copy in box 7, Minow Papers; *New York Times*, 19 and 20 May 1961, 18 June 1961; address by Landis, 9 Nov. 1961, p. 11, box 148, Landis Papers, LC.

19 Hugh Russell Frazier, undated columns, *Los Angeles Times* and *San Francisco Daily Commercial News*, clippings in box 16, Minow Papers.

20 Berkman, "A Modest Proposal," 34; Barbara Matusow, "When Push Comes to Shove," *Channels of Communication* 1 (Aug.-Sept. 1981), 34. Congressmen's files invariably included reams of correspondence concerning their radio and television reports to constituents. See, for example, Cy Tuma to Page Belcher, 17 Dec. 1958, Belcher to Tuma, 25 Feb. 1959, Belcher to Martin Ferguson, 17 March 1959, box 49, Belcher

Papers; Wendell Elliott to Frank Carlson, 18 Jan. 1965, box 399, Carlson Papers.

21 Press release, 25 Jan. 1958, group 12, box 10-4-28, Harris Papers. *Broadcasting* (17 April 1961), 62, 64, listed 12 House members holding an interest in a broadcast station. Of the 12, only 1—Keogh of New York—voted for the plan.

22 *San Francisco Chronicle*, 22 June 1961; *Grand Rapids Press*, 25 June 1961.

23 *Sponsor* (22 May 1961), 25; editorial, *Christian Science Monitor*, 19 June 1961. Two perhaps surprisingly penetrating analyses are Drew Pearson, "How to Pull Wires and Influence Government," *Show Business Illustrated* (5 Sept. 1961), 120-22, which discusses the plan number two struggle, and Al Toffler, "How Congressmen Make Up Their Minds," *Redbook* 118 (Feb. 1962), 56-57, 126-31.

24 Frank Stanton, interview with author; Alfred R. Beckman to William Avery, 5 Dec. 1961, box 9, Avery Papers.

25 *Television Digest* (24 June 1961), 5, ABC, "Issue and Answers," 18 June 1961, transcript, p. 16, copy in box 46, Minow Papers.

26 Polenberg, *Reorganizing Roosevelt's Government*, 193; Pemberton, *Bureaucratic Politics*.

27 *Grand Rapids Press*, 25 June 1961; Peabody et al., *To Enact a Law*, 30; Bailey, *Congress Makes a Law*, 148-49, 185f; Warren E. Miller and Donald E. Stokes, "Constituency in Congress," *American Political Science Review* 57 (March 1963), 47, 54-55. Examples of station managers' letters, many, also arranging the congressmen's air time, include Leslie C. Johnson to Paul H. Douglas, c. May 1961, box 86, Douglas papers; W.N. McKinney to Oren Harris, 6 May 1961, group 3, box 4-5-17, Harris Papers; George Stevens to A.S. "Mike" Monroney, 25 May 1961, Edgar T. Bell to Monroney, 18 May 1961, box 8, Monroney Papers; Ralph T. Weir, Jr., to Andrew F. Schoeppel, 13 June 1961, Thad M. Sandstrom to Schoeppel, 22 May 1961, Schoeppel Papers, KSHS. On May 16, Senator Schoeppel sent out a form letter to Kansas broadcasters to assure them of his opposition to plan number two.

28 Minow and other commission chairmen in "Regulatory Agencies Panel" (1964) Oral History, JFKL, 6-7, 8-12; Minow, interview with author, 22 May 1978.

29 Minow to Pastore, 23 Oct. 1961, box 34, Minow Papers;
    memorandum, Henry Geller to Commission, 6 June 1961,
    and 19 June 1961, invoice 57-A-433, box 226, FCC Records,
    GSA; address by Ford, 19 Oct. 1964, copy in box 31, pp. 7-8,
    Henry Papers; memoranda, Charles P. Howze, Jr., chief
    counsel, to Oren Harris and members of the special subcom-
    mittee on regulatory agencies 12 June 1961, Kurt Borchardt
    to Harris, 28 June 1961, group 17, box 16-1-37, Harris Papers.
    Congressional Quarterly Almanac, 1961, 360-62; *Public
    Utilities Fortnightly* 68 (14 Sept. 1961), 395; James R. Bailes,
    William H. Hardie, Jr., and Alexander H. Slaughter, "The
    Progress of Federal Agency Reorganization under the Ken-
    nedy Administration," *Virginia Law Review* 48 (March
    1962), 325, 333-34. The new amendments allowed a commis-
    sion majority to delegate authority in some cases to in-
    dividual commissioners or staff. In the long run, this provi-
    sion did give the agency more time for important pro-
    ceedings, though it did not take effect until August 1962. See
    James O. Freedman, "Review Boards in the Administrative
    Process," *University of Pennsylvania Law Review* 117 (Feb.
    1969), 546-77.
30 *Show Business Illustrated* (19 Sept. 1961), 89, Minow, hand-
    written notes, c. late 1963, box 1, Laurent Papers.
31 *Variety* (13 Dec. 1961), 42; remarks by Rosel Hyde at NAB
    panel discussion, 4 April 1962, box 6, NAB Papers.
32 Minow in "Regulatory Agencies Panel" (1964), Oral History,
    JFKL, 160-162; Minow, interview with author, 22 May 1978;
    Ford, interview with author, 19 June 1978.
33 Two later studies, one statistical and the other impres-
    sionistic, suggest that partisan affiliations did not predict
    commissioners' votes: Canon, "Voting Behavior on the FCC";
    Cole and Oettinger, *Reluctant Regulators,* vi. Cf. Quirk, *In-
    dustry Influence.*
34 *Television Digest* (13 July 1959), 4; Ford, interview with
    author, 19 June 1978.
35 Minow, interview with author, 22 May 1978; Ford, interview
    with author, 15 June 1978.
36 Quinlan, *The Hundred Million Dollar Lunch,* 70; Minow, in-
    terview with author, 8 Aug. 1978; *Broadcasting* (24 July
    1961), 50-51 (27 June 1966), 29, 31; "The Reminiscences of

Rosel Hyde" (1974), Oral History, Broadcast Pioneers Library, Washington, D.C., pp. 16, 21-22.

37 Robert E. Lee, interview with author; Robert Griffith, *The Politics of Fear: Joseph R. McCarthy and the Senate* (Lexington, Ky. 1970), 40, 54-55 235-37; press release, FCC, 6 Oct. 1953, copy in box 119, Du Mont Laboratories Records, LC; Thomas C. Reeves, *The Life and Times of Joe McCarthy* (New York, 1982), 227-28, 512.

38 *Television Age* (9 March 1959), 111; Quinlan, *The Hundred Million Dollar Lunch*, 70-71; Lee to author, 24 April 1979; Lee, interview with author; Welborn, "Presidents," 9; *Chicago Sun-Times*, 18 March 1962; *Washington Post*, 7 July 1967.

39 "The Reminiscences of Clifford J. Durr" (1967), FLOHC, 22, 23; Minow, interview with author, 22 May 1978; Minow, interview with Sterling Quinlan, 27 Dec. 1972, tape in box 12, Quinlan Papers.

40 Robert Bartley, interview with Sterling Quinlan, 9 Dec. 1972, tape in box 12, Quinlan Papers.

41 The wag was unidentified but wrote the comments on a list of commissioners, box 2, Henry Wilson Papers. See also *Broadcasting* (17 March 1958), 54, 126.

42 Suggestive in this regard are McCraw, "Regulation in America," 182; Robert J. Shapiro, "Politics and the Federal Reserve," *Public Interest*, no. 66 (Winter 1982), 128.

43 Peter Shuebruk to Mary Jane Morris, 25 March 1960, George Gearon to Commission, 13 Feb. 1961, Mrs. Rudolph Schwenzer to Commission, 19 April 1961, ABC, "Opposition of American Broadcasting Co." [to JCET petition, 15 Dec. 1958]. ibid., "Comments of ABC in Support of Proposed Rule Making," [18 April 1961]; Mrs. Albert B. Craig, Jr., to Minow, 18 Oct. 1961, docket 18359, vols. 1-3, FCC Records, NA; Joseph C. Wilson to Harold Ostertag, 26 Jan. 1962, box 18, Ostertag Papers; editorial, *Honolulu Star-Bulletin*, 6 Sept. 1961, copy in box 52, Minow Papers; FCC, *Reports and Orders* 41 (1961), 997. Of the 76 area viewers who wrote the FCC regarding the Rochester matter, 72 favored an ETV VHF reservation, 2 favored ABC's position, and 2 made no sense.

44 John Kenneth Galbraith, *The New Industrial State*, paper ed. (New York, 1967), 202-3.

45 FCC, *Reports and Orders* 44 (1962), 2778, 2786-88.

46 "The Reminiscences of E. William Henry" (1966), Oral
History, JFKL, 39-40; John McClellan and J. William Fulbright
to Kennedy, 6 Feb. 1962, copy in group 3, box 5-2-18, Harris
Papers; *Wall Street Journal*, 8 Dec. 1961. Cross had wed the
daughter of former congressman Claude Fuller of Arkansas.
Senate Commerce Committee, *Appointments to the
Regulatory Agencies*, 112-113.

47 Cotton to Sterling Campbell Conn, 1 March 1961, box 47,
Cotton Papers.

48 *Wall Street Journal*, 11 May 1961. For other critical
editorials, see *Richmond News Leader*, 11 May 1961, *Peoria
Journal Star*, 17 May 1961, *Baltimore Sun*, 12 May 1961, and
Charleston (West Virginia) *Daily Mail*, 15 May 1961, clippings in invoice 63-A-83, box 239, FCC Records, GSA.

49 *Washington Star*, 11 and 8 May 1961. See also George E.
Sokolsky for a less decipherable critique, *New York Journal-
American*, 11 May 1961.

50 *Broadcasting* (19 June 1961), 103.

51 *Newsweek* (11 Sept. 1961), 62; Ward L. Quaal to Minow, 15
May 1961, box 4, Minow Papers; Janet Kern to Minow, 29
Aug. 1961, box 24, ibid.

52 Minow to Gould, 13 Aug. 1961, box 17, Minow Papers.

53 Monroe to Minow, 13 May 1961, box 26, ibid.

54 Pierson in Coons, *Freedom and Responsibility*, 84-95; Pierson to Minow, 4 Nov. 1961, box 4, Minow Papers; address
by Pierson, "The Active Eyebrow—A Changing Style of Censorship," *Television Quarterly* 1 (Feb. 1962) 14-21.

55 Jaffe in Coons, *Freedom and Responsibility*, 173. See also,
ibid., 35, 37, 42; *New York Times*, 4 Aug. 1961; Jaffe to
Minow, 5 Aug. 1961, box 23, Minow Papers; Saul Carson,
"Television," *Nation* (12 Aug. 1961), 85-86.

56 Kern to Minow, 29 Aug. 1961, box 24, Minow Papers.

57 ACLU, *Annual Reports*, vol. 41 (1961), pp. 5-16, vol. 42 (1962),
p. 12 (reprint ed., New York, 1970); docket 12782, vol. 4,
Proceedings, vol. 3, pp. 688ff, FCC Records, Dockets Room,
FCC; Charles L. Stewart, Jr., to Dorothy Dunbar Bromley, 21
Feb. 1961, box 228, ACLU Papers, Princeton Univ.; Minow,
Equal Time, 67; *Television Digest* (13 March 1961), 2.

58 Minow, interview with author, 22 May 1978; address by

Fairfax M. Cone, 10 Oct. 1961, box 135, Cone Papers; *Broadcasting* (19 Oct. 1961), 28.

59 *New York Times*, 13 Aug. 1961.

60 Coons, *Freedom and Responsibility*, 28.

61 Minow to Kern, 9 Sept. 1961, box 24, Minow Papers.

62 Minow to Madeline Carr, 18 Aug. 1961, box 9, ibid.

63 Minow, *Equal Time*, 115.

64 Gans, *Deciding What's News*, 9.

65 Sorensen, *Kennedy*, 325; Newton N. Minow, John Bartlow Martin, and Lee Mitchell, *Presidential Television* (New York, 1973), 38-39; Henry Fairlie, "J.F.K.'s Television Presidency," *New Republic* (26 Dec. 1983), 11-13, 16.

66 Truman and Eisenhower had allowed TV cameras during their conferences but not live transmission. Salinger, *With Kennedy*, 54-60; Cornwell, *Presidential Leadership*, 188, 190ff.

67 Barnouw, *A History of Broadcasting*, III:224-57; Salinger, *With Kennedy*, 116; Benjamin Bradlee, *Conversations with Kennedy* (New York: 1975), 54-58. When CBS and NBC expanded their nightly news programs to 30 minutes in Sept. 1963, the president rewarded the networks by allowing the anchors of the programs to interview him at the White House.

68 Karl E. Meyer, "For Polemical Passion in the Press," *Nieman Reports* 16 (Dec. 1963), 15-17; David L. Sallach, "Class Domination and Ideological Hegemony," *Sociological Quarterly* 15 (Winter 1974), 38-50.

69 Minow, interview with author, 22 May 1978.

70 Minow's testimony is in Senate Judiciary Committee, · *Juvenile Delinquency*, 87th Cong., 1st sess., pp. 2217ff.

71 Minow, *Equal Time*, 98-112; *Variety* (27 Sept. 1961), 24, 50; *Washington Star*, 22 Sept. 1961; *Chicago Tribune*, 23 Sept. 1961; *New York Times*, 23 Sept. 1961, 1 Oct. 96. Characteristically critical was *Broadcasting* (2 Oct. 1961), 98.

72 Treyz to Minow, 10 Oct. 1961, box 2, Minow Papers; Minow, *Equal Time*, 103-4; Minow, interview with author, 22 May 1978; *Variety* (4 Oct. 1961), 26; *Sponsor* (9 Oct. 1961), 7; memorandum to files, B.D., 9 July 1962, box 30, Heckscher Papers.

73 *Chicago Daily News*, 13 Oct. 1962.

74   Minow, *Equal Time*, 52; *Variety* (27 Sept. 1961), 25 (13 Dec. 1961), 1; *Television Digest* (22 May 1961), 4.

75   *New York Times*, 18 June 1961; *Milwaukee Journal*, 4 June 1961; *Miami News*, 12 June 1961, clippings in box 53, Minow Papers; *Media Agencies Clients* (25 March 1963), clipping in box 58, ibid.; John Bartlow Martin, "The Battle of the Big Three," *Saturday Evening Post* (28 Oct. 1961), 62; Morgan, "Crisis, Conflict, and Change, 51.

76   Bailey, "Examination of Prime Time," 74 and *passim*; Carroll, "Economic Influences"; Fred W. Friendly, interview with author; Michael Dann, interview with author; Richard Salant to author, 12 June 1979.

77   Script production notes, 30 May 1961 and 22 Oct. 1961, box 34, Salkowitz Papers.

78   *Chicago Tribune*, 8 Oct. 1961.

79   *Milwaukee Journal*, 13 June 1961, clipping in box 53, Minow Papers.

80   *Variety* (13 Dec. 1961), 1, 42; *New York Times*, 14 Dec. 1961.

81   Page Belcher to Quinn Dickason, 7 Dec. 1961, box 58, Belcher Papers.

82   *Printer's Ink* (15 Dec. 1961), 12; *Variety* (13 Dec. 1961), 26; Stanton to Minow, 17 Jan. 1963, box 41, Minow Papers; docket 12782, vol. 18, *Proceedings*, vol. 53, pp. 7998-8000, FCC Records, Dockets Room, FCC; *San Francisco Examiner*, 24 Dec. 1961; *Seattle Times*, 17 Dec. 1961, clippings in box 53, Minow Papers.

83   Minow, *Equal Time*, 127.

84   Docket 12782, vol. 18, *Proceedings*, vol. 53, p. 7999, FCC Records, Dockets Room, FCC. See also *Detroit Free Press*, 27 Dec. 1961, clipping in box 52, Minow Papers; Sarnoff, "What Do You Want from TV?"

85   Quoted in Leo Bogart, *Strategy in Advertising*, 242.

86   Schlesinger to Minow, 15 Dec. 1961, box 7, Minow Papers.

87   Minow, interview with author, 22 May 1978.

88   Al Capp, "Yawn along with Ike," syndicated column, United Features wire, 5 Feb. 1962, copy in box 7, Minow Papers.

89   Hy Goldin to Minow, 29 March 1961, box 6, Minow Papers.

90   Docket 12782, vol. 18, *Proceedings*, vol. 53, p. 8118, FCC Records, Dockets Room, FCC.

91 *San Francisco Chronicle*, 26 Dec. 1961.
92 Minow, interview with Sterling Quinlan, 27 Dec. 1972, Quinlan Papers.
93 Transcript of press conference, copy in box 26, Minow Papers; *New York Times*, 1 Feb. 1962
94 For examples of Minow's curbing his references to specific programs, see interviews, *Wilmington Journal*, 7 June 1962; *Weekly News Review*, 3 Dec. 1962, clippings in box 54, Minow Papers; James J. Dailey, "Minow Charts a Course," *TV Guide* (29 Dec. 1962), 4-7.

CHAPTER 6

1 House Commerce Committee, *All-Channel Television*, hearings, 184.
2 William C. Koplovitz to James M. Landis, 23 Nov. 1960, box 3, Landis Papers, JFKL.
3 Senate Commerce Committee, *All-Channel Television*, report 1526, p. 3; U.S. Congress, House of Representatives, Committee on Appropriations (hereafter House Appropriations Committee), Subcommittee on Independent Offices, *Independent Offices Appropriations, 1963*, p. 627; *Channel 1* (April 1962), 1, copy in box 25, Minow Papers.
4 House Commerce Committee, *All-Channel Television*, hearings, 76, 102, 453-55.
5 *Ft. Lauderdale News*, 4 May 1962, clipping in box 54, Minow Papers.
6 House Commerce Committee, *All-Channel Television*, hearings 136, 184; memorandum, General Counsel to Commission, 16 Nov. 1960, invoice 67-A-83, box 26, FCC Papers, GSA; Senate Commerce Committee, *The Television Inquiry; Television Network Practices*, 85th Cong., 1st sess., 1957; Brinton, "The Regulation of Broadcasting," 298.
7 "Darkened Channels."
8 *Variety* (15 June 1960), 23 (15 March 1961), 25 (3 June 1962), 26; docket 12782, vol. 21, *Proceedings*, vol. 61, p. 9664, FCC Records, Dockets Room, FCC. In 1960 an NBC vice president discouraged rotating coverage of the presidential debates on the grounds that ABC's chain of affiliates was so weak that many Americans would be denied adequate coverage when

that network carried a debate. Senate Commerce Committee, *Presidential Broadcasting Act*, 275.

9   Glynn, "Public Policy" 89-90; Robert Kintner to Magnuson, reprinted in Senate Commerce Committee, *The Television Inquiry*, hearings, 2507-8 and 2468-507; House Judiciary Committee, *Monopoly Problems in Regulated Industries*, 4774-80; ABC, petition, 7 Oct. 1955, docket 11532, FCC Records, NA; "Darkened Channels," 1593; FCC, *Reports and Orders* 41 (1960), 803.

10 House Commerce Committee, *All-Channel Television*, hearings, 297-314, 319; "Statement of Oliver Treyz, president of ABC, before FCC," 5 Feb. 1962, and ABC, "Progress and Problems," copies in box 2, Minow Papers; ABC comments, [19] February 1962, docket 14239, vol. 7, FCC Records, NA; House Appropriations Committee, *Independent Offices Appropriations, 1962*, pp. 607, 616, 619; AB-UP, *Annual Report* (1961), 8; Cunniff, "Mediocrity's Mahatma," 96.

11 *Variety* (5 Oct. 1960), 53; ABC, comments, 18 April 1961, docket 13859, FCC Records, NA.

12 Mayer, "ABC: Portrait of a Network," 59-60; John Bartlow Martin, "The Battle of the Big Three," 62.

13 Docket 12782, vol. 21, *Proceedings*, vol. 61, pp. 9357-58, 9707, FCC Records, Dockets Room, FCC; *Wall Street Journal*, 6 Feb. 1962.

14 See their remarks in *Washington Star*, 9 May 1961, *New York Post*, 10 May 1961, *Christian Science Monitor*, 11 May 1961, *Television Digest* (15 May 1961), 2.

15 ABC, "Progress and Problems"; *Wall Street Journal*, 12 May 1961; *Christian Science Monitor*, 24 Oct. 1962; Robert Lewis Shayon, "Hagerty's Lullaby," *Saturday Review* (26 Aug. 1961), 27.

16 Press release, ABC, "Adlai Stevenson Reports," 16 May 1961, copy in box 41, Minow Papers and 29 June 1961, copy in box 68, Martin Mayer Papers; *New York Times*, 2 and 22 Oct. 1961; *Newsweek* (9 Oct. 1961), 66; John E. Drewry to Stevenson, 16 March 1963, box 864, Stevenson Papers.

17 Minow, broadcast interview with Harold E. Ostertag, 10 June 1962, transcript in box 46, Minow Papers.

18 John Walker Powell, *Channels of Learning: The Story of Educational Television* (Washington, D.C., 1962), 154-55 and

ch. 4; Schramm, Lyle, and Pool, *The People Look*, 35; Mrs. Myrl Cypher to Frieda Hennock, 24 May 1955, box 2-29, Hennock Papers, Schlesinger Library, Radcliffe College.

19 "Educational Television for Wisconsin—Discussion Guide," paper, c. 1954, box 2-7, WCCET Papers; John Benjamin Haney, "A Study of Public Attitudes toward Tax-Support for Educational Television Activities in the Detroit Metropolitan Area" (Ph.D. diss., Univ. of Michigan, 1959), esp. 21, 22, 113-14.

20 JCET, "Current Developments in Educational Television," manuscripts, 1960, box 2A-13-3, NETRC Records; Schramm, *The Impact of Educational Television*, 19; Robert J. Blakely, *To Serve the Public Interest: Educational Broadcasting in the United States* (Syracuse, 1979), 81-142.

21 Address by Abraham Ribicoff, 9 May 1961, copy in box 28, Minow Papers.

22 Lippmann, *New York Herald Tribune*, 5 Jan. 1960; Mannes, *Who Owns the Air?* 12-13; Crosby, "What You Can Do," 135.

23 Memorandum, Minow to Frederick G. Dutton, 7 Sept. 1961, box 45, Minow Papers; address by Robert E. Lee, 7 March 1961, box 67-101, Lee Papers; Schramm, Lyle and Pool, *The People Look*, ch. 10; William Harlan Hale, "A Legacy from the Model T to the Age of ETV," *Reporter* (30 May 1957), 10-15; Fund for the Advancement of Education, *Decade of Experiment* (New York, 1961), 53-63; *Christian Science Monitor*, 13 May 1961; House Commerce Committee, *Educational Television*, hearings, 85th Cong., 2d sess., 1958, pp. 19, 54-55, 172-73, and 87th Cong., 1st sess., 1961, pp. 20-30, 42-48; Siepmann, *TV and Our School Crisis*, 100-5 and passim.

24 Quoted in Wylie, *Clear Channels*, 11.

25 Ithiel de Sola Pool and Barbara Adler, "Educational Television: Is Anyone Watching?" *Journal of Social Issues* 18, no. 2 (1961), 50-61; Schramm, *Impact of Educational Television*, 20-21, 30-33; Schramm to Robert B. Hudson, 20 Sept. 1961, box 2A-12-10, NETRC Records; Schramm, Lyle, and Pool, *The People Look*, ch. 5 and p. 109. These findings were attacked as betraying an upper-class bias. Kent Geiger and Robert Sokol, "Educational Television in Boston," in Schramm, ed.,

Impact of Educational Television, 39-67

26 Minow, interview with author, 8 Aug. 1978; notes for *Equal Time,* by Minow, in box 1, Laurent Papers; Emanuel Celler to Minow, 5 April 1961, box 265, Celler Papers; Tedson J. Meyers, interview with author; docket 14006, 3 vols., FCC Records, NA; FCC, *Reports and Orders* 44 (1961), 2563, 2579. Only Cross dissented in the final vote; Minow was criticized for high-handedness in the transfer procedure and for taking away New Jersey's only VHF assignment. (memorandum, Leo Carlin et al. to Kennedy, n.d. [c. Sept. 1961], Tom Graves to Bill Cary, 14 Sept. 1961, WHSF, box 991, Kennedy Papers; Cox, interview with author; Jack Guthman, "The Channel 13 Case: FCC Intervention in a 310(b) Transfer," manuscript, Yale Univ. Law School Forum, copy in Laurent Papers; Reich, "The New Property," 750; *Barron's* [1 Jan. 1962], 1 [10 Dec. 1962], 1).

27 See chapter 5.

28 Minow, interview with author, 22 May 1978; Cox, interview with author; comments of Times-Mirror Broadcasting Co., 31 May 1961, docket 14006, vol. 1 FCC Records, NA.

29 Address by Minow before the NAEB, 23 Oct. 1961, copy in box 47, Minow Papers, and remarks in Coons, *Freedom and Responsibility,* 184.

30 Minow, interview with author, 22 May 1978; William G. Harley to Oren Harris, 15 Nov. 1961, box 73-485-86, NAEB Records; House Commerce Committee, *All-Channel Television,* hearings, 138-39; House Appropriations Committee, *Independent Offices Appropriations, 1962,* pp. 610, 636; memorandum, Chief Counsel to Commission, 16 Jan. 1961, invoice 67A83, box 27, FCC Records, GSA; NETRC, "Proposal for Financing National Educational Television," Sept. 1961, manuscript, copy in box 11, Minow Papers; Shayon, "The Coming Breakthrough," 41, 50; *TV Guide* (11 March 1961), A-7; Geller, interview with author; press release, FCC, 1 Jan. 1961, copy in box 8, Monroney Papers; Jack McBride to Roman Hruska, 22 May 1962, box 82, Hruska Papers.

31 House Commerce Committee, *All-Channel Television,* hearings, 164.

32 Minow, broadcast interview with Harold E. Ostertag, 10 June 1962, transcript in box 46, Minow Papers; House Commerce

Committee, *All-Channel Television*, hearings, 122-23; Senate Commerce Committee, *All-Channel Television*, 4; FCC, *Reports and Orders* 45 (1962), 144; memorandum, David Z. Robinson to Landis, 17 May 1961, box 42, Landis Papers, JFKL.

33 House Commerce Committee, *All-Channel Television*, hearings, 105; *Broadcasting* (5 Nov. 1962), 70-71; Seymour N. Siegel, "UHF Works," NAEB *Journal* 21 (Nov. 1962), 21-34.

34 Minow, interview with author, 8 Aug. 1978; Webbink, "All-Channel Receiver Law," iv; Le Duc, *Cable Television*, chs. 4-5; *Business Week* (1 Sept. 1962), 96-98.

35 *Variety* (7 Feb. 1962), 30; Ashmore, *Fear in the Air*, 68. In the broadcast field, this was the closest a Kennedy appointee came to advocating deregulation, which within twenty years became fashionable at virtually all regulatory agencies. At the time, however, only some conservative economists (whose analyses only eventually overwhelmed public interest sentimentalism) urged markedly less regulation. There was an exception: transportation regulation. In an April 1962 message, the president asked without success that Congress lessen the regulatory hold on the railroad and airline industries to increase the power of market forces in setting rates and service areas. See *Congressional Quarterly Almanac, 1962* (Washington, D.C., 1963), 901; Lindley H. Clark, Jr., "Some Lessons from Airline Deregulation," *Wall Street Journal,* 22 Nov. 1983; Hoogenboom and Hoogenboom, *A History of the ICC*, 163-65.

36 Trienens to Minow, 24 Nov. 1961, box 43, Minow Papers.

37 Minow, "More Regulation or More Competition," *AAUW Journal* 55 (March 1962), 147.

38 Minow in "The Regulatory Agencies Panel" (1964), Oral History, JFKL, 13; *Variety* (7 Feb. 1962), 30.

39 Carson, "Television and Your Place in the Picture," 77.

40 Rosel Hyde, interview with Dwight Macdonald, c. Feb. 1962, notes in box 124, Macdonald Papers; Hyde to Morris L. Ernst, 27 Nov. 1959, box 557, Ernst Papers; *Business Week* (20 Jan. 1962), 93-94.

41 NAB-FCC panel discussion, 18 March 1959, transcript in box 6, NAB Papers; Lee to author, 24 May 1979.

42 Memorandum, CBS to Commission, 9 Sept. 1955, invoice

72-A-1986, box 13, FCC Records, GSA.

43   Address by Lee, 7 March 1961, box 67-101, Lee Papers;
House Appropriations Committee, *Independent Offices Appropriations, 1962*, p. 610; House Commerce Committee,
All-Channel Television, hearings, 134, 199-207; Robert E.
Lee, "Let's Put the Show on the Road," *NAEB Journal* (Jan.-
Feb. 1961), 34-36; Erwin G. Krasnow and Lawrence L.
Longley, *The Politics of Broadcast Regulation* (New York,
1973), 98; Emanuel Celler to Oren Harris, 5 March 1962, box
306, Celler Papers.

44   FCC, *Reports and Orders* 41 (1961), 926, 950-51.

45   Minow to Myer Feldman, 2 June 1961, WHSF, box 992, Kennedy Papers; Hodges to Minow, [2 Nov. 1961], invoice
57A433, box 226, FCC Records, GSA; Robert E. Giles to
Minow, 18 Dec. 1961, box 1, Minow Papers.

46   *Congressional Quarterly Almanac, 1962*, p. 892; memorandum, Max D. Paglin et al. to Minow, [12 Jan. 1962], box 1,
Minow Papers; Minow, *Equal Time*, 137-44.

47   House Commerce Committee, *All-Channel Television*, hearings, 131, 139, 160; House Appropriations Committee, *Independent Offices Appropriations, 1962*, pp. 608-9, 625;
Senate Commerce Committee, *All-Channel Television*,
report, 6.

48   *Printer's Ink* (19 May 1961), 13.

49   Bruce Lannes Smith to Minow, 20 June 1961, invoice 63A83,
box 242, FCC Records, GSA.

50   *Show* (Dec. 1961), 26; docket 12782, vol. 6, *Proceedings*, vol.
43, p. 6562, FCC Records, Dockets Room, FCC.

51   John McKnight to Alan Reitman, 4 Feb. 1961, box 228, ACLU
Papers, Princeton Univ.

52   Speech, 10 Oct. 1961, box 135, Cone papers; *Broadcasting*,
(16 Oct. 1961), 29.

53   *Washington Post*, 16 Jan. 1962. In Great Britain, the royal
commission on broadcasting also offered competition as a
solution to its deficiencies. See *Report of the Committee on
Broadcasting, 1960* (London, 1962), esp. 286; *Economist* (30
June 1962), 1288.

54   Norris Cotton to James Hanrahan, 4 June 1962, box 47, Cotton Papers.

55   James Wechsler, "The Minow Show," *New York Post*, 19

Oct. 1961. See also Shayon, "The Coming Breakthrough," for a similarly guarded statement.

56 House Commerce Committee, *All-Channel Television,* hearings, 443-50; House Appropriations Committee, *Independent Offices Appropriations, 1962,* p. 619; *Broadcasting* (4 Dec. 1961), 78; L.M. Sandwick to Celler, 30 April 1962, box 406, Celler Papers; Grand Gardner to Paul H. Douglas, 7 May 1962, box 434, Douglas Papers; E.R. Taylor of Motorola to Pastore, 19 Feb. 1962, Ross D. Siragusa to Pastore, 19 Feb. 1962, copies in box 1, Minow Papers; Meyers, interview with author. Minow argued that the cost would decline as more all-channel receivers were sold. House Commerce Committee, *All-Channel Television,* hearings, 33.

57 Thad M. Sandstrom to Frank Carlson, 23 May 1962, box 236, Carlson Papers.

58 *New York Times,* 1 April 1962.

59 House Appropriations Committee, *Independent Office Appropriations, 1962,* p. 619; House Commerce Committee, *All-Channel Television,* hearings, 164, 443.

60 House Commerce Committee, *All-Channel Television,* hearings, 273; Minow, interview with author, 8 Aug. 1978; note from memo pad, Office of David Sarnoff, and Minow to Sarnoff, 21 Feb. 1962, box 37, Minow Papers; John F. Cushman to William L. North, 26 Feb. 1962, box 9, ibid.

61 Minow, interview with author, 8 Aug. 1978; Everett H. Erlick to author, 13 June 1979.

62 House Commerce Committee, *All-Channel Television,* hearings, 297, 319; press release, ABC, 9 March 1962, copy in box 5B-13-8, NETRC Records; petition for reconsideration, [ABC], app. H, 1 July 1963, docket 14231, FCC Records, NA.

63 House Appropriations Committee, *Independent Offices Appropriations, 1962,* p. 616; House Commerce Committee, *All-Channel Television,* hearings, 225, 320-21; Collins to Minow, 23 April 1962, box 28, Minow Papers.

64 House Commerce Committee, *All-Channel Television,* hearings, 136, 139, 184; House Appropriations Committee, *Independent Offices Appropriations, 1962,* pp. 606, 624.

65 House Commerce Committee, *All-Channel Television,* hearings, p. 314; ABC comments, [19] Feb. 1962, docket 14239, vol. 7, pp. 4, 222, FCC Records, NA; Senate Commerce Com-

mittee, *All-Channel Television*, report, 9; Norman P. Bagwell to A.S. Mike Monroney, 8 Feb. 1962, Bill Hoover to Monroney, 12 Feb. 1962, box 15, Monroney Papers; folder 8b, box 61, Belcher Papers; William J. Bryan Dorn to Minow, 8 Aug. 1961, *Florence (S.C.) Morning News*, 11 Nov. 1961, clipping in Dorn Papers.

66 See docket 14239, FCC Records, NA.

67 W.W. Wessel to Ben F. Waple, 27 Dec. 1961, docket 14244, vol. 5, FCC Records, NA.

68 See, for example, constituent mail in boxes 6-108-2 and 6-108-3, Alexander H. Wiley Papers; Mrs. Emma Parish to Minow, 22 Aug. 1961, docket 14239, vol. 1, FCC Records, NA.

69 Address by Gale McGee, 6 June 1962, copy in box 2A-11-4, NETRC Records.

70 William Clark to Commission, 3 Nov. 1961, docket 14244, vol. 4, FCC Records, NA; Senate resolution, 18 Oct. 1961, docket 14244, vol. 29, ibid.; Cox, interview with author.

71 Dirksen and Arends filed separate comments [19 Feb. 1962] for docket 14244, vol. 29, as did Congressman Peter F. Mack, Jr., a Democrat, and Congressman William Springer, a Republican, both on the House Commerce Committee. On the orchestration of anti-FCC letters, see Mrs. Ann Miles to FCC, 2 Aug. 1961, Edward L. Staff to editor, *Urbana News-Gazette*, 31 July 1961, and related materials, docket 14244, vol. 1, FCC Records, NA; *Broadcasting* (15 Jan. 1962), 58; House Appropriations Committee, *Independent Offices Appropriations, 1962*, p. 608; House Commerce Committee, *All-Channel Television*, hearings, 35-36.

72 House Commerce Committee, *All-Channel Television*, hearings, 11-12, 23, 51-52.

73 Ibid., 35-36, 134; *Providence Journal*, 14 June 1962, clipping in Pastore Papers.

74 Minow to Oren Harris, 15 March 1962, box 1, Minow Papers; materials filed: "Legislation, 1962," in invoice 67A433, box 26, with "approved" note, [March 1962], FCC records, GSA; Ford, interview with author, 19 June 1978, and his remarks in House Appropriations Committee, *Independent Offices Appropriations, 1962*, p. 619; House Commerce Committee, *All-Channel Television*, hearings, 23, 35-36, 43,

44, 142-43, 195-98; House Commerce Committee, *All-Channel Television*, report 1559, pp. 6, 13-19; *Variety* (28 Feb. 1962), 23 (21 March 1962), 26, 48; *New York Times*, 1 April 1962; *Broadcasting* (7 May 1962), 54; FCC, *Reports and Orders* 45 (1962), 211, 457; Meyers, interview with author; *Congressional Quarterly Almanac, 1962*, pp. 576-79, 608-9; Lawrence D. Longley, "The FCC and the All-Channel Receiver Bill of 1962," *Journal of Broadcasting* 13 (Summer 1969), 293-303.

75 *New York Times*, 1 April 1962.

CHAPTER 7

1   Address by Minow, 2 Feb. 1962, box 47, Minow Papers. See also Ted Mills to Robert E. Lee, 1 March 1962, docket 14546, vol. 1, *Proceedings*, vol. 2, pp. 42, 56, 65, 144, 175, 247, FCC Records, NA; Harriet Van Horne, "The Chicago Touch," *Theatre Arts* (July 1951) 36-39, Joel Sternberg, "Television Town," *Chicago History* 4 (Summer 1975), 108-17.

2   FRC, *Annual Report* (1929), 32-35; FCC, *Public Service Responsibilities of Broadcast Licensees* (1946); *RR*, 1st ser., 20 (1960), 1901. "Local, live" stood for any program produced by a station utilizing live talent more than 50 percent of the time and using the facilities of the station (statement of presiding officer, docket 14863, vol. 2, pp. 6-7, FCC Records, NA).

3   Report of the presiding officer, docket 14863, 24 Oct. 1963, p. 54, FCC Records, NA. Percentages, based on FCC data listed in *Broadcasting Yearbook*, may be found in Sterling and Haight, *The Mass Media*, 308.

4   Buell, "The History and Development of WSAZ-TV," 69-79; *Television Magazine* (Aug. 1957), 61-63; ibid. (Aug. 1961), special issue on local telecasting; *Broadcasting* (1 April 1963), 70; FCC, *Public Service Responsibilities*, 12; "WTMJ—Pioneering Tradition," supplement to *Milwaukee Journal*, 9 Oct. 1966, copy in box 70-49, *Milwaukee Journal* Stations Records.

5   *Variety* (13 Feb. 1963), 21. See also Tim Onosko, "The ZIV Tradition," in Fireman, *TV Book*, 77-78.

6   Sterling and Kittross, *Stay Tuned*, 575.
7   Janet Kern, *Chicago American*, 20 March 1961; docket 14863, *Proceedings*, vol. 3, pp. 505-6, FCC Records, NA.
8   These are "above the line" data from *Variety* (10 Jan. 1962), 107. They do not include time charges for technical costs (of AT&T) for sending out the program. See also docket 14546, *Proceedings*, vol. 3, p. 1009, FCC Records, NA. See also *Variety* (29 May 1963), 21; House Commerce Committee, *Network Broadcasting*, House Report 1297, 85th Cong., 2d sess., 1958, pp. 46-47.
9   C.G. Thompson to Minow, 15 May 196, invoice 63A83, box 240, FCC Records, GSA.
10 *Variety* (6 Dec. 1961) 23; *New York Times*, 5 Dec. 1961; Senate Judiciary Committee, *Juvenile Delinquency*, hearings, 87th Cong., 1st sess., 1961, pp. 2340-341; Peter E. Kane to Robert E. Lee, 20 March 1962, docket 14645, vol. 3, FCC Records, NA.
11 Oliver Treyz to Minow, 10 Oct. 1961, box 2, Minow Papers.
12 *Detroit Free Press*, 12 May 1961; George Fearon to Commission, 13 Feb. 1961, docket 13859, vol. 1, FCC Records, NA.
13 Richard L. Tobin, "The Tyranny of the Local TV Station," *Saturday Review* (9 Sept. 1961), 41.
14 Kahn to Minow, 17 May 1961, invoice 63A83, box 240, FCC Records, GSA.
15 Notes of interview with Willie Grant, n.d., box 66, Mayer Papers. See also, National Association of Broadcasters, "Television Financial Report 1963," pamphlet, box 9, NAB Papers, for information on station profits.
16 Quoted in John Bartlow Martin, "The Big Squeeze," *Saturday Evening Post* (11 Nov. 1961), 62. Such assessments seem harsh. But other observers of the industry found a similar orientation. See Manny Lucoff, "Le Roy Collins and the National Association of Broadcasters" (Ph.D. diss., Univ. of Iowa, 1971), 242-72. Suggestive on the background of the station manager are Bunzel, *The American Small Businessman*; Winick, "The Television Station Manager."
17 Jones, *Licensing of Major Broadcast Facilities by the Federal Communications Commission*, 216. Sample "breakdowns" for two stations are reprinted in FCC, *Reports and Orders* 36 (1964), 423-28, and 37 (1964), 476-81; docket 14546, *Pro-*

ceedings, vol. 4, p. 1718, FCC Records, NA.

18 Buckley, "Partial Insight," 442.

19 *RR*, 1st ser., 20 (1960), 1901; Ford, "The Meaning of the 'Public Interest.' "

20 NBC, "David Brinkley's Journal," transcript of telecast, 27 May 1963, copy in group 3, box 5-4-32, Harris Papers.

21 Docket 14006, vols. 1, 4, FCC Records, NA; FCC, *Reports and Orders* 31 (1961), 16.

22 *Norfolk Virginian-Pilot*, 25 July 1961, *Portland Oregonian*, 18 July 1961, clippings in box 53, Minow Papers.

23 *Broadcasting* (4 Dec. 1961), 58-59 (3 Dec. 1962), 29-32 (1 April 1963), 70 (7 Feb. 1966), 90; Coons, *Freedom and Responsibility*, 92; Kenneth A. Cox, "The FCC"; idem, "FCC's Role in TV Programming Regulation," *Villanova Law Review* 14 (Summer 1969), 642; Cox and Johnson, *Broadcasting in America*, 5-6; Hurt, "FCC: Free Speech," 34. A copy of one "letter of inquiry is reprinted in *RR*, 1st ser., 25 (1963), 486-87.

24 Kintner, "Television and the World of Politics," 132; *Nation's Business* (Feb. 1963), 44; Epstein, *News from Nowhere*, 60-61; telephone interview with W. Theodore Pierson, 23 Jan. 1980.

25 Cox, "FCC's Role," 642.

26 Goldin, " 'Spare the Golden Goose,' " 1022; Lucoff, "Le Roy Collins," 66.

27 McKerns and Robertson, "Disciplinary Powers," lists license suspensions, actions on some of which were pending when the article was published. To complete this compilation, the commission's files on each station were checked. See also Robert Lewis Shayon, "An End to Laissez-Faire?" *Saturday Review* (24 March 1962), 35; F. Leslie Smith, "The Charlie Walker Case," *Journal of Broadcasting* 23 (Spring 1979), 137-51; FCC, *Reports and Orders* 31 (1961), 16; *Miami News*, 12 July 1961, *Denver Post*, 2 Aug. 1961, clippings in box 53, Minow Papers.

28 Minow, interview with author, 8 Aug. 1978; Rosenbloom, interview with author; Geller, interview with author. The station in question was apparently KCOP, later cited for over-commercialization. Compare Minow's claim with remarks in Coons, *Freedom and Responsibility*, 28; *Newsweek*, (11 Sept.

1961), 63. See also Jones, *Licensing of Major Broadcast Facilities*, 216, 28-20; *Broadcasting* (4 Dec. 1961), 58-59 (28 Feb. 1966), 30-31.

29 There was also the question of whether the courts would uphold the revocation on broader criteria. The judiciary had supported the commission's earliest revocations. Gould of the *New York Times*, for one, thought the commissioners hesitated for fear that the courts would only support the revocation of licenses of stations engaged in flagrant violation of earlier public service pledges to the agency (*New York Times*, 1 April 1962). The prospect of the courts' disapproval may have cautioned the chairman's colleagues; Minow, however, contended that the judiciary would have endorsed the FCC's more ambitious policing (*Newsweek* [11 Sept. 1961], 65; Minow, interview with author, 22 May 1978).

30 FCC, *Reports and Orders* 44 (1962), 2778, 2782-85.

31 Ibid. 36 (1964), 701, 708; see also, ibid. 38 (1965), 1143, 1154.

32 Minow, *Equal Time*, 57.

33 Quoted in Carson, "Television and Your Place in the Picture," 78.

34 Interview in *Show Business Illustrated* (Sept. 1961), 35.

35 *Variety* (4 April 1962), 26.

36 Docket 14546, *Proceedings*, vol. 2, pp. 54-56, 171-72, 183, 294, FCC Records, NA. The networks' Chicago stations also did less local, live telecasting than their Los Angeles outlets. Report of the presiding officer, docket 14546, *Proceedings*, vol. 2, p. 12, FCC Records, NA.

37 Docket 14546, *Proceedings*, vol. 2, pp. 252, 597, FCC Records, NA; *Chicago Daily News*, 17 March 1962 and 18 April 1962; *Chicago Tribune*, 22 July 1959 and 12 Dec. 1961; *Chicago Sun-Times*, 13 Feb. 1959.

38 *Variety* (11 Oct. 1961), 7. See also *Chicago Daily News*, 17 March 1962 and 18 April 1962.

39 *Chicago Tribune*, 22 July 1959, 10 Oct. 1961, 12 Dec. 1961; *Variety* (11 Oct. 1961), 27 (28 Feb. 1962), 27, 46 (21 March 1962), 31 (28 March 1962), 27 (25 April 1962), 25; *Chicago Daily News*, 17 March 1962; docket 14546, *Proceedings*, vol. 1, pp. 178-79, FCC Records, NA; Paul H. Douglas to David Sarnoff, 2 Feb. 1957, Raymond A. Jones et al. to Douglas, 8

Nov. 1958, box 277, Douglas Papers.

40 FCC, *Reports and Orders* 44 (1959), 1870.

41 Terry Turner, *Chicago Daily News*, 17 March 1962; docket 14546, notice of inquiry, 21 Feb. 1962, vol. 1, *Proceedings*, vol. 1, pp. 4-5, FCC Records, NA.

42 Docket 14546, *Proceedings*, vol. 11, p. 1661, FCC Records, NA.

43 Ibid., vol. 6, pp. 1007-09, vol. 8, pp. 1192-93, vol. 11, pp. 1660, 1668-69, 1695-96; *Chicago American*, 18 April 1962.

44 Hurt, "FCC: Free Speech," 33.

45 Docket 14546, report of presiding officer, 125, FCC Records, NA.

46 Docket 14546, *Proceedings*, vol. 3., p. 505, FCC Records, NA.

47 Ibid., pp. 486-89, 500-2, 505-6, 521-23, vol. 8, pp. 1192-93, 1228, 1232.

48 Docket 14546, report of presiding officer, esp. 12, 125-27; FCC Records, NA; *Wall Street Journal*, 13 Nov. 1962. Lee's style of interrogation suggests, however, that he was not enthusiastic about the hearings. *Chicago Sun-Times*, 24 and 25 March 1962.

49 *Variety* (9 Jan. 1963), 89 (23 Dec. 1964), 25 (7 April 1965), 51.

50 Cox, interview with author; Henry, interview with author.

51 See docket 14863, notice of inquiry, 21 Nov. 1962, vol. 1, FCC Records, NA, for Hyde's views. Ford's views are outlined in his address of 20 April 1963, copy made available to the author by Mr. Ford.

52 Memorandum, Henry H. Wilson to O'Brien, 15 March 1962, box 170, Kennedy Papers.; McClellan et al. to Kennedy, 6 Feb. 1962, Cross to Fulbright, 12 March 1962, Cross to Harris, 4 April 1962, group 3, box 5-2-18, Harris Papers.

53 Cross to Fulbright, 12 March 1962, group 3, box 5-2-18, Harris Papers; *Sponsor* (18 June 1962), 59; Fulbright to Cross, 19 March 1962, box 25, Fulbright Papers; Cox, interview with author; Minow in "Regulatory Agencies Panel," (1964) Oral History, JFKL, 36-40.

54 Robert Lewis Shayon, "Appointment in Suspense," *Saturday Review* (25 Aug. 1962), 22.

55 Robert Kennedy had been hoping to name Henry to an independent agency—almost any agency—since 1961. Henry, interview with author, and "The Reminiscences of E.

William Henry" (1966), Oral History, JFKL, 1-3, 28-29, 32. Not knowing Henry, Minow had not recommended him, but the nomination pleased the chairman anyway. Minow, interview with Graham and Kramer, 29 April 1973, tape in INSPIRE Papers.

56 So lacking was Henry in expertise that the FCC actually listed his college broadcasting experience in its official biography of him, attached with memorandum, Gillingham to Minow, 28 Sept. 1962, box 18, Minow Papers. See also, Senate Commerce Committee, *Sundry Nominations*, 87th Cong., 2d sess., 1962; "The Reminiscences of E. William Henry," Oral History, JFKL, 31.

57 Henry, interview with author; "The Reminiscences of E. William Henry," Oral History, JFKL, 33, 38; docket 14863, notice of inquiry, 21 Nov. 1962, vol. 7, FCC Records, NA. See also two speeches by Henry, 13 Dec. 1962 and 3 May 1963, copies in box 18, Minow Papers. Each is a ringing affirmation of the local hearing process and are heavily and affirmatively annotated by Minow.

58 R.B. White to Commission, 22 Jan. 1963, Mrs. R.H. Muchemore to FCC, 21 Jan. 1963, docket 14863, vol. 1, FCC Records, NA.

59 Ibid., *Proceedings*, vol. 1, p. 4; FCC, *Reports and Orders* 45 (1962), 422, 424-25.

60 Henry made this remark in a televised interview, 29 Jan. 1963. See *Omaha World-Herald*, 30 Jan. 1963 and 20 Feb. 1963; *Broadcasting* (4 Feb. 1963), 21, 30-32.

61 Henry to M.K. Haller, 20 Jan. 1963, docket 4863, vol. 6, FCC Records, NA.

62 *Omaha World-Herald*, 28 Jan. 1963.

63 *Broadcasting* (4 Feb. 1963), 30-31; Roman Hruska to Henry, 21 Jan. 1963, Carl Curtis to Minow, 25 Jan. 1963, copies in docket 14863, vol. 1, FCC Records, NA; J.P. McGlynn and William Moulton of Nebraska legislature to Henry, 1 Feb. 1963, box 55, Henry Papers; docket 14863, *Proceedings*, vol. 1, pp. 116-18, FCC Records, NA; Gerre Jones to Hruska, 28 Nov. 1962, Hruska to Robert L. Shrum, 28 Jan. 1963, box 184, Hruska Papers.

64 Docket 14863, *Proceedings*, vol. 5, pp. 1096-97, FCC Records, NA; memorandum, Bob Kutak to Dean Pholenz, 17 Dec.

1962, box 184, Hruska Papers.

65 Anthony Mueller [a pseudonym], "Inquiry or Inquisition," *Ave Maria* (3 Aug. 1963), 23, copy in box 55, Henry Papers.

66 Docket 14863, *Proceedings*, vol. 3, pp. 498-517, 552, 562, 565, FCC Records, NA.

67 Ibid., vol. 6, pp. 1111-112, vol. 5, pp. 1569-570.

68 Report of the presiding officer, docket 14863, 24 Oct. 1963, FCC Records, NA; San Francisco *Chronicle*, 16 Nov. 1963.

69 Frank N. Magid Associates, "Attitudes and Opinions Toward Television Stations, Omaha," April 1965, [report prepared for WOW], copy in box 55, Henry Papers.

70 Minow, *Equal Time*, 57.

71 Mueller, "Inquiry or Inquisition," 21. See also, Harold Seidman, *Politics, Position, and Power: The Dynamics of Federal Organization*, 2d ed. (New York, 1975), 173.

72 Situation comedies with working-class characters, though common in the 1950s with such programs as "The Life of Riley" and "The Honeymooners," were inexplicably absent from the schedules of the early 1960s. See Brooks and Marsh, *The Complete Directory*. One of the few series for this period with lower-class roles was "I'm Dickens, He's Fenster," favorably reviewed in *Variety* (3 Oct. 1962), 35.

73 Jones, *Licensing of Major Broadcast Facilities*, 219.

74 Margaret Ernest to Henry, 17 Jan. 1963; Susan Stone to Minow, 9 Feb. 1962, box 43, Minow Papers; Terry Turner, *Chicago Daily News*, 21 March 1962; docket 14546, *Proceedings*, vol. 4, pp. 1192-93, 1659-60; docket 14863, *Proceedings*, vol. 5, pp. 1655-45, FCC Records, NA.

75 On this point, see Charles V. Hamilton, "Blacks and the Crisis of Political Participation," *Public Interest*, no. 34 (Winter 1974), esp. 207; Dorothy Wickenden, "Mental Health's Malady," *New Republic* (15 Aug. 1981), 19-22; Theodore J. Lowi, *The End of Liberalism: Ideology, Policy, and the Crisis of Public Authority* (New York, 1969), 230-49.

76 Fairlie, *The Kennedy Promise*, 207.

77 Clare Boothe Luce to Minow, 1 Aug. 1961, box 26, Minow Papers.

78 Torre, *Don't Quote Me*, 142-43.

79 *Omaha World-Herald*, 3 Feb. 1963.

80 For example, see *Washington Post*, 22 May 1961.

81   Lee, "Let's Give the Public a Chance," 104. In fiscal year 1963, four times as many people wrote the FCC regarding the Rev. Carl McIntyre's religious broadcasts than had about Minow's talk (*Broadcasting* [27 Jan. 1964] 44).

82   Brown, *Television*, 258-59.

83   Sterling and Haight, *The Mass Media*, 308; *Broadcasting Yearbook 1963*, p. 19; *Broadcasting Yearbook 1964*, p. 26, the last of which reveals that local, live programs did increase notably for independent stations. Calculations of local, live programs include local taped productions as well.

84   Goldin, " 'Spare the Golden Goose,' " 1022.

85   Brown, *Television*, 167, 326.

CHAPTER 8

1   *Nation* (4 Jan. 1964), 2-3.

2   Mackey, "The National Association of Broadcasters"; idem, "The Development of the National Association of Broadcasters," *Journal of Broadcasting* 1 (Fall 1957), 305-25; memorandum, Ashbrook P. Bryant to the Commission, 13 April 1960, invoice 67A433, box 227, FCC Records, GSA.

3   *New York Times* 9 Nov. 1959; *New York Journal-American*, 9 Nov. 1959; *Christian Science Monitor*, 3 Nov. 1959; *Advertising Age* (1 Feb. 1960), 90; Donald G. McGannon to Norris Cotton, 7 Dec. 1959, box 45, Cotton Papers; press release, NAB, 16 Oct. 1959, box 10, NAB Papers; *Broadcasting* (11 April 1960), 48; remarks by McGannon, 18 Nov. 1959, copy in box 9, William H. Avery Papers.

4   Edwin H. James, "No Man's Collar But His Own," *Television Magazine* (May 1961), 59-60, 62, 65-71, 73; *Broadcasting* (3 Oct. 1960); 27-29; "The Reminiscences of Le Roy Collins" (1965), Oral History, JFKL, 37-40 and passim; *Baltimore Sun*, 27 Sept. 1960; *Miami Herald*, 4 Dec. 1960; *Television Digest* (4 Jan. 1961), 2; *Current Biography 1956* (New York, 1957), 122-24; Numan V. Bartley, *The Rise of Massive Resistance: Race Politics in the South during the 1950s* (Baton Rouge, 1969), 24, 141-44, 278-79.

5   Addresses by Collins, 17 May 1963, copy in box 80, Henry Papers, and 26 April 1963, copy in box 48, Minow Papers; James, "No Man's Collar," 71; John Bartlow Martin, "The

Big Squeeze," 66.

6   Speeches by Collins in box 6, NAB Papers.

7   *Television Digest* (13 Feb. 1961), 1; *Variety* (22 March 1961), 41.

8   Minow to Oren Harris, 31 March 1961, box 18, Minow Papers; Minow, interview, *Television Magazine* (July 1961), 63.

9   Minow, *Equal Time*, 50, 59, 61, 62.

10   NAB, *Code of Good Practice*, reprinted in *Broadcasting Yearbook, 1961-62* (Washington, D.C., 1962).

11   Minow, *Equal Time*, 61-63; confidential and unsigned memorandum, to Minow, n.d., c. April-May, 1961, box 28, Minow Papers.

12   Roscoe Barrow, quoted in Coons, *Freedom and Responsibility*, 71.

13   Draft of statement, c. Nov. 1962, Warren Braren to Frank Gavitt, n.d., and Frank Gavitt to John S. Cushman, 30 Nov. 1962, box 43, Minow Papers.

14   Addresses by Collins, 8 May 1961 and 19 Nov. 1962, copies in box 48, Minow Papers; address by Robert Swezey, NAB Code Authority Director, 13 Feb. 1962, copies in ibid.

15   Collins to Robert F. Kennedy, 21 June 1961, Lee Loevinger to Collins, 30 Oct. 1961, copies in box 28, Minow Papers.

16   *Broadcasting* (27 May 1963), 28-29; Robert Shepherd Morgan, "The Television Code of the National Association of Broadcasters: The First Ten Years" (Ph.D. diss., Iowa State Univ., 1964) 230; address by Robert Swezey, 18 Sept. 1962, copy in box 48, Minow Papers.

17   Address by Robert Swezey, 20 March 1962, 18 Sept. 1962, copies in box 48, Minow Papers; Morgan, "The Television Code," 277, 279.

18   Address by Robert Swezey, 15 Oct. 1962, copy in box 48, Minow Papers; Winick, *Taste and Censor in Television*, 24; docket 15083, vol. 11, *Proceedings*, vol. 1, pp. 98, 107, FCC Records, NA.

19   Docket 15083, vol. 12, *Proceedings*, vol. 2, pp. 272-73, FCC Records, NA.

20   *Broadcasting* (27 May 1963), 29.

21   Lucoff, "Le Roy Collins," 65-66, 202, 276.

22   Ibid., 108, 111-12, 276-77, 279; *Broadcasting* (April 1962),

5 (9 April 1962), 5 (16 April 1962), 51; Collins to Stanton, 10 May 1962, copy in box 28, Minow Papers; Senate Judiciary Committee, *Juvenile Delinquency*, hearings, 87th Cong. 2d sess., 1962, pp. 2418ff, 2540-41, 2588-89.

24 Lucoff, "Le Roy Collins," 4-5, 7, 15-16, 29-49, 58, 275, 296; *Variety* (22 March 1961), 43; *Broadcasting* (15 May 1961), 5 (16 Oct. 1961), 61 (20 Jan. 1964), 53; "The Reminiscences of E. William Henry" (1966), Oral History, JFKL, 40-41.

25 *Variety* (10 May 1961), 1; *Broadcasting* (20 Jan. 1964), 53; Lucoff, "Le Roy Collins," 58.

26 *Broadcasting* (16 Oct. 1961), 62; Lucoff, "Le Roy Collins," 82-83, 93, 170, 180-81, 190-91, 242-72.

27 Address by Collins, 3 April 1962, box 6, NAB Papers.

28 *Variety* (11 April 1962), 34; Lucoff, "Le Roy Collins," 101.

29 Minow, *Equal Time*, 62, 170, 256-57.

30 Memorandum, Max Paglin to Minow, 18 Sept. 1961, box 37, Minow Papers; Minow to author, 9 Aug. 1978. See also House Commerce Committee, *National Association of Securities Dealers*, Subcommittee print, 86th Cong., 1st sess., 1959; Parrish, *Securities*, 214-18; Robert Sobel, *N.Y.S.E.* (New York, 1975), 119, 247-48, 254.

31 Minow, *Equal Time*, 258.

32 *Broadcasting* (8 April 1963), 126, (20 April 1963), 50-56. *TV Guide* (11 May 1963), 2, spoke kindly of the NASD idea.

33 *Business Week* (20 April 1963), 38. Henry favored the proposal. Bernard Koteen, interview with Martin Mayer, n.d., box 65, Mayer Papers.

34 NAB, *Code of Good Practice.*

35 NBC, *Meet the Press* 6 (22 July 1962), 8; Dailey, "Minow Charts a Course," 6; Minow, *Equal Time*, 169-70, 256.

36 *Buxiness Week*, (20 April 1963), 40. See also *Printer's Ink* (1 March 1963), 68; *Los Angeles Times*, 1 Aug. 1963.

37 On Lee's reasoning, see two speeches, 16 Nov. 1963 and 28 Jan. 1965, box 68-131, Lee Papers; *Television Age*, (9 March 1959), 11. Like most within the FCC, Lee held to uninformed economic opinion. There was very little empirical proof that advertising appreciably raised the cost of goods. See Francis A. Lees and Charles Yneu Yang, "The Redistributional Effect of Television Advertising," *Economic Journal* 76 (June

1966), 328-36.

38 *Broadcasting* (26 Nov. 1962), 5; *Sponsor* (25 Feb. 1963), 31.

39 Press release, White House, 10 Dec. 1962, copy in box 45, Minow Papers; *Broadcasting* (3 Dec. 1962), 36; Henry Geller, interview with author. Of Cox's liberalism, one Washington observer commented, "Cox lacks one of the fundamental things in our society—he's not a complete man—he's not greedy." (Bernard Koteen, interview with Martin Mayer, n.d., box 65, Mayer Papers).

40 *Business Week* (20 April 1963), 38; *Printer's Ink* (1 March 1963) 68.

41 *Broadcasting* (1 April 1963), 63 (20 May 1963), 52-55; *Wall Street Journal*, 20 May 1963; *Atlanta Constitution*, 29 March 1963; *Washington Post*, 2 Aug. 1963.

42 *Business Week* (20 April 1963) 38.

43 Minow to Kennedy, 22 March 1963, 1 and 31 May 1963, WHSF, box 170, Kennedy Papers; *Broadcasting* (31 Dec. 1962), 5 (11 Feb. 1963), 23 (18 Feb. 1963), 36; *New York Times*, 15 May 1963; Minow, interview with author, 8 Aug. 1978; Minow, interview with Graham and Kramer, 29 April 1973, tape in INSPIRE Papers.

44 "The Reminiscences of Lee Loevinger" (1966), Oral History, JFKL, 35-36; Anthony Lewis, *New York Times*, 15 May 1963; Navasky, *Kennedy Justice*, 297; Senate Commerce Committee, *Appointments to the Regulatory Agencies*, 204-9, 275, Dan Fenn, interview with Graham and Kramer, 15 March 1973, notes in INSPIRE Papers; Lee White, interview with Graham and Kramer, 9 Nov. 1973, tape in INSPIRE Papers; Loevinger, interview with Graham and Kramer, 29 March 1973, tape in INSPIRE Papers; Geller, interview with author. Loevinger had too many friends among Minnesota's powerful Democrats, including Agriculture Secretary Orville Freeman and Senate Majority Whip Hubert H. Humphrey, to be removed completely from the administration (Humphrey to Ralph Demgen, 29 March 1968, box 904, Humphrey Papers).

45 Docket 14863, "Report of the Presiding Officer," 24 Oct. 1963, p. 54, FCC Records, NA; Minow, interview with Graham and Kramer, 29 April 1973, tape in INSPIRE Papers.

46 *Variety* (15 May 1963), 29 (22 May 1963), 23; *Business Week* (18 May 1963), 28; *Printer's Ink* (24 May 1963), 14; *Broad-*

casting (8 April 1963), 5 (13 May 1963), 64.

47   Address by Henry, 13 Dec. 1962, copy in box 18, Minow Papers.

48   Address by Henry, 24 Sept. 1963, box 77, Henry Papers.

49   *Broadcasting* (8 April 1963), 5.

50   Kenneth P. O'Donnell, interview with Graham and Kramer, c. 1973, tape in INSPIRE Papers.

51   *Wall Street Journal*, 22 Nov. 1963.

52   *Broadcasting* (2 Dec. 1963), 72; *Sponsor* (2 Dec. 1963), 65; *Wall Street Journal*, 4 Dec. 1963 and 13 Jan. 1964. Johnson's treatment of the FCC is discussed at length in the next chapter.

53   Cox, interview with author; Henry, interview with author.

54   Docket 15083, vol. 11, *Proceedings*, vol. 26 (Aug. 1964), 180, copy in box 1, Loevinger Papers; Loevinger to John de J. Pemberton, 11 May 1964, box 379 ACLU Papers, Princeton University; Loevinger to W.H. Ferry, 20 July 1964, box 351, ibid.; Loevinger, "Role of Law." Loevinger had given little hint of this approach to regulation. Senate Commerce Committee, *Sundry Nominations*, hearings, 88th Cong., 1st sess., 1963.

55   Harris to Henry, 10 Dec. 1963, box 17, Henry Papers; Lloyd Bentsen to Rogers, 13 Oct. 1963, copy in Departmental Files, Ancher Nelsen Papers; House Commerce Committee, *Lack of Authority of the Federal Communications Commission to Make Rules*.

56   Termination order, 15 Jan. 1964, docket 15083, vol. 15, FCC Records, NA; *New York Times*, 16 Jan. 1964; *Washington Post*, 17 Jan. 1964.

57   FCC, *Reports and Orders* 36 (1964), 48-49; *RR*, 2d ser., 1 (1964), 1606, 1160.

58   *Washington Star*, 21 Jan. 1964.

59   *Congressional Quarterly Almanac, 1964* (Washington, D.C., 1965), 560-61, 610-11; *New York Times*, 24 Nov. 1963 and 10 April 1964; address by Walter Rogers, 28 April 1964, copy in box 78, Henry Papers; Kenneth A. Roberts, "Should the Government Regulate Radio-Television Commercials?" *American Legion Magazine* (March 1964), 27; John de J. Pemberton to Henry, 28 April 1964, and minutes, ACLU radio-TV committee, box 351, ACLU Papers, Princeton Univ.;

Frank L. Baird, "Program Regulation on the New Frontier," *Journal of Broadcasting* 11 (Summer 1967), 231-43; Lawrence D. Longley, "FCC's Attempt to Regulate Commercial Time," ibid. (Winter 1966-67), 83-89.

60 Henry, interview with author; Cox, interview with author; NET, "At Issue," transcript, 6 Jan. 1966, p. 2, copy in box 39, Henry Papers; *Broadcasting* (18 Jan. 1964), 40 (17 Feb. 1964), 94; Cox, "FCC's Role," 644.

61 Leonard Zeidenberg, "Is the FCC Obsolete?" 57; Norris Cotton to Mr. and Mrs. William J. Bradley, 8 April 1964, box 50, Cotton Papers; Roman Hruska to Charles Thone, 6 March 1964, box 144, Hruska Papers.

62 Robert J. Kutak to Charles Thone, 27 March 1964, box 144, Hruska Papers; Gerald C. Roth & Co., "Television Broadcasting Industry Networks and Owned Stations," report prepared for ITT, April 1964, docket 16828, vol. 27, invoice 173-75-9, box 190, FCC Records, GSA; Geller, interview with author.

63 Geller, interview with author.

64 Henry Steele Commager to Leverett Saltonstall, 8 March 1964, copy in box 2, Henry Papers.

65 For similar arguments, see Long, "Bureaucracy and Constitutionalism"; Newman and Keaton, "Congress and the Faithful Execution of Laws."

66 Collins to John O. Pastore, copy in box 16, Henry Papers; Lucoff, "Le Roy Collins," 188ff; Collins to all NAB members, copy in box 2, Henry Papers; NAB, "Comments," 30 Sept. 963, docket 15083, FCC Records, NA.

67 *Sponsor* (25 Feb. 1963), 31-32, 46; docket 15083, vol. 11, *Proceedings*, vol. 2, pp. 264ff, FCC Records, NA; C.W. Montgomery to Henry, 6 Sept. 1963, box 2, Henry Papers; Arthur M. Swift to Ancher Nelsen, 12 Nov. 1963, N.L. Bentson to Nelsen, 1 Nov. 1963, Sherman K. Headley to Nelsen, 3 Oct. 1963, Departmental Files, Nelsen Papers. See also telegrams and other correspondence from six New York City radio and television station managers to Congressman Emanuel Celler, in box 306, Celler Papers.

68 Statement, Theodore C. Bastic, NAB Code Review Board, 10 and 11 July 1963, p. 2, copy in box 2, Henry Papers; Otto Ulrich to Roman Hruska, 27 June 1963, box 184, Hruska

Papers.

69 Statement by Sherman K. Headley, c. Oct. 1963, copy in Departmental Files, Nelsen Papers. See also Matusow, "When Push Comes to Shove," 33-35, 38-39.

70 Two studies dealing primarily with the Senate suggest that orchestrated lobbying efforts such as that employed by the NAB have at best marginal influence, *unless* congressmen find a self-interest (in this instance, access to the airwaves) in supporting the lobbyist's position (Bauer, Pool, and Dexter, *American Business and Public Policy*, ch. 12, and Donald R. Matthews, *U.S. Senators and Their World*, ch. 8).

71 Peabody et al., *To Enact a Law*, 30. Cf. Miller and Stokes, "Constituency in Congress," 47, 54-55.

72 See Schwerin Research Corporation poll of 1,720 viewers, cited in *Television Digest* (7 March 1960), 11; Irene Kawin to Lawrence Spivak, 8 Dec. 1963, box A-13, Spivak Papers; docket 15083, vol. 11, *Proceedings*, vol. 1, pp. 162, 177, FCC Records, NA; *Printer's Ink* (9 Feb. 1962), 26-27, 32-33; Steiner, *The People Look*, ch. 7, esp. 221-22. Although maintaining that most Americans "favored" broadcast advertising, one survey indicated an increasing disaffection between 1953 and 1961 with advertising (Greyser and Bauer, "Americans and Advertising").

73 Tom Steed et al. to FCC, 6 Sept. 1963, A.S. Mike Monroney to Ward L. Quaal, 14 Oct. 1963, box 31, Monroney Papers. A review of the collections of two members of Oklahoma's delegation confirms this observation. Occasionally citizens did write about TV but rarely concerning overcommercialization.

74 Docket 15083, vol. 11, *Proceedings*, vol. 1, p. 44, FCC Records, NA; Karl H. Grossman to Celler, 9 Nov. 1963, box 306, Celler Papers.

75 Constituent newsletter, Congressman Thomas J. Gill of Hawaii, 3 March 1964, copy in box 2, Henry Papers.

76 Rapoport, "And Now, A Brief Word," 26-27.

77 Robert W. Hemphill to G. Richard Shafto, 19 Feb. 1963, box 3, Hemphill Papers. See also Peabody et al., *To Enact a Law*, 17; Matthews, *U.S. Senators*, 229-30.

78 Berkman, "A Modest Proposal."

79 Telegram, Joseph P. Dougherty to Fogarty, 12 Feb. 1964,

Fogarty to Dougherty, 13 Feb. 1964, box 72, Fogarty Papers.

80 Peabody et al., *To Enact a Law*, 65, 68; Bailey, *Congress Makes a Law*, 126, 148-49, 185-87.

81 Roll call compared with listing in *Broadcasting* (6 May 1963), 58-59.

82 Robert E. Lee to Bernard Hollander, 24 Feb. 1964, Department Files, file 60-211-62, sec. 6, Department of Justice Records.

CHAPTER 9

1 John W. Macy, Jr., interview with Graham and Kramer, 12 June 1973, tape in INSPIRE Papers; Senate Commerce Committee, *Appointments to the Regulatory Agencies*, 260, 389.

2 Press release, NAB, 27 Jan. 1965, copy in box 49, Henry Papers. *Broadcasting* (6 July 1964), 5 (13 July 1965), 44-46.

3 Howard H. Bell to Henry, 13 Feb. 1964, Henry to Bell, 8 Dec. 1965, box 50, Henry Papers.

4 *Broadcasting* (24 Jan. 1966) 40 (14 Feb. 1966), 32.

5 George Gerbner, "The Structure and Process of Television Program Content Regulation in the United States," in Comstock and Rubinstein, *Television and Social Behavior*, I: *Media Conent and Control*, 410; *Chicago Tribune*, 19 Sept. 1967; Robert Lewis Shayon, "Morality Building with the FBI," *Saturday Review* (30 July 1966), 42.

6 *Broadcasting* (13 Jan. 1964), 40 (20 Jan. 1964), 34 (17 Feb. 1964), 36; *Denver Post*, 17 Feb. 1964; memorandum to Henry, n.d., box 50, Henry Papers.

7 Henry to Oren Harris, 19 Dec. 1963, box 17, Henry Papers.

8 *Broadcasting* (6 July 1964), 38-39.

9 FCC Public Notice of 24 July 1964; Loevinger, "The Role of Government in the Field of Advertising," ABA Antitrust Section, *Proceedings*, vol. 26 (Aug. 1964), copy in box 1, Loevinger Papers.

10 *Broadcasting* (5 July 1965), 40; Cox and Johnson, *Broadcasting in America*, 5; Carl R. Ramey, "Federal Communications Commission and Broadcast Advertising: An Analytical Review," *Federal Communications Bar Journal* 20, no. 2 (1966), 109. See also *Broadcasting* (12 July 1965), 33-34 (6 Dec. 1965) 40-41 (28 Feb. 1966), 30-31; Cox, "FCC's Role,"

643.

11 Arlen, *Living-Room War*, 163-67.

12 Data cited in address by Henry, 23 March 1965, box 77, Henry Papers. See also Robert E.R. Huntley and Charles E. Phillips, Jr., "Community Antenna Television: Some Issues of Public Policy," *Alabama Law Review* 18 (Spring 1966) 2, 309; George W. Darlington, "The Many Worlds of Local TV," *Television Magazine* 24 (Aug. 1967), 34-43, 60.

13 Cox and Johnson, *Broadcasting in America*, passim.

14 Jaffe, "Program Control," 619.

15 Henry, interview with author.

16 Brown, *Television*, 181, 258-59.

17 Minow, *Equal Time*, 26-28; Ashmore, *Fear in the Air*, 77-78; Fred W. Friendly, *The Good Guys*, ch. 7.

18 FCC, *Reports and Orders* 38 (1965), 1135, 1154; Henry, interview with author; Geller, interview with author.

19 *Office of Communication of the United Church of Christ v. FCC*, 359, F.2d. (1966), 994, 1003.

20 Ibid., at 1008.

21 *Broadcasting* (29 March 1965), 50; *Variety* (31 March 1965) 28; 28; *Washington Star*, 25 March 1965.

22 *Broadcasting* (29 March 1965), 50; Loevinger, "Religious Liberty"; Cox wrote a rejoinder, *George Washington Law Review* 34 (Dec. 1965), 196-218.

23 Quoted in Edith Efron, "He Has Seen Pig Pens Better Run," *TV Guide* 12 (3 July 1965), 5-19. Loevinger quickly apologized for this remarks (Loevinger to Editor, *TV Guide*, 29 June 1965, copy in box 45, Henry Papers). For other examples of Loevinger's opinions on broadcast regulation, see his "Role of Law"; idem, "The Issues in Program Regulation."

24 *Variety* (31 March 1965), 28, 50; *Broadcasting* (29 March 1965), 58.

25 *Wall Street Journal*, 19 Nov. 1964; Ford, interview with author, 15 June 1978; *Broadcasting* (29 March 1965), 37 (11 April 1966), 34; Robert Kintner to Johnson, 21 April 1966, unsigned memorandum to Johnson, 12 June 1967, WHCF, EX, 228/A, Johnson Papers; Senate Commerce Committee, *Appointments to the Regulatory Agencies*, ch. 16.

26 Senate Commerce Committee, *Appointments to the Regulatory Agencies*, 251; memoranda, Ernest Goldstein to

Johnson, 26 Dec. 1967, Doug Nobles to W. Marvin Watson, 11 Jan. 1968, WHCF, EX, FG 228, Johnson Papers; Hubert Humphrey to Ralph Demgen, 29 March 1968, box 904, Humphrey Papers; "The Reminiscences of Lee Loevinger" (1966), Oral History, JFKL, esp. 36.

27 Senate Commerce Committee, *Appointments to the Regulatory Agencies*, 247-49; *Broadcasting* (29 March 1965), 37. Although he failed to discuss Wadsworth's designation with Henry, Johnson did call Robert Kintner, then NBC president. Kintner to Johnson, 26 March 1965, WHCF, EX, FG, 228, Johnson Papers.

28 Quoted in Drew, "Is the FCC Dead?" 32.

29 *Broadcasting* (11 April 1966), 34; Senate Commerce Committee, *Appointments to the Regulatory Agencies*, 251; telephone interview with Sterling Quinlan, Loevinger, 21 Dec. 1972, notes in box 12, Quinlan Papers; Bob Adams, interview with Quinlan, 23 Jan. 1973. Cf. Harold B. Meyers, "FCC's Expanding, Demanding Universe," *Fortune* 73 (June 1966), 150-53.

30 "The Reminiscences of Newton N. Minow" (1971), Oral History, LBJL, 21-22.

31 Henry, interview with author; *Wall Street Journal*, 4 Dec. 1963, 13 Jan. 1964.

32 *Broadcasting* (2 Dec. 1963), 72.

33 "The Reminiscences of Leonard Marks" (1970), Oral History, LBJL, 5, 13-15: *Wall Street Journal*, 23 and 24 March 1964, 30 April 1964, 9 April 1967; Goldman, *Tragedy of Lyndon Johnson*, 417.

34 Goldman, *Tragedy of Lyndon Johnson*, 27; *Wall Street Journal*, 13 Jan. 1964, 24 March 1964; David Delanis, interview with Martin Mayer, n.d., notes in box 65, Mayer Papers; *Broadcasting* (25 Nov. 1963), 9 (20 July 1964), 5; Laurence Stern, "LBJ and the FCC."

35 *Chicago Tribune*, 16 Dec. 1963; *Broadcasting* (25 Nov. 1963), 9; *Wall Street Journal*, 13 Jan. 1964.

36 Armon Glenn, "Lucrative Channels," *Barron's* (27 Jan. 1964), 12.

37 *Wall Street Journal*, 29 Nov. 1963 and 13 Jan. 1964; *Printer's Ink* (29 Nov. 1963), 11.

38 Joseph P. Harris, "The Senatorial Rejection of Leland Olds: A

Case Study," 690-91; Ronnie Dugger, *The Politician: The Life and Times of Lyndon Johnson*, 2 vols. (New York; 1982-), I:350-54; Goldman, *Tragedy of Lyndon Johnson*, 44-45; Kearns, *Lyndon Johnson and the American Dream*, 373, 386; Robert Caro, "The Years of Lyndon Johnson," *Atlantic* (Oct. 1981), 39-45 (April 1982), 36-38, 75; George Norris Green, *The Establishment in Texas Politics: The Primitive Years, 1938-1957* (Westport, Conn., 1979), 12-15, 113; V.O. Key, Jr., *Southern Politics in State and Nation* (New York, 1949), ch. 22.

39 Kearns, *Lyndon Johnson and the American Dream*, 108, 121-24, 133, 136-37, 373, 384; Jeanne Kirkpatrick, review of Kearns, *Commentary* 62 (Aug. 1976), 76; James Reston, *New York Times*, 8 Jan. 1964; T. Harry Williams, "Huey, Lyndon, and Southern Radicalism," *Journal of American History* 60 (Sept. 1973), 290; Ralph K. Huitt, "Democratic Party Leadership in the Senate," *American Political Science Review*, 55 (June 1961), 337, 338.

40 Hobart Rowan, *The Free Enterprisers: Kennedy, Johnson, and the Business Establishment*, 279-81, 291; *Wall Street Journal*, 29 Nov. 1963 and 9 Jan. 1964; Hamby, *The Imperial Years*, 305. Johnson's ostensible penchant for penny-saving led him on Nov. 29 to send a strongly worded memo demanding reductions in departmental and commission expenses (E. William Henry to bureau heads and staff officers, 3 Dec. 1963, and Lyndon B. Johnson to department and agency heads, 30 Nov. 1963, box 76, Henry Papers).

41 John Morton Blum, *The Progressive Presidents: Roosevelt, Wilson, Roosevelt, Johnson* (New York, 1980), 180; William Appleman Williams, *Some Presidents: Wilson to Nixon* (New York, 1972), 91-92; Rowland Evans and Robert Novak, *Lyndon B. Johnson and the Exercise of Power* (New York, 1966), 484-89; Herbert S. Parmet, *The Democrats: The Years after FDR* (New York, 1976), 228-29; *U.S. News and World Report* (11 May 1964), 58; *Business Week* (18 Jan. 1964), 282-29 (7 Nov. 1964), 37; Jack Bell, *The Johnson Treatment* (New York, 1965), 120; Rosen, "Johnson and the Businessmen"; Levitt, "The Johnson Treatment"; Harold B. Meyers, "L.B.J.'s Romance with Business," *Fortune* (Sept. 1964), 131-33, 222, 226, 230. Allen J. Matusow, *The Unraveling of America: A*

History of Liberalism in the 1960s (New York, 1984), sees little difference between Kennedy and Johnson in their courting of the business community; Johnson was simply better at it. See also Kim McQuaid, *Big Business and Presidential Power: From FDR to Reagan* (New York, 1982), ch. 7; David T. Bazelon, "Big Business and the Democrats," *Commentary* (May, 1965), 39-46.

42 Theodore Lowi, "The Public Philosophy: Interest Group Liberalism," *American Political Science Review* 61 (March 1967), 21. See also Richard J. Barber, "The New Partnership.

43 Address by Henry, 23 March 1965, box 77, Henry Papers; *New York Herald Tribune*, 24 March 1965. For related criticisms, see Cecil Smith, *Los Angeles Times*, 15 Oct. 1964; *Baltimore Sun*, 19 May 1963: *New Orleans States-Item*, 8 April 1963; *New York Herald Tribune*, 28 April 1963. Henry's dark view tends to be supported by a comparison of the March 1961 and March 1965 NBC and CBS schedules in Hyman H. Goldin, " 'Serious' Commercial Network Programming: Statistical Notes on Trend and Scope," report for the Carnegie Commission on Educational Television, 17 March 1965, box 2-7, Carnegie Commission Papers.

44 Humphrey, for example, had stood with Minow during the controversy over the FCC's reorganization in June 1961. Memorandum, James M. Landis to Lawrence F. O'Brien and Michael Manitos, 24 June 1961, box 19, Landis Papers, JFKL.

45 Address by Humphrey, 28 March 1965, box 1287, Humphrey Papers.

46 Ibid.

47 Ibid.; *Wall Street Journal*, 24 March 1965; *Broadcasting* (29 March 1965), 76-77. Humphrey echoed this theme in a March 25 address to the American Society of Magazine Editors, copy in box 1287, Humphrey Papers. For accounts of Humphrey's NAB talk, see *Broadcasting* (29 March 1965), 76-77. Also see Ways, " 'Creative Federalism.' "

48 *Wall Street Journal*, 24 March 1965.

49 Memorandum, Theodore Koop to Frank Stanton, 3 March 1965, copy in WHCF, Name File, Johnson Papers.

50 Route slip, Jack Valenti to Henry, 15 March 1965, UT 1-1, Johnson Papers. Henry did not later recall this snub (Henry, interview with author).

51   Henry, interview with author.

52   Henry, interview with author; Evans and Novak, *Johnson*, 339, 341, 343-44. Johnson's reticence did not result from a lack of interest or familiarity with the activities of the FCC. The president's mastery of the minutiae of government constantly amazed commissioners and sublevel agency officials. Johnson knew what was going on in every part of official Washington, including the FCC. "The Reminiscences of Nicholas Johnson" (1969), Oral History, LBJL, 4-5; memorandum, Robert Kintner to Lyndon Johnson, 6 July 1966, WHCF, CF, UT 1-1.

53   "The Reminiscences of Nicholas Johnson," Oral History, LBJL, 44; Henry, interview with author; Rosel Hyde, interview with Sterling Quinlan, 1972, tape in box 12, Quinlan Papers; *Broadcasting* (9 Nov. 1964), 30; memorandum to files, Robert Kintner, 3 Sept. 1966, WHCF, Gen, UT 1-1, Johnson Papers; Loevinger interview, WCBS Radio, "WCBS Looks at Television," 19 July 1965, transcript in WCBS Radio Papers.

54   Senate Commerce Committee, *Appointments to the Regulatory Agencies*, 254, 256-57, 260, recounts such tutorials held for Commissioners Hyde, Johnson, and Lee.

55   Halberstam, *The Powers That Be*, 440-41.

56   *Wall Street Journal*, 23 March 1964; Stanton to Walter Jenkins, 9 Dec. 1963, Jenkins to Stanton, 12 Dec. 1963, WHCF, Gen, UT 1-1, Johnson Papers; Johnson to Stanton, 24 Feb. 1964, George Reedy to Stanton, 14 April 1964, Bill Moyers to Johnson, 16 July 1964. Jack Valenti to Moyers, 4 Aug. 1964, WHCF, Name File, Johnson Papers; Joseph Califano to Johnson, 11 Jan. 1966, 25 July 1967, WHCF, EX, FG 228, ibid. When Johnson finally agreed to speak before the NAB in April 1968, Stanton edited the president's speech. (Douglass Cater to Johnson, 31 March 1968, WHCF, Name File, ibid.)

57   Quoted in Barnouw, *A History of Broadcasting*, III:144.

58   Record of long-distance call to New York City, Johnson to Sarnoff, 3 Sept. 1965, Johnson Papers; Robert W. Sarnoff to Johnson, 13 Sept. 1965, WHCF, Name File, ibid.

59   Kintner to Johnson, 27 Nov. 1963, Johnson to Jean Kintner, 25 Nov. 1964, Kintner to Moyers, 17 March 1965, Hayes Redmon to Moyers, 29 July 1965, Moyers to Kintner, 3 Aug. 1965, telegram from Kintner to Moyers, 25 Aug. 1965,

Kintner to Moyers, 16 June 1966, WHCF, Name File, Johnson
Papers. Robert Kintner to Moyers, 16 June 1966, Kintner to
Johnson, 20 June 1966, WHCF, FG 11-8-1, ibid.; Cassie Mackin
feature for Hearst Headline Service, dated 19 June 1966, clipping in ibid; *New York Times*, 23 Dec. 1980.

60 Kintner to Sarnoff, 25 Feb. 1966, copy in box 51, Henry
Papers; Edwin L. Weisl to Valenti, 4 Feb. 1966, Moyers to
Johnson, 25 Feb. 1966, Kintner to Marvin Watson, 15 April
1966, WHCF, Name File, Johnson Papers; Kintner to Johnson,
14 June 1966, WCHF, UT 11-8-1, Johnson Papers.

61 Moyers to Kintner, 8 April 1966, WHCF, CF, Staff Aides File,
FG 11-8-1, Johnson Papers; Kintner to Harry McPherson, 18
Jan. 1967, WHCF CF, UT 1-1, ibid.; Grossman and Kumar,
Portraying the President, 165-66; Milton Viorst, "The Rise
and Fall of Robert Kintner," *Washingtonian* (June 1967),
35-36.

62 Moyers complained to Stanton of inadequate attention in a
CBS newscast to the administration's position on the Viet-
nam war, 14 Feb. 1966, WHCF, Name File, Johnson Papers.
On Johnson's efforts to woo the broadcast media, see
Grossman and Kumar, *Portraying the President*, 285,
William C. Spragens, "The Myth of the Johnson 'Credibility
Gap,'" *Presidential Studies Quarterly* 10 (Fall 1980); 629-35;
Culbert, "Johnson and the Media."

63 Johnson to Thomas Wolf, 13 Jan. 1969, WHCF, Name File,
Johnson Papers; *Variety* (9 Dec. 1964), 1.

64 Review of Richard Rovere, *The Goldwater Caper*, New York
Herald Tribune Book Review, c. March 1965, clipping in box
8, Rovere Papers; Goldman, *Tragedy of Lyndon Johnson*,
37-38, 42; William E. Leuchtenburg, "The Genesis of the
Great Society," *Reporter* (21 April 1966) 36-39.

65 Richard K. Doan, "All's Quiet on the Status Quo," *New
York Magazine* (26 July 1964), 36; Arthur M. Schlesinger, Jr.,
interview with author; *Broadcasting* (27 Jan. 1964), 55.

66 *New York Times*, 27 Sept. 1965 and 17 Oct. 1965; *Variety*
(14 Nov. 1962), 22 (24 April 1963), 28-29. The half-hearted efforts to present "better" children's fare all but ended in
mid-1963: CBS cancelled "The Reading Room," NBC cancelled
"Exploring," and ABC relegated "Discovery" to a weekly basis
(*Baltimore Sun*, 19 May 1963).

67 *Chicago Sun-Times*, 13 and 14 Feb. 1964; Ben Waple to ABC,

4 March 1964, docket 14546, vol. 10, FCC Records, NA.

68   From survey used in Frank Wolf, "Some Determinants of Public Affairs Programming on Commercial Television in the United States" (Ph.D. diss., Columbia University, 1971), 100n.

69   Using data from the A.C. Nielsen Company, Henry's aides calculated that the number of network news and informational programs dropped from 271 hours in the 1960-61 season to 210 in 1963-64. Art Schatzow to Henry, 11 May 1965, box 70, Henry Papers. Stanton of CBS disputed such calculations, but he counted the four days the networks covered Kennedy's assassination. Stanton to Henry, 27 May 1965, ibid. Figures cited in *Variety* (6 Oct. 1965), 35, 51, detail the decline of public service network telecasts for the 964-65 and 1965-66 seasons.

70   *Variety* (6 Oct. 1965), 35, 51.

71   The best single analysis of the scheduling of news programs is Epstein, *News from Nowhere.*

72   Production notes for NBC's coverage, 17 and 18 Feb. 1966, box 5, Ashman Papers.

73   Stanton to John de J. Pemberton, Jr., 28 Feb. 1966, box 412, ACLU Papers, Princeton Univ.; *Broadcasting* (7 March 1966), 58. I found no evidence that Stanton played a role in Schneider's decision, which probably related more to Paley's unhappiness over lower earnings growth than Stanton's close ties to the Johnson administration. Halberstam, *The Powers That Be*, 503-6, implies otherwise.

74   Fred W. Friendly, *Due to Circumstances*, 169-84 and chs. 9-10; Arlen, *Living-Room War*, 191; Small, *To Kill a Messenger*, 118; Joseph C. Harsch to William McAndrew, 6 April 1966, 1968 Addition, box 4, Harsch Papers; *Broadcasting* (14 Feb. 1966), 9. For Commissioner Loevinger's sarcastic view of Friendly's resignation, see address, 2 April 1967, Loevinger Papers, which industry groups reprinted in *New York Times*, 24 April 1967.

75   *Broadcasting* (21 Feb. 1966), 74.

76   Kintner to Johnson, 14 June 1966, WHCF, CF, FG -8-1, Johnson Papers.

77   Kintner to Robert Sarnoff, 25 Feb. 1966, copy in box 51, Henry Papers. See also Kintner address, reprinted in *Broad-*

casting (12 Dec. 1966), 52.

78 *Variety* (27 Oct. 1965), 39; *TV Guide* (26 Nov. 1966), A-1.

79 *New York Times*, 9 April 1966; *Broadcasting* (11 April 1966), 33-35, 134; Henry to Johnson, 5 April 1966, Johnson to Henry, 11 April 1966, WHCF, EX, FG 228/A, Johnson Papers; Henry interview with author.

80 Eric F. Goldman, interview with author

81 Editorial, *New York Times*, 20 June 1966; *Business Week*, (25 June 1966), 42; *Broadcasting* (27 June 1966), 29, 31; Joseph Califano, interview with Graham and Kramer, 5 June 1973, notes in INSPIRE Papers.

82 Kintner to Johnson, 21 April 1966, 20 June 1966, WHCF, CF, FG 228, Johnson Papers; Kintner to Johnson, 30 June 1966, FG 228/A, ibid.

83 *Los Angeles Times*, 26 Sept. 1966.

84 Zeidenberg, "Is the FCC Obsolete?" 56; Drew, "Is the FCC Dead?" 33; *Broadcasting* (7 Feb. 1966), 90.

85 Nicholas Johnson, interview with author; Califano, interview with Graham and Kramer, 5 June 1973, notes in INSPIRE Papers; memorandum, James M. Graham to file, 24 April 1973, ibid.

86 Wadsworth, reply to questionnaire, n.d. [1973], INSPIRE Papers; "The Reminiscences of Nicholas Johnson," (1969) Oral History, LBJL, 41, 43-44; Senate Commerce Committee, *Appointments to the Regulatory Agencies*, 256-57; W. Marvin Watson to Johnson, 5 April 1965, WHCF, Name File, Johnson Papers.

87 *Broadcasting* (21 Feb. 1966), 74.

88 Stanton, interview with author.

89 Nicholas Johnson, "CATV: Promise and Peril," *Saturday Review* (11 Nov. 1967), 87-88; idem, "Media Barons and the Public Interst," *Atlantic* (June 1968), 43-51; idem, "What You Can Do to Improve TV," *Harper's* (Feb. 1969), 14.

90 See, for example, address before Iowa Association of Broadcasters, 13 May 1967, reprinted in Pennybacker and Braden, *Broadcasting and the Public Interest*, 22-40.

91 "A New Fidelity to the Regulatory Ideal," *Georgetown Law Journal* 59 (March 1971), 883. For a harsh and provocative assessment of Johnson's FCC years, see Kolson, "Broadcasting in the Public Interest."

92   Quinlan, *The Hundred Million Dollar Lunch*, 121.
93   Senate Commerce Committee, *Appointments to the Regulatory Agencies* 257.
94   Henry, interview with author.
95   Joseph Califano to Johnson, 22 May 1967, WHCF, Name File, Johnson Papers; Senate, *Appointments to the Regulatory Agencies*, 260.
96   Wolf, "Some Determinants," 100.

CHAPTER 10

1   John O. Pastore, "TV Allocations: A National Problem," draft of article, 3 April 1964, Pastore Papers.
2   David Potter, "The Historical Perspective," in Donner, *The Meaning of Commercial Television*, 66-67. See also *Los Angeles Times*, 11 Dec. 1963; Clair Wilcox, *Public Policies toward Business*, 462; address by Minow, 22 Jan. 1963, box 47, Minow Papers.
3   Loevinger, "The Issues in Program Regulation," 11; address by idem, "The Role of Law in Broadcasting," 4 May 1964, Loevinger Papers, reprinted in *Journal of Broadcasting* 8 (Spring 1964), 113-24.
4   Address, 23 March 1965, box 77, Henry Papers.
5   *RR*, 2d ser., 11 (1967), 968; FCC, *Reports and Orders*, 2d ser. 10 (1967), 823; Wolf, "Some Determinants," 94-95; Anne Coffey, "The 'Top 50 Market Policy': Fifteen Years of Non-Policy," *Federal Communications Law Journal* 31 (Spring 1979), 303-39.
6   ABC, press release, 7 Dec. 1965, copy in box 3, Henry Papers; idem, preliminary notice of annual meeting of stockholders, n.d., Goldenson to Harold S. Geneen, 18 March 1966, docket 16828, vol. 1, invoice 173-75-9, box 182, FCC Records, GSA; *Broadcasting* (6 Dec. 1965), 27-30 (13 Dec. 1965), 33-35; Carol J. Loomis, "That Long, Lively Pursuit of A.B.C.," *Fortune* (March 1969), 131.
7   Docket 16828, vol. 24, *Proceedings*, vol. 1, pp. 70, 73-74, 96ff, 105-6, 252, 259, box 189, FCC Records, GSA . The chairman of ABC argued that the merger would so greatly aid UHF that the establishment of a fourth commercial network would soon follow. This new network would rely on UHF

outlets for affiliates and be able to provide the diverse programming that the first three networks had long abandoned
or limited. See ibid., 107-8, 316-18.

8   Opinion of hearing examiner, 25 July 1966, docket 16828,
box 189, FCC Records, GSA.

9   *RR*, 2d ser., 9 (1966), 23-24, and 10 (1967), 290-91, 304-05,
319. Three commissioners, Bartley, Cox, and Johnson, voted
against the merger, which they held would unduly concentrate the industry.

10 William Putnam to McGeorge Bundy, 29 Oct. 1965, and 9
Nov. 1965, WHCF, CF, UT-1-1, Johnson Papers; James E.
Bailey to Norris Cotton, 26 Sept. 1958, box 42, Cotton
Papers. Such concerns seemed confirmed in preliminary
research on CATV's effects on UHF. Fisher and Ferrall, "Com-
munity Antenna Systems."

11 Morris J. Gelman, " 'U' as in Upward," *Television Magazine*
(Oct. 1965), 65; Vincent J. Wasilewski to A.S. Mike
Monroney, 21 Jan. 1966, box 66, Monroney Papers; A. James
Ebel to Roman Hruska, 29 March 1965, Jim Ballas to
Hruska, 1 March 1966, box 188, Hruska Papers.

12 FCC, *Reports and Orders* 32 (1962), 459; *RR* 2d ser., 4 (1965),
1679, and 6 (1966), 1717, 1779; Henry to Charles McC.
Mathias, 11 March 1966, box 18, Henry Papers; Charles O.
Verrill, Jr., "CATV's Emerging Role: Cablecaster or Common
Carrier?" *Law and Contemporary Problems* 34 (Summer
1969), 592ff. The Supreme Court upheld the commission's
right to regulate CATV in *U.S.* v. *Southwestern Cable*, 392
U.S. (1968), 157. The Rules required that cable systems first
apply to the FCC for permission to transmit the signals of
any licensed frequency. The very process of petitioning invariably invited delay, since the FCC promised to ponder the
potential ill effects to local UHF stations; the regulatory lag
often consumed available start-up capital while enriching
Washington lawyers specializing in communications law. In
addition, would-be cable processes had to carry any UHF
channels situated in the area served. Finally, the FCC forbade
CATV companies from duplicating programming (a rerun of
"December Bride," for example) carried by the local UHF
outlet. Thus, a CATV system offering a Chicago channel also
airing "December Bride" had to black out those 30 minutes

and originate their own substitute fare. For an elaboration on the FCC's CATV policies, see Le Duc, *Cable Television.*

13   *RR*, 2d ser., 6 (1966), 1717, 1779, 1785; FCC, "Administrative History: CATV," manuscript 1968, 10-12, copy in Johnson Papers; Le Duc, *Cable Television* 139, 215.

14   Webbink, "The Impact of UHF Promotion," 545-46, 548-49; *FYI* [Time Inc. Newsletter], 9 Aug. 1963, copy in box 86, Robert Desmond Papers, SHSW.

15   Webbink, "Impact of UHF Promotion," 545; Senate Commerce Committee, *All-Channel Television*, report 1526, 87th Cong., 2d sess., 1962, p. 3.

16   *Broadcasting* (7 March 1966), 61; *New York Times* 2 June 1967.

17   Robert Lewis Shayon, "UHF Breakthrough in Chicago?" WFLD," *Saturday Review* (13 Aug. 1966), 55; Kenneth D. Tiven, "UHF: The Sleeping Giant"; Michael Alan Stoller, "The Economics of UHF Television: Effects of Government Policy" (Ph.D. diss., Washington Univ., 1977).

18   Herman W. Land Associates, *Television and the Wired City*, esp. ch. 2; Bunce, *Television in the Corporate Interest* 27-28; James A. Wollert and Wirth, "UHF Television Program Performance," 140ff; Darlington, "The Many Worlds of Local TV," 36.

19   Loren Mathre, interview with Martin Mayer, n.d., notes in box 62, Mayer Papers.

20   David Lachenbruch, "The $200,000,000 Experiment," *TV Guide* (11 Dec. 1965), 7.

21   Gelman, " 'U' as in Upward," 50.

22   Levin, "Program Duplication," 88 and passim.

23   Henry to F. Bradford Morse, 31 July 1964, box 55, Henry Papers; *Broadcasting* (20 July 1964), 23-24; *Business Week* (13 July 1963), 131-32; Bernard Asbell, "Pay TV: The Way to Free TV?" *The Progressive* 23 (Oct. 1959), 41-44.

24   Sylvester L. Weaver, Jr., "Why Suppress Pay-TV? The Fight in California," *Atlantic* (Oct. 1964), 55; *Broadcasting* (20 Jan. 1964), 61 (10 Feb. 1964), 52 (20 July 1964), 27 (9 Nov. 1964), 21-24 (24 May 1965), 46, 48, 50; Weaver to Henry, 8 Sept. 1964, box 55, Henry Papers; Janet Kippen Voelker to Robert Lewis Shayon, 23 March 1965, box 11, Shayon Papers; *New York Times*, 15 Nov. 1964; David H. Ostroff, "A History of

STV, Inc., and the 1964 California Vote against Pay Television," *Journal of Broadcasting* 27 (Fall 1983), 371-86.

25 *Congressional Quarterly Almanac, 1962,* 226-28; memorandum, Robert W. Lishman to members of House Commerce
Committee, Subcommittee on Communications and Power,
28 July 1967, box 57, Ancher Nelsen Papers; *Congressional
Record,* vol. 110, p. 20, 21 Sept. 1967, p. 26382; House Commerce Committee, *Public Television,* hearings, 178.

26 WCBS Radio, "WCBS Radio Looks at Television," 3 Aug.
1966, transcript, John F. White interview, p. 13, WCBS Papers.
See also address by Henry, 2 Oct. 1964, box 77, Henry
Papers; Senate Commerce Committee, *Public Television,*
248; Gordon F. Andrus, "ETV in St. Louis: The Rise and Fall
of Channel 9," *Focus/Midwest* 6 (1968), 31 and passim;
Gerald L. Appy to Gregory G. Harney, April 1966, box 1,
Carnegie Commission Papers; Lawrence Laurent, unpublished report on WETA, Washington, Nov. 1966, Alan Levy, unpublished report on WNED, Buffalo, Sept. 1966, and WTHS,
Miami, Nov. 1966, box 4, ibid.

27 J. W. Kiermaier to Emanuel Celler, 5 Sept. 1967, box 306,
Celler Papers; Henry to Eric F. Goldman, 8 Dec. 1964, Henry
to Morris Ernst, 8 Feb. 1965, box 22, Henry Papers; *Broadcasting* (24 March 1965), 47; *Business Week* (22 Sept. 1962),
95. Cf. John C. Schwarzwalder, "Myths of Educational
Television."

28 Hy Goldin to Chief, Broadcast Bureau, 12 Nov. 1965, copy in
box 60, Henry Papers; House Commerce Committee, *Public
Television,* hearings, 290; Douglass Cater, introduction in
Cater and Michael J. Nyham, eds., *The Future of Public
Broadcasting* (New York, 1976), 1-2; Joseph M. Cahalan,
"Congress, Mass Communications and Public Policy—The
Public Broadcasting Act of 1967" (Ph.D. diss., New York
University, 1971), 132; Stephen White, "Carnegie, Ford, and
the Public Interest," in MacAvoy, *The Crisis of the
Regulatory Commissions,* 118.

29 Henry to Goldman, 8 Dec. 1964, Cater to Henry, 8 March
1965, Henry to E.B. Crosland, 11 June 1965, 19 July 1965,
box 22, Henry Papers; Henry, interview with author; "The
Reminiscences of Douglass Cater" (1969), Oral History, LBJL,
2-3.

30 Cater to President, 19 May 1965, box 13, Cater Papers.

31 Carnegie Commission on Educational Television, *Public Television: A Program for Action* (Cambridge, Mass, 1967); Senate Commerce Committee, *Public Television*, 134ff.

32 Hyman H. Goldin, "Financing Public Broadcasting," *Law and Contemporary Problems* 34 (Summer 1969), 650; Calahan, "Congress, Mass Communications, and Public Policy," 111, 112, 150-51, 155; memorandum, JPJ to Page Belcher, n.d., box 117, Belcher Papers.

33 Cater to President, c. Oct. 1965, box 16, Cater Papers.

34 Johnson's remarks written on memorandum, Cater to President, 13 Oct. 1967, ibid.; Minow to Cater, 13 March 1967, WHCF, Legislation, Gen. LE/ED 5, Johnson Papers; Cater to Minow, 17 March 1967, Gen. UT 1-1, ibid.,

35 Cater to President, 25 Jan. 1967, box 15, Cater Papers; Cater to President, 28 Feb. 1967, box 16, ibid.; Joseph Califano to President, 27 Feb. 1967; telegram, Donald McGannon to Cater, 22 Sept. 1967, WHCF, Name File, Johnson Papers; *Wall Street Journal*, 11 Sept. 1967; Robert M. Pepper, "The Formation of the Public Broadcasting Service," (Ph.D. diss., University of Wisconsin, 1975), 43n.

36 Presidential aides agreed to an eight-to-seven partisan division of the CPB board and to forbid CPB stations to editorialize. Ralph Huitt to Cater and Barefoot Sanders, 19 July 1967, Jerome T. Murphy to Charles Roche, 18 Sept. 1967, WHCF, LE/ED 5, Johnson Papers; Cater to President, 2 Aug. 1967, Leonard Marks to President, 26 Sept. 1967, box 17, Cater Papers; memorandum, Lewis E. Berry to minority members, House Commerce Committee, Subcommittee on Communications and Power, 16 Aug. 1967, Departmental Files, Box 57, Ancher Nelsen Papers; memorandum JPJ to Belcher, n.d., box 117, Belcher Papers.

37 Cater, introduction,in Cater and Nyham, *The Future of Public Broadcasting*, 2; Cahalan, "Congress, Mass Communications and Public Policy," 112-13; Ralph K. Huitt to Cater and Barefoot Sanders, 19 July 1967, WHCF, LE/ED 5, Johnson Papers.

38 *Public Papers of Lyndon B. Johnson 1967*, 2 vols. (Washington, D.C., 1968), II:995. See also *Wall Street Journal*, 11 Sept. 1967; Senate Commerce Committee, *Public Televi-*

sion, 448

39 Berkman, "A Modest Proposal."

40 Drew, "Is the FCC Dead?" See also Zeidenberg, "Is the FCC Obsolete?", Martin Mayer, "The F Stands for Frustration," *TV Guide* (19 Nov. 1966), 6-10; *Business Week* (18 Nov. 1967), 66-68, 70, 72, 74. The FCC's ill repute may also be seen as part of a larger intellectual dissatisfaction in the late 1960s with federal bureaucracies, a disenchantment relating to the failings of the war-on-poverty programs. See Wilson, "The Bureaucracy Problem," 3-9.

41 Annotated copy of Drew in box 513, Celler Papers.

42 FCC, *Reports and Orders* 34 (1963), 1103. On the failings of the option time ban, see *Atlanta Constitution*, 13 and 14 Sept. 1965. Stations freed of option time agreements generally refused to carry certain network programs in favor of reruns of old network programs or old feature films. The commission had hoped for more programming from stations and non-network sources. In Omaha, the CBS affiliate bumped "CBS Reports," for example, for recent films. One night, an Elvis Presley movie displaced a "CBS Reports" discussion of the Vietnam War.

43 Carnegie Commission, *Public Television*, 34; Senate Commerce Committee, *Public Television*, 136.

44 George Bluestone, "Life, Death, and 'Nature' in Children's TV," in Hazard, *TV as Art*, 157-76.

45 Senate Commerce Committees, *Public Television*, hearings, 18.

46 House Commerce Committees, *Public Television*, hearings, 521-22.

47 *Congressional Record*, vol. 110, pt. 20, 21 Sept. 1967, p. 26414.

48 Such were the findings of a special report prepared for the Carnegie Commission, comparing the March 1961 and March 1965 CBS and NBC schedules. Goldin, " 'Serious' Commercial Network Programming."

49 Senate Commerce Committee, *Public Television*, 53, 476.

50 Lester Markel, "A Program for Public-TV," *New York Times Magazine*, 12 March 1967, reprinted in Senate Commerce Committee, *Public Television*, 401.

51 Address, 17 Feb. 1964, copy in box 78, Henry Papers.

52 Address by Richard D. Heffner, 2 June 1965, copy in box 79, ibid. See also Kendrick, *Prime Time*, 515.

53 Berkman, "A Modest Proposal," 36.

54 Vidal, "See It Later," 27.

55 William Benton, "Big Brother's TV Set," Marya Mannes, "TV's Fascinating Fourth Network," *Ladies' Home Journal* (July 1963), 100,103; Vance Packard, "New Kinds of Television," *Atlantic* (Oct. 1963), 68-74; Packard's discussion of advertising and TV is in *The Hidden Persuaders* (New York, 1957), 132-33.

56 *Los Angeles Times* 6 Oct. 1964. Gould simiarly took up ETV. Young, "One Medium," 54.

57 Cousins to Johnson, 20 Nov. 1967, WHCF, EX, LE/EDS, Johnson Papers. See also R.H. Coase and Edward W. Barrett, *Educational Television: Who Should Pay?* (Washington, D.C., 1968), 20-21.

58 Docket 12782, vol. 15, *Proceedings*, vol. 40, pp. 6143ff, FCC Records, Dockets Room, FCC.

59 Friendly to Minow, 16 May 1963, box 36, Minow Papers.

60 Fred W. Friendly, "World without Distance," *NAEB Journal* 26 (Jan.-Feb. 1967), 3-12.

61 "The Reminiscences of Fred W. Friendly" (1967), FLOHC, 2; Friendly, interview with author, 11 March 1977. Howard K. Smith of ABC News, another old Murrow hand, suffered a similar disillusionment. In an Aug 1962 article, Smith had written optimistically about TV's potential for informational programming by the late sixties. See Smith, "What TV Will Be Like in 1970," *Sponsor* (27 Aug. 1962), 41-43. A Johnson aide met with Smith early in 1967 and reported that Smith "is fed up with television." Cater to Johnson, 22 March 1967, box 16, Cater Papers.

62 William J. McGill et al., *A Public Trust: The Report of the Carnegie Commission on the Future of Public Broadcasting* (New York, 1979).

CHAPTER 11

1 Huntington, "The Marasmus of the ICC"; Marver H. Bernstein, *Regulating Business*; Kolko, *The Triumph of Conservatism*; idem, *Railroads and Regulation*, Murray Edelman,

The Symbolic Uses of Politics, 24, 56. For a convoluted variation on this theme, see Vincent Mosco's thinly research-ed *Broadcasting in the United States: Innovative Challenge and Organizational Control.*

2   Fellmuth, *The Interstate Commerce Commission*; McCraw, "Regulation in America," 162-64; Kohlmeier, *The Regulators*; Stigler, "Theory of Economic Regulation,"3.

3   For similar assessments of the FCC and other independent agencies, see Edelman, *Licensing of Radio Services*; Williams, "Politics of American Broadcasting"; Gerald Thain, "Suffer the Hucksters to Come Unto the Little Children? Possible Restrictions of Television Advertising to Children under Section 5 of the Federal Trade Commission Act," *Boston University Law Review* 56 (July 1976), 666; Shapiro, "Politics and the Federal Reserve."

4   *Rocky Mountain Cervi's Journal*, 24 May 1961.

5   Minow, interview with author, 24 May 1978.

6   Minow, interview with Sterling Quinlan, 27 Dec. 1972, notes and tape in boxes 12 and 13, Quinlan Papers; U. S. Congress, Senate, Committee on Governmental Affairs, *Study on Federal Regulation*, vol. 4: *Delay in the Regulatory Process*, report, 95th Cong., 1st sess., doc. 95-72, 1977, pp. xiii, 1, 2.

7   Freedman, *Crisis and Legitimacy*, 261,263. See also Emmette S. Reford, "Perspectives"; Friedrich and Sternberg, "Congress"; Quirk, *Industry Influence*, 87 and passim.

8   *Congressional Quarterly Almanac, 1964* (Washington, 1965), 248; *Congressional Quarterly Almanac, 1965* (Washington, 1966), 344-451, 987-79, 1050; Thomas Whiteside, "Cutting Down,"; 43; A. Lee Fritschler, *Smoking and Politics: Policymaking and the Federal Bureaucracy* (New York, 1969).

9   *Congressional Quarterly Almanac, 1965*, 351.

10 Cited in *Sponsor* (20 Dec. 1958), 15. See also Steiner, *The People Look*, 126-29, 139, 140-41, 149-50, 151, 155; Rolf Meyersohn, "Television and the Rest of Leisure," *Public Opinion Quarterly* 32 (Spring 1968), 102-12.

11 Henry, interview with author.

12 McCraw, "Regulation in America," 178. See also Marver H. Berstein, *Regulating Business*, 285; Freedman, *Crisis and Legitimacy*, 264; David M. Lenny, "The Case for Funding

Citizen Participation in the Administrative Process," *Administrative Law Review* 28 (Summer 1976), 484-87.

13 Television Bureau of Advertising, "Trends in Television for the First Half of the Year, 1959-1963," unpublished paper, c. Aug. 1963, copy in box 73, Henry Papers; Bower, *Television and the Public;* George Comstock et al., *Television and Human Behavior,* ch. 3.

14 Work and the social whirl of the capital kept most congressmen away from the set (Norris Cotton to Harry H. Gilmanton, 3 March 1960, box 45, Cotton Papers; Senate Commerce Committee, *Nomination of Newton N. Minow,* 6, 20; Steinberg, *Sam Rayburn,* 297).

15 Johnson to Thomas Wolfe, 13 Jan. 1969, WHCF, Name File, Johnson Papers; *Variety* (9 Dec. 1964), 1.

16 Address by Henry, 2 Oct. 1964, Box 77, Henry Papers.

17 Wright, constituent newsletter, 12 June 1961, copy in Box 10, Minow Papers; Norris Cotton to Sterling Campbell Conn 1 March 1961, Box 47, Cotton Papers.

18 William Brackett to Board of Directors, ACLU, Illinois Division, c. Jan. 1962, box 37, ACLU Papers, Illinois Division, Univ. of Chicago; Kalven, Jr., and Rosenfield, "Minow Should Watch His Step."

19 *Philadelphia Inquirer,* 18 April 1962, clipping in Box 54; Minow Papers; Gilbert Seldes, *The Public Interest* (Lexington, Va., 1963).

20 Kristol, "Of Newton Minow and Matthew Arnold."

21 *The Public Papers and Addresses of Franklin D. Roosevelt,* 5 vols. (New York, 1938) V:16.

22 Ashmore, *Fear in the Air;* Porter, *Assault on the Media;* Jonathan Schell, *Time of Illusion* (New York, 1976) 56, 69, 86-87, 109, 110-111, 126-27, 132, 302-3; Lee, interview with author; *Time* (21 Nov. 1969), 22; *New York Post,* 26 Feb. 1979; Peter Steinfels, "A Tale of Two Speeches," *Commonweal* 91 (28 Nov. 1969), 272.

23 Minow, interview with author, 24 May 1978.

24 UPI wire, 3 April 1965, based on interview with Henry, 26 March 1965, copy in Box 39, Henry Papers. Minow often expressed his liking for popular programs, such as *The Untouchables,* a violent gangbusters series. *Variety* (9 Jan. 1963), 86.

25 Address by Weaver, 19 Jan. 1956, copy in ser. B-3, box 1, NBC Records; Thomas Whiteside, "The Communicator," *New Yorker* 30 (16 Oct. 1954), 47.

26 Quoted in *Variety* (27 Dec. 1961), 19, 26

27 Suggestive is James Q. Wilson, "The Bureaucracy Problem."

28 Cole and Oettinger, *Reluctant Regulator*; Thomas L. Schuessler, "FCC Regulation of the Network Television Program Procurement Process: An Attempt to Regulate the Laws of Economics?" *Northwestern University Law Review* 73 (May-June 1978); 227-306; Geoffrey Cowan, *See No Evil: The Backstage Battle over Sex and Violence on Television* (New York, 1979); *New York Times*, 1 Jan. 1979; Goldberg and Couzens, "'Peculiar Characteristics,'" 9-33.

29 David Vogel, "The 'New' Social Regulation in Historical Perspective," in McCraw, *Regulation in Perspective*, 170. comments by Everett C. Parker, Tenth Annual Telecommunications Policy Research Conference, Annapolis, 27 April 1982.

30 Comments by Richard Wiley, Tenth Annual Telecommunications Policy Research Conference, Annapolis, 26 April 1982; Quirk, *Industry Influence*, 84-85.

31 *Washington Post*, 13 Oct. 1978; *New York Times*, 3 April 1979.

32 Linda Jo Lacey, "The Electric Church: An FCC 'Established' Institution;" Frances FitzGerald, "A Disciplined, Charging Army," *New Yorker* (18 May 1981), 54.

33 FCC, Network Inquiry Staff, *A Review of the Proceedings of the Federal Communications Commission Leading to the . . . Prime Time Access Rule*, mimeo, Oct. 1979, esp. p. 50; *Variety* (1 March 1978), 1, 111 and (13 Jan. 1982), 143; *TV Guide* (22 Sept. 1973), 4; *Milwaukee Journal*, 18 June 1980; *New York Times*, 28 Sept. 1977 and 28 Nov. 1977.

34 Le Duc, *Cable Television*, 215; FCC, *Reports and Orders*, 2d ser., 71 (1979), 632; Levin, *Fact and Fancy*, esp. ch. 12; *Business Week* (1 Sept, 1962), 96-98, (22 June 1968), 138. Cf. *New York Times*, 24 Nov. 1983.

35 Levin, *Fact and Fancy*, 140ff; *TV Guide* (19 Aug. 1978), A-4; *Broadcasting* (26 Feb. 1979), 43-44, *Backstage*, (15 Sept. 1978); special issue; *Wall Street Journal*, 8 Jan. 1980 and 4 March 1982; Stoller, "Economics of UHF Television";

Wollert and Wirth, "UHF Television Program Performance."
36 Sally Bedell, *Up the Tube: Prime-Time TV and the Silverman Years* (New York, 1981).
37 *Broadcasting* (4 April 1977), 34. See also his comments in *Boston Herald-American*, 5 March 1978; *Detroit Free Press*, 22 July 1982.
38 Sobel, *The Manipulators*, ch. 11; Sheldon Zalaznick, "The Rich, Risky Business of TV News," *Fortune* 79 (May 1969), 92-97, 143-45; *New York Times*, 5 Feb. 1978 and 21 Feb. 1982; *Wall Street Journal*, 2 Jan. 1980. The audience for TV news programming, including the nightly newscasts, is subject to much exaggeration. See Robert L. Stevenson and Kathryn P. White, "The Cumulative Audience of Network Television News," *Journalism Quarterly* 57 (Autumn 1980), 477-81; Lawrence W. Lichty, "Video versus Print," *Wilson Quarterly* 6 (Special Issue, 1982), 49-57. Since the 1950s, however, advertisers have increased their patronage of news programming, if only because the total demand for television time has risen dramatically.
39 Saul Braun, "What Makes *60 Minutes* Tick?" *TV Guide* (20 Oct. 1973), 16-18; *Variety* (30 Sept. 1981), 60; *Broadcasting* (12 Sept. 1977), 38.
40 Henry Geller interview, *New York Times*, 18 July 1978; Johnson and Meyer, "A Debate on TV Licensing."
41 Skowronek, *Building a New American State*, 286-90; Kristol, *On the Democratic Idea.*
42 Besen, "Deregulating Tele-communications"; Bazelon, "The First Amendment"; Stuart N. Brotman, "Judge David T. Bazelon: Making the First Amendment Work," *Federal Communications Law Journal* 33 (Winter 1981), 50-52; *Cleveland Plain Dealer*, 22 March 1982; *Variety* (1 Oct. 1980), 77, 97 (30 Sept. 1981), 1, 108; *Washington Post*, 27 June 1981; *Wall Street Journal*, 24 June 1982, 7 Dec. 1983; *Milwaukee Journal*, 28 Feb. 1980; Timothy J. Brennan, "Economic Efficiency and Broadcast Content Regulation," *Federal Communications Law Journal* 35 (Summer 1983), 117-38; Patricia Brosterhous, "*United States v. National Association of Broadcasters*: The Deregulation of Self-Regulation," ibid. 35 (Fall 1983), 313-46.

Bibliography

MANUSCRIPT COLLECTIONS

Sherman Adams Papers. Eisenhower Library.
American Civil Liberties Union Papers. Princeton University.
American Civil Liberties Union Papers. Illinois Division,
    University of Chicago.
Americans for Democratic Action Papers. State Historical Society
    of Wisconsin.
Robert Areeda Papers. Eisenhower Library.
Robert Ashman Papers. State Historical Society of Wisconsin.
William H. Avery Papers. Kansas State Historical Society.
Erik Barnouw Papers. Columbia University.
Page Belcher Papers. University of Oklahoma.
Robert Bendiner Papers. State Historical Society of Wisconsin.
John B. Bennett Papers. University of Michigan.
Chester Bowles Papers. Yale University.
Alan S. Boyd Papers. Johnson Library.
John W. Bricker Papers. Ohio Historical Society.
Clarence J. Brown Papers. Ohio Historical Society.
Joseph Califano Papers. Johnson Library.
Frank Carlson Papers. Kansas State Historical Society.
Carnegie Commission on Educational Television Papers. State
    Historical Society of Wisconsin.
Douglass Cater Papers. Johnson Library.

Emanuel Celler Papers. Library of Congress.

Zechariah Chafee Papers. Harvard Law School Library, Harvard University.

Fairfax M. Cone Papers. University of Chicago.

Norris Cotton Papers. University of New Hampshire.

Louis Cowan Papers. Columbia University.

Kenneth A. Cox Papers. State Historical Society of Wisconsin.

John Charles Daly Papers. State Historical Society of Wisconsin.

Elmer Davis Papers. Library of Congress.

Democratic National Committee Records. Kennedy Library.

John C. Doerfer Papers. State Historical Society of Wisconsin.

William Jennings Bryan Dorn Papers. University of South Carolina.

Paul H. Douglas Papers. Chicago Historical Society.

Du Mont Laboratories Records. Library of Congress.

Dwight D. Eisenhower Papers. Eisenhower Library.

Morris Ernst Papers. Western Humanities Center, University of Texas.

Myer Feldman Papers. Kennedy Library.

John Fischer Papers. State Historical Society of Wisconsin.

James Lawrence Fly Papers. Columbia University.

John E. Fogarty Papers. Providence College.

Felix Frankfurter Papers. Harvard Law School Library, Harvard University.

J. William Fulbright Papers. University of Arkansas.

Fund for the Republic Papers. Princeton University.

James Gaither Papers. Johnson Library.

John Kenneth Galbraith Papers. Kennedy Library.

James Haggerty Papers. Eisenhower Library.

Oren Harris Papers. University of Arkansas.

Joseph C. Harsch Papers. State Historical Society of Wisconsin.

August Heckscher Papers. Kennedy Library.

Robert W. Hemphill Papers. University of South Carolina.

Frieda Hennock Papers. Schlesinger Library, Radcliffe College.

Frieda Hennock Papers. Truman Library.

E. William Henry Papers. State Historical Society of Wisconsin.

Herbert Hoover Papers. Hoover Library.

Roman Hruska Papers. Nebraska State Historical Society.

Hubert Humphrey Papers. Minnesota Historical Society.

Institute for Public Interest Representation Papers. Broadcast

Pioneers Library, Washington, D. C.

Walter H. Judd Papers. Minnesota Historical Society.

John F. Kennedy Papers. Kennedy Library.

Arthur Krock Papers. Princeton University.

James M. Lambie, Jr., Papers. Eisenhower Library.

James M. Landis Papers. Kennedy Library.

James M. Landis Papers. State Historical Society of Wisconsin.

Robert E. Lee Papers. State Historical Society of Wisconsin.

Lester W. Lindow Papers. State Historical Society of Wisconsin.

Walter Lippmann Papers. Yale University.

Lee Loevinger Papers. State Historical Society of Wisconsin.

Dwight Macdonald Papers. Yale University.

Peter F. Mack Papers. Illinois State Historical Society.

Henry R. McPhee Papers. Eisenhower Library.

Loring Mandel Papers. State Historical Society of Wisconsin.

Marya Mannes Papers. Boston University.

Groucho Marx Papers. Library of Congress.

Martin Mayer Papers. Columbia University.

Robert E. Merriam Papers. Eisenhower Library.

William E. Miller Papers. Cornell University.

Milwaukee Journal Stations Records. State Historical Society of Wisconsin.

Newton N. Minow Papers. State Historical Society of Wisconsin.

A. S. Mike Monroney Papers. University of Oklahoma.

Gerald D. Morgan Papers. Eisenhower Library.

Frank J. Murphy Papers. Bentley Historical Library, University of Michigan.

Edward R. Murrow Papers. Tufts University

National Association of Broadcasters Papers. State Historical Society of Wisconsin.

National Association of Educational Broadcasters Records. State Historical Society of Wisconsin.

National Educational Television and Radio Center Records. State Historical Society of Wisconsin.

Ancher Nelsen Papers. Minnesota Historical Society.

Lawrence F. O'Brien Papers. Kennedy Library.

Ohio Educational Television Commission Records. Ohio Historical Society.

Harold Ostertag Papers. Cornell University.

John O. Pastore Papers. Providence College.

W. Theodore Pierson Papers. State Historical Society of Wisconsin.

Joseph Pulitzer II Papers. Library of Congress.

Sterling H. Quinlan Papers. Boston University.

Dan Rather Papers. Boston University.

Hubbell Robinson Papers. State Historical Society of Wisconsin.

Harold Rodman Papers. State Historical Society of Wisconsin.

Franklin D. Roosevelt Papers. Roosevelt Library.

Richard Rovere Papers. State Historical Society of Wisconsin.

Sy Salkowitz Papers. State Historical Society of Wisconsin.

Arthur M. Schlesinger, Jr., Papers. Kennedy Library.

Rod Serling Papers. State Historical Society of Wisconsin.

Eric Sevareid Papers. Library of Congress.

Robert Lewis Shayon Papers. Boston University.

Theodore Sorensen Papers. Kennedy Library.

Lawrence F. Spivak Papers. Library of Congress.

Adlai E. Stevenson Papers. Princeton University.

David Susskind Papers. State Historical Society of Wisconsin.

Harry S. Truman Papers. Truman Library.

U. S. Department of Justice Records. Department of Justice.

U. S. Federal Communications Commission Records. Dockets Room, Federal Communications Commission.

U. S. Federal Communications Commission Records. General Service Administration.

U. S. Federal Communications Commission Records. National Archives.

WCBS Radio Papers. State Historical Society of Wisconsin.

Wallace White Papers. Library of Congress.

Ann C. Whitman Papers. Eisenhower Library.

Alexander H. Wiley Papers. State Historical Society of Wisconsin.

Charles F. Willis, Jr., Papers. Eisenhower Library.

Henry Wilson Papers. Johnson Library.

Wisconsin Citizens' Commission for Educational Television Papers. State Historical Society of Wisconsin.

Max Wylie Papers. Boston University.

BOOKS

Allen, Steve. *Mark It and Strike It: An Autobiography*. New York, 1960.

Anderson, Kent. *Television Fraud: The History and Implications of the Quiz Show Scandals.* Westport, Conn., 1978.

Arlen, Michael J. *Living-Room War.* New York, 1969.

_____. *The View from Highway 1.* New York, 1976.

Ashmore, Harry S. *Fear in the Air: Broadcasting and the First Amendment.* New York, 1972.

Aurthur, Robert Alan, et al. *The Relation of the Writer to Television.* New York, 1960.

Bagdikian, Ben H. *The Information Machines: Their Impact on Men and the Media.* New York, 1971.

Bailey, Stephen Kemp. *Congress Makes a Law: The Story behind the Employment Act of 1946.* New York, 1950.

Barnouw, Erik. *A History of Broadcasting in the United States.* 3 vols. New York, 1966-70.

_____. *The Sponsor: Notes on a Modern Potentate.* New York, 1978.

_____. *Tube of Plenty: The Evolution of American Television* New York, 1975.

Bauer, Raymond; Pool, Ithiel de Sola; and Dexter, Lewis Anthony. *American Business and Public Policy.* New York, 1963.

Baumol, William J., and Bowen William G. *Performing Arts—The Economic Dilemma.* New York, 1966.

Bazelon, David T. *Power in American: The Politics of the New Class.* New York, 1967.

Bentley, Arthur F. *The Process of Government.* Chicago, 1908.

Bernstein, Irving. *The Economics of Television Film Production and Distribution.* Hollywood, 1960.

Bernstein, Marver H. *Regulating Business by Independent Commission.* Princeton, 1955.

Bibby, John, and Davidson, Roger, eds. *On Capitol Hill: Studies in the Legislative Process.* New York, 1967.

Bliss, Edward, Jr.,ed. *In Search of Light: The Broadcasts of Edward R. Murrow, 1938-1961.* New York, 1967.

Bogart, Leo. *The Age of Television.* 2d. ed. New York, 1958.

_____. *Strategy in Advertising.* New York, 1967.

Boorstin, Daniel J. *Democracy and Its Discontents: Reflections on Everyday America.* New York, 1976.

_____. *The Image: A Guide to Pseudo-Events in America.* New York, 1964.

Bower, Robert T. *Television and the Public.* New York, 1973.

Boyer, William W. *Bureaucracy on Trial: Policy-Making by Government Agencies*. Indianapolis, 1964.

Briggs, Asa. *Mass Entertainment: The Origins of a Modern Industry*. Adelaide, 1960.

Britton, Florence, ed. *Best Television Plays, 1957*. New York, 1957.

Brooks, John. *The Great Leap: The Past Twenty-Five Years in America*. New York, 1966.

Brooks, Tim, and Marsh, Earle. *The Complete Directory of Prime Time Network TV Shows, 1946—present*. New York, 1979.

Brown, Les. *Television: The Business Behind the Box*. New York, 1971.

Bunce, Richard. *Television in the Corporate Interest*. New York, 1976.

Bunzel, John H. *The American Small Businessman*. New York, 1962.

Burns, Joan Simpson. *The Awkward Embrace: The Creative Artist and the Institution in America*. New York, 1975.

Cantor, Muriel G. *The Hollywood TV Producer: His Work and His Audience*. New York, 1971.

Carnegie Commission on Educational Television. *Public Television: A Program for Action*. Cambridge, Mass., 1967.

Carnegie Commission on the Future of Public Television. *A Public Trust*. New York, 1979.

Cary, William L. *Politics and the Regulated Agencies*. New York, 1967.

Center for the Study of Democratic Institutions. *Broadcasting and Government: Regulation in a Free Society*. New York, 1959.

Chafee, Zechariah, Jr. *Government and Mass Communications: A Report from the Commmmission on Freedom of the Press*. 2 vols. Chicago, 1947.

Chayefsky, Paddy. *Television Plays*. New York, 1955.

Coase, R. H. *British Broadcasting: A Study in Monopoly*. Cambridge, Mass., 1950.

Cole, Barry, and Oettinger, Mal. *Reluctant Regulators: The FCC and the Broadcast Audience*. Reading, Mass., 1978.

Comstock, George, et al. *Television and Human Behavior*. New York, 1978.

Comstock, George A., and Rubinstein Eli A., eds. *Television and*

Social Behavior: Reports and Papers. I: *Media Content and Control.* Rockville, Md., 1972.

Cone, Fairfax M. *With All Its Faults: A Candid Account of Forty Years in Advertising.* Boston, 1969.

Coons, John E., ed. *Freedom and Responsibility in Broadcasting.* Evanston, 1961.

Cornwell, Elmer E. *Presidential Leadership of Public Opinion.* Bloomington, 1965.

Cox, Kenneth A., and Johnson, Nicholas. *Broadcasting in America and the FCC's License Renewal Process: An Oklahoma Case Study.* Washington, D. C., 1968.

Crosby, John. *Out of the Blue.* New York, 1952.

Cushman, Robert E. *The Independent Regulatory Commissions.* New York, 1941.

_____. *The Problem of the Independent Regulatory Commission.* Studies in Administrative Management in the Government of the United States. No.3. Washington, D. C., 1937.

Davis, Fred. *Yearning for Yesterday: A Sociology of Nostalgia.* New York, 1979.

De Grazia, Alfred, ed. *Congress: The First Branch of Government.* Garden City, N.Y., 1967.

De Grazia, Sebastian. *Of Time, Work, and Leisure.* New York, 1962.

Diamond, Edwin. *The Tin Kazoo.* Cambridge, Mass., 1975.

Donner, Stanley T., ed. *The Meaning of Commercial Television.* Austin, 1966.

Edelman, Murray. *The Licensing of Radio Services in the United States, 1927 to 1947: A Study in Administrative Formulation of Policy.* Urbana, 1950.

_____. *The Symbolic Use of Politics.* Urbana, 1964.

Elliott, William Y., ed. *Television's Impact on American Culture.* East Lansing, 1956.

Epstein, Edward Jay. *News from Nowhere: Television and the News.* New York, 1973.

Ernst, Morris. *The First Freedom.* New York, 1946.

Fainsod, Merle, and Gordon, Lincoln. *Government and the American Economy.* 2d ed. New York, 1948.

Fairlie, Henry. *The Kennedy Promise: The Politics of Expectation* Garden City, N. Y., 1972.

Fellmuth, Robert C., [ed.]. *The Interstate Commerce Commis-*

sion: *The Public Interest and the ICC.* New York, 1970.

Fireman, Judy, ed. *TV Book: The Ultimate Television Book.* New York, 1970.

Foreman, Robert. *The Hot Half Hour.* New York, 1958.

Freedman, James O. *Crisis and Legitimacy: The Administrative Process and American Government.* Cambridge, 1978.

Friendly, Fred W. *Due to Circumstances beyond Our Control.* New York, 1967.

———. *The Good Guys, the Bad Guys, and the First Amendment: Free Speech vs. Fairness in Broadcasting.* New York, 1976.

Friendly, Henry J. *The Federal Administrative Agencies: The Need for Better Definition of Standards.* Cambridge, Mass., 1962.

Frier, David A. *Conflict of Interest in the Eisenhower Administration.* Ames, 1969.

Galbraith, John Kenneth. *The Affluent Society.* Boston, 1958.

Gans, Herbert J. *Deciding What's News: A Study of CBS Evening News, NBC Nightly News, Newsweek and Time.* New York, 1979.

———. *Popular Culture and High Culture: An Analysis and Evaluation of Taste.* New York, 1974.

Gates, Gary Paul. *Air Time: The Inside Story of CBS News.* New York, 1978.

Goals for Americans. Englewood Cliffs, N. J., 1960.

Goldman, Eric F. *The Crucial Decade—and After: America, 1945-1960.* New York, 1960.

———. *The Tragedy of Lyndon Johnson.* New York, 1969.

Goodman, Walter. *All Honorable Men: Corruption and Compromise in American Life.* Boston, 1963.

———. *The Clowns of Commerce.* New York, 1957.

Gross, Ben. *I Looked and I Listened: Informal Recollections of Radio and TV.* New York, 1954.

Grossman, Michael Baruch, and Kumar, Martha Joynt. *Portraying the President: The White House and the News Media.* Baltimore, 1981.

Guimary, Donald L. *Citizens' Groups and Broadcasting.* New York, 1975.

Halberstam, David. *The Powers That Be.* New York, 1979.

Hazard, Patrick D., ed. *TV as Art: Some Essays in Criticisms.*

Champaign, 1966.

Heath, Jim F. *John F. Kennedy and the Business Community.* Chicago, 1969.

Heckscher, August. *The Public Happiness.* New York, 1962.

Hoogenboom, Ari, and Hoogenboom, Olive. *A History of the ICC: From Panacea to Palliative.* New York, 1976.

Hoover, Herbert. *The Memoirs of Herbert Hoover.* Vol. II: *The Cabinet and the Presidency, 1920-1933.* New York, 1952.

Horton, Robert W. *To Pay or Not to Pay: A Report on Subscription Television.* New York, 1960.

Johnson, Nicholas. *How to Talk Back to Your Television Set.* Boston, 1970.

Jones, William K. *Licensing of Major Broadcast Facilities by the Federal Communications Commission.* New York, 1962.

Kariel, Henry S. *The Decline of American Pluralism.* Stanford, 1961.

Kearns, Doris. *Lyndon Johnson and the American Dream.* New York, 1976.

Kendrick, Alexander. *Prime Time: The Life of Edward R. Murrow.* Boston, 1969.

Key, V. O., Jr. *Politics, Parties, and Pressure Groups.* 5th ed. New York, 1964.

_____. *Public Opinion and American Democracy.* New York, 1961.

Kirkendall, Richard S., ed. *The Truman Period as a Research Field, a Reappraisal, 1972.* Columbia, Mo., 1974.

Klapper, Joseph T. *The Effects of Mass Communication.* New York, 1960.

Kohlmeier, Louis M. *The Regulators: Watchdog Agencies and the Public Interest.* New York, 1968.

Kolko, Gabriel. *Railroads and Regulation, 1977-1916.* Princeton, 1965.

_____. *The Triumph of Conservatism: A Reinterpretation of American History, 1900-1916.* New York, 1963.

Kovaleff, Theodore P. *Business and Government during the Eisenhower Administration: A Study of the Antitrust Division of the Justice Department.* Athens, Ohio, 1980.

Krasnow, Erwin G.; Langley, Lawrence D; and Terry, Herbert A. *The Politics of Broadcast Regulation.* 3d ed. New York, 1982.

Kraus, Sidney, ed. *The Great Debate: Background—Perspective—*

Effects. Bloomington, 1962.

Krislov, Samuel, and Musolf, Lloyd D., eds. *The Politics of Regulation*. Boston, 1964.

Krooss, Herman. *Executive Opinion*. New York, 1970.

Lacy, Dan. *Freedom of Communications*. 2d ed. Urbana, 1965.

Landis, James M. *The Administrative Process*. New Haven, 1938.

Lazarsfeld, Paul F. *The People Look at Radio*. Chapel Hill, 1946.

Le Duc, Don L. *Cable Television and the FCC: A Crisis in Media Control*. Philadelphia, 1973.

Leuchtenburg, William E. *A Troubled Feast: American Society since 1945*. Rev. ed. Boston, 1979.

Levin, Harvey J. *Broadcast Regulation and Joint Ownership of Media*. New York, 1960.

_____. *Fact and Fancy in Television Regulation: An Economic Study of Policy Alternatives*. New York, 1980.

Levy, David. *The Chameleons*. New York, 1964.

Lichty, Lawrence W., and Topping, Malachi C., eds. *American Broadcasting: A Source Book on the History of Radio and Television*. New York, 1975.

Lindley, Lester G. *The Constitution Faces Technology: The Relationship of the National Government to the Telegraph, 1866-1884*. New York, 1975.

Long, Stewart Louis. *The Development of the Television Network Oligopoly* New York, 1979.

Lyons, Eugene. *David Sarnoff: A Biography*. New York, 1966.

MacAvoy, Paul W., ed. *The Crisis of the Regulatory Commissions*. New York, 1970.

McCarthy, Charles. *The Wisconsin Idea*. New York, 1912.

McCraw, Thomas K., ed. *Regulation in Perspective: Historical Essays*. Boston, 1981.

Macdonald, Dwight. *Against the American Grain*. New York, 1962.

McPherson, Harry. *A Political Education*. Boston, 1972.

Mannes, Marya. *But Will It Sell?* Philadelphia, 1964.

_____. *More in Anger*. Milwaukee, 1960.

_____. *Who Owns the Air?* Philadelphia, 1964.

Marias, Augilera Julian. *America in the Fifties and Sixties*. University Park, Pa., 1972

Martin, Albro. *Enterprise Denied: Origins of the Decline of American Railroads, 1897-1917*. New York, 1971.

Martin, John Bartlow. *The Life of Adlai Stevenson.* 2 vols. Garden City, N. Y., 1977-1978.

Matthews, Donald R. *U. S. Senators and Their World.* Chapel Hill, 1960.

Mayer, Martin. *About Television.* New York, 1972.

———. *Madison Avenue, USA.* New York, 1958.

Mehling, Harold. *The Great Time Killer.* Cleveland, 1962.

Mickelson, Sig. *The Electric Mirror: Politics in the Age of Television.* New York, 1972.

Mileur, Jerome M., ed. *The Liberal Tradition in Crisis: American Politics in the Sixties.* Lexington, Mass., 1974.

Miller, Douglas T., and Nowak, Marion. *The Fifties: The Way We Really Were.* Garden City, N. Y., 1977.

Miller, Merle, and Rhodes, Evan. *Only You, Dick Darling! or, How to Write One Television Script and Make $50,000,000.* New York, 1964.

Minow, Newton N. *Equal Time: The Private Broadcaster and the Public Interest.* New York, 1964.

Miroff, Bruce. *Pragmatic Illusions: The Presidential Politics of John F. Kennedy.* New York, 1976.

Montgomery, Robert. *An Open Letter from a Television Viewer.* New York, 1968.

Morstein Marx, Fritz, ed. *Elements of Public Administration.* Englewood Cliffs, N. J., 1946.

Mosco, Vincent. *Broadcasting in the United States: Innovative Challenge and Organizational Control.* Norwood, N. J., 1979.

Navasky, Victor S. *Kennedy Justice.* New York, 1971.

Newfield, Jack, and Greenfield, Jeff. *A Populist Manifesto.* New York, 1971,

Noll, Roger G.; Peck, Merton J.; and McGowan, John J. *Economic Aspects of Television Regulation.* Washington, D. C., 1973.

Nossiter, Bernard D. *The Mythmakers.* Boston, 1964.

O'Connor, John E., ed. *American History/American Television.* New York, 1983.

O'Neill, William. *Coming Apart: An Informal History of America in the 1960s.* Chicago, 1971.

Owen, Bruce M. *Economics and Freedom of Expression: Media Structure and the First Amendment.* Cambridge, Mass., 1975.

Owen, Bruce M.; Beebe, Jack H.; and Manning, Willard G., Jr. *Television Economics.* Lexington, Mass., 1974.

Packard, Vance. *The Hidden Persuaders.* New York, 1957.

Paley, William S. *As It Happened: A Memoir.* Garden City, N. Y., 1979.

Parmet, Herbert S. *Jack: The Struggles of John F. Kennedy.* New York, 1980.

Parrish, Michael E. *Securities Regulation and the New Deal.* New Haven, 1970

Patterson, Thomas E., and McClure, Robert D. *The Unseeing Eye: The Myth of Television Power in Presidential Politics.* New York, 1976.

Peabody, Robert L., et al. *To Enact a Law: Congress and Campaign Financing.* New York, 1972.

Peabody, Robert L., and Polsby, Nelson W., eds. *New Perspectives on the House of Representatives.* Chicago, 1963.

Pease, Otis. *Responsibilities of American Advertising: Private Control and Public Influence, 1920-1940.* New Haven, 1958.

Pemberton, William E. *Bureaucratic Politics: Executive Reorganization during the Truman Administration.* Columbia, Mo., 1979.

Pennybacker, John H., and Braden, Waldo W., eds. *Broadcasting and the Public Interest.* New York, 1969.

Polenberg, Richard. *Reorganizing Roosevelt's Government: The Controversy over Executive Reorganization, 1936-1939.* Cambridge, Mass., 1966.

Pollard, James E. *The President and the Press: Truman to Johnson.* Washington, D. C., 1964.

Porter, William E. *Assault on the Media: The Nixon Years.* Ann Arbor, 1976.

Pritchett, C. Herman. *The Roosevelt Court: A Study in Judicial Politics and Values.* New York, 1948.

Pusateri, C. Joseph. *Enterprise in Radio: WWL and the Business of Broadcasting in America.* Washington, D. C., 1980.

Quinlan, Sterling H. *The Hundred Million Dollar Lunch.* Chicago, 1974.

_____. *Inside ABC.* New York, 1979.

Quirk, Paul J. *Industry Influence in Federal Regulatory Agencies.* Princeton, 1981.

Reeves, Rosser. *Reality in Advertising.* New York, 1962.

Ritchie, Donald A. *James M. Landis: Dean of the Regulators.*

Cambridge, Mass., 1980.

Rivers, William L. *The Opinionmakers*. Boston, 1965.

Robinson, Thomas Porter. *Radio Networks and the Federal Government*. New York, 1943.

Roe, Yale. *The Television Dilemma: Search for a Solution*. New York, 1962.

Rosen, Philip T. *The Modern Stentors: Radio Broadcasting and the Federal Government, 1920-1934*. Westport, Conn., 1980.

Rovere, Richard H. *The American Establishment and Other Reports, Opinions and Speculations*. New York, 1962.

Rowen, Hobart, *The Free Enterprisers: Kennedy, Johnson, and the Business Establishment*. New York, 1964.

Rucker, Bryce W. *The First Freedom*. Carbondale, 1968.

Salinger, Pierre. *With Kennedy*. Garden City, N. Y., 1966.

Sarnoff, David. *Looking Ahead: The Papers of David Sarnoff*. New York, 1968.

Schlesinger, Arthur M., Jr. *A Thousand Days: John F. Kennedy in the White House*. Boston, 1965.

_____. *The Vital Center*. Boston, 1962.

Schramm, Wilbur. *Responsibility in Mass Communication*. New York, 1957.

_____, ed. *The Impact of Educational Television*. Urbana, 1960.

Schramm, Wilbur; Lyle, Jack; and Parker, Edwin B. *Television in the Lives of Our Children*. Stanford, 1961.

Schramm, Wilbur; Lyle, Jack; and Pool, Ithiel de Sola. *The People Look at Educational Television*. Stanford, 1963.

Schubert, Glendon A. *The Public Interest: A Critique of the Theory of a Political Concept*. Glencoe, Ill., 1960.

Schwartz, Bernard. *The Professor and the Commissions*. New York, 1959.

Seldes, Gilbert, *The Public Arts*. New York, 1956.

Shayon, Robert Lewis. *Open to Criticism*. Boston, 1971.

_____. *Television and Our Children*. New York, 1951.

Shayon, Robert Lewis, et al. *The Eighth Art: Twenty-Three Views of Television Today*. New York, 1962.

Shulman, Arthur, and Youman, Roger. *The Golden Age of Television: How Sweet It Was*. New York, 1966.

Siepmann, Charles A. *Radio, Television, and Society*. New York, 1950.

_____. *Radio's Second Chance*. Boston, 1946.

_____. *TV and Our School Crisis.* New York, 1958.

Simmons, Steven J. *The Fairness Doctrine and the Media.* Berkeley, 1978.

Skowronek, Stephen. *Building a New American State: The Expansion of National Administrative Capacities, 1877-1920.* Cambridge, 1982.

Sloan Commission on Cable Communications. *On the Cable: The Television of Abundance.* New York, 1971.

Small, William. *To Kill a Messenger: Television News and the Real World.* New York, 1970.

Smith, Ralph Lee. *The Wired Nation, Cable TV: The Electronic Communications Highway.* New York, 1972.

Sobel, Robert. *The Age of Giant Corporations: A Microeconomic History of American Business, 1914-1970.* Westport, Conn., 1972.

_____. *The Manipulators: America in the Media Age.* Garden City, N. Y., 1976.

Sopkin, Charles. *Seven Glorious Days, Seven Fun-Filled Nights: One Man's Struggle to Survive a Week Watching Commercial Television in America.* New York, 1968.

Sorensen, Theodore C. *Kennedy.* New York, 1968.

Stanley, David T.; Mann, Dean E.; and Doig, Jameson W. *Men Who Govern: A Biographical Profile of Federal Political Executives.* Washington, D. C., 1967.

Stavins, Ralph L., ed. *Television Today: The End of Communication and the Death of Community.* Washington, D. C., 1969.

Steiner, Gary A. *The People Look at Television: A Study of Audience Attitudes.* New York, 1963.

Sterling, Christopher H., and Haight, Timothy R., eds. *The Mass Media: The Aspen Guide to Communication Industry Trends.* New York, 1977.

Sterling, Christopher H., and Kittross, John M. *Stay Tuned: A Concise History of American Broadcasting.* Belmont, Calif., 1978.

Stigler, George J. *The Citizen and the State.* Chicago, 1975.

Torre, Marie. *Don't Quote Me.* Garden City, N. Y. 1965.

Tuchman, Gaye, ed. *The TV Establishment: Programming for Power and Profit.* Englewood Cliffs, N. J., 1974.

Vidal, Gore, ed. *Best Television Plays.* New York, 1956.

White, David Manning, ed. *Pop Culture in America*. Chicago, 1970.

Wilcox, Clair. *Public Policies toward Business*. 3d ed. Homewood, Ill., 1966.

Wilk, Max. *The Golden Age of Television: Notes from the Survivors*. New York, 1976.

Williams, Raymond. *Television: Technology and Cultural Form*. Cambridge, Mass., 1975.

Winick, Charles. *Taste and the Censor in Television*. New York, 1959.

Woll, Peter. *Administrative Law: The Informal Process*. Berkeley, 1963.

_____. *American Bureaucracy*. New York, 1963.

Wylie, Max. *Clear Channels: Television and the American People*. New York, 1955.

ARTICLES

Anello, Douglas, and Cahill, Robert V. "Legal Authority of the FCC to Place Limits on Broadcast Advertising." *Journal of Broadcasting* 7 (Fall 1963), 285-304.

Bailes, James R.; Hardie, William H., Jr.; and Slaughter, Alexander H. "The Progress of Federal Agency Reorganization under the Kennedy Administration." *Virginia Law Review* 48 (March 1962), 300-77.

Bailyn, Lotte, ed. "The Uses of Television." *Journal of Social Issues* 18, no. 2 (1962), 1-61.

Baker, Kenneth. "An Analysis of Radio's Programming." In Paul F. Lazarsfeld and Frank N. Stanton, eds., *Communications Research, 1948-1949*. New York, 1949.

Barber, Oren G. "Competition, Free Speech, and FCC Radio Regulation." *George Washington Law Review* 12 (May 1943), 34-53.

Barber, Richard J. "The New Partnership: Big Government and Big Business." *New Republic* (13 Aug. 1966), 17-22.

Barrow, Roscoe L. "Antitrust and the Regulated Industry: Promoting Competition in Broadcasting." *Duke Law Journal* (Spring 1964), 282-306.

_____. "The Attainment of Balanced Program Service in Television." *Virginia Law Review* 52 (May 1966), 633-66.

————. "Network Broadcasting—The Report of the FCC Network Study Staff." *Law and Contemporary Problems* 22 (Autumn 1957), 611-25.

Bauer, Raymond A. "The Initiative of the Audience." *Journal of Advertising Research* 3, no. 2 (1963), 2-7.

————. "The Limits of Persuasion." *Harvard Business Review* 36 (Sept.-Oct. 1958), 105-10.

Baughman, James L. "The National Purpose and the Newest Medium: Liberal Critics of Television, 1958-60." *Mid-America* 64 (April-July 1983). 41-55.

————. *"See It Now* and Television's Golden Age, 1951-58." *Journal of Popular Culture* 15 (Fall 1981), 106-15.

————. "'The Strange Birth of *CBS Resports'* Revisited." *Historical Journal of Film, Radio, and Television* 2 (March 1982), 27-38.

Bazelon, David L. "The First Amendment and the 'New Media'—New Direction in Regulating Telecommunications." *Federal Communications Law Journal* 31 (Spring 1979), 201-13.

Beebe, Jack H. "Institutional Structure and Program Choices in Television Markets." *Quarterly Journal of Economics* 91 (Feb. 1977), 15-37.

Bell, Daniel. "Modernity and Mass Society: On the Variety of Cultural Experiences." *Studies in Public Communication* no. 4, (Autumn 1962), 3-34.

Bendiner, Robert. "Could You Stand a Four-Day Week?" *Reporter* 17 (8 August 1957), 10-14.

————. "The FCC—Who Will Regulate the Regulators?" *Reporter* 17 (19 Sept. 1957), 26-30.

Benton, William. "Big Brother's TV Set." *Esquire* (March 1964), 98-99.

Berelson, Bernard. "The Great Debate On Cultural Democracy." *Studies in Public Communication* no. 3 (Summer 1961), 3-14.

Berkman, Dave. "A Modest Proposal: Abolishing the FCC." *Columbia Journalism Review* 4 (Fall 1965), 34-36.

Bernstein, Marver H., ed. "The Government as Regulator." *Annals of the American Academy of Political and Social Science* 400 (March 1972).

Blachly, Frederick F., and Oatman, Miriam E. "Sabotage of the Administrative Process." *Public Administration Review* 6 (Summer 1946), 213-27.

Blank, David M. "The Quest for Quality and Diversity in Television Programming." *American Economic Association Papers and Proceedings* 56 (May 1966), 448-56.

Bliss, Edward, Jr. "Remembering Edward R. Murrow." *Saturday Review* (31 May 1975), 17-20.

Bookman, George. "Loevinger vs. Big Business." *Fortune* (Jan. 1961), 137.

———. "Regulation by Elephant, Rabbit, and Lark." *Fortune* (June 1961), 137.

Borchardt, Kurt. "Congressional Use of Administrative Organization and Procedures for Policy-Making Purposes: Six Case Studies and Some Conclusions." *George Washington Law Review* 30 (March 1962) 429-66.

Bourjaily, Vance. "The Lost Art of Writing for Television." *Harper's.* (Oct. 1959), 151-57.

Braeman, John. "The New Deal and the 'Broker State': A Review of the Recent Scholarly Liberature." *Business History Review* 46 (Winter 1972), 409-29.

Brenner, Daniel L. "Government Regulation of Radio Program Format Changes." *University of Pennsylvania Law Review* 127 (Nov. 1978), 56-110.

Brogan, D. W. "The Problem of High Culture and Mass Culture." *Diogenes,* no. 5 (Winter 1954), 1-13.

Bryant, Ashbrook P. "Historical and Social Aspects of Concentration of Program Control in Television." *Law and Comtemporary Problems* 34 (Summer 1969), 610-35.

Buckley, William F., Jr. "The Partial Insight of Mr. Minow." *National Review* 14 (4 June 1963), 447.

Caldwell, Louis G. "The Standard of Public Interest, Convenience, or Necessity as Used in the Radio Act of 1927." *Air Law Review* 1 (July 1930), 295.

Canon, Bradley C. "Voting Behavior on the FCC." *Midwest Journal of Political Sciences* 13 (Nov. 1969), 587-612.

Carroll, Raymond L. "Economic Influences on Commercial Network Television Documentary Scheduling." *Journal of Broadcasting* 23 (Fall 1979), 411-25.

Carrow, Milton M. "Dean Landis and the Regulatory Process." *George Washington Law Review* 29 (April 1961), 718-38.

Carson, Saul. "Television and Your Place in the Picture." *Theatre Arts* (Dec. 1961), 65-67, 76-79.

Cater, Douglass. "The Kennedy Look in the Arts." *Horizon* (Sept. 1961), 4-17.

Celler, Emanuel. "Antitrust Problems in the Television Broad-casting Industry." *Law and Contemporary Problems* 22 (Autumn 1957), 549-71.

Chamberlain, E. H. "Product Heterogeneity and Public Policy." *American Economic Review* 40 (May 1950), 85-92.

Clark, David G., and Blankenburg, William B. "Trends in Violent Content in Selected Mass Media." In George A. Comstock and Eli A. Rubinstein, eds., *Television and Social Behavior: Reports and Papers* 6 vols. Rockville, Md., 1972.

Coase, R. H. "The Economics of Broadcasting and Advertising: The Economics of Broadcasting and Government Policy." *American Economic Association Papers and Proceedings* 56 (May 1966), 440-47.

_____. "Evaluation of Public Policy Relating to Radio and Television Broadcasting: Social and Economic Issues." *Land Economics* 41 (May 1965), 161-67.

_____. "The Federal Communications Commission." *Journal of Law and Economics* 2 (Oct. 1959), 1-40.

Cochran, Thomas C. "Media as Business: A Brief History." *Journal of Communication* 25 (Autumn 1975), 155-65.

Coffin, Thomas E. "Television's Impact on Society." *American Psychologist* 10 (Oct. 1955), 630-41.

Cohn, Marcus. "Religion and the FCC." *Reporter* (14 Jan. 1965), 32-34.

Cone, Fairfax M. "What's Bad for TV Is Worse for Adver-tisers." *Fortune* (July 1965), 102.

Cort, David. "Arms and the Man." *Nation* (23 May 1959), 475-77.

Cox, Kenneth A. "Broadcasters as Revolutionaries." *Television Quarterly* 6 (Winter 1967), 13-20.

_____. "Competition in and among the Broadcasting, CATV, and Pay-TV Industries." *Antitrust Bulletin* 13 (Fall 1968), 911-26.

_____. "The FCC, the Constitution, and Religious Broadcast Programming." *George Washington Law Review* 34 (Dec. 1965), 196-218.

Crandall, Robert W. "The Economic Effect of Television Net-work Program Ownership." *Journal of Law and Economics* 141 (Oct. 1971), 385-412.

_____. "FCC Regulation, Monopsony, and Network Television Program Costs." *Bell Journal of Economics and Management Science* 3 (Autumn 1972) 483-508.

_____. "Regulation of Television Broadcasting: How Costly is the 'Public Interest'?" *Regulation* 2 (Jan.-Feb. 1978), 31-39.

Crosby, John. "It Was New and Wc Were Very Innocent." *TV Guide* (22 Sept. 1973), 5-8.

_____. "What You Can Do to Make Poor TV Better." *Ladies Home Journal* (Nov. 1960), 74 75. 135.

Culbert, David. "Johnson and the Media." In Robert A. Divine, ed., *Exploring the Johnson Years*. Austin, 1981.

"Darkened Channels: UHF Television and the FCC." *Harvard Law Review* 75 (June 1962). 1578-507.

Davis, G. Cullom "The Transformation of the Federal Trade Commission, 1914-1929." *Mississippi Valley Historical Review* 49 (Dec. 1962), 437-55.

Decter, Midge. "Kennedyism." *Commentary* 49 (Jan. 1970). 19-27.

"Diversification and the Public Interest: Administrative Responsibility of the FCC." *Yale Law Journal* 66 (Jan. 1957). 365-96.

Dodds, Wendell H., and Harwood, Kenneth. "Governmental Issues in U. S. Broadcasting, 1946-1955." *Journal of Broadcasting* 1 (Spring 1957), 161-67.

Doerfer, John C. "Legislation Affecting the Federal Regulatory Process." *Federal Communications Bar Journal* 17, no. 1 (1959), 5-20.

Dominick, Joseph R., and Pearce, Millard C. "Trends in Network Prime-Time Programming." *Journal of Communication* 26 (Winter 1976), 70-80.

Drew, Elizabeth Brenner. "Is the FCC Dead?" *Atlantic* (July 1967), 20-36.

Durr, Clifford J. "The Forgotten Client of the Agencies." *New Republic* (30 June 1958), 8-9.

Duscha, Julius. "New Voices for Consumers." *Progressive* 25 (Nov. 1961). 17-20.

Eck, Robert. "The Real Masters of Television." *Harper's* (March 1967), 45-52.

Elman, Philip. "Administration Reform of the Federal Trade Commission." *Georgetown Law Journal* 59 (March 1971), 777-860.

"*Ex Parte* Contacts with the Federal Communications Commission." *Harvard Law Review* 73 (April 1960), 1178-199.

Fainsod, Merle. "Some Reflections on the Nature of the Regulatory Process." In Carl J. Friedrich and Edward S. Mason eds., *Public Policy, 1940*. Cambridge, Mass., 1940.

Fairlie, Henry. "The Philosophy of Pilkington." *Spectator* 209 (6 July 1962), 9, 11.

"FCC Regulation of Competition among Networks." *Yale Law Journal* 51 (Jan. 1942), 448-65.

"The FCC's Role in TV Programming Regulation." *Villanova Law Review* 14 (Summer 1969).

Ferry, W. H. "Masscomm as Educators." *American Scholar* 35 (Spring 1966), 293-302.

Fielder, Leslie. "The Middle Against Both Ends." *Encounter* 5 (Aug. 1955), 16-23.

Fischer, John. "TV and Its Critics." *Harper's* (July 1959), 10-14.

Fisher, Ben C. "Communications Acts Amendments, 1952—An Attempt to Legislate Administrative Fairness." *Law and Contemporary Problems* 22 (Autumn 1957), 672-96.

Fisher, Franklin M., and Ferrall, Victor E., Jr. "Community Antenna Systems and Local Television Audience." *Quarterly Journal of Economics* 80 (May 1966), 227-51.

Fly, James Lawrence. "The Network Bluff." *Nation* 194 (10 March 1962), 210-12.

Ford, Frederick W. "The Meaning of the 'Public Interest, Convenience, or Necessity.'" *Journal of Broadcasting* 5 (Summer 1961), 205-18.

_____. "Some Current Problems in Broadcast Regulation." *Federal Communications Bar Journal* 17, no. 2 (1960), 76-82.

Friederich, Carl J., and Sternberg, Evelyn. "Congress and the Control of Radio-Broadcasting." *American Political Science Review* 37 (Oct. 1943), 797-818; (Dec. 1943), 1014-026.

Fuess, Claude M. "The Retreat from Excellence." *Saturday Review* (26 March 1960), 21-23.

Gans, Herbert J. "The Mass Media as an Educational Institution." *Television Quarterly* 6 (Spring 1967), 20-37.

Garvey, Daniel E. "Secretary Hoover and the Quest for Broadcast Regulation." *Journalism History* 3 (Autumn 1976), 66-70.

Godfrey, Donald G. "The 1927 Radio Act: People and Politics." *Journalism History* 4 (Autumn 1977), 74-78.

_____. "Senator Dill and the 1927 Radio Act: People and Politics." *Journalism History* 4 (Autumn 1977), 74-78.

Goldberg, Henry, and Couzens, Michael. "'Peculiar Characteristics': An Analysis of the First Amendment Implications of of Broadcasting Regulation." *Federal Communications Law Journal* (Winter 1978), 1-50.

Goldin, Hyman H. "Economic and Regulatory Problems in the Broadcast Field." *Land Economics* 30 (August 1954), 223-33.

_____. "'Spare the Golden Goose'—The Aftermath of WHDH in FCC License Policy." *Harvard Law Review* 83 (March 1970), 1014-037.

Goldman, Eric F. "Good-By to the Fifties—and Good Riddance." *Harper's* (Jan. 1960), 27-29.

_____. "What Is Prosperity Doing to Our Political Parties?" *Saturday Review* (8 Oct. 1955), 9-10.

Goodman, Paul. "A Few Questions for Mr. Minow." *New Republic* (2 March 1963), 35-37.

Gormley, William T., Jr. "A Test of the Revolving Door Hypothesis at the FCC." *American Journal of Political Science* 23 (Nov. 1979), 665-83.

"Government Control of the Content of Radio Programs." *Columbia Law Review* 47 (Sept. 1947), 1041-052.

Greenberg, Edward, and Barnett, Harold J. "TV Program Diversity—New Evidence and Old Theories." *American Economic Association Papers and Proceedings* 61 (May 1971), 89-93.

Greyser, Stephen A., and Bauer, Raymond A. "Americans and Advertising: Thirty Years of Public Opinion." *Public Opinion Quarterly* 30 (Spring 1966), 69-78.

Harris, Joseph P. "The Senatorial Rejection of Leland Olds: A Case Study." *American Political Science Review* 45 (Sept. 1051), 674-92.

Harris, Oren. "Improving the Regulatory Process." *Public Utilities Fortnightly* 64 (2 July 1959), 19-23.

Harwood, Kenneth, "Broadcasting and the Theory of the Firm." *Law and Contemporary Problems* 34 (Summer 1969), 485-504.

Hawley, Ellis W. "Herbert Hoover, the Commerce Secretariat, and the Vision of an 'Associative State." *Journal of American History* 61 (June 1974), 116-40.

Heady, Ferrel. "The New Reform Movement in Regulatory Administration." *Public Administration Review* 19 (Spring 1959), 89-100.

Henry, E. William. "Educational TV Is Still Just a Promise." *American Education* 1 (Feb. 1965), 26-28.

Hentoff, Nat. "Irrigating the Wasteland," *Commonweal* 75 (11 Aug. 1961), 445-47.

Herring, E. Pendleton. "Politics and Radio Regulation." *Harvard Business Review* 13 (Jan. 1935), 167-78.

Holt, Derrel. "The Origin of 'Public Interest' in Broadcasting." *Educational Broadcasting Review* 1 (Oct. 1967), 15-49.

Hoover, Herbert. "Radio Gets a Policeman." *American Heritage* (Aug. 1955), 73-76.

Howe, Irving. "Notes on Mass Culture." *Politics* 5 (Spring 1948), 120-23.

Huntington, Samuel P. "The Marasmus of the ICC: The Commission, the Railroads, and the Public Interest." *Yale Law Journal* 61 (April 1952), 467-509.

Hurt, Robert M. "FCC: Free Speech, 'Public Needs,' and Mr. Minow." *New Individualist Review* 2 (Spring 1963), 24-37.

"The Impact of the FCC's Chain Broadcasting Rules." *Yale Law Journal* 60 (Jan. 1951), 78-111.

"Indirect Censorship of Radio Programs." *Yale Law Journal* 40 (April 1931), 967-73.

Jaffe, Louis L. "The Effective Limits of the Administrative Process: A Reevaluation." *Harvard Law Review* 67 (May 1954), 1105-035.

_____. "Independent Agency—a New Scapegoat." *Yale Law Journal* 65 (June 1956), 1068.

_____. "James Landis and the Administrative Process." *Harvard Law Review* 78 (Dec. 1964), 319-28.

_____. "Program Control." *Villanova Law Review* 14 (Summer 1969), 619-22.

_____. "The Scandal in TV Licensing." *Harper's* (Sept. 1957), 77-79, 82, 84.

Jeffries, John W. "The 'Quest for National Purpose' of 1960." *American Quarterly* 30 (Fall 1978), 451-70.

Johnson, Nicholas. "Consumer Rights and the Regulatory Crisis." *Catholic University Law Review* 20 (Spring 1971), 424-48.

_____. "A New Fidelity to the Regulatory Ideal." *Georgetown*

Law Journal 59 (March 1971), 869-908.

Johnson, Nicholas, and Meyer, Karl E. "A Debate on TV Licensing." *Nation* (30 Sept. 1978), 298-302.

Kalven, Harry, Jr., and Rosenfield, Maurice. "Minow Should Watch His Step in the Wasteland." *Fortune* (Oct. 1962), 116.

Kintner, Robert E. "Broadcasting and the News." *Harper's* (April 1965), 49-55.

———. "The Television and the Real World." *Harper's* (June 1965), 94-98.

———. "Television and the World of Politics." *Harper's* (May 1965), 121-23, 126, 128.

Kirshner, Charles. "The Color Television Controversy." *University of Pittsburgh Law Review* 13 (Fall 1951), 65-84.

Klapper, Joseph T. "Mass Communication Research: An Old Road Resurveyed." *Public Opinion Quarterly* 27 (Winter 1963), 515-27.

Kolson, Kenneth L. "Broadcasting in the Public Interest: The Legacy of Federal Communications Commissioner Nicholas Johnson." *Administrative Law Review* 30 (Winter 1978). 133-65.

Koppes, Clayton R. "The Social Destiny of the Radio: Hope and Disillusionment in the 1920s." *South Atlantic Quarterly* 68 (Summer 1969). 363-76.

Kristol, Irving. "Of Newton Minow and Matthew Arnold." *New Leader* 46 (7 Jan. 1963), 18-20.

Lacey, Linda Jo. "The Electric Church: An FCC 'Established' Institution?" *Federal Communications Law Journal* 31 (Spring 1979) 235-76.

Landis, James M. "The Administrative Process: The Third Decade." *Journal of the American Bar Association* 47 (Feb. 1961), 135.

———. "The Place of Administrative Law." *Connecticut Bar Journal* 13 (April 1939), 71-81.

———. "Remarks." *Antitrust Law Symposium* (1961), 48-54.

Lang, Gladys Engel, and Lang, Kurt. "Van Doren as Victim: Student Reaction." *Studies in Public Communication*, no. 3 (Summer 1961), 50-58.

Larrabee, Eric. "The Imaginary Audience." *Horizon* (March 1960), 46-51.

Lazarsfeld, Paul F. "Remarks on Administrative and Critical

Communications Research." *Studies in Philosophy and Social Science* 9 (1941), 2-16.

Lessing, Lawrence. "The Television Freeze." *Fortune* (Nov. 1949), 123-27.

Levin, Harvey J. "Broadcast Structure, Technology, and the ABC-ITT Merger Decision." *Law and Contemporary Problems* 34 (Summer 1969), 452-84.

_____. "Program Duplication, Diversity, and Effective Viewer Sources: Some Empirical Findings." *American Economic Association Papers and Proceedings* 61 (May 1971), 81-88.

_____. "Regulatory Efficiency, Reform and the FCC." *Georgetown Law Journal* 50 (Fall 1961), 1-45.

_____. "Workable Competition and Regulatory Policy in Television Broadcasting." *Land Economics* 34 (May 1958), 101-12.

Levitt, Theodore. "The Johnson Treatment." *Harvard Business Review* 45 (Jan. 1967), 114-28.

Lichty, Lawrence W. "An Analysis of the FCC Membership." *Public Utilities Fortnightly* 68 (Nov. 1961), 828-33.

_____. "The Impact of FRC and FCC Commissioners' Backgrounds on the Regulation of Broadcasting." *Journal of Broadcasting* 6 (Spring 1962), 97-110.

_____. "Members of the Federal Radio Commission and Federal Communications Commission." *Journal of Broadcasting* 6 (Winter 1961-1962), 23-34.

Lishman, Robert W. "'Independence' in Independent Regulatory Agencies." *Administrative Law Review* 13 (Winter 1960), 135-40.

Loevinger, Lee. "The Issues in Program Regulation." *Federal Communications Bar Journal* 20, no. 1, (1966), 3-15.

_____. "Religious Liberty and Broadcasting." *George Washington Law Review* 33 (March 1965), 631-59.

_____. "The Role of Law in Broadcasting." *Journal of Broadcasting* 8 (Spring 1964), 113-26.

Long, Norton E. "Bureaucracy and Constitutionalism." *American Political Science Review* 46 (Sept. 1952), 808-18.

McCarran, Pat. "Improving 'Administrative Justice': Hearings and Evidence; Scope of Judicial Review." *Journal of the American Bar Association* 32 (Dec. 1946), 827-31.

McCoy, Harold D. "Communication Act Amendments, 1952, Certain Aspects of Interest to I. C. C." *ICC Practitioners*

Journal 20 (Oct. 1952), 8-21.

McCraw, Thomas K. "Regulation in America: A Review Article." *Business History Review* 49 (Summer 1975), 159-83.

Macdonald, Dwight. "A Theory of Mass Culture." *Diogenes*, no. 3 (Summer 1953), 1-17.

McFarland, Carl. "Landis' Report: The Voice Of One Crying in the Wildnerness." *Virginia Law Review* 47 (April 1961), 373-438.

McKerns, Charles J., and Robertson, Charles J. "Disciplinary Powers under the Commuications Act Amendments of 1960." *Federal Communications Bar Journal* 19, no. 2 (1964-65), 3-26.

McKerns, Joseph P. "Industry Skeptics and the Radio Act of 1927." *Journalism History* 3 (Winter 1976-77), 128-31.

MacLeish, Archibald. "The Great American Frustration." *Saturday Review* (13 July 1968), 13-16.

Manheim, Jarol B. "Can Democracy Survive Television?" *Journal of Communication* 26 (Spring 1976), 84-90.

Mannes, Marya. "The Networks and the FCC." *Reporter* 26 (29 March 1962), 19-23.

———. "The TV Pattern—Signs of Revolt." *Reporter* 16 (2 May 1957), 19-22.

Martin, John Bartlow. "Television, U. S. A." *Saturday Evening Post* 234 (21 Oct. 1961), 19-24; (28 Oct. 1961), 56-58, 60-62; (4 Nov. 1961), 31, 36-38; (11 Nov. 1961); 62.

"Mass Culture and Mass Media." *Daedalus* 89 (Spring 1960).

Mayer, Martin. "ABC: Portrait of a Network." *Show* 1 (Oct. 1961), 58-63.

———. "CBS: The Networks and the Mind Machines." *Show* 2 (April 1962) 62-65, 104-05.

———. "How Good Is TV at Its Best?" *Harper's* (Aug. 1960), 82-86; (Sept. 1960), 85-90.

———. "Television's Lords of Creation." *Harper's* (Nov. 1956), 25; (Dec. 1956), 45.

Meyer, Karl E. "Don't Annoy the Sponsor." *Progressive* 27 (Dec. 1963). 26-29.

Meyer, Richard J. "Reaction to the Blue Book." *Journal of Broadcasting* 6 (Fall 1962), 295-312.

Miller, Warren E., and Stokes, Donald E. "Constituency in Congress." *American Political Science Review* 57 (March 1963), 45-56.

Mott, Frank Luther. "A Twentieth Century Monster: The Mass Audience." *Saturday Review* (8 Oct. 1960), 59-60.

Nathanson, N. L. "Mr. Justice Frankfurter and Administrative Law." *Yale Law Journal* 67 (Dec. 1957), 240-65.

Newman, Frank C., and Keaton, Harry J. "Congress and the Faithful Execution of Laws—Should Legislators Supervise Administrators?" *California Law Review* 41 (Winter 1953-54), 565-95.

Nielsen, Ted. "Television: Chicago Style." *Journal of Broadcasting* 9 (Fall 1965), 302-12.

Nix, Mindy. "The Meet the Press Game." *MORE* (Feb. 1973), 12-14.

Neuchterlein, James A. "Arthur M. Schlesinger, Jr., and the Discontents of Postwar American Liberalism." *Review of Politics* 39 (Jan. 1977), 3-40.

Owen, Bruce M. "Regulating Diversity: The Case of Radio Formats." *Journal of Broadcasting* 21 (Summer 1977), 305-19.

Pusateri, C. Joseph. "The Stormy Career of a Radio Maverick: W. K. Henderson of KWKH." *Louisiana Studies* 15 (Winter 1976), 389-407.

Rapoport, Daniel. "And Now, A Brief Word from Our Sponsor." *Reporter* (4 June 1964), 26-28.

Redford, Emmette S. "Perspective for the Study of Government Regulation." *Midwest Journal of Political Science* 6 (Feb. 1962). 1-18.

Reeves, Byron, and Baughman, James L. "'Fraught with Such Great Possibilities': The Historical Relationship of Communication Research to Mass Media Regulation." In Oscar Gandy, Paul Espinosa, and Janusz Ordover, eds., *Proceedings of the Tenth Annual Telecommunications Policy Research Conference.* Norwood, N. J., 1983.

"Regulation of Program Content by the FCC." *Harvard Law Review* 77 (Feb. 1964), 701-16.

Reich, Charles A. "The New Prosperity." *Yale Law Journal* 73 (April 1964), 753-87.

Robinson, Glen O. "FCC and the First Amendment: Observations on 40 Years of Radio and Television Regulation." *Minnesota Law Review* 52 (Nov. 1967), 67-163.

Rolla, Edward Park. "Television Station Performance and Revenues." *Educational Broadcasting Review* 5 (June 1971) 43-49.

Rosen, Gerald R. "Johnson and the Businessmen." *Dun's Review* 85 (May 1967), 40, 42-43, 79-80.

Rosenblum, Victor G. "How to Get into TV: The Federal Communications Commission and Miami's Channel 10." In Alan F. Westin, ed., *The Uses of Power.* New York, 1962.

Rosenberg, Herbert H. "Program Content—A Criterion of Public Interest in FCC Licensing." *Western Political Quarterly* 2 (Sept. 1949), 373-401.

Sarnoff, Robert W. "What Do You Want From TV?" *Saturday Evening Post* (1 July 1961), 13-15, 44-46.

Scher, Seymour. "Conditions for Legislative Control." *Journal of Politics* 25 (Aug. 1963), 526-51.

_____. "Congressional Committee Members as Independent Agency Overseers." *American Political Science Review* 54 (Dec. 1960), 911-20.

Schickel, Richard. "The Television Problem." *Commentary* 34 (Dec. 1962), 461-69.

Schiro, Richard. "Diversity in Television's Speech: Balancing Programs in the Eyes of the Viewer." *Case Western Reserve University Law Review* 27 (Fall 1976), 336-53.

Schlesinger, Arthur M., Jr. "The Challenge of Abundance." *Reporter* (3 May 1956), 8-11.

_____. "Government and the Arts: A New Era." *Show* (Oct. 1962), 74, 101.

_____. "Which Road for the Democrats?" *Reporter* (20 Jan. 1953), 31-34.

Schwartz, Bernard. "The Administrative Agency in Historical Perspective." *Indiana Law Journal* 36 (Spring 1961), 263-81.

_____. "Antitrust and the FCC: The Problem of Network Dominance." *University of Pennsylvania Law Review* 107 (April 1959), 753-95.

_____. "Comparative Television and the Chancellor's Foot." *Georgetown Law Journal* 47 (Summer 1959), 655-99.

Schwarzwalder, John C. "The Myths of Educational Television." *NAEB Journal* 24 (May-June 1965), 51-60.

Shils, Edward C. "Daydreams and Nightmares: Reflections on the Criticism of Mass Culture." *Sewanee Review* 65 (Autumn 1957), 586-608.

Smith, Bernard B. "A New Weapon to Get Better TV." *Harper's* (July 1962), 27-34.

_____. "Television: There Ought to Be a Law." *Harper's* (Sept. 1948), 34-42.

Smith, Richard Austin. "TV: The Coming Showdown." *Fortune* (Sept. 1954), 138-39.

_____. "TV: The Light That Failed." *Fortune* (Dec. 1958). 78-81.

Smythe, Dallas W., and Smythe, Jennie N. "Menace of Pay TV." *Nation* (4 Jan. 1958), 5-9.

Steiner, Peter O. "Program Patterns and Preferences, and the Workability of Competition in Radio Broadcasting." *Quarterly Journal of Economics* 66 (May 1952), 194-223.

Stern, Laurence. "LBJ and the FCC." *Progressive* 28 (June 1964), 21-24.

Stern, Robert H. "Regulatory Influences upon Television's Development: Early Years Under the Federal Radio Commission." *American Journal of Economics and Sociology* 22 (July 1963), 347-62.

Sternberg, Joel. "Television Town." *Chicago History* 4 (Summer 1975), 108-17.

Sternsher, Bernard. "Liberalism in the Fifties: The Travail of Redefinition." *Antioch Review* 22 (Fall 1962), 315-31.

Stukas, William B. "The Federal Communications Commission and Program Regulation—Violation of the First Amendment?" *Nebraska Law Review* 41 (June 1962), 826-46.

Sultzer, Elmer G., and Johnson, George C. "Attitudes towards Deception in Television." *Journal of Broadcasting* 4 (Spring 1960), 97-109.

Susskind, David. "The Mental Midgets Take Over." *Saturday Evening Post* (24 March 1962), 12, 18.

Swados, Harvey. "Less Work—Less Leisure." *Nation* (22 Feb. 1958), 153-58.

Tedlow, Richard S. "Intellect on Television: The Quiz Show Scandals of the 1950s." *American Quarterly* 28 (Fall 1975), 483-95.

Thomas, Lowell S., Jr. "The Federal Communications Commission: Control of 'Deceptive Programming.'" *University of Pennsylvania Law Review* 108 (April 1960), 868-92.

Tiven, Kenneth D. "UHF: The Sleeping Giant." *Television Quarterly* 9 (Winter 1970), 40-49.

Van Horne, Harriet. "The Chicago Touch," *Theatre Arts* (July, 1951) 36-39.

Vidal, Gore. "See It Later." *New York Review of Books* 9 (7 Dec. 1967), 24-29.

Ways, Max "'Creative Federalism' and the Great Society." *Fortune* (Jan. 1966), 121-23, 222.

Webbink, Douglas W. "The Impact of UHF Promotion: The All-Channel Receiver Law." *Law and Contemporary Problems* 34 (Summer 1969), 535-61.

Welborn, David M. "Presidents, Regulatory Commissions, and Regulatory Policy." *Journal of Public Law* 15, no. 1 (1966), 3-29.

Wertenbaker, Charles. "The World on His Back." *New Yorker* (26 Dec. 1953), 28-30, 32-45.

White, David Manning. "What's Happening to Mass Culture?" *Saturday Review* (3 Nov. 1956), 11-13.

White, Stephen. "Carnegie, Ford, and the Public Interest." *Public Interest* no. 5 (Fall 1967), 8-19.

Whiteside, Thomas. "The Communicator." *New Yorker* (16 Oct. 1954), 37-38; (23 Oct. 1954), 43-44.

———. "Cutting Down." *New Yorker* (19 Dec. 1970). 42-48.

Whitfield, Stephen J. "The 1950's: The Era of No Hard Feelings." *South Atlantic Quarterly* 74 (Summer 1975), 289-307.

Whitworth, William. "An Accident of Casting." *New Yorker* (3 Aug. 1968), 34-60.

Wilensky, Harold L. "Mass Society and Mass Culture." *American Sociological Review* 29 (April 1964), 173-96.

Wilson, James Q. "The Bureaucracy Problem." *Public Interest* no. 6 (Winter 1967), 3-9.

Williams, Robert J. "Politics and the Ecology of Regulation." *Public Administration* 54 (Autumn 1976), 319-31.

———. "The Politics of American Broadcasting: Public Purposes and Private Interests." *Journal of American Studies* 10 (Dec. 1976), 329-40.

Winick, Charles E. "The Television Station Manager." *Advanced Management Journal* 31 (Jan. 1966). 53-60.

Woll, Peter. "Administrative Law Reform: Proposals and Prospects." *Nebraska Law Review* 41 (June 1962). 687-722.

Wollert, James A., and Wirth, Michael O. "UHF Television Program Performance: Continuing Questions on Spectrum Use." *Journalism Quarterly* 56 (Summer 1979) 346-52.

Young, Elizabeth. "One Medium: Two Critics." *Journal of*

casting 11 (Winter 1966-67), 41-55.

Zeidenberg, Leonard. "Is the FCC Obsolete?" *Television Magazine* (Oct. 1966), 27-31, 51-57.

GOVERNMENT PUBLICATIONS

U. S. Commission on Organization of the Executive Branch of the Government. *Task Force on Regulatory Commissions.* 1949.

U. S. Congress. *Congressional Record.*

U. S. Congress. House of Representatives. Committee on Appropriations. Subcommittee on Independent Offices. *Independent Offices Appropriations for 1962.* Hearings. 87th Cong. 1st sess., 1961.

————. *Independent Offices Appropriations for 1963.* Hearings. 87th Cong., 2d sess., 1962.

————. Committee on Government Operations. *Reorganization Plans Nos. 1, 2, 3, and 4 of 1961.* Hearings. 87th Cong., 1st sess., 1961.

————. Committee on Interstate and Foreign Commerce. *Administrative Process and Ethnical Questions.* Hearings. 85th Cong., 2d sess., 1958.

————. *All-Channel Television Receivers.* Report no. 1559. 87th Cong., 2d sess., 1962.

————. *All-Channel Television Receivers and Deintermixture.* Hearings. 87th Cong., 2d. sess., 1962.

————. *Broadcast Advertisements.* Hearings. 88th Cong., 1st sess., 1963.

————. *Communications Act Amendments.* Hearings. 86th Cong., 2d sess., 1960.

————. *Educational Television.* Hearings. 85th Cong., 2d sess., 1958.

————. *Educational Television.* Hearings. 86th Cong., 1st sess, 1959.

————. *Educational Television.* Hearings. 87th Cong., 1st sess., 1961.

————. *Educational Television.* Report no. 999, 87th Cong., 1st sess., 1961.

————. *History of the National Association of Securities Dealers.*

Committee Report. 86th Cong., 2d sess., 1960.

_____. *Investigation of Regulatory Commissions and Agencies.* Hearings. 85th Cong., 2d sess., 1958.

_____. *Investigation of Television Quiz Shows.* Hearings. 86th Cong., 1st sess., 1959.

_____. *Lack of Authority of the Federal Communications Commission to Make Rules Relating to the Length or Frequency of Broadcast Commercials.* Report no. 1054. 88th Cong., 1st sess., 1963.

_____. *Public Television Act of 1967.* Hearings. 90th Cong., 1st sess., 1967.

_____. *Public Television Act of 1967.* Report no. 572. 90th Cong., 1st sess., 1967.

_____. *Regulation of Broadcasting: Half a Century of Government Regulation of Broadcasting.* Committee print. 85th Cong., 2d sess., 1958.

_____. *Responsibilities of Broadcasting Licenses and Station Personnel.* Hearings. 86th Cong., 2d sess., 1960.

_____. *Subscription Television.* Hearings. 85th Cong., 2d sess., 1958.

_____. *Television Network Program Procurement.* Report no. 281. 88th Cong., 1st sess., 1963.

_____. Subcommittee on Legislative Oversight. *Interim Report.* 86th Cong., 2d sess., 9 Feb. 1960.

_____. Committee on the Judiciary. *Monopoly Problems in Regulated Industries.* Hearings. Pt. 2: *Television.* 84th Cong., 2d sess., 1956.

_____. Select Committee on Small Business. *Activities of Regulatory and Enforcement Agencies Relating to Small Business: The Federal Communications Commissions.* Hearings. 89th Cong., 2d sess., 1966.

U. S. Congess. Senate. Committee on Government Operations. *Reorganization Plans Nos. 1, 2, 3, and 4.* Hearings. 87th Cong., 1st sess., 1961.

_____. Committee on Interstate and Foreign Commerce. *All-Channel Television.* Report no. 1526. 87th Cong., 2d sess., 1962.

_____. *Appointments to the Regulatory Agencies: The Federal Communications Commission and the Federal Trade*

Commission (1949-1974). Committee staff report. 94th Cong., 2d sess., 1976.

———. *A Bill to Provide for the Regulation of Interstate and Foreign Communications by Wire or Radio, and for Other Purposes, S. 2910*. Hearings. 73d Cong., 2d sess., 1934.

———. *Communications Act Amendments 1960*. Report no. 1857. 86th Cong., 2d sess., 1960.

———. *Educational Television*. Hearings. 87th Cong., 1st sess., 1961.

———. *Educational Television*. Report no. 65. 87th Cong., 1st sess., 1961.

———. *Investigation of Television Networks and the UHF-VHF Problem*. Committee Report. 84th Cong., 1st sess., 1955.

———. *The Network Monoply*. Report prepared by John W. Bricker. Committee print. 84th Cong., 2d sess., 1956.

———. *Nomination of Newton N. Minow to be Chairman of the Federal Communications Commission*. Hearings. 87th Cong., 1st sess., 1961.

———. *Presidential Broadcasting Act*. Hearings. 86th Cong., 2d sess., 1960.

———. *Proposed Amendments to the FCC Act of 1934*. Hearings 86th Cong., 1st sess., 1959.

———. *The Public Television Act of 1967*. Hearings. 90th Cong., 1st sess., 1967.

———. *Regulation of Radio Transmission*. Report no. 772. 69th Cong., 1st sess., 1926.

———. *Status of UHF and Multiple Ownership of TV Stations*. Hearings. 83rd Cong., 2d sess., 1954.

———. *Sundry Nominations*. Hearings. 88th Cong., 1st sess., 1963.

———. *Sundry Nominations . . . February 8, 1962 through October 4, 1963*. Hearings. 87th Cong., 2d sess., 1962.

———. *The Television Inquiry: Television Network Practices*. 84th Cong., 2d sess., 1956.

———. *The Television Inquiry: Television Network Practices*. Committee report. 85th Cong., 1st sess., 1957.

———. *Television Network Regulation and the UHF Problem*. Memorandum prepared by Harry M. Plotkin, special counsel. Committee print. 84th Cong., 1st sess., 1955.

———. Committee on the Judiciary. *Juvenile Delinquency*. Hearings. 83d Cong., 2d sess., 1954.

———. *Juvenile Delinquency*. Hearings. 84th Cong., 1st sess., 1955.

———. *Juvenile Delinquency*. Hearings. 87th Cong., 1st and 2d sess., 1961-62.

———. Subcommittee on Administrative Practice and Procedure. *Report on the Regulatory Agencies to the President-Elect*. Prepared by James M. Landis. Committee Print. 86th Cong., 2d sess., 1960.

U. S. Department of Justice. Attorney General's Committee on Administrative Procedure. *Federal Communications Commission*. 2 vols. 1940.

———. *Report to the President by the Attorney General on Deceptive Practices in Broadcasting Media*. 30 Dec. 1969.

U. S. Federal Communications Commission. *Annual Report* (1946-1970).

———. *An Economic Analysis of Community Antenna Systems and the Television Broadcasting Industry*. Report prepared by Martin H. Seiden. 1965.

———. *Public Service Responsibilities of Broadcast Licensees*. 1946.

———. *Report on Chain Broadcasting*. 1941.

———. *Reports and Orders*.

———. Office of Network Study. *Network Broadcasting*. 1957.

———. *Television Network Program Procurement*. 2d interim report. 1965.

———. Network Inquiry Special Staff. "An Analysis of the Network-Affiliate Relationship in Television." 1979.

———. "FCC Jurisdiction to Regulate Commercial Television Network Practices." 1979.

———. "FCC Rules Governing Commercial Television Network Practices." 1979.

———. "The Historical Evolution of the Commercial Network Broadcast System." 1979.

U. S. Federal Radio Commission. *Annual Reports* (1927-33).

U. S. Federal Trade Commission Bureau of Competition. *Symposium on Media Concentration*. 2 vols. 1978.

U. S. National Commission on the Causes and Prevention of Violence. *Mass Media and Violence*. Staff report, 1969.

U. S. President's Task Force on Communications Policy. *Final*

Report. 1968.

THESES AND DISSERTATIONS

Anderson, James Kent. "Fraudulence in Television: The History and Implications of the Quiz Show Scandals, 1955-1960." Ph.D. diss. University of Washington, 1975.

Bailey, Robert Lee. "Examination of Prime Time Network Television Special Programs." Ph.D. diss., University of Wisconsin, 1967.

Baird, Frank Lorenzo. "Congress' Role in Regulation: Radio and Television Programming." Ph.D. diss., University of Texas, 1964.

Boekemeier, Barbara S. "The Genesis of WNDT: A Non-Commercial Channel on a Commercial Channel." M.F.A. thesis, Columbia University, 1963.

Brinton, Avard Wellington. "The Regulation of Broadcasting by the FCC: A Case Study in Regulation by Independent Commission." Ph.D. diss. Harvard University, 1962.

Buell, Stephen David. "The History and Development of WSAZ-TV, Channel 3, Huntington, West Virginia." Ph.D. diss., Ohio State University, 1962.

Burke, John Edward. "An Historical-Analytical Study of the Legislative and Political Origins of the Public Broadcasting Act of 1967." Ph.D. diss. Ohio State University, 1971.

Cahalan, Joseph M. "Congress, Mass Communications and Public Policy—The Public Broadcasting Act of 1967." Ph.D. diss., New York University, 1971.

Day, Charles W. "The Television Adult Western: A Pilot Study." M. A. thesis, University of Chicago, 1958.

Dougall, Thomas J. "Newton N. Minow, 'Advocate of the Public Interest,' An Evaluative Study of the Effect Produced on the Balance of Commercial Television Programming by the Public Addresses of Newton N. Minow." Ph.D. diss., Wayne State University, 1967.

Grunewald, Donald. "The Entrepreneur and the Federal Communications Commission: A Study of Comparative Television Licensing." Ph.D. diss., Graduate School of Business Administration, Harvard University, 1962.

Haney, John Benjamin. "A Study of Public Attitudes toward Tax-

Support for Educational Television Activities in the Detroit Metropolitan Area." Ph.D. diss., University of Michigan, 1959.

Hess, Gary Newton. "An Historical Study of the Du Mont Television Network." Ph.D. diss., Northwestern Univeristy, 1960.

Kahn, Frank Jules. "The FCC's Regulation of Economic Injury in Broadcasting, 1934-1966." Ph.D. diss., Northwestern University, 1960.

Kittross, John Michael. "Television Frequency Allocation Policy in the United States." Ph.D. diss., University of Illinois, 1960.

Lally, Emmett W. "A Descriptive Analysis of the Influence of Newton N. Minow upon Major Issues in Broadcasting While Chairman of the FCC." M.S. thesis, Boston University, 1966.

Larka, Robert. "Television's Private Eye: An Examination of Twenty Years of a Particular Genre, 1949-1969." Ph.D. diss., Ohio University, 1973.

Lucoff, Manny. "Le Roy Collins and the National Association of Broadcasters: Experiment in the Public Interest." Ph.D. diss., University of Iowa, 1971.

Mackey, David R. "The National Association of Broadcasters—Its First Twenty Years." Ph.D. diss., Northwestern University, 1956.

Maltese, Anthony Michael. "A Descriptive Study of Children's Programming on Major American Television Networks from 1950 through 1964." Ph.D. diss., Ohio University, 1967

Morgan, Robert Shepherd. "The Television Code of the National Association of Broadcasters: The First Ten Years." Ph.D. diss., Iowa State University, 1964.

Pepper, Robert M. "The Formation of the Public Broadcasting Service." Ph.D. diss., University of Wisconsin, 1976.

Perry, David. "Diversity and the Demand for Television Broadcasting." Ph.D. diss., University of Pennsylvania, 1974.

Peterson, Gale Eugene. "President Harry S. Truman and the Independent Commission, 1945-1952." Ph.D. diss., University of Maryland, 1973.

Silverman, Fred. "An Analysis of ABC Television Network Programming from February 1953 to October 1959." M. A. thesis, Ohio State University, 1959.

Stern, Robert H. "The Federal Communications Commission and Television: The Regulatory Process in an Environment of

Rapid Technological Innovation." Ph.D. diss., Harvard University, 1950.

Stoller, Michael Allan. "The Economics of UHF Television: Effects of Government Policy." Ph.D. diss., Washington University, 1977.

Webbink, Douglas William. "The All-Channel Receiver Law and the Future of Ultra-High Frequency Television." Ph.D. diss., Duke University, 1968.

Wellman, John Floyd. "Storer Broadcasting Company—Its History, Organization, and Operation." Ph.D. diss., University of Michigan, 1973.

Wolf, Frank. "Some Determinants of Public Affairs Programming on Commercial Television in the United States." Ph.D. diss., Columbia University, 1971.

INDUSTRY SOURCES

American Broadcasting Co.-United Paramount Theatres (later American Broadcasting Companies), *Annual Report.* 1951-79.

Arthur D. Little, Inc. *Television Program Production Procurement, Distribution, and Scheduling.* Boston, 1969.

Broadcasting Yearbook. Washington, D. C., 1951-1975.

Columbia Broadcasting System. *Annual Report.* 1950-68.

_____. *An Analysis of Senator John W. Bricker's Report Entitled 'The Network Monopoly'.* New York, 1956.

_____. *Network Practices: Memorandum Supplementing Statement of Frank Stanton, President.* New York, 1956.

Columbia University Graduate School of Journalism. *The Network Project, Notebook.* Nos. 1-10. Oct. 1972-Winter 1975.

Cunningham and Walsh, Inc. *Videotown: Annual Census of TV and Its Effects on Family Life in a Typical American City.* New York, 1953-58.

Herman W. Land Associates. *Television and the Wired City: A Study of the Implications of a Change in the Mode of Transmission.* Washington, D. C., 1969.

Radio Corporation of America. *Annual Report.* 1951-68.

The Roper Organization, Inc. *Emerging Profiles of Television and Other Mass Media: Public Attitudes, 1959-1967.* Washington, D. C., 1967

_____. *New Trends in the Public's Measure of Television and*

Other Media. New York, 1964.

_____. *What People Think of Television and Other Mass Media, 1959-1972.* New York, 1973.

ORAL HISTORIES

William Benton. Kennedy Library
Richard Boone. Popular Arts Project, Columbia University.
Edward Brecher. James Lawrence Fly Project, Columbia University.
Douglass Cater. Johnson Library
Children's Television Workshop Project. Columbia University.
Norman M. Clapp. Kennedy Library.
Marcus Cohn. James Lawrence Fly Project, Columbia University.
Le Roy Collins. Kennedy Library.
Louis Cowan. Radio Pioneers Project, Columbia University.
Paul Rand Dixon. Kennedy Library.
Clifford J. Durr. James Lawrence Fly Project, Columbia University
Fred W. Friendly. James Lawrence Fly Project, Columbia University.
Fred W. Friendly. Radio Pioneers Project, Columbia University.
Oren Harris. Johnson Library.
Oren Harris. Kennedy Library.
August Heckscher. Kennedy Library.
William Hedges. Radio Pioneers Project, Columbia University.
E. William Henry. Kennedy Library.
Luther Hodges. Kennedy Library.
John Jay Hooker. Kennedy Library.
Francis Keppel. Kennedy Library.
James M. Landis. Columbia University.
William Lawrence. Kennedy Library.
Peter Lisagor. Kennedy Library.
Lee Loevinger. Kennedy Library.
J. Leonard Marks. Johnson Library.
Neville Miller. James Lawrence Fly Project, Columbia University.
Newton N. Minow. Adlai Stevenson Project, Columbia University.
Newton N. Minow. Johnson Library.

Newton N. Minow. Regulatory Agencies Panel, Kennedy Library.
Harry Plotkin. James Lawrence Fly Project, Columbia University.
Paul A. Porter. James Lawrence Fly Project, Columbia University.
Joseph Rauh. James Lawrence Fly Project, Columbia University.
James Rowe. James Lawrence Fly Project, Columbia University.
Robert Lewis Shayon. Radio Pioneers Project, Columbia
    University.
Peter Shuebruk. James Lawrence Fly Project, Columbia
    University
Frank Stanton. Columbia University.
Rod Steiger. Popular Arts Project, Columbia University.
Telford Taylor. James Lawrence Fly Project, Columbia
    University.

PERSONAL INTERVIEWS

Kenneth A. Cox, 14 June 1978.
Michael Dann, 14 June 1979.
Frederick W. Ford, 15 June 1978, 19 June 1978.
Fred W. Friendly, 11 March 1977.
Henry Geller, 30 June 1981.
Eric F. Goldman, 12 Sept. 1978.
E. William Henry, 21 June 1978.
Nicholas Johnson, 8 Jan. 1980
Robert E. Lee, 20 June 1978.
Tedson J. Meyers, 30 June 1981.
Newton N. Minow, 22 May 1978, 24 May 1978, 9 Aug. 1978.
Joel Rosenbloom, 25 June 1981.
Arthur M. Schlesinger, Jr., 5 Oct. 1978.
Bernard Schwartz, 13 Nov. 1978.
Frank Shakespeare, 12 June 1979.
Frank N. Stanton, 16 Nov. 1978.

Index

Televisions's Guardians was composed into type on a Compugraphic phototypesetter in nine point Trump Mediaeval with three-point spacing between the lines. The book was designed by Cameron Poulter, typeset by Byron's Graphic Arts, printed offset by Thomson-Shore, Inc., and bound by John H. Dekker & Sons. The paper on which the book is printed is designed for an effective life of at least three hundred years.

THE UNIVERSITY OF TENNESSEE PRESS : KNOXVILLE